MW01147219

SERGIO M. FITA

Jesus and You, Woman

Ignatian Retreat for Women under the guidance of
Edith Stein

✝

Soli Deo honor et gloria

To Darlene, hoping that this book helps you get closer to Jesus through Mary.

God bless you, Darlene.

Sergio Fita ™

First edition

ISBN: 978-1-7374373-2-1

Editing by Stephen Phelan
Translation by Norma Guzman
Translation by Jean Estes-Gonzales

Contents

THE ROMAN CATHOLIC
DIOCESE OF PHOENIX

February 8, 2022

Rev. Father Sergio M. Fita
St. Ann's Roman Catholic Parish

Dear Father Sergio:

Upon receiving a *nihil obstat* from Rev. Father Eugene Mary of the Trinity, Frem. Dio., S.T.L., who served as the censor and reviewed the texts that were submitted, I hereby grant my *imprimatur* for the publication of the following text, as of the date of this letter: *"Jesus and You. Woman: An Ignatian Retreat for Women under the guidance of Edith Stein"*.

I share your hope that the publication of this work will greatly benefit readers to grow in their knowledge and love of our Lord Jesus.

Sincerely yours in Christ,

Thomas J. Olmsted

+ Thomas J. Olmsted
Bishop of Phoenix

vii

To the holiest and most beautiful of all women, my Mother.

AUTHOR'S PROLOGUE

1. Let's travel back in time. In June 2019, Catholics in Action, a young adult ministry, asked me to lead a retreat for women based on St. Ignatius's Spiritual Exercises. It was to be held at Prince of Peace Benedictine Abbey in California. It seemed appropriate to prepare each of the reflections according to an idea I had been thinking about for a long time: using the Ignatian method based on the encounters of the Lord Jesus with various female figures throughout the New Testament. This effort led to the book that you now hold in your hands.

The unanimous response of the participants in those days of silent prayer was overwhelmingly positive. They were the first to encourage me to share the meditations I had prepared for the retreat; however, it seemed to me at the time that the work was incomplete. The brevity of that retreat meant leaving out some very rich gospel stories, and I had not been able to respect the structure of the Exercises as much as I had wished. It was therefore necessary to fill in these gaps and to revise the work already done to give it better balance as a whole.

This project has taken two long years of my life. As I write these words, I am pastor of a wonderful community in the Diocese of Phoenix, Arizona. St. Anne is a huge parish, and thank God, there is always work to be done. In order to complete this task, it was necessary to find time where there was none, to work through the small hours, and to immerse myself once again in this daunting task during the turbulent circumstances of the Covid pandemic. Added to all this are my own personal limitations, which have been the real battle that I have had to overcome in order to finally offer in these pages the fruit of so many sleepless nights.

2. The two pillars that support this work are the Sacred Scriptures and the Spiritual Exercises of the great Ignatius of Loyola, in that order: first, the Word of God, joyfully understood according to the living interpretation of the Apostolic Tradition; and secondly, the orientation and guidance of the founder of the Society of Jesus. If the Ignatian Exercises were the mold into which the content of the message was poured, the spiritual nourishment comes entirely from the Gospel.

Perhaps a third stream could be pointed out, not as dominant as the previous two, but equally necessary to understand the work as a whole. I am referring to the writings of the saintly German philosopher and religious sister, Edith Stein, on the mystery of woman. Edith, later St. Teresa Benedicta of the Cross, was Jewish, converted to Catholicism, and later died as a Carmelite nun in the concentration camp of Auschwitz in 1942.

I remember reading her essays in their Spanish version while I was studying philosophy in my seminary years. From the first moment, I was overcome by the depth and the wisdom of those reflections. I am still surprised today that more use is not made of her work, which paints, with the brush of her precise language, the fundamental traits of the feminine soul. It is difficult to imagine that one could better express what Edith affirms about women. I have not found anything else comparable to it.

3.The reader should not, however, think that this is an abstract and complex book. It is, in fact, an *eminently simple and concrete work*. Simply put, it is a book of prayer, which aims to accompany the woman who desires to find Jesus Christ. Its sole purpose is to bring souls to God and to serve the Holy Spirit in touching hearts and drawing them to the Lord. This work is intended to help initiate an interior conversation with the Master who speaks in silence and who has the words of eternal life (Jn 6:68). I must confess that it was born of prayer, it was written in prayer, and that it is intended to lead the reader to a deeper experience of prayer. This is the main reason that led me to maintain the simple dialogue style of the first presentations that can be seen in the pages of this book. In these words, I am speaking to you familiarly, as a friend. I do not intend to give a sterile description of the various Gospel passages. I want, with your permission, to speak to you personally, and from there, to lead you to God.

An note about the personal memories inserted here from time to time: I am well aware that the message, not the messenger, is the only important thing. It is the Word alone that must be received in the soul, while the voice, the envelope that delivers it, fades into silence. I know that "he must increase, and I must decrease" (Jn. 3:30), but I also believe in the importance of everything that is genuinely human as a vehicle for the transmission of grace. Is this not the very logic of the Incarnation?

An experience that has marked me deeply, and appears frequently throughout, is my pilgrimage to the Holy Land. In

2018, the Lord granted me the undeserved grace of walking for three months, backpack over shoulder, throughout the Holy Land. From February to May, I walked the distance between Egypt and Syria, crossed Palestine from top to bottom, walked the wastelands of Jordan and crossed, from south to north, the entire state of Israel.

To date, it has been the only time I have been able to visit the place chosen by God to manifest himself to us in the flesh. More than three years have passed and I still don't know what happened to me there, but *something did happen.* Be that as it may, it is evident that in a book that revolves around evangelical scenes, that pilgrimage had to have an impact on my way of contemplating and explaining those events. I hope that bringing up those experiences will not end up becoming a distraction. On the contrary, for me that adventure was the gateway to a better understanding of Sacred Scripture. I trust that for the reader it will also be an opportunity for grace that will give the feeling that in some way she is walking with me, and that the only content of our conversation is, ultimately, Jesus.

4. The book is structured in two sections. The first part is the meditations that constitute the true core of this work; the second is made up of a series of appendices containing complimentary readings for some of the reflections. The book is intended to be used primarily in the context of a silent retreat, and I wanted to offer a kind of *all-in-one* for anyone undertaking such an experience.

I do not, however, mean to suggest that mine is the only book to have when spending a few days with the Spiritual Exercises. In fact, I wish here and now to recommend three others, of which this one is intended only as an introduction:

- First and foremost, the written Word of God is an indispensable stream of clear water and an essential wellspring for those who wish to enter into authentic dialogue with the Lord.
- It would also be useful to have at hand the *Spiritual Exercises* of St. Ignatius of Loyola, so that the reader can turn to them when she wishes to enter more deeply into the truly God-given wisdom of the holy founder.
- Finally, Edith Stein's essays on the mystery of woman, which have been published in English in an extraordinary edition by the *Institute of Carmelite Studies under the name The Collected Works of Edith Stein, vol. 2, Essays on Woman* (Washington, DC: ICS Publications 2017).

5. *Who is this book for?* First of all, of course, for women – for women *who are thirsty and desire a work that will help them discover who they are and what God wants of them.* It is a book for personal prayer, both for use in daily life and to take along on a few days of retreat in solitude and silence.

By extension, it can be equally useful for those who are preparing prayer materials for women, either in the context of spiritual exercises or as a presentation in shorter retreats.

Finally, it goes without saying that much of the content offered here is *for absolutely everyone*, man or woman. God addresses his Revelation to every person who has ears to hear him.

6. Some *practical considerations* before beginning. For greater

ease in reading, I have chosen to reference in the body of the text only those quotations that come from Sacred Scripture or from the Spiritual Exercises of St. Ignatius. All other notes can be found at the end of the book, including those that refer to magisterial documents found on the official Vatican website.

I would like to recommend that those who use this book during a silent retreat begin by reading the first of the appendices, which contains some advice to orient the person who is experiencing this type of retreat for the first time to take better advantage of the meditations that are presented.

7. I conclude with the joyful duty of *thanks*. The first names that come to my mind and heart are those of Norma Guzman and Jean Estes-Gonzales. These women have dedicated hours, effort, and more time than they probably should have to the tasks of translating and proofreading. I have no words to adequately express my admiration for these two women who represent well many of the feminine qualities that this book explores and honors.

My heartfelt thanks also to Steve Phelan who has worked on the editing of the English version. His contribution has been invaluable to the successful completion of this enormous task.

In a special way, I am deeply grateful to the *Institute of Carmelite Studies* for their generosity in allowing me to use the texts of Edith Stein that appear in this book. With their permission to use the words of St. Teresa Benedicta of the Cross, they have allowed her to be the true "traveling companion" of all the women who will one day read this book.

My sincere thanks also to Bishop Thomas J. Olmsted for granting me the honor of endorsing these simple meditations.

I would like to give infinite thanks to Fathers Valverde and Mendizábal, of the Society of Jesus and both now deceased, for having always guided me in the ways of the Spirit. The reader will find them generously mentioned herein since the best ideas of this book came from them.

Finally, thank you, dear reader, for your trust in me, and for desiring to find in the pages of this book some light for the path of your life.

I was going to end my prologue here, but I beg to be allowed, even at the risk of sounding a bit ridiculous, to thank the work itself, which has filled my solitude and accompanied me in very dark hours for the Church and the world. In a letter to his Salesian sons dated March 19, 1885, St. John Bosco describes a good book as a "faithful friend."[1] I must admit that this work has certainly been, in this sense, a friend also to me. When the tumult of recent events pounded at my door and tried to rob me of my peace, this book was the refuge in which I always found shelter and warmth. Working on it has been a great blessing for me, and I am undoubtedly the first beneficiary of its words. In them, the Lord has also spoken to me, and for them, I am also infinitely grateful.

I now offer them to you, my friend, in the hope that they may be useful to you and to others. You can be sure of one thing: they were born and written *ad maiorem Dei gloriam* —, for the greater glory of God and the salvation of souls.

May He, Mary, and Joseph bless you,
Father Sergio

Gilbert (Arizona), May 1st, 2021, Memorial of St Joseph the Worker

INTRODUCTORY LETTER

A FEW CONSIDERATIONS ON THE UPCOMING RETREAT[2]

I would like to start by congratulating you on your decision to participate in this retreat during the last week of June organized by Catholics in Action. I thank Catholics in Action for their effort to promote this initiative, which tries to help women like you to a deeper encounter with the Lord. I also thank each one of you for having given God space and silence so that he can speak to your heart. For a long time, I have been entrusting in my poor prayer the fruit of these Spiritual Exercises and I encourage you to ask for the grace of an intimate and transforming encounter with Christ.

What we are doing with this retreat

As you know, this retreat is inspired by the Spiritual Exercises of Saint Ignatius of Loyola. It is important to underline the word "inspired." The usual Ignatian experience is four weeks and has characteristics that are simply impossible to adapt to a retreat of five days. We are going to keep in mind the structure that Saint Ignatius proposes and we are going to take from him the advice that he offers in his Exercises.

During this retreat, you will have a generous amount of time to devote to meditation, as I will cover fewer subjects and speak less than would be required if we had covered the full range offered by St. Ignatius. This more leisurely pace allows for greater depth in personal reflection.

Some of the reasons to choose the less ambitious format are the following:

- In several places of his Exercises, Saint Ignatius proposes to dedicate four or five hours to personal meditation. It seems to me that this point is important and that we should follow this recommendation because the fruit of these days depends, to a large extent, on that generosity and time for personal and meditative prayer.
- In Saint Ignatius' method, what he calls "repetitions" are very important: it is about returning to the same meditation to see what the Holy Spirit is inviting us to pay attention to in our spiritual life. In a retreat with too many presentations, it is impossible to return to what has been meditated on previously, because one has the impression that the train is going very fast and if one gets off ... maybe when she returns it has already left the station!
- In my personal experience, listening to the director speak for a long time ends up becoming a distraction. Instead of helping the union with God, it disperses the mind and the person ends up very tired.
- I am also of the opinion that, when time is left for personal prayer and the director speaks little, the emphasis shifts to the action of God and to the personal response of the participant and *that* is *precisely* the heart of the Ignatian experience.
- Saint Ignatius himself advises in the second annotation

of his Exercises the following: *"The second is that the person who gives to another the way and order in which to meditate or contemplate, ought to relate faithfully the events of such Contemplation or Meditation, going over the points with only a short or summary development. For, if the person who is making the Contemplation, takes the true groundwork of the narrative, and, discussing and considering for himself, finds something which makes the events a little clearer or brings them a little more home to him whether this comes through his own reasoning, or because his intellect is enlightened by the Divine power—he will get more spiritual relish and fruit, than if he who is giving the Exercises had much explained and amplified the meaning of the events. For it is not knowing much, but realizing and relishing things inside, that contents and satisfies the soul"* (SE 2).

· In a practical sense, it has to be an authentic purgatory to listen to me speak for a long time in my poor English for five days. Do not worry, I will not subject you to that torture.

With all this in mind, I am going to limit myself to speaking three times: in two daily meditations, one in the morning, another in the afternoon, and during the Holy Mass. Each day you will have four hours in the schedule for personal prayer. You can add if you want one more hour at the end of the day. I will not be tempted to "want to say it all" because in that too can be a sign (as I see it) of some pride or distrust of God's work in the soul. We must leave the person who exercises in the hands of God and trust that he or she will respond to what God is communicating.

The official schedule will always end with the prayer of Compline at 8 p.m. After that time, there will be "something else" that will vary every day and that, in any case, will not be mandatory. The backbone of the Exercises will be the meditations of the morning and afternoon. The last activity of the day is voluntary and is offered for those who wish to participate in it.

In addition, of those four hours of meditation, two hours will be of silent adoration before the Blessed Sacrament. This also has to do with the proposal of Saint Ignatius: frequently, he concludes the prayer with what he calls "colloquy." For St. Ignatius, it is evident that the new life presented to us in the Exercises is impossible without the help of grace. The reason for this conversation with the Lord, or with Mary, or with the guardian angel, is to ask for help to receive from God the strength and love we need to "be born again." In that same line of thought, praying for a long time before the Blessed Sacrament is a way of insisting on that aspect: "without Me, you can do nothing" (Jn 15:5).

Maybe some of you are thinking that four hours is too long to pray—that you have never prayed so much and that you are unlikely to be able to do so. In this regard, I also want to quickly point out several things:

- The first is not to exaggerate the difficulty of praying for so long. It is perfectly possible, even easy, to meditate four or five hours during a week. Experience shows that, although challenging, it is possible for everyone.
- If it costs us, for whatever reasons, it is worth noting that the Exercises of Saint Ignatius of Loyola are an expe-

rience that counts on the effort of the person who makes them. This effort is the expression of the generosity of those who wish to take advantage of these days of retreat and it is already a sign of the action of the Holy Spirit in the soul. As he explains: "as strolling, walking, and running are bodily exercises, so every way of preparing and disposing the soul to rid itself of all the disordered tendencies, and, after it is rid, to seek and find the Divine Will as to the management of one's life for the salvation of the soul, is called a Spiritual Exercise" (SE 1).

· In fact, the idea of shortening the hour of meditation should be considered *as a temptation to be resisted*: "the enemy is not used to try and make one cut short of the hour of such contemplation, meditation, or prayer" (SE 12). Saint Ignatius, who was always a soldier, proposes to overcome the test by striking back: "the person who is exercising himself, in order to act against the desolation and conquer the temptations, ought always to stay somewhat more than the full hour; so as to accustom himself not only to resist the adversary, but even to overthrow him" (SE 13).

· In this sense, I insist with the Spanish Saint that the retreatant take full advantage of the times of prayer. It would not make sense to seek such an encounter with God—which is the reason you wanted to participate in this retreat—only to let ourselves be carried away by fatigue, desolation, or dryness and fail in the fundamental thing—*being with Christ.*

As an aid to completing the hour of meditation, I advise you to bring your prayer books, those in which the Lord has told you something in the past. I encourage you to use them freely if you need them to find material for your personal prayer. I will also occasionally give you some reading for use during your prayer or during moments of rest. And, of course, you will always have the Holy Scriptures.

During the presentations, do not try to write word for word what I say: limit yourself to writing down what you want to take with you later to your meditation, that toward which you feel that the Holy Spirit is inclining you.

Last days before the exercises

I want to conclude this email by encouraging you to ask for the fruits of it. Actually, *five days alone with God can mean the beginning of a new Christian life.* You must think that the Lord wants to give you a very important grace and you must dispose yourself from now on, asking for greatness of soul. That attitude of the heart is a grace—we must beg for it in prayer: "Lord, make me generous." "Jesus, give me the grace to trust you." "Mary, help me say yes to God." "Touch my heart and change it." "I want to love you as you love me." These little prayers or aspirations should be preparing your heart so that God can enter in a new way in your life.

If you are generous, the retreat will be very fruitful. God is not outdone in generosity—indeed, He offers abundant encouragement and joy!

Thank you very much for your patience and your confidence.

I entrust you to the Blessed Virgin Mary and I ask our Mother to grant you the graces you need to receive Jesus in your heart as she welcomed him in her womb and in her soul.

God bless you,
Fr. Sergio

I

MEDITATIONS

1

WIDOW AT THE TEMPLE & QUEEN ESTHER

AN INTRODUCTORY MEDITATION – INITIAL DISPOSITIONS

"Merciful Father, fill our hearts with your love and keep us faithful to the gospel of Christ. Give us the grace to rise above our human weakness." (Friday, Third Week of Lent)

I want to begin these Spiritual Exercises by welcoming you all in the name of the Lord. You are here because Jesus has invited you and you have accepted his invitation.

God has brought you here to *speak to your heart.* As the prophet Hosea says: "I will lead her into the desert and speak to her heart" (Hos. 2:13). In the world, in your daily life, there is a lot of noise and the Lord wanted this week for you to step away from all of that.

3

There is a verse in the New Testament that I always like to quote at the beginning of a retreat like this. It says: "He said to them, 'Come away by yourselves to a deserted place and rest a while.' People were coming and going in great numbers, and they had no opportunity even to eat" (Mk. 6:31). Such is your life as women, mothers, and daughters. Many times, just as the apostles, you do not have time for yourselves.

The people in your life—your family, your friends, your ministry collaborators, and co-workers—come to you for many things, and it is hard for you to find time for the Lord. So, Jesus invites you to come with Him to a place like this, a deserted place, to rest in Him and with Him.

1.In this first presentation, I want to explain the agenda for the few next days. As you know from the letter that I sent you, in these Spiritual Exercises you will not hear very much talking from me. The emphasis is on your *inner conversation with God.* You will have the opportunity to talk with Jesus. Above all, you are here *to listen*, to place yourself in the hands of God. "You, Lord, are our Father. We are the clay and you are the potter. We are the work of your hands" (Is. 64:8).

Along with the prophet Isaiah, I invite you to truly become clay in the hands of the Lord. The Spiritual Exercises are a spiritual journey: there must be a progression, an advancement, a transformation. In *The Interior Castle*, Saint Teresa of Jesus uses the analogy of the worm that within the silk cocoon becomes a butterfly.[3] You must start with that desire, with that intensity: with the determination to take full advantage of these days of retreat.

In the twentieth annotation of his Spiritual Exercises,

Saint Ignatius of Loyola describes the correct attitude when he speaks of the person *"who desires to get all the profit he can."* Ask of God—and this is the most important thing of this introduction—that He will give you the attitude of wanting to get all the profit you can from these days. It is the attitude of the widow who, in the temple and in the sight of Jesus, gave everything she had. (Lk. 21:1-4) It would be good to meditate on the example of this woman today and tomorrow in prayer and to ask yourself: *Have I come to this retreat with the same attitude? Am I willing to give everything?* Ask God for the grace to make a gift of yourself, as this woman did, during these exercises.

As I wrote in the letter, this retreat will be inspired by the spirituality of Saint Ignatius, but we are going to adapt it because we cannot condense a month into a few days. Thinking about how we could organize this spiritual journey, in my private prayer an idea became evident to me that, I must confess, I have had in my heart for many years.

2. The full title of the Spiritual Exercises of Saint Ignatius is "Spiritual Exercises to conquer oneself and regulate one's life without determining oneself through any tendency that is disordered." Ignatius was a soldier and, in his Spiritual Exercises, he summons us to battle. You've come to conquer yourself. You have come to open your heart and let the Will of God, only the Will of God, guide your life.

The Will of God is the most beautiful and wonderful adventure possible. Sometimes we are afraid of God because deep down we think we would be happier if we did what we wanted and not what He wants. It is the old temptation of Adam and Eve in Eden. Rather, we must see in God a friend, and in his loving Will the most wonderful project and the only one that can make us fully happy. He is our Father, Jesus is our Brother, and the Most Holy Trinity loves us and knows us. As a good Father, God invites us to communion with him. In that communion we find life, peace, joy, grace, mercy, and love.

God's plan for each person is different. You have come to embrace that mission, that vocation that the Lord has given to each one of you.

How does one know the Will of God? The way is always Jesus. This is what Saint Ignatius proposes: from the four weeks of Exercises, the last three are basically dedicated to the contemplation of Jesus Christ. "The Pastoral Constitution on the Church in the Modern World (*Gaudium et Spes*)" has an affirmation that St. John Paul II often repeated: "Only in the mystery of the Incarnate Word does the mystery of man take on light".[4] You have to enter into a vital relationship with Christ—only then will you discover who you are and what you are called to.

* * *

In these Spiritual Exercises, we will slowly contemplate scenes from Holy Scripture, especially from the Gospels, in which the Lord interacts with women. In these biblical women, I ask you to see yourself. I am convinced that in them, God has revealed a way of being a woman and a way in which women should relate to God in Christ. In his Apostolic Letter *Mulieris Dignitatem*, St. John Paul II affirms that:

In the person and mission of Jesus Christ, we also recognize what the reality of the Redemption means for the dignity and the vocation of women. This meaning becomes clearer for us from Christ's words and from his whole attitude towards women, an attitude which is extremely simple, and for this very reason extraordinary, if seen against the background of his time. It is an attitude marked by great clarity and depth. Various women appear along the path of the mission of Jesus of Nazareth, and his meeting with each of them is a confirmation of the evangelical "newness of life" already spoken of.[5]

A little later, the Pope continues:

Jesus' attitude to the women he meets in the course of his Messianic service reflects the eternal plan of God, who, in creating each one of them, chooses her and loves her in Christ. (Eph. 1: 1–5) Each woman is therefore "the only creature on earth which God willed for its own sake". Each of them from the "beginning" inherits as a woman the dignity of personhood. Jesus of Nazareth confirms this dignity, recalls it, renews it, and makes it a part of the Gospel and of the Redemption for which he is sent into the world. Every word and gesture of Christ about women must therefore be brought into the dimension of the Paschal Mystery. In this way everything is completely explained.[6]

In these evangelical women, you will be able to discover yourself, finding what Edith Stein called "woman's soul", that which is genuinely feminine and that therefore forms part of the vocation that God wants for you. Jesus should make you feel like more of a woman, and here in this retreat, He wants to show you the kind of woman He wants you to be in your families and communities, but above all, in your relationship with Him.

I want to put before your eyes Edith Stein's description of the soul of the woman. I ask you to discover this soul in each woman of the Holy Scripture that we will consider, and that you ask God to discover it perfected by God's grace. As you know, Edith Stein is the Jewish name of Saint Teresa Benedicta of the Cross, martyr of Auschwitz, who was one of the most important philosophers in early twentieth-century Europe. It is a description that I invite you to keep in mind throughout these Spiritual Exercises so that you can see it reflected in the Gospel passages that we are going to consider and so that you try to reflect it yourself in your life and your behavior from now on.

Woman's nature is determined by her original vo-cation of spouse and mother. One depends on the other. The body of woman is fashioned "to be one flesh" with another and to nurse new human life in itself. A well-disciplined body is an accommodating instrument for the mind, which animates it; at the same time, it is a source of power and a habitat for the mind. Just so, woman's soul is designed to be subordinate to man in obedience and support. It is also fashioned to be a shelter in which other souls may unfold. Both spiritual companionship and spiritual motherliness are not limited to the physical spouse and mother relationships, but they extend to all people with whom woman comes into contact.

The soul of woman must therefore be expansive and open to all human beings; it must be quiet so that no small weak flame will be extinguished by stormy winds; warm so as not to benumb fragile buds; clear, so that no vermin will settle in dark corners and recesses; self-contained, so that no invasions from without imperil the inner life; empty of itself, in order that extraneous life may have room in it; finally, mistress of itself and also of its body, so that the entire person is readily at the disposal of every call.

That is an ideal image of the gestalt of the feminine soul. The soul of the first woman was formed for this purpose, and so, too, was the soul of the Mother of God. In all other women since the Fall, there is an embryo of such development, but it needs particular cultivation if it is not to be suffocated among weeds rankly shooting up around it.[7]

3. At the outset of this retreat, I want to put before your eyes the example of two women, one from the Old Testament and one from the new. Of the latter, we have already spoken: the widow in Luke 21:1-4 who gave everything. As I pointed out in my letter, the Spiritual Exercises do not depend on how beautiful the meditations are or how wise the director is, but *on your generosity.* God is never outdone in generosity. Imagine that moment when the old woman

drops every coin she had into the temple box. Contemplate the widow standing in line, perhaps embarrassed because she had almost nothing to offer and saw others make larger donations by throwing in more money. In your prayer, witness the moment in which she releases the coin before the loving and admiring look of Jesus. I invite you to spend time in that second. If the Lord had not said anything, this act would have been left only between that woman and God. But Jesus wanted us to have it now and *to measure ourselves with the generosity of that woman.*

You can ask yourself these questions, while still looking at the Gospel scene: *Am I giving everything in my Christian life? Have I come here willing to empty myself for Jesus? Or, on the contrary, is there some part of me that does not want to give myself to Jesus?* Above all, meditate first on the look of Jesus toward that woman. Contemplate the admiration and love in Jesus' eyes. Can the Lord look at you in the same way because he finds in you the same generosity and trust? In your personal prayer, offer yourself to Jesus and tell Him: "Lord, I also want to put myself completely in your hands. Help me to trust You and give you everything. Help me believe that you want my happiness and know what I need to be happy. Take the reins and lead the way."

4. The second woman we find in the Old Testament: I speak of Queen Esther. She is a very dear character to me because, unlike other women from the Old Testament, Esther is a woman full of sweetness and fear—she feels fragile but overcomes that fragility with the strength of her faith.

You know her story: A Jewish woman who becomes the wife of the King of Persia during the Babylonian exile around the year 586 BC. A family member, Mordecai, had educated her after the death of her parents. She was of extraordinary beauty, so that, when King Ahasuerus repudiates his first wife, Esther is chosen from among all the women of the Kingdom to succeed her as Queen of the entire empire.

The army commander, Haman, began a persecution to kill all the Jewish people. Mordecai asks Esther, who is a queen and whose Jewish origin is unknown in court, to help her persecuted people. "Save us from death," says Mordecai in a message to her.

At first, Ester refuses to help her people, replying to Mordecai in a message: "All the servants of the king and the people of his provinces know that any man or woman who goes to the king in the inner court without being summoned is subject to the same law—death. Only if the king extends the golden scepter will such a person live. Now as for me, I have not been summoned to the king for thirty days" (Est. 4:11).

Mordecai's response is clear: "Do not imagine that you are safe in the king's palace, you alone of all the Jews. Even if you now remain silent, relief and deliverance will come to the Jews from another source; but you and your father's house will perish. Who knows—perhaps it was for a time like this that you became queen?" (v. 13-14)

Esther sent back to Mordecai this response: "Go and assemble all the Jews who are in Susa; fast on my behalf, all of you, not eating or drinking, night or day, for three days. I and my maids will also fast in the same way. Thus prepared, I will go to the king, contrary to the law. If I perish, I perish" (v. 16).

I invite you to read the beautiful prayer of Queen Esther in

11

the Old Testament. (4:14-30) She confesses several times that she is afraid: "deliver me from my fear." The Word of God says: "Queen Esther, seized with mortal anguish, likewise had recourse to the Lord." (4:12). It also states in the next chapter: "her heart was shrunk with fear" (5:5). Indeed, she fainted out of fear before the King.

She prays and fasts: "Taking off her splendid garments, she put on garments of distress and mourning. In place of her precious ointments, she covered her head with dung and ashes. She afflicted her body severely and in place of her festive adornments, her tangled hair covered her. Then she prayed to the Lord, the God of Israel." (4:13-14)

You know the end of the story, which you can find in your Bible: the intercession of the Queen obtains the salvation of her people.

I think there are many similarities between Queen Esther and you as you proceed with the Spiritual Exercises. I will point out only a few:

- Just as she was, you are called to make a journey. The woman who appears at the end of the story is different from the one who begins the story. I hope the woman you are at the beginning of this retreat is different from the woman you'll be at the end of it.
- Just as she was aware of her fears, you also have weaknesses, and the Lord wants to take you beyond those limitations, which block you and prevent you from doing the Will of God.
- Just as God saved Israel thanks to Esther, the Lord wants to change your hearts to be able to bring eternal life to your family and the people around you.

- Just as Esther was led by God's Providence to be Queen and in this way become an instrument of salvation, the Lord has also been taking you through your life with his Providence and has placed you where you are to be the salvation for your families
- Just as Esther prayed and fasted for three days, you are here this week to pray and offer sacrifices for God to transform you and for your salvation to come first to you, and then through you, to other people.
- Queen Esther had the generosity of which we spoke earlier that is fundamental to the fruit of this retreat: "If I perish, I perish." She was willing to die for her faith and for her people. From her you can learn to have this disposition of the heart. And if you do not have it, imitate the Queen by asking God at the beginning of this retreat to grant you that courage, generosity, and love.

I ask you to take these days *with the same seriousness* with which Queen Esther took those three days of prayer and fasting. Like Queen Esther, in our Christian life or in a Spiritual Exercises like these, God can ask us for sacrifices, even great sacrifices.

In *The Glories of Mary*, St. Alphonsus de Liguori uses the example of Esther to speak of Mary: just as Esther interceded and with her intercession saved her people, so Mary, who is also a beautiful Queen, saves us, her children, with her intercession. As in Cana (Jn 2:5), She tells each of you, in your heart: "Do whatever He tells you." Whatever He tells you. That is to say, the premise is that *Jesus is going to talk to you.* Listen to him.

5. In these days of the retreat, think of Queen Esther, and dedicate yourself to taking advantage of this week as if your lives were at stake. I invite you to turn off your phones and forget everything. I assure you that nothing will happen to your family if they don't hear from you for a few days. These are days of prayer and silence. You will find God if you focus on the Lord and do not get distracted. Without recollection, you will not find what you are looking for.

My experience on my pilgrimage to the Holy Land made a big impression on me in that sense: I already knew the importance of silence, but there I discovered something new that I cannot express, that I do not know how to describe. Embrace the silence and let God speak to you.

2

MARTHA AND MARY

DAY 1 (MORNING) – SECOND MEDITATION – PRINCIPLE AND FOUNDATION I

"Prompt our actions with your inspiration, we pray, O Lord, and further them with your constant help, that all we do may always begin from you and by you be brought to completion. Through our Lord Jesus Christ. Amen." (Thursday after Ash Wednesday)

Good morning to all. We begin our first day of Spiritual Exercises by placing ourselves in the presence of God. We ask Him to help us obtain "an intimate knowledge of our Lord, who has become man for me, that I may love Him more and follow Him more closely" (SE 104).

Allow me to remind you again, with Saint Ignatius, that "it is not knowing much, but realizing and relishing things inside, that contents and satisfies the soul" (SE 2). St. Teresa

15

of Jesus is of the same opinion: "the soul's progress does not lie in thinking much but in loving much."[8]

So do not try to meditate on everything I say now: let your prayer be gentle, serene, quiet, without hurry. What you do not meditate on here, you can take with you and use it for your prayer when you return to your homes. So, in a way, these days of retreat will be extended and you will continue to receive benefit from these Spiritual Exercises even after we finish in a few days.

The first meditation of the Spiritual Exercises is the "Principle and Foundation." On a personal level, it may have been the meditation that has most influenced my entire life. When I did the month of Exercises in 2003, I dedicated nine days to this meditation alone.

It is often said that it is the most important meditation because, as the name suggests, it establishes the foundation of all the Spiritual Exercises and is the gateway to the Ignatian experience. In fact, it establishes the foundation of the whole Christian life. In the Ignatian Exercises, all meditations are related. There is a progression that has been masterfully planned by the rational mind of Saint Ignatius. In a way, it is like a pyramid in which some meditations are built on the previous ones. The meditation that is below and on which all are sustained, is this meditation of Principle and Foundation.

The text of Saint Ignatius says the following:

> *Man is created to praise, reverence, and serve God our Lord, and by this means to save his soul. The other things on the face of the earth are created for man to help him in attaining the end for which he is created.*

16

Hence, man is to make use of them in as far as they help him in the attainment of his end, and he must rid himself of them in as far as they prove a hindrance to him.

Therefore, we must make ourselves indifferent to all created things, as far as we are allowed free choice and are not under any prohibition. Consequently, as far as we are concerned, we should not prefer health to sickness, riches to poverty, honor to dishonor, a long life to a short life. The same holds for all other things. Our one desire and choice should be what is more conducive to the end for which we are created. (SE 23)

Actually, I am tempted to say that I need not add anything more. I could get up and go back to Arizona right here. Everything is really in these words of Saint Ignatius. He is telling us that man is created for God. That the end of man is God. That everything we do should take us to God and glorify God. That "the other things on the face of the Earth" were made by God for us to make use of them in as much as they help us get to God and glorify him. In the second paragraph, he establishes a criterion for judging things and events with a view of faith: "good" is that which leads us to a greater union with the Lord; everything that separates us from him and the end for which we are created is "bad".

We evaluate things, almost without realizing it, according to human criteria. We mourn when a family loses their home. We suffer when a young person becomes seriously ill. It hurts us to find out that someone is having a bad time due to any circumstance. In the Exercises, we must be transformed by the Holy Spirit in such a way that He changes even our way of evaluating and judging things. If a disease, for example, leads the person to conversion, is it good or bad? Is a long life good if the person departs from God and uses his time to do bad things? If someone loses everything and that experience of detachment helps them to unite and love God more, can we say that their "misfortune" was bad or, on the contrary, the greatest blessing of their life?

What St. Ignatius told us we must apply to the consideration of our own life *as it is today*. We must ask God to enlighten us, to show us what elements of our life are leading us to him and what other things or relationships are, little by little, taking us away from him. Is there a stone in your life over which you are always stumbling? Do you have an activity, or a passion, or a relationship with someone that blocks your union with God? St. Paul says: "*Whatever you do*, do from the heart, for the Lord and not for others, knowing that you will receive from the Lord the due payment of the inheritance; be slaves of the Lord Christ" (Col 3:23-24). Do we do everything for Jesus? What parts of our life are illuminated by Christ and what parts are in darkness?

This meditation should also help us in the life we will begin from now on. Before beginning any activity, however small it may seem, at every moment, every step, every second, we should have this kind of holy obsession. We must ask ourselves: "What I am about to do, is it God's Will *for me*?" "Jesus, do you want me to do this?" "The action that I am about to take, does it take me to the Lord or away from Him?" Let us never do anything deliberately that we know displeases God or that, even without it being a sin, is not His Will for us.

The consequence of meditation is evident: we must ask for grace and have the determination to put our whole life, without exceptions, in the service of God. We must resolve, with the help of the Lord, to remove from our lives everything that is preventing union with God. We must strengthen and allow to take root that which helps us in our union with Christ.

* * *

Everything that we have just said of the Principle and Foundation is shown to us in a scene from the Gospel that undoubtedly has a particular warmth. It is when Jesus allows himself to be welcomed by two women and one of them loses sight of what is truly important. As you can imagine, I am referring to the encounter of Jesus Christ with Mary and Martha in Bethany that is found in the Gospel of Saint Luke, at the end of Chapter 10. Let's meditate together on this mystery in the life of Jesus because, as with the meditation of Principle and Foundation, *here is the secret of holiness*.

"As they continued their journey he entered a village where a woman whose name was Martha welcomed him. She had a sister named Mary, who sat beside the Lord at his feet listening to him speak. Martha, burdened with much serving, came to him and said, "Lord, do you not care that my sister has left me by myself to do the serving? Tell her to help me." The Lord said to her in reply, "Martha, Martha, you are anxious and worried about many things. There is

need of only one thing. Mary has chosen the better
part and it will not be taken from her" (10:38-42).

Bethany is a place that I have always felt powerfully attracted
to and I return to this page of the Gospel practically every week to help me understand what is really important.
Bethany was one of the places where Jesus was comfortable,
to which he went to rest with his disciples and to avoid the
noise of Jerusalem. Maybe it reminded him of his city of
Nazareth, and whenever he could he went there to get out of
the spotlight.

During the preparation for my pilgrimage to the Holy Land,
the desire to visit Bethany was always there. I searched
everywhere on the map and could not find it anywhere. It
was as if Bethany had been swallowed up by the earth. I did
not know then that in honor of Lazarus, this place is now
known by its Arabic name: *Al Azariyeh*. It is a village located
in Palestine on the other side of the wall that separates that
territory from the state of Israel. In a straight line it is
about four kilometers from Jerusalem, however, it is difficult
to get there, especially if you are traveling alone. Once I
arrived in the Holy City, I really did not know how to get to
Bethany, although I still had the desire to visit that small
corner of the world sanctified by the presence of the Lord. I
remember asking a priest from the Franciscan Monastery
of San Salvador for information and he strongly advised me
against the trip: "There is almost nothing to see and it's very
difficult to get there. You would have to take public transport,
and the church is in a Muslim neighborhood. You have to be
careful. The people there only speak Arabic and you will not
be able to communicate with anyone. The border controls

are very thorough and you will have to deal with the soldiers at Customs. Nowadays practically no one goes there because of all these difficulties."

Without realizing it, that friar was enumerating many of the reasons that made me want to go there, so instead of discouraging me, his words only increased my desire to try the adventure.

Thanks be to God, I spent one of the most memorable days of my trip in Bethany. I was able to celebrate Holy Mass, alone, in the house of Martha, Mary and Lazarus. In the adjoining church, without the interruption of rushed or bad-mannered tourists, the hours flew by as I meditated with devotion on the Lord's visit to that place. Indeed, almost nobody goes to Bethany, but this relative obscurity seems to have granted an atmosphere of intimacy to the village that it surely had in the time of Jesus. The floods of pilgrims that fill the bustling streets of Jerusalem do not reach this secluded place. Isolation has restored its primitive charm and increased the pious delight of those fortunate enough to be able to visit it today. Since my arrival in Jerusalem coincided with the holiest days of the Christian calendar (Holy Week and the Octave of Easter), I was able to experience the contrast between the hustle and bustle of the city – especially crowded by the influx of tourists - and the stillness of this secluded and silent village.

Spring was just beginning. The light was soft and golden on that April morning, and how merrily the sparrows chirped with laughter! At the entrance to the church, a tethered camel, bored and indifferent, oversaw the scant activity of the courtyard. I also remember a peaceful garden with a leafy vine and a lovely fresh breeze running through its green leaves. I said to myself: "Lord, now I understand a little why you liked this place so much." It was the simple beauty of nature, silence, hospitality, and genuine friendship that attracted Christ to that tiny corner of Judea. Yes, Jesus found rest there and I too experienced a heavenly peace in that charming little town. Undoubtedly, something of Christ remains in the supernaturally simple atmosphere of Bethany.

I tell you this to help you imagine the town a little bit. Your composition of place has to imagine a charming place. A place sanctified not only by the presence of Jesus, but also because it was a special place for him. Listen to the birds; feel the fresh morning breeze on your face and let the bright sunshine, whose light gives life and joy to everything, warm you.

In this story, I invite you to consider several things:

1. *Our God is a hidden God and only in concealment can we find him.* Jesus loved Bethany because of the contrast between the noise of the big city and the tranquility of that little village. The Gospel tells us that Jesus and his disciples went there when they made a pilgrimage to Jerusalem. The Lord slept there, climbed the Mount of Olives, and went to Gethsemane early to pray alone on the other side of the mountain; and after his prayer, he crossed the Kidron Valley and entered the city. At the end of the day, he used to return to Bethany with this remarkable family formed by Martha, Mary, and Lazarus.

The historical evolution of Jesus is wrapped in silence. He is conceived without anyone knowing. He is born in the solitude of a stable. He disappears from the scene when he and his parents emigrate to Egypt. He spends most of his thirty-three years in the hidden life of Nazareth. Even during his public life, we see him look for the mountains to pray alone, retire to Bethany to avoid the crowds, go to the desert far from everything and to get away from the people when they cheered him and wanted to proclaim him king.

This is something we must learn. We must learn the *style of Jesus*. Be like him. Love what he loved. It is not enough just to "be silent," you have to "hide" with Christ. Saint Paul says, "For you have died, and your life is hidden with Christ in God." (Col 3:3)

Jesus has to be your hideout, just as Bethany was Jesus' hideout.

Saint John of the Cross speaks precisely about this hiding in his Spiritual Canticle:

> *Yet you inquire: Since he whom my soul loves is within me, why don't I find him or experience him? The reason is that he remains concealed and you do not also conceal yourself in order to find and experience him. If you want to find a hidden treasure you must enter the hiding place secretly, and once you have discovered it, you will also be hidden just as the treasure is hidden. Since, then, your beloved Bridegroom is the treasure hidden in a field for which the wise merchant sold all his possessions [Mt. 13:44], and that field is your soul, in order to find him you should forget all your possessions and all creatures and hide in the secret inner room of your spirit and there, closing the door behind you (your will to all*

things), you should pray to your Father in secret [Mt. 6:6]. Remaining hidden with him, you will experience him in hiding, that is, in a way transcending all language and feeling.

Come, then, O beautiful soul! Since you know now that your desired Beloved lives hidden within your heart, strive to be really hidden with him, and you will embrace him within you and experience him with loving affection. Note that through Isaiah he calls you to this hiding place: Come, enter into your inner rooms, shut the door behind you (your faculties to all creatures), hide yourself a little, even for a moment [Is. 26:20], for this moment of life on earth. If, O soul, in this short space of time you keep diligent watch over your heart, as the Wise Man advises [Prv. 4:23], God will undoubtedly give you what he also promises further on through Isaiah: I will give you hidden treasures and reveal to you the substance and mysteries of the secrets [Is. 45:3]. The substance of the secrets is God himself, for God is the substance and concept of faith, and faith is the secret and the mystery. And when that which faith covers and hides from us is revealed—that which is perfect concerning God, spoken of by St. Paul [1 Cor. 13:10]—then the substance and mysteries of the secrets will be uncovered to the soul.[9]

This concealment is the path of humility. It is to want people not to count on us, to be left in the last place, to close the windows of the soul to everything that does not lead us to God: to disappear, not to be sad when we are not taken into account, to live our hidden life with joy, to seek silence whenever possible. It is the union with God in which nothing is sought but God.

2. *Jesus enters your house.* Jesus enters your soul. "A woman whose name was Martha welcomed him." The Scripture scholars explain that Lazarus was almost certainly a young man, reasoning that at that time, the name of the male used to precede that of the women. In the Gospel, however, whenever these siblings are mentioned, they are given the same order: Martha, Mary, and Lazarus. It seems that the best explanation of this order of precedence is that Lazarus was the youngest, perhaps much younger than his sisters, a son of old age. This explains why the parents never appear in the Gospel—probably both would have died when Lazarus was a child and his sisters took care of him. This also explains the attention that both gave him when he falls ill—he was their little brother, the legacy of their parents, the one they had cared for since childhood.

Following this line of thought, let us think that Martha is the older sister. Precisely for this reason, she feels responsible for the house and the family, and she welcomes Jesus to her home with warmth and hospitality. In her home. Imagine what joy when the sisters (Lazarus was not at home at that moment) hear the voice of Jesus at the door. We can even imagine the first word of the Lord, the one he taught his disciples, the one he pronounced when he visited them after his resurrection, and the same word that Jews continue to use today to say hello: "Shalom!" *"Peace to this house."* (Lk 10:5). *"Peace be with you"* (Jn 20:19). That word, on the lips of Jesus, is more than a greeting: *it is the gift that He brings to the soul that receives Him.* Only Jesus gives us peace. Do you

25

live in this peace?

In the episode of the resurrection of Lazarus, we read: "When Martha heard that Jesus was coming, she went to meet him; but Mary sat at home" (Jn 11:20). We can imagine something similar: Martha hears the voice of Jesus and she goes to him. This is what Jesus says in chapter ten of the Gospel of St. John: "My sheep hear my voice and follow me" (10:3). Martha is one of his sheep, because she follows him, and because Jesus calls his own sheep by name. At the end of this passage, Jesus addresses her by her name: *Martha, Martha ...*

What a joy when they meet! In the episode of the resurrection of Lazarus, St. John tells us: "Jesus loved Martha and her sister and Lazarus." (Jn 11: 5) And that love of Jesus for Martha is expressed in the joy of the encounter. Martha is glad to see him. Jesus is glad to see her. Martha, both in this passage and in the resurrection of Lazarus, uses the same word to address Jesus: "Adonai", Lord. She also calls him "Rabbi", teacher, master. Therefore, there is a great affection between the two, but there is also enormous respect. The love between Jesus and Martha is more than love, it is friendship, it is intimacy, as evidenced by the fact that Christ goes to her house and addresses her by name: "Martha, Martha".

You are Martha, and Jesus comes to your house. With his presence, he brings you his peace, and his joy, and his love. You have come to these Exercises because you are also one of His sheep, you have heard his voice and you have followed Him here. He calls you by your name. He knows who you are, he knows you, and he loves you.

Think of this presence of Jesus in your soul. All your

happiness must be in the love and presence of Jesus in your life. If you are not happy, it is because you are looking outside for what you have inside. Do you have the Lord in your heart because of grace?

It is again Saint John of the Cross who says in the Spiritual Canticle:

Oh, then, soul, most beautiful among all creatures, so anxious to know the dwelling place of your Beloved so you may go in search of him and be united with him, now we are telling you that you yourself are his dwelling and his secret inner room and hiding place. There is reason for you to be elated and joyful in seeing that all your good and hope is so close as to be within you, or better, that you cannot be without him. Behold, exclaims the Bridegroom, the kingdom of God is within you [Lk. 17:21]. And his servant, the apostle St. Paul, declares: You are the temple of God [2 Cor. 6:16].

It brings special happiness to a person to understand that God is never absent, not even from a soul in mortal sin (and how much less from one in the state of grace).

What more do you want, O soul! And what else do you search for outside, when within yourself you possess your riches, delights, satisfaction, fullness, and kingdom—your Beloved whom you desire and seek? Be joyful and gladdened in your interior recollection with him, for you have him so close to you. Desire him there, adore him there. Do not go in pursuit of him outside yourself. You will only become distracted and

*wearied thereby, and you shall not find him, or enjoy
him more securely, or sooner, or more intimately than
by seeking him within you.*[10]

3. *"Mary sat beside the Lord at his feet, listening to him speak"*
(Lk 10:39). Imagine the rest of that scene. The disciples are
not with the Lord at that moment, which gives even more
intimacy to this scene. Where were they? We do not know. In
the passage of the Samaritan woman, which we will meditate
on this evening, it is said that "his disciples had gone into
the town to buy food" (Jn 4:8). Maybe they had gone to
Jerusalem that is so close, although I have a different theory,
which I will tell you a little later.

The fact is that Jesus enters the house and there he finds
Mary. Again, as in the episode of the resurrection of Lazarus:
First Martha goes to Jesus, and then Jesus meets Mary. In
the passage of the resurrection of Lazarus, when Martha
returns home she says to her sister: "The teacher is here
and is asking for you." (Jn 11:28) Probably, Jesus did the
same here. He would ask Martha: "Where are your brother
and sister?" We can imagine an answer similar to this one:
"Lazarus has not yet returned, but Mary is here. Come in and
stay with us."

I said before that you are Martha. Now, let me tell you that,
in these Spiritual Exercises, *you are especially Mary.* You are
here listening to him speak. Jesus is speaking to you. He is
going to speak to you, and you have to be sitting at his feet,
capturing every word that comes from his lips and from his
Heart. You can imagine in these days being at His feet, giving
Him all your attention and all your time.

Mary of Bethany is a wonderful woman. In the gospel, we

always find her *at the feet of Jesus.* So we see it here, and in the episode of the resurrection of Lazarus ("when Mary came to where Jesus was and saw him, she fell at his feet," (Jn 11:32), and in the anointing in the house of Simon the Leper that appears in the synoptic gospels and in Chapter twelve of Saint John. It is the position of the disciple who listens and learns from the teacher. Mary is all for Jesus, and Jesus is everything for Mary. What an honor, what a privilege to have Jesus only for her, to listen in silence as if there were nothing else!

Mary is the quiet soul who contemplates Jesus. Yesterday I read to you a text by Edith Stein, in which she says that the soul of the woman is called to be quiet. This is how she explains it:

> *"The soul has to be quiet, for the life which it must protect is timid and speaks only faintly; if the soul itself is in tumult, it will not hear this life which will soon be completely silenced and will disappear from the soul. I wonder whether one can say that the feminine soul is fashioned by nature for this? At first sight, the contrary seems to be true. Women's souls are in commotion so much and so strongly; commotion itself makes much noise; and, in addition, the soul is urged to express its agitation. Nevertheless, the faculty for this quiet must be there; otherwise, it could not be so profoundly practiced as it is, after all, by many women: those women in whom one takes refuge in order to find peace, and who have ears for the softest and most imperceptible little voices."*[11]

29

It is beautiful to apply these last words of Edith Stein to the scene we are contemplating. "Those women in whom one takes refuge in order to find peace and who have been for the softest and most imperceptible little voices." Mary is one of those women and here, Jesus takes refuge in her, not in order to find peace, but in order to give her true peace.

Ask yourself if your soul is quiet or if the world and your occupations are taking peace away from your woman's soul. Ask yourself if you enjoy your encounters with Jesus, if you live at his feet, if he is your teacher. Ask yourself what you should change in your life, what Jesus is asking you to change so that you can hear his voice. How is your prayer life? Is it a furnace where the fire of the Heart of Christ transforms you or, do you pray distractedly and poorly or late and little?

4. *"Martha, burdened with much serving, came to him and said, "Lord, do you not care that my sister has left me by myself to do the serving? Tell her to help me."* (Lk 10:40)

It's funny. Martha was the one who invited Jesus to her home, but when she has him inside, she leaves him with her sister because she has many things to do. It would probably be cleaning, or preparing a banquet as was common—all good things, but in the end, she is "burdened with much serving."

Here *we are all portrayed.* Martha represents the person who is good, who loves Jesus, who has invited the Lord into her life, but who later, through the things of daily life, ends up getting tepid in the love of God. Here is what Saint Ignatius of Loyola told us before: instead of our activity taking us to God, we allow our activity to take us away from God when we are trapped in the realities of this world.

Are you now in that state? Did you tell Jesus one day that you would love him with all your heart and, almost without realizing it, you have ended up distracted, trapped in the trap of occupations and the many things you have to do? That would be very sad.

What happens to Martha is well illustrated in the message of God to the church in Ephesus found in the book of Revelation:

> *"To the angel of the church in Ephesus, write this: "The one who holds the seven stars in his right hand and walks in the midst of the seven gold lampstands says this: "I know your works, your labor, and your endurance, and that you cannot tolerate the wicked; you have tested those who call themselves apostles but are not, and discovered that they are impostors. Moreover, you have endurance and have suffered for my name, and you have not grown weary. Yet I hold this against you: you have lost the love you had at first. Realize how far you have fallen. Repent, and do the works you did at first. Otherwise, I will come to you and remove your lampstand from its place, unless you repent" (2:1–5).*

This is a message full of sadness. Translated for today, it might read: "Yes, I know your works, your labor and your endurance. Yes, I know that you have suffered for me, that everything you do, you do for me. You go out to work and offer your work for me. That the service to your parish and your ministry and your family you do for me. Yes, you have been serving me for a long time. Yet *I hold this against you*: you have lost the love you had at first. *You no longer love me as you loved me at the beginning of your Christian life.* Why do everything you do if your heart grows lukewarm?"

In the *Spiritual Canticle*, Saint John of the Cross says:

> *"Because we said that God makes use of nothing other than love, it may prove beneficial to explain the reason for this before commenting on the stanza. The reason is that all our works and all our trials, even though they be the greatest possible, are nothing in the sight of God. For through them we cannot give him anything or fulfill his only desire, which is the exaltation of the soul. Of these other things he desires nothing for himself, since he has no need of them. If anything pleases him, it is the exaltation of the soul. Since there is no way by which he can exalt her more than by making her equal to himself, he is pleased only with her love. For the property of love is to make the lover equal to the object loved."*[12]

Martha, too, overwhelmed by work, has forgotten her position: if her sister Mary was at the feet of Jesus as a disciple, Martha approaches the Lord demanding what he has to do: "Tell her to help me." The Master is Jesus, but how many times do we want to tell God what he has to do and where he should lead our life? Who is the Lord and who is the disciple? When we turn away from God because of the worries of life, we inevitably turn our love away from our neighbor. We become angry, like Martha with her sister. We get angry because things do not go as we want. Could it be that the lack of patience with others is born of being burdened with so much serving?

5. *"Martha, Martha, you are anxious and worried about many things"* (Lk 10:41).

Jesus responds with meekness. He knows that Martha is good and that she loves him. Probably, she was doing housework for Jesus. "Those whom I love, I reprove and chastise. Be earnest, therefore, and repent" (Rev 3:19).

Think that Jesus *is telling you these words*: He looks you in the eye, calls you by your name and tells you, "You are anxious and worried about many things." Ask yourself in the peace of your prayer, what things make you feel anxious and worried. What things get you out of that presence of God that you have in your soul? The phone? What you hear on television? What you read or see on the Internet? News that makes you angry? Maybe the uncertain future? Do you have too many things on your plate, and is the Lord asking you to leave something? Is there a relationship in your life with someone that makes you grow in anxiety? Maybe some apostolate? Is there too much noise in your life? How do you spend your time?

The devil deceives good souls like Martha: he keeps them busy. He knows that this way, trapped in a tangle of multiple and excessive obligations they may not do something very bad, but *they will stop doing all the good things to which they are called by God.* They will not be able to grow in the love of the Lord.

Think about it slowly, as you listen again to Jesus saying: "You are anxious and worried about many things." Jesus wants to give you the grace to find peace and make the necessary changes, but in this retreat you have to be sincere and see in the presence of God the decisions you have to make.

6. *"There is need of only one thing"* (Lk 10:42). These are the most important words of the passage—the conclusion, the moral, the teaching of Jesus for you today. I invite you to listen many times in your personal prayer to these words: "there is need of only one thing." After you have told Jesus all those things that make you feel anxious, listen to Jesus tell you gently, in the softest voice: "There is need of only one thing."

These words of Jesus are *the beginning of a revolution in your life.* You know that, if you take them seriously, you will have to change commitments, priorities, attachments. These words of Jesus are an invitation to establish different priorities: "There is need of only one thing." It is also a way to simplify our lives, to detach bonds and return to the fundamental, to the important, to the only necessary thing. Forget about the superfluous, the superficial, and focus on the only important thing.

Commenting on Chapter 15 of Saint John, where it says that the Father prunes the branches of the vine (verse 2), Saint Thomas Aquinas affirms that a tree cannot grow very tall when it has many branches.[13] You have to prune the tree, remove branches so that it can reach its maximum height. That is what the Lord is teaching you here in Bethany: your life has too many branches, cut them all and *leave only one.* We cannot give ourselves generously to the Lord if we are involved in a thousand things. We simply cannot. If someone wants to stand out in a particular discipline he knows has to focus on that. If I want to be a great pianist, I have to dedicate six, seven, eight hours a day to the instrument. If you do many things, if you waste your time on less important things, you will never excel.

In the spiritual life, something similar happens. Kierkegaard said that "purity of intention is *to will one thing*."[14] If Christ were our *one thing*, if our *only one thing* was "to praise, reverence, and serve God our Lord," as Saint Ignatius tells us, *we would be saints*.

From this perspective, we can give a definition of holiness: the saint is the one who wants only one thing. As Pope Paul VI said, *"souls of a single love."*[15] Those of us who are not saints are the ones who want too many things, we are scattered among many things—maybe not bad things, or maybe some of them are bad, but we get lost in the jumble of projects, commitments and tasks that do not allow us to grow. This meditation on "Principle and Foundation" aims to turn us into people who look only to God, who care only about God.

Jesus was a radical, and his radicalism is expressed in the word, *one*: "There is need of only ONE thing." The Lord is not saying that there are more important and less important things: He is saying that listening to Him is the *only* important thing and that *everything else, in God's eyes, is not*. Do we judge reality according to this criterion of Jesus?

We live in a world that is continually inviting us to stay tangled, like Martha, in things, activities, projects, and initiatives. Perhaps now, more than ever, we need to return to Bethany at the feet of Jesus and forget everything.

I believe that Jesus is inviting you to this spiritual revolution. The Lord is pointing out to you the primacy of the whole reality *as He sees it,* which is the personal Truth, the Truth made man:

- The primacy of your relationship with Him above all else.
- The primacy of your fidelity to prayer over any other activity.
- The primacy of the spiritual life over the material life.
- The primacy of the eternal over what ends in this life.
- The primacy of being over doing.
- The primacy of listening over speaking.
- The primacy of silence over the noise of the world.
- The primacy of receiving first to give later.
- The primacy of personal relationships over the realization of projects. Sometimes we are so busy with *things* that we forget about the *people* in our family.

Ask Jesus for a change of heart, *metanoia*, to see the world, your life, everything, as he sees it.

7. *"Mary has chosen the better part and it will not be taken from her"* (Lk 10:42).

The conclusion of this meditation is left to Saint Ambrose. In commenting on this episode, Saint Ambrose urges his faithful and us too:

> *"Let us too seek to have what cannot be taken from us, dedicating diligent, not distracted, attention to the Lord's word. The seeds of the heavenly word are blown away if they are sown along the roadside. May the wish to know be an incentive to you too, as it was*

36

to Mary; this is the greatest and most perfect act."[16]

These are the seven points that I bring to your consideration. For your personal reading, I am going to leave you with a beautiful passage from Edith Stein. Earlier I said that, in your prayer, you must see yourself in both Martha and Mary. It is evident that you cannot be "*only*" Mary or "*only*" Martha. Better said, you must *always* be Mary, having her heart and always at the feet of Jesus, although you are also called to the activity of your life like Martha. Edith Stein's text is a page of her personal writings, which she wrote when she was still a lay woman in the world. It seems to me that it is one of the best practical applications on this passage that you can read. In her writing, she tries to find the balance between the active and contemplative dimensions of her life. Surely it will give you much light.[17]

* * *

I will finish here with one last application of the Gospel that we have meditated on and that I could only begin to understand while in the Holy Land. I do not know if some biblical scholar has noticed before (I am sure, good ideas that come out of my head are rarely original) but it helps me a lot, and that is why I share it with you.

The story of Martha and Mary in Bethany begins with the words: "*As they continued their journey* He entered a village where a woman whose name was Martha welcomed him." Those first words "As they continued their journey ..." seem to relate this passage to the one immediately preceding. In addition, St. Luke tells us at the onset of his Gospel, "I too have decided, after investigating everything carefully from the beginning, to write it down *in an orderly sequence* for you, most excellent Theophilus" (Lk 1:3). That is to say, that Saint Luke has been diligent to investigate what he writes and to write it *in an orderly sequence*, that is, respecting the chronology of events.

What is the story immediately before the story of Bethany? The parable of the Good Samaritan. This parable begins when a "scholar of the law" asks Jesus: "Teacher, what must I do to inherit eternal life?" (Lk. 10:25) In this passage, Jesus also appears as a teacher, but the attitude of this man is completely different from Mary's. Mary was at the feet of Jesus, listening; this man, says the Scripture, "stood up to test him."

As a scholar of the law, that man was familiar with Sacred Scripture. We can say that God was the most important thing in his life and he had dedicated his whole life to study the revealed Word of God. That is why Jesus answers him with the question of what is written in the law: "How do you read it?" That is, how do you understand it? What do you think about it? "He said in reply, 'You shall love the Lord, your God, with all your heart, with all your being, with all your strength, and with all your mind, and your neighbor as yourself.'"

Jesus is satisfied with the answer and says so: "You have answered correctly, do this and you will live." But the scholar of the law continues: "But because he wished to justify himself, he said to Jesus, 'And who is my neighbor?'" The Lord answers with the parable that we all know. The first words of Jesus are: "A man fell victim to robbers as he went down from Jerusalem to Jericho." It is very likely that this conversation with the scholar of the law took place in the same city of Jericho. The first reason is that in the previous chapter it is said that Jesus had determined "to journey to Jerusalem." (9:51) Jericho was on the way to the Holy City and we know that it was a city of residence for the priests of the tribe of Levi who served in the temple and for the scholars of the law because of its proximity to Jerusalem, only fifteen miles away. We also know that there was a path that connected both cities and that is the path Jesus refers to at the beginning of the parable. I had the grace to walk half of it, in the direction of Jericho: now it cannot be completed because the border between Palestine and Israel divides it into two. The road runs through a very deep gorge that cuts through the arid landscape.

Now, having been there, this is how I do my particular "composition of place:"[18] Jesus speaks with the scholar of the law in Jericho and from there, they continue to-wards Jerusalem, stopping in Bethany, which is just outside Jerusalem. The road from Jericho to Jerusalem is brutal. It is uphill and there is no shade. Jericho is the lowest-lying city in the world, 250 meters below sea level, where Jerusalem is located at almost 800 meters above sea level: a climb of more than 1,000 meters. To give you an idea, that's almost the difference in elevation between the bottom of the Grand Canyon and the top. That is why I said before that I believe that Jesus came first to Bethany while the apostles fell behind and that the conversation with Martha and Mary took place while he was waiting for them.

But what I wanted to say with these two stories is that, deep down, the Lord is giving us *the same teaching, but he is putting the accents in different places.* Jesus reminds the scholar of the law, who had devoted himself to serving God in the Scriptures, that love for God is the most important thing, but he must also have concern for his brother.

To Martha, who was dedicated to service, Jesus reminds her of the same thing but emphasizes the dedication to the "only important thing," which is listening to the Word of God.

I think it is important to see where each of us fits, whether by nature or by vocation. There may be among us people who, because of their obligations to their family and their many other obligations, need to especially listen to the words of the Lord to Martha. Jesus reminds you that a relationship with him is the most important thing. To those who have more time and who find it easier to pray, because you are unmarried or widowed, or because your children are grown and have already left home, or whatever your circumstances may be, the Lord may ask you to take care of the brother who needs you and who is at your side.

I do not believe that the Lord reproached Martha for her service. Jesus says that he himself had come to serve (Mt. 20:28). The Lord's rebuke to his friend is because she *has forgotten love* and become so engrossed in her tasks that she lost sight of Him. I remember a Jesuit priest, Fr. Luis María Mendizábal, saying that perhaps Jesus' response would have been very different if Martha had said to him: "Lord, what a joy that you are teaching my sister! I am very happy for her and I want her to continue listening to you. I would very much like to hear you, too. Why don't you come into the kitchen and talk while I finish the dishes? That way I could listen to you too."

In this time of prayer that lies before you, may you place yourself at the feet of Jesus. May you have the courage to recognize what may be distracting you from Him. Ask for the grace to seek no other foundation for your life than that which has already been established—Jesus Christ. (1 Cor. 3:11)

3

WOMAN'S EUCHARISTIC LIFE

DAY 1 – HOMILY (Gn 13:2. 5-18; Mt 7:6. 12-14)

Today's first reading has a special meaning for me this year. On March 12 of last year, I prayed before the Terebinth (Oak) of Mamre, in the Palestinian city of Hebron. The Lord told Abram: "Get up and walk through the land, across its length and breadth, for I give it to you" (Gn. 13:2) God also granted me the privilege of walking in that land, through its length and breadth, and to pray before the grave of this great patriarch, who is the father of all believers.

I have always been impressed by this generosity of Abram: the Jordan Valley is the most fertile part of the Holy Land. It is a green area, full of orchards that produce fruit and abundant crops. Maybe that's why Lot chose it for himself and his family. For his part, Abram yields it to Lot with equanimity and as a reward for his faith and his generosity, he receives from God, a double promise: the land and the offspring: "all the land that you see I will give it to you and your descendants forever."

God is the one we can trust. Abram left his home at the age of seventy-five and set out on a thousand-mile journey to the Land that God wanted to show him. In our first reading, the Lord indicates that he has finally reached that Promised Land and Abram is finally settled on it.

Abram always listens to the Word of God. In the book of Genesis, we see him constantly attentive to the voice of God, like Mary in this morning's meditation. It is the position of the believer, who before the mystery of God's revelation accepts and welcomes the revealed Word and carries it into practice.

Yes, Abraham in his faithful obedience to the Word that is revealed to him and Mary, at the feet of Jesus, invite us to listen to God and live only for him. That is fulfilled, in a preeminent way, in the Eucharist. Here Christ comes to us, and in the silence of this Sacrament speaks to us and listens to us.

"A woman's life must be a Eucharistic life." This affirmation of Edith Stein allows us to unite this morning's meditation, Abraham's example, today's Gospel and the mystery of the Eucharist. If you will allow me an interpretation, the narrow gate and the constricted road that lead to life are a sincere devotion to Jesus in the Eucharist, *"and those who find it are few."* In the Eucharist, we learn to listen. In the Eucharist, we also place ourselves at the feet of Jesus and contemplate him. In the Eucharist, we receive the promises of God and he fills us with divine life. For you, Catholic women who want to live a deep Christian life, the Eucharist is the source of your strength and a place of rest.

This is what Edith Stein tells us, and I finish with her words that express what I am trying to say better than I can on my own:

> *It is most important that the Holy Eucharist becomes life's focal point: that the Eucharistic Savior is the center of existence; that every day is received from His hand and laid back therein; that the day's happenings are deliberated with Him. In this way, God is given the best opportunity to be heard in the heart, to form the soul, and to make its faculties clear-sighted and alert for the supernatural.[19]*

> *Whoever wants to preserve this life continually within herself must nourish it constantly from the source whence it flows without end—from the holy sacraments, above all from the sacrament of love. To have divine love as its inner form, a woman's life must be a Eucharistic life. Only in daily, confidential relationship with the Lord in the tabernacle can one forget self, become free of all one's own wishes and pretensions, and have a heart open to all the needs and wants of others. Whoever seeks to consult with the Eucharistic God in all her concerns, whoever lets herself be purified by the sanctifying power coming from the sacrifice at the altar, offering herself to the Lord in this sacrifice, whoever receives the Lord in her soul's innermost depth in Holy Communion cannot but be drawn ever more deeply and powerfully into the flow of divine life, incorporated into the Mystical Body of Christ, her heart converted to the likeness of the divine heart.[20]*

May Jesus teach us today to delight in his Eucharistic presence and to hear his voice; to listen and obey as did Abraham and Mary. In our familiar, close, and desired relationship with the Blessed Sacrament, may we find the "only one necessary thing" that we considered in this morning's meditation: our friendship with the living person of Jesus.

4

THE SAMARITAN WOMAN

DAY 1 (AFTERNOON) – THIRD MEDITATION – PRINCIPLE AND FOUNDATION II

"Grant, almighty God, through the yearly observance of holy Lent that we may grow in understanding of the riches hidden in Christ and by worthy conduct pursue their effects. Through our Lord Jesus Christ. Amen."
(First Sunday of Lent)

Good afternoon. We continue on this first day within the Spiritual Exercises framework, meditating on the Principle and Foundation. Taking as a biblical basis the episode of Jesus' conversation with Martha at Bethany, we reflected on the fact that our life consists in the service of God, in listening to his Word, in loving God with all our heart and our neighbor as ourselves, in always living dedicated to the only important thing. Indeed, *"there is need of only one thing."*

I told you this morning that the meditation of Principle

and Foundation should be present in all the reflections of the Exercises. Here is what that means in practical terms: Saint Ignatius includes two petitions: one is general, and is the same in all the meditations of the Exercises; the second is particular, and it is the specific grace that you want to ask of God in the present meditation.

The general request, which we have to ask every step of the way, the ultimate goal of this experience we are in, has its origin in the Principle and Foundation. It is the following prayer:

> *"The Preparatory Prayer is to ask grace of God our Lord that all my intentions, actions, and operations may be directed purely to the service and praise of His Divine Majesty" (SE 46).*

The "conquer oneself" in the title of the Spiritual Exercises applies to this Principle and Foundation, according to which "man is created to praise, reverence, and serve God, our Lord, and by this means to save his soul," translates into this preparatory prayer saying that "all my intentions, actions and operations may be directed purely to the service and praise of His Divine Majesty." That is the grace we seek: that our whole life be *ad maiorem Dei gloriam*, "for the greater glory of God," as He always liked to say, knowing that, in a life given to God, true happiness is found.

We are going to go deeper into this because it is important. If the Principle and Foundation is not well understood, then when we say that man is created to serve God it may sound as if God has made us for his self-glorification, to give glory to himself, as if he were a king creating a court of subjects to praise him, thinking exclusively of himself and not of us.

It is not like that. It is true that the purpose of all creation is the glory of God, but we cannot increase the glory of God because the glory of God is infinite. It existed before creation and we cannot "add" glory to the Lord. That would be in fact a heresy. As I said, the glory that the Divine Persons give and receive from them is infinite: "Glorify me, Father, with you, with the glory that I had with you before the world began." (Jn. 17: 5)

What are we talking about, when we say, "give glory to God" or "glorify God"?

First, the *Catechism of the Catholic Church*, quoting Saint Bonaventure, says that God created all things "not to increase his glory, but to show it forth and to communicate it".[21] God's purpose in creating us was not to give himself more glory than he already had—something that is impossible. He creates to share that glory with beings other than himself. Is this not beautiful? The creation of the world and of man is explained by love. "*Aperta manu clave amoris, creaturae prodierunt* (Creatures came into existence when the key of love opened his hand)," says Saint Thomas Aquinas. Therefore, it is not the egoism of an self-obsessed God that moves him to create out of nothing this wonderful world in which we live, but the love of a God who wanted to share his light and reflect it in his creatures, especially man. "*Gloria Dei vivens homo* (The glory of God is man fully alive)," says St. Irenaeus.

The glory of God consists in glorifying man. We are his children, and he wants to see us filled with life. We glorify him not when we serve him in the manner of servants, but when, as his children, we live with joy in our dependence on him. This is important to underscore in today's world, where maturity is measured by our degree of independence. Young people want to live away from their parents and we teach them to "take care of themselves." The ideal person is independent. We do not like to depend on others. We do not like to be dependent economically or existentially because we think that makes us weak. A little child depends on his parents for everything and we think that as we grow up the normal thing is to become autonomous. The word "autonomous" comes from the Greek: auto means "self" and "nomos" means law. The one who gives the law to himself is autonomous. That's what we want: no one to tell us what we have to do, to give ourselves our own laws.

Saint Ignatius of Loyola, along with the whole Church, teaches us precisely the opposite: in the supernatural order, the ideal is the *absolute dependence on God*. That is the attitude of the Son with regard to his Father: "Amen, amen, I say to you, a son cannot do anything on his own, but only what he sees his father doing, for what he does, his son will do also" (Jn. 5:19).

"Let the children come to me, and do not prevent them, for the kingdom of heaven belongs to such as these" (Mt. 19:14).In the spiritual life, the ideal is not to grow, it is to remain children. Saint Therese of Lisieux said that what He likes to see is the way we love our littleness. She explains this dependence on God:

> *It is to recognize our nothingness, to look for every-thing from God as a little child looks for everything from his father; it is to be disquieted about nothing, and not to be set on gaining our fortune. Even among*

50

the poor, they give the child all he needs until he grows up; then his father will no longer support him, and says to him: 'Go out to work now, for you are able to look after yourself.' It is to avoid hearing this that I have desired not to grow up, because I realized I should never be able to earn my own living, the eternal life of heaven! I have, then, always remained little, and have had no other occupation than that of gathering flowers, the flowers of love and sacrifice. These I have offered to the good God simply for His own pleasure.[22]

The best explanation of what I have tried to say comes from a holy Church Father for whom I have great affection, Saint Irenaeus. He explains that our glory consists in friendship with God, that we add nothing to the glory of God, that it is He who wants to glorify us, that our glory is in communion with Him. These are His words:

Our Lord, the Word of God, first drew men to God as servants, but later he freed those made subject to him. He himself testified to this: 'I do not call you servants any longer, for a servant does not know what his master is doing. Instead I call you friends, since I have made known to you everything that I have learned from my Father.' Friendship with God brings the gift of immortality to those who accept it.

In the beginning God created Adam, not because he needed man, but because he wanted to have someone on whom to bestow his blessings. Not only before Adam but also before all creation, the Word was glorifying the Father in whom he dwelt, and was himself being glorified b y t he F ather. T he Word himself said: Father, glorify me with that glory I had with you before the world was.

Nor did the Lord need our service. He commanded us to follow him, but his was the gift of salvation. To follow the Savior is to share in salvation; to follow the light is to enjoy the light. Those who are in the light do not illuminate the light but are themselves illuminated and enlightened by the light. They add nothing to the light; rather, they are beneficiaries, for they are enlightened by the light.

The same is true of service to God: it adds nothing to God, nor does God need the service of man. Rather, he gives life and immortality and eternal glory to those who follow and serve him. He confers a benefit on his servants in return for their service and on his followers in return for their loyalty, but he receives no benefit from them. He is rich, perfect, and in need of nothing.

The reason why God requires service from man is this: because he is good and merciful he desires to confer benefits on those who persevere in his service. In proportion to God's need of nothing is man's need for communion with God.

This is the glory of man: to persevere and remain in the service of God. For this reason the Lord told his disciples: 'You did not choose me but I chose you.' He meant that his disciples did not glorify him by following him, but in following the Son of God they were glorified by h im. As he s aid: I wish that where I am they also may be, that they may see my glory."[23]

So, we must understand the Principle and Foundation of Saint Ignatius. We have to serve God as children and friends. And this we will see reflected in a passage of the New Testament that I invite you to meditate on in this context: the encounter of Jesus with the Samaritan woman.

* * *

One of the most important people in my spiritual journey has been Fr. Luis María Mendizábal, whom I am certain will be canonized by the Church someday. Fr. Mendizábal was a Jesuit priest, Spanish and Basque, who died in 2017 at ninety-two years of age, having spent seventy-seven of those years in the Society of Jesus. He spent his novitiate in Loyola, studied in Germany and was a professor of asceticism and mysticism at the Gregorian University in Rome for ten years. He directed the month-long Spiritual Exercises for many years in Toledo, Spain. He was a spiritual director without equal, but stands out in a special way for being the great propagator of the message of the Sacred Heart of Jesus in Spain in the twentieth century. His penetration of the Mystery of the Heart of Christ is unlike anything I have ever known. He was a man who lived within the Heart of Jesus, who spoke of the Heart of Jesus as one intimately united to him. The Heart of Jesus and he were one and Fr. Mendizábal knew his friend Jesus with that "interior knowledge" of which Saint Ignatius speaks. What I am going to say about the Samaritan woman is based on what he himself said about this episode in the Spiritual Exercises that he directed and also in the Commentary of St. Thomas Aquinas on this passage.[24]

Father Mendizábal used this passage from the Samaritan woman at the beginning of his Spiritual Exercises precisely to talk about the Principle and Foundation. The meditation of St. Ignatius must be understood in the light of Christ. St. Paul writes: "for no one can lay a foundation other than the one that is there, namely, Jesus Christ" (1 Cor. 3:11).

Christ is the foundation, the stone on which we are to build our life (Mt. 7: 24-27).I remember the words of Pope Benedict on his trip to Poland in 2006:

To build on Christ and with Christ means to build on a foundation that is called 'crucified love.' It means to build with Someone who, knowing us better than we know ourselves, says to us: 'You are precious in my eyes and honored, and I love you' (Is. 43:4). It means to build with Someone, who is always faithful, even when we are lacking in faith, because he cannot deny himself (cf. 2 Tim. 2:13). It means to build with Someone who constantly looks down on the wounded heart of man and says: 'I do not condemn you, go and do not sin again' (cf. Jn. 8:11). It means to build with Someone who, from the Cross, extends his arms and repeats for all eternity: 'O man, I give my life for you because I love you.' In short, building on Christ means basing all your desires, aspirations, dreams, ambitions and plans on his will. It means saying to yourself, to your family, to your friends, to the whole world and, above all to Christ: 'Lord, in life I wish to do nothing against you, because you know what is

best for me. Only you have the words of eternal life'
(cf. Jn 6:68). My friends, do not be afraid to lean on
Christ! Long for Christ, as the foundation of your life!
Enkindle within you the desire to build your life on
him and for him! Because no one who depends on the
crucified love of the Incarnate Word can ever lose.[25]

If we do not build our life on Christ, we are building it on sand. The Samaritan woman had built her life on sand until she met the Lord. As you know, this passage occupies practically all of Chapter 4 of the Gospel of St. John.

I invite you to read it and let the Lord speak to you through it. Here I will comment on some key points that I hope will help you.

1. Let me tell you that last year on my pilgrimage through Palestine, I personally received the immense grace of praying at Jacob's Well, where this scene took place. It is another of those places where there are almost no visitors since it is in Palestine, in the city of Nablus, which is located in what is called "Area A" in the Oslo Accord. More than 80% of the West Bank is militarily controlled by the State of Israel in Areas B and C. Area A represents less than 20% of the entire West Bank, and is the only area controlled by the Palestinian Authority. It is, therefore, the only part of the country in which Palestinians feel "free" because they are "out" of Israel's control.

All the trips or pilgrimages that are organized to the Holy Land avoid going to Area A because it is considered dangerous. In Areas B and C, the pilgrims are under the shadow of the wings of Israel. When entering Area A, there is a sign written in Arabic, Hebrew and English, with the following "friendly" words of welcome: "This road leads to Area A, under the Palestinian Authority. The entrance for Israeli citizens is forbidden, dangerous to your lives and is against the Israeli Law." When you cross that point, you accept the risk and enter under your own responsibility.

We arrived in Nablus on March 19, 250 miles after beginning our journey by the Red Sea. Maybe this name, Nablus, does not ring a bell, but in the time of Jesus, its name was Sychar. "He had to pass through Samaria. So he came to a town of Samaria called Sychar, near the plot of land that Jacob had given to his son Joseph. Jacob's well was there. Jesus, tired from his journey, sat down there at the well. It was about noon." (Jn 4: 4-6)

The first words are noteworthy: "He had to pass through Samaria." What do they mean? Saint John is telling us that, because of the Pharisees, Jesus decided to retire to Galilee from Judea, where he was with his disciples. To get there, there were at least three roads: the one that crossed Samaria, which was chosen by the Lord; the path that climbed the Jordan River, which Jesus used in other occasions; and the most important and well known of all, the one that is called in the Gospel, *"way of the sea"* (Mt. 4:15).That is the literal translation of the Latin *Via Maris*, which ran along the coast of the Mediterranean and reached Galilee after crossing the Jezreel valley. It was the closest thing to a modern highway in those days, a path used by merchants and armies that connected Egypt with Syria. I had the grace to go to walk two of them last year.

From the geographical point of view, Jesus *did not have to pass through Samaria.* In fact, it was the least recommended way for him, as a Jew. *"Jews use nothing in common with Samaritans,"* says Saint John to put it mildly (v. 9).Several times the Gospel tells us that the Samaritans rejected Jesus. Perhaps the clearest passage is in the Gospel of St. Luke, where it is said that "they would not welcome him" (9:51-53).It is the moment when, angry at this rejection, the meek James and John say to Jesus: "Lord, do you want us to call down fire from heaven to consume them?"

If Jesus knew that he was not welcomed there and had other options to get to Galilee, why does Saint John say, "He had to pass through Samaria?"

Father Mendizábal gives a beautiful explanation. He had to pass through Samaria *in order to encounter this woman.* In other words, he was looking for her. The words of Saint John should not be understood in a geographical sense, as if that were the only way to get there, but in an *intentional* sense: he is speaking to us of the Heart of Jesus, of his desire to save this woman! Jesus had no *physical* need to go through Samaria: it is his love that forces him to pass through there.

This gives us the frame to read this passage. It is part of the "composition of place" that you must do because you have to contemplate this scene not from without, but *from within the Heart of Jesus.* It is no coincidence that Jesus came across this woman. It wasn't that He was tired, sat down by the well, and the woman just happened to arrive to get water while the Lord was sitting and waiting for his apostles.

No: this scene is that of the Good Shepherd who leaves his ninety-nine sheep, or his twelve sheep, and goes in search of the one that had been lost to him. Jesus wants to find that woman who was lost in her broken life. Jesus seeks her.

From this perspective, I invite you to make an effort to imagine in your prayer what happens immediately before this page of the Gospel, in her life before meeting Christ. Think, for example, of the day before this encounter: imagine the woman in her house, a day like any other in her life. She had no idea who Jesus was, but while she was still in her ordinary life, *Jesus was on his way to meet her!* The Lord did know her, and walked towards that woman he loved, and his Heart is thirsty for her. Imagine Jesus walking to find her, like someone who goes to meet the person he loves. Imagine the face of Jesus, try to feel what the Heart of Jesus feels on his way to her. Possibly Jesus' fatigue has to do with his fast pace, which expresses his desire to save that lost woman: "I have come to set the earth on fire, and how I wish it were already blazing!" (Lk. 12:49)The lost sheep is the treasure of Jesus, as we will also see in the film tonight. Jesus took that detour to find her. Meanwhile, she could not have suspected that the Lord was approaching her.

The Lord does the same with you today, in your life. He seeks you with a heart in love. He looks for a meeting with you. He wants to talk to you, quench your thirst, and transform you. While he is here, the Lord is not still. He is looking for you with his grace, he is preparing future encounters with you just as he has prepared this one. He wants to look you in the eyes to tell you, "I am who loves you." It is the invitation to the friendship that Saint Irenaeus spoke about, a friendship that gives you eternal life. The Church says in one of its Latin hymns: "*quaerens me, sedisti lassus* (Seeking me, you sat down wearily)."That's exactly what this woman is going to experience.

"So he came to a town of Samaria called Sychar, near the

plot of land that Jacob had given to his son, Joseph. Jacob's well was there." Jacob's well was a gift from father to son, and in this setting the gift of our heavenly Father to his children will be presented to us: Jesus Christ. He is the inheritance that the Father gives us. In him there is also a deep well, a source of living water: his Heart pierced.

2. "Jesus, tired from his journey, sat down there at the well. It was about noon." Another wonderful point explained by Father Mendizábal, and also suggested by Saint Thomas Aquinas, is that Saint John is seeing this encounter between Jesus and this woman *as a prefigurement of the Passion of Jesus.*

The first sign that Saint John gives us is the indication of time: "It was about noon." These are the same words Saint John uses at the moment of the Passion: "When Pilate heard these words he brought Jesus out and seated him on the judge's bench in the place called Stone Pavement—in Hebrew, Gabbatha. It was preparation day for the Passover, and it was about noon. And he said to the Jews, "Behold, your king!" (Jn. 19:14)For St. John, it is a diptych: this Jesus who is sitting by the well is Christ in his Passion. This Jesus who is sitting by the well at noon is the same Jesus who is sitting on the judge's bench at noon. In both cases, it is a Jesus "tired from his journey." This present weariness is a symbol of the pains of his Passion, of his weariness after having been destroyed by the scourging, by the crowning of thorns, by the crucifixion. In both cases, it is a thirsty Jesus, who here says: "Give me a drink," and on the cross he exclaims: "I thirst." In both episodes, there is a well and water: here, the well of Jacob, and on Calvary, the well of his pierced Heart from which flows blood and water.

In both cases, it is the hour of mercy. It is Christ, exhausted, tired, at the well, begging for mercy. It is also the Christ of the Eucharist, of the Tabernacle, before which people pass without paying attention to it, without accepting his message, without responding to his request for mercy: "Give me a drink."

3. "A woman of Samaria came to draw water" (v. 7).Imagine the woman just before she arrived there. Jesus is already at the well, waiting for her! With the desire to give her eternal life, the gift of God. Imagine the woman holding the water pitcher, just like any other day, and setting out toward the well.

That woman... is you. Do not lose sight of that. While it is true that the Samaritan woman represents all people, in a special way she is representing those of you who are women. In the Exercises, you should see yourself *in her*, not just representing you. Jesus is seeing you in her; he is asking you to drink. He is inviting you.

Who is this woman? Someone who wants to be loved. This page of the Gospel may seem, at first glance, a bit fragmented. In the conversation between Jesus and this woman, there is a first part in which the main theme is water and thirst. Suddenly, the conversation changes direction completely when Jesus tells the woman point blank: "Call your husband." It seems an abrupt comment, and if it unsettles us, it unsettles this woman even more. And, finally, there is the part in which Jesus speaks of true worship of God: "true worshipers will worship the Father in Spirit and truth" (v. 23).

How do we find unity in this dispersal? Is there something in common in these three parts? Apparently not, and yet there is unity. The unity of the story is in the desire.

Thirst is an image of love and desire. The woman went to the well *"to draw water."*

And Jesus is going to talk about another water that satisfies forever. They are two different waters, two different ways to quench the thirst of the heart.

This woman, who is you, has tried to quench her thirst in the people and things of this world. She has sought her happiness there, but she cannot fill her heart. She has sought to satisfy her heart in human love, marrying five times, but she has always remained unsatisfied. This woman is us—is you—seeking to fill yourself h ere. The prophet Jeremiah says, "Two evils have my people done: they have forsaken me, the source of living waters; They have dug themselves cisterns, broken cisterns, that hold no water" (2:13).How many times have you felt disappointed? How many times have you wanted something and have not found what you wanted? How many times have you wanted to quench your thirst in something or in someone, and discovered that you were still parched and dry? How many times have you sought your happiness in sin, represented by those five husbands, that result from those sad experiences? To this day, where are you looking to quench your thirst? From which well are you trying to draw water? In your family? In some person? In some hobby or in some activity?

The work of Jesus in your heart wants to reach the bottom, and wants to heal the root of your unhappiness, which is desire. You have desired bad things, or you have desired good things but they do not fill the heart. Jesus wants to heal

61

you by loving you. When we are loved by a good love, by a good friendship, we are transformed by that love. And that is what Jesus offers this woman: a love that not only loves her, but transforms her. That is what Jesus is offering here, to you. Are you going to let him?

4. *The Encounter.* Imagine Jesus from the perspective of the woman approaching the well. Imagine the first exchange of looks on the ledge of that well. That well still exists in the lower part of an Orthodox church that is respected by Muslims and Christians as a sacred place. "The cistern is deep," says the woman in the Gospel. I can attest to that: I remember pouring water into the well and having to wait several seconds until I heard the sound of the water hitting the bottom. It is a well, made of stone, which you can find in many images on the Internet. It is awesome to be there and to think that Jesus was sitting right there. From the archaeological point of view, it is one of those places in the Holy Land that offers no doubt about its authenticity. I had seen the well that Abraham had made in Bersheeba and now I could see the one that his grandson, Jacob, had opened there. The patriarchs dug as many wells as they could. For them, in such an arid place, it was a matter of life or death. Digging a well has a meaning: they wanted to express a willingness to settle in, to take root, to have a place they could call home.

This is again Pope Benedict:

> *"My friends, in the heart of every man there is the desire for a house. Even more so in the young person's heart there is a great longing for a proper house, a stable house, one to which he can not only return with*

joy, but where every guest who arrives can be joyfully welcomed. There is a yearning for a house where the daily bread is love, pardon and understanding. It is a place where the truth is the source out of which flows peace of h eart. There is a longing for a house you can be proud of, where you need not be ashamed and where you never fear its loss. These longings are simply the desire for a full, happy, and successful life. Do not be afraid of this desire! Do not run away from this desire! Do not be discouraged at the sight of crumbling houses, frustrated desires, and faded longings. God the Creator, who inspires in young hearts an immense yearning for happiness, will not abandon you in the difficult construction of the house called life."[26]

The well is also a place of meeting and joy: the place where people went to talk and to rest after a long trip as Jesus does here.

The *Catechism* uses this passage to talk about prayer. We said yesterday that prayer is a gift. Yes, it is a gift to arrive at the well and to find Jesus there. See that God comes to meet man and seeks us. The *Catechism* says something very beautiful that we can apply to the contemplation of this scene of the Gospel:

The wonder of prayer is revealed beside the well where we come seeking water: there, Christ comes to meet every human being. It is he who first seeks us and asks us for a drink. Jesus thirsts; his asking arises from the depths of God's desire for us.

Whether we realize it or not, prayer is the encounter of God's thirst with ours. God thirsts that we may thirst for him.[27]

When the woman arrives, Jesus is there. God is waiting for her in the love of that human Heart, in that face that she can see, in those eyes that are looking at her. "In this is love: not that we have loved God, but that he loved us. We love because He first loved us" (1 Jn. 4:10,19).

In my pilgrimage, one of the ideas that occupied my mind every day was the very fact of Revelation—the fact that God wanted to reveal himself, open his Heart and invite us into intimacy. I was walking through all those places and thinking: "all this, all this manifestation, the whole history of your encounters with man, on this earth, everything is grace. Everything you have done to attract us to you and bring us to eternal life with you—without us deserving anything."

Like the Samaritan woman, Jesus was waiting for you here and wants to talk to you. His love precedes you. He has created you, he loved you before you existed, he has revealed himself to you and now he finds you. In Him is ALL that that woman can desire.

5. "Give me a drink" (v. 7). Here, in these four words, I lose myself. In your prayer, close your eyes and find the eyes of Jesus, "the eyes I have desired," as Saint John of the Cross says. The look of Jesus is unique, it is the gaze of God. It is the look of One who knows what is in the heart of man (cf. Jn. 2:24). A look that sees from within, eyes "which I bear sketched deep within my heart," says Saint John of the

Cross.

In that look, you must discover all the love of God. And in that request, the depth of God's desire for you, as the *Catechism* has said. "Prayer is the encounter of God's thirst with ours. God thirsts that we may thirst for him."

The *Catechism* also says that in prayer, we are all beggars before God[28]. The truth is that in prayer, God is a beggar before us. He is asking you for a drink.

The amazement of seeing God at our feet should make us cry in confusion and joy. The woman says later: "How can you, a Jew, ask me, a Samaritan woman, for a drink?" (v. 9) She is amazed that this man asks her for a drink because he is Jewish. You should say with infinitely greater astonishment, "How can you, a God, ask me, a sinner, for a drink? How can you, a God, desire me, an unfaithful creature? How can you, who has everything, ask me who am nothing, for my love? You have to be out of your mind to love someone like me."

Saint Bernard writes: "when God loves, all he desires is to be loved in return; the sole purpose of his love is to be loved, in the knowledge that those who love him are made happy by their love of him."[29]

Be astounded by Christ's desire for you. Be amazed that the fountain is thirsty. Ask yourself if you want Jesus, if your thirst for him is the thirst he has for you.

6. *Dialogue and words of Jesus.* We cannot reflect on all the words of the Lord with the Samaritan woman. I invite you to read them in light of what we have said so far.

The purpose of Jesus is to make the woman feel desire for Him. Jesus is going to win her over. The Lord wants—in her heart that is arid because it is full of human desires—to plant the seed of a desire that she does not have. "If you knew the gift of God and who is saying to you, 'Give me a drink,' you would have asked Him and He would have given you living water" (v. 10).

The ordering of our spiritual life, of our desires, is the fruit of the Holy Spirit. When we meet the Lord for the first time, our heart still desires many things, some of which may be bad or disordered. The Christian life consists in letting the Holy Spirit heal and order those desires. He does it inwardly, through grace, giving us other things to desire: the gift of God (the Holy Spirit)and the Person of Christ. The Lord is the source of living water: "Let anyone who thirsts come to me and drink. Whoever believes in me, as scripture says: 'Rivers of living water will flow from within him'" (Jn. 7:37-38).

> *Jesus said to her, "Go call your husband and come back." The woman answered and said to him, "I do not have a husband." Jesus answered her, "You are right in saying, 'I do not have a husband.' For you have had five husbands, and the one you have now is not your husband. What you have said is true (v. 16–18).*

Jesus changes the conversation suddenly by bringing up the subject of her husband. Just before, she told him: "Sir, give me this water, so that I may not be thirsty or have to keep coming here to draw water" (v. 15). Without knowing what she was saying, but captivated by this mysterious Jew, she has made her request. She has already begun her salvation and meets Jesus' surprising and uncomfortable request that she go find her husband.

Why does the Lord choose this issue? We have already said that one reason is to help her understand that her heart is also thirsty and she has gone to quench that thirst without finding full s atisfaction. But there is also another reason here. Jesus is meaning to say: "I know who you are."

Maybe at the beginning of the conversation, when Jesus began to say such beautiful words, and told her about the gift of God, and that other water, the woman thought, "If he knew who I am . . . surely he would not be telling me these things." And when Jesus talks to her about her husband, possibly she thought, "How well the conversation had been going until now . . ."

The Lord is telling her here: *I am making this invitation to you, personally, in the life that you have. I know your story.* Jesus prepares her by making her understand that the wonderful life he was talking about *is for her.* His invitation was not by mistake. He knew who he was talking to, whom he had asked to drink. The Son of God is not ashamed to ask for water from a sinful woman. He presents himself by offering her friendship and divine communion!

Jesus also knows your story. Knows perfectly where you are in your life. It is an invitation that personally addresses you. Addresses you by your name, with your sins and miseries. He invites you to a new life. He invites you to a friendship with Him. Jesus is thirsty for you, to turn your desert into springs of living water.

The Church is the place where we take people where they are and help them get to where God wants us to be. That's what Jesus does here: takes his lost sheep from where she is to the life he wants to give her. That is what the Lord does with you now: to love you so that you may be born again, so that you may be born in his love, as a child is born of the love of his parents. And for that you must present yourself to Him in the truth of your life as it is, in your sinfulness, so that it is a true encounter and he can heal you.

In this way, with his infinite gentleness, Jesus lifts the woman, each time to higher levels: he begins talking to her about the material water, then he follows with another, better water, and ends talking about adoration in Spirit and truth to the Father.

The theme of adoration, with which the dialogue with this woman is closed, is the conclusion of all that has been said. Jesus tells this woman that her desire and love will only be satiated in the personal relationship with the God who has been revealed to her *personally*: Jesus said to her, "I am he, the one who is speaking with you" (v. 26).

Only then will you find happiness, the water your heart seeks: *"With joy you will draw water at the fountain of salvation"* (Is. 12:3).As Saint Augustine writes at the beginning of his *Confessions*: *"fecisti nos ad te ...* You made us for yourself, and our hearts are restless until they rest in you."

This is important for you as women. Neither your husbands, nor your family, nor your friends, nor your work, nor your activities, will give you ultimate happiness. Do not look for in those things what they will never be able to give you. Women need to feel loved, but only God can fill your hearts. Edith Stein explains it well:

> *To speak to Him [God] is easier by nature for woman*
> *than for man because a natural desire lives in her to*
> *give herself completely to someone. When she has*
> *once realized that no one other than God is capable*

> *of receiving her completely for Himself and that it is*
> *sinful theft toward God to give oneself completely to*
> *one other than Him, then the surrender is no longer*
> *difficult and she becomes free of he rself. Then it is*
> *also self-evident to her to enclose herself in her castle,*
> *whereas, before, she was given to the storms which*
> *penetrated her from without again and again; and*
> *previously she had also gone into the world in order to*
> *seek something abroad which might be able to still her*
> *hunger. Now she has all that she needs; she reaches*
> *out when she is sent, and opens up only to that which*
> *may find admission to her.*[30]

I say to you with the words of Edith Stein: a natural desire lives in you to give yourself completely to someone but not one other than God is capable of receiving you completely for Himself. As you see, the Lord tells you the same thing he said to the Samaritan woman. He tells you *in her.* If you wonder who is the only one who will make you happy, who is the only one on whom you will find the only foundation that does not disappoint, the Lord will tell you today in the sentence: *"I am he, the one who is speaking with you."*

7. *Conclusion.* It has always saddened me a little not knowing what happened to this woman after her encounter with Christ. She disappears into oblivion.

The Gospel states that when the disciples came to the well, they were amazed that he was talking to a woman (v. 27). Saint John Paul II uses this verse to talk about the novelty and respect with which Jesus treated women.[31] I imagine that when twelve men arrived at the well, that woman left because the last words of Jesus, "I am he," were like arrows of fire that melted her heart. The Lord had revealed himself to her and she rushed out to look for her acquaintances: "The woman left her water jar and went into the town" (v. 28).

It is her joy that wants to be communicated. This feature is, again, deeply feminine. Again, Edith Stein returns to comment, and to warn you of the danger that is in this desire if it is not harnessed properly:

> Woman's soul should be expansive; nothing human should be alien to it. Evidently, it has a natural predisposition to such an end: on average, its principal interest is directed to people and human relations. But, if one leaves the natural instinct to itself, this is expressed in a manner apart from its objective. Often the interest is chiefly mere curiosity, mere desire to get to know people and their circumstances; sometimes it is real avidity to penetrate alien areas. If this instinct is simply indulged in, then nothing is won either for the soul itself or for other souls. It goes out of itself, so to speak, and remains standing outside of itself. It loses itself, without giving anything to others. This is unfruitful, indeed, even detrimental. Woman's soul will profit only if it goes abroad to search and to bring home the hidden treasure which rests in every human soul, and which can enrich not only her soul but also others; and it will profit only if it searches and bears home the well-known or hidden burden which is laid on every human soul. Only the one who stands with wholesome awe before human souls will search in such a manner, one who knows that human

70

souls are the kingdom of God, who knows that one may approach them only if one is sent to them. But whoever is sent will find that which she is seeking, and whoever is so sought will be found and saved. Then the soul does not remain standing on the outside but, on the contrary, carries its booty home; and its expanses must widen in order to be able to take in what it carries.[32]

It seems that this woman, with her woman's soul, brought the Gospel to many other people. While I was there in Nablus, they told me that tradition has it that she, along with her two sons and her four sisters, evangelized in Carthage and Rome and died a martyr during the persecution of Nero. The same tradition has kept her name, which does not appear in the Gospel: Photina, which in Greek means, "Enlightened." Maybe because of her name, the Church says of her in the preface of the third Sunday of Lent: "So ardently did he thirst for her faith, that he kindled in her the fire of divine love." In the Church of Nablus fragments can be seen of her skull and they are venerated as those of a saint. She really loved Christ and gave her life for Him.

If the encounter in these Spiritual Exercises is authentic, God will give you an expansive soul like that of Photina, a soul which will witness the encounter with Christ wherever you are. Like the Samaritan woman, you will also take your families and friends to Jesus and they will be able to say like the people in the Gospel, "We know that this is truly the savior of the world" (v. 42).

71

5

JESUS' LOOK

DAY 1 (NIGHT) – EXCERPTS FROM THE MOVIE "JESUS OF NAZARETH"[33]

Tonight, we are going to see part of the film, *Jesus of Nazareth.* We will watch only about thirty-five minutes of the film because I think watching the whole movie would be tiring and perhaps distracting from our mission. The part we are going to see is a very good transition between the meditations we have had today and what, God willing, we are going to consider tomorrow.

It may seem strange to see a movie during Spiritual Exercises. But I think that it is very appropriate because, as we said yesterday, Saint Ignatius presents a way of praying that could even be described as "cinematographic," above all because of the importance it gives to the imagination of the person who makes the Spiritual Exercises and for the effort that it requires to envision the place in which each particular mystery or event unfolds in what he calls (and I have been calling) "composition of place." From this perspective, the representation of what we are going to see can help you in your personal prayer and in your contemplation of Christ in this retreat.

In this part that we are going to see, everything revolves around the call of the first apostles. Personally, it's the part I like most about this movie and I think it's made with great finesse. I have been moved to tears watching these scenes. At the same time, we are going to listen to the Lord perform miracles such as filling the apostles' nets with fish, the healing of the demon-possessed, and the healing of the paralytic.

We are going to see this piece of film with a contemplative view. I want to give you several points so that you have them in mind and take them into your heart.

1. *The admiration of the crowds*: Something that is revealed in this part of the film is the novelty that Jesus brings. It is not only what he teaches, but also his very person who "unsettles" everyone: Pharisees, disciples, and simple people. Jesus is not like others, does not speak like others, does not behave like others. And that novelty causes in some the desire to follow him because they perceive that, for this man, it is worth leaving everything. In others his novelty causes fear, because it forces them to change their opinions and their way of life. In others it creates enthusiasm, but does not lead them to act.

Just like then, today Jesus also comes to meet you at this time in the Exercises. What does this encounter with Christ cause in you? In whom do you see yourself? In the apostles who risked everything and followed him? Or in those who listened to him with pleasure, but then returned to their lives as they were before? Or in those who did not allow themselves to be transformed by the Lord?

2. *The looks of Jesus and others:* It's something that really catches my attention in this movie. The Italian director, Franco Zeffirelli, puts the emphasis on the looks or gazes of the characters with long close-ups where the look is everything. This mannerism is so important that Saint Peter says to Jesus, "What are you staring at?"

The look of human beings, unlike that of animals, is intentional, expressive, and reflects a state of the soul. That is why I encourage you to examine yourselves in those looks. The look of Saint Matthew when Jesus enters his house, the look of Saint Peter when he is alone on the beach, the look of Saint John when he is invited by Jesus to follow him. When you see, for example, the crowd that listens to Jesus in silence ask yourself, "Do I have that attitude before the word of Jesus?" When you see the disciples excited, ask: "Do I feel that excitement when I receive the message of Jesus? Do I perceive it as good news that brings me joy?"

In a special way, look at the gaze of Jesus: his love when he looks at his disciples (he smiles at them), his seriousness when he exorcises the young man possessed by the devil. Look at the interactions between Jesus and the characters: the look of Jesus is healing. Ask yourself, "How does Jesus look at me? Jesus, how are you looking at me in these Exercises?"

3. *The mercy of Jesus.* It is wonderful, as I said before, to see the way Jesus treats everyone. They feel valued and loved. When he enters the house of Saint Matthew, the good

Jews and the other disciples all stay outside so as not to be "contaminated." Yet, Jesus enters, eats with them, lets himself be loved by them.

In particular, I ask you to pay close attention to the moment when Jesus tells the story of the prodigal son. In my opinion, it is the summit of the film because of the way it is represented. Tomorrow we are going to consider the reality of sin and it is important to keep in mind what the Lord says. The director portrays this scene masterfully: the scenery, the drama, the movement of the camera, the looks while Jesus speaks, the sound in which only the voice of Jesus is heard and the noise of the wind that, to me, appears to symbolize the Holy Spirit. And remember the phrase Jesus says just before, "The heart of the law is mercy."

It is very clearly seen that one of the most striking things in Jesus is his mercy, and that will be important when we meditate on our own miseries. Jesus receives everyone, speaks with everyone, gives everyone an opportunity. By the way, the woman sitting to the left of Jesus when the parable begins is Mary Magdalene.

4. *The relationship between Peter and Matthew.* To me, this part is brilliantly portrayed. Here the director and screenwriter compose a scene based in part on data of the Gospel, but with some variations. It could have happened this way, or maybe even in a different way. The actors that play Saint Peter and Saint Matthew are in my opinion the best that I have seen in these roles. They cannot do better.

Saint Matthew is transformed by the love of Jesus that makes him feel loved, that does not judge him like the others, that treats him with dignity. Peter, who is his enemy, is scandalized when Jesus agrees to go to the house of the tax collector—he realizes that Jesus is not like him, that Jesus receives everyone.

In the Spiritual Exercises, most of the work is placed on our personal relationship with God. But this passage reminds us of something fundamental: to accept Christ, we must be reconciled not only with God, but also with our brothers and sisters. We cannot call ourselves Disciples of Christ and we cannot really follow him if we hold a grudge against someone. We must love like Jesus to be his followers: *"This is how you will know that you are my disciples, if you have love for one another"* (Jn 13:35). Saint Peter is aware that in order to accept Jesus' invitation, he has to change, and he does not want to change. Saint Peter says: "Matthew is my blood-sucking enemy. I hate Matthew!"

To follow Jesus, conversion is necessary, and conversion has consequences in all dimensions of our being. It is accepting the totality of Jesus; I cannot keep one part and leave another. Saint Peter knows this. Ask yourself if you are in the situation of this disciple—if you cannot follow him because there is something or someone in your life where you do not let the love of God act. I am struck by the moment in which Saint Peter grabs the fishing nets and shouts at the other disciples: "This is my life! My nets, my boat! This is where I belong." Sometimes we are like Peter - The Lord offers us something wonderful and we remain tied to our past life, to our little life, instead of putting Christ first.

In these Exercises, we must allow Jesus to heal us, just as he healed and reconciled Matthew and Peter.

5. *Final scene.* The final scene is not in the Gospels. I left it because it too seems extraordinary. It is a dialogue between Saint Peter and Saint Matthew by the fire, while Jesus is asleep. Saint Matthew makes Peter understand that nothing will be the same now that he has knows Christ; that he will not return to his old life, that they are the first of many who will follow Jesus. The last image of that scene is the two of them looking at Jesus sleeping by the fire.

I invite you to think in the same way. You cannot finish these days of retreat and "return to your life" as it was before coming here. If you really meet Christ, if you renew your surrender to Him and decide to follow Him to the end, you cannot just go back. Everything has to be different after this retreat.

When we finish viewing the film, we will pray a Hail Mary and go quietly to our rooms or to the chapel.

6

SINFUL WOMAN

DAY 2 (MORNING) – FOURTH MEDITATION – OUR OWN SINS

"Almighty and most gentle God, who brought forth from the rock a fountain of living water for your thirsty people, bring forth we pray, from the hardness of our heart, tears of sorrow, that we may lament our sins and merit forgiveness from your mercy. Through our Lord Jesus Christ. Amen." (Mass for the Forgiveness of Sins).

Good morning to all. Little by little we have been entering into Saint Ignatius' method of prayer. Yesterday we considered, in a special way, the meditation on the Principle and Foundation. We have been created by God with a purpose. Fulfilling that purpose for which God brought us out of nothingness is the only way to be happy: obedience to our calling and the mission we have received is the only way to achieve what our heart desires.

We saw how Christ must be our foundation. As we will hear in the Gospel, God invites us to build our lives on rock: *"heaven and earth will pass away, but my words will never pass away"* (Mt 24:35). Everything we do should lead us to an intimate union with the mystery of the Most Holy Trinity: with the Father, in the Son, and by the Holy Spirit. We have been invited to that friendship, to that communion of life, to that love which is the only one that completely quenches our thirst. As we saw yesterday in the passage of the Samaritan Woman, only at the side of the crucified Christ can we drink living water.

We also said that before doing anything, before making any decision, we should always ask ourselves: "What does Christ want from me now?" "In view of this decision or activity that I must do, what is the Will of my Lord?" We must start "training" ourselves in this way: When we get up, when we go to eat, when we rest, when we work, we must always begin rectifying the intention, offering ourselves to the Lord in it, always working in his presence. As the book of Genesis says: "When Abram was ninety-nine years old, the LORD appeared to him and said, "I am God Almighty, walk before me and be blameless" (17:1). We always have to "walk before God." In doing so, we will be blameless.

1. In that relationship of friendship with Christ, sin always appears as an obstacle. Sin is a resistance to the love of God. As you know, the structure of the Spiritual Exercises of Saint Ignatius is four weeks in length, with the first being a *week of purification.* In the remaining three weeks, the main objective

of the person who makes the Exercises is to contemplate the life of Jesus Christ, from his Incarnation until his Ascension into Heaven: a week for the contemplation of the life of Christ until the Passion; a week dedicated to the Passion of the Lord, and the last week in the company of the risen Christ. This is the overarching structure, but then there are other meditations within it.

In this great structure, Saint Ignatius is already teaching us something very important: We cannot "see" Jesus if our eyes are not prepared to contemplate him. Yes, we can all grab a Bible and read the Gospels, but that is not "seeing." Remember that here we are trying to achieve an "interior knowledge of Christ". I can "see" a person from the outside, but if there is no love, I remain on the surface and do not enter into his mystery. In a similar way, I must be purified in order to know the Lord inwardly, love him and follow him. As we say at every Mass: "Let us acknowledge our sins and so prepare ourselves to celebrate the Sacred Mysteries." We are now at that moment of our Exercises.

I imagine you have come here to start over. In some way, you are looking for the same thing: the grace of *conversion*. One of the terms that Scripture uses to refer to conversion is metanoia, which, in Greek, literally means "change of mind." Conversion, therefore, is not simply changing some parts of my life, it is not about making tweaks in my Christian life. Conversion is an organ transplant surgery where the Holy Spirit is the surgeon and you are the patient. God wants to take your brain and your heart out of your body and give you the mind and Heart of Jesus. After this surgery, we have among ourselves the same attitude that is also ours in Christ Jesus (Phil 2: 5) and we have the mind of Christ (1Co 2:16). It is evident that this change, which makes us truly say with St. Paul: *"I live, no longer I, but Christ lives in me"* (Gal 2:20) will also be the beginning of new actions, of decisions made in a different way, of new relationships with the people around us. But all that is the tip of the iceberg, the fruit of an inner and deeper transformation. If we do different things, even better things, but we do not change our heart and our mind, it does not help.

Pope Benedict XVI explained it in an unbeatable way with these words:

> *To repent [or convert] is to change direction in the journey of life: not, however, by means of a small adjustment, but with a true and proper about turn. Conversion means swimming against the tide. Where the "tide" is the superficial lifestyle, inconsistent and deceptive, that often sweeps us along, overwhelms us and makes us slaves to evil or at any rate prisoners of moral mediocrity. With conversion, on the other hand, we are aiming for the high standard of Christian living, we entrust ourselves to the living and personal Gospel, which is Jesus Christ. He is our final goal and the profound meaning of conversion, he is the path on which all are called to walk through life, letting them- selves be illumined by his light and sustained by his power which moves our steps. In this way conversion expresses his most splendid and fascinating Face: it is not a mere moral decision that rectifies our conduct in life, but rather a choice of faith that wholly involves us in close communion with Jesus as a real and living Person. To repent and believe in the Gospel are not*

two different things or in some way only juxtaposed, but express the same reality. Repentance is the total "yes" of those who consign their whole life to the Gospel, responding freely to Christ who first offers himself to humankind as the Way, the Truth and the Life, as the only One who sets us free and saves us. This is the precise meaning of the first words with which, according to the Evangelist Mark, Jesus begins preaching the "Gospel of God": "The time is fulfilled, and the Kingdom of God is at hand; repent, and believe in the Gospel." (Mk 1: 15)[34]

We have to continually ask for this grace and, during these days, you have to think that God offers it to you so that you can begin again, so that you can be "born from above," as Jesus tells Nicodemus (Jn 3:3). That is the grace that we should look for.

2. Father Mendizábal talks about "emotional conversion." It is something that we may already have known, but that God allows us to see in a new way, with a new light, something that hits us and shakes us off interiorly. We do not come to these Exercises to listen to new ideas that we have never heard before and that will eventually move us to love God with all our hearts. Conversion is a *grace*: what we do is *prepare* our hearts and beg God to grant us an *experience* of his love or his Word in a new way, whenever he wants and in the way he wishes.

Saint Teresa speaks about this in *The Way of Perfection* when she writes:

"Now it seems to me that those whom God brings to a certain clear knowledge love very differently than do those who have not reached it. This clear knowledge is about the nature of the world, that there is another world, about the difference between the one and the other, that the one is eternal and the other a dream; or about the nature of loving the Creator and loving the creature (and this seen through experience, which is entirely different from merely thinking about it or believing it); or this knowledge comes from seeing and feeling what is gained by the one love and lost by the other, and what the Creator is and what the creature is, and from many other things that the Lord teaches to anyone who wants to be taught by Him in prayer, or whom His Majesty desires to teach."[35]

I want to emphasize these words: "this seen through experience, which is entirely different from merely thinking about it or believing it." I can, for example, believe that Christ has died for me. I believe it. I do not doubt it. I can even think and reflect on it, says Saint Teresa, but that is very different from "having the experience that Christ has died for me." The Holy Spirit shakes me off, helps me to LIVE it in a way that, that experience, transforms me. I can believe that this world is temporary and that the other is eternal, as Saint Teresa said. I believe it, I know. But one day, God gives me the experience of that truth that I knew and accepted, and everything changes.

I think the best example of this is the conversion of Saint Francis of Borgia. He was the Viceroy of Catalonia and Duke of Gandia in the sixteenth century, during the reign of King

84

Charles I of Spain. He was very close to the King of Spain, who named him as Queen Isabella's chamberlain, or manager of household. When the Queen died, her corpse was transferred from Toledo to Granada to be buried. The Queen, who died at the age of thirty-six, was an extraordinary woman and had a reputation for being very holy and very beautiful. When the funeral procession finally arrived at the Cathedral of Granada, Francis of Borgia was asked to confirm that the body was that of the Queen. When they opened the coffin, the face of that beautiful young woman was corrupt and rotten. Saint Francis de Borgia said: "Had I not accompanied the bier all the way from Toledo, I could not say that this was the Empress."

In his *Life of Father Francis of Borgia*, his first biographer, Fr. Ribadeneyra, who met both Saint Ignatius of Loyola and Saint Francis in person, wrote the following:

> *[Francis] recognized the vanity of all that the world prizes so highly; and it inspired him with disdain for all that is transient and with a good, efficacious desire to know what is true and enduring and to bring it about, be it at the cost of great hardship, suffering and persecution.*[36]

When he was alone after the burial, Saint Francis exclaimed:

> *What shall we do, Soul, what shall we seek? Have you not seen, Soul, how the brightest and most precious things of earth end? If death treats earth's splendor so, who can resist it? That same death has his arrow directed at you. Is it not well to die to the world in life*

in order to live with God in death? Give me, O God,
give me Your light, give me Your Spirit. ... Nevermore
will I serve a master who can die on me.[37]

That was the beginning of a new life, a life of extraordinary holiness. Upon the death of his wife, Saint Francis entered the Jesuits and became an intimate friend of St. Ignatius and his successor as the head of the Society of Jesus.

At the root of his conversion is the moment when he sees the face of the queen in the cathedral of Granada. In that moment, he *experiences* a reality that he already knew, but he does it with a force of such intensity that it is capable of changing his whole life. Nothing new was revealed to him, but what he already knew, he saw in a new way. Saint Teresa said: *"this seen through experience, which is entirely different from merely thinking about it or believing it."*

It is what Saint John of the Cross, at the beginning of his Spiritual Canticle, calls "growing aware." These are some notable words, which always impress me when I read them:

The soul at the beginning of this song has grown
aware of her obligations and observed that life is short
[Jb. 14: 5], the path leading to eternal life constricted
[Mt. 7:14], the just one scarcely saved [1 Pt. 4:18], the
things of the world vain and deceitful [Eccl. 1: 2], that
all comes to an end and fails like falling water [2 Sm.
14:14], and that the time is uncertain, the accounting
strict, perdition very easy, and salvation very difficult
[...] Touched with dread and interior sorrow of heart
over so much loss and danger, renouncing all things,
leaving aside all business , and not delaying a day

86

or an hour, with desires and sighs pouring from her
heart, wounded now with love for God ...[38]

3. In this way we want to contemplate the reality of sin in our life. We already know that we are sinners and that we have often offended the Lord, but this morning we ask the grace of "growing aware" of our sins as they are in the eyes of God, the grace of knowing through experience what we have done when we deliberately said no to God's infinite love. We want to see the truth of who we are with peace, in order to draw from that sorrow for our sins, the strength to start a holy life.

We already know the general prayer that Saint Ignatius asks us to do every step of the way: "to ask grace of God our Lord that all my intentions, actions and operations may be directed purely to the service and praise of His Divine Majesty" (SE 46).

For the meditations of sins, Saint Ignatius invites us "to ask for shame and confusion about myself" (SE 48), and in another place he says, "we must ask for growing and intense sorrow and tears for our sins" (SE 55).

As you can see, Saint Ignatius wants us to have a particularly profound *experience* of our sins. He does not speak of a simple pain, as we can have it when we confess regularly. We have to ask for "*intense sorrow.*" We have to ask for the gift of tears, "*tears for my sins.*" There's no shame in crying over one's sins. The tears shed for our sins, when they come from the Holy Spirit, wash us, purify us, open us to the love of God. They can be external tears, but it is not necessary. The heart also cries, and we know when it is crying. Saint Ignatius speaks many times in the Exercises of tears, and he himself is said to have had the "*gift of tears.*" From his spiritual diary, we know that he cried practically every day, sometimes in contrition for his sins, sometimes moved by the love of God in such a way that doctors feared that his gift of tears might cause him to lose his eyesight.

That is precisely why today's Mass will be the " Mass for the Forgiveness of Sins." The real name in Latin is *Missa ad Petendam Compunctionem Cordis*, which would be better translated as *Mass Requesting Sorrow or Compunction of Heart.* The first prayer we have made belongs precisely to that Mass. It will be a Mass that today I will offer in reparation for all our sins, the sins of your past life and also the most recent sins. I ask you, in a special way, to weep at the feet of Jesus for all the evil we have done.

Precisely because of the subject of this meditation and for the moment at which we are in the Spiritual Exercises, I am going to invite you to contemplate the episode in which a woman washes the feet of Jesus. You will find it in the Gospel of St. Luke (7:36-50).

* * *

4. "*A Pharisee invited him to dine with him, and he entered the Pharisee's house and reclined at table*" (v. 36). Today we are going to the house of this Pharisee, where Jesus is at the table. The composition of place is *that place,* which you can imagine full of good Jews who are observant of the law, the majority of whom are Pharisees, Orthodox men jealously guarding the traditions of their parents. Imagine their faces,

88

the noise of celebration, the smell of food that comes and goes. The Holy Spirit works also in our senses and grace will move your imagination according to the Will of God if you let Him guide you.

5. *"Now there was a sinful woman in the city who learned that he was at table in the house of the Pharisee"* (v. 37). A "sinful woman." Is that not an accurate definition of who you are in the eyes of God? Obviously, and this is what tradition has understood, with that expression it was meant that she was a prostitute. A woman who made a living by letting men find sexual satisfaction in her. Pope Saint Paul VI, in his encyclical *Humanae Vitae*, says talking about contraception:

> *Another effect that gives cause for alarm is that a man who grows accustomed to the use of contraceptive methods may forget the reverence due to a woman, and, disregarding her physical and emotional equilibrium, reduces her to being a mere instrument for the satisfaction of his own desires, no longer considering her as his partner whom he should surround with care and affection.*[39]

Edith Stein has some words that help us to enter into the heart of this woman who lived her prostitution and her encounters with these men in a very different way than they did. Men and women do not experience sexual life or our bodies in the same way:

> *I would also like to believe that even the relationship of soul and body is not completely similar in man*

and woman; with woman, the soul's union with the body is naturally more intimately emphasized [...] Woman's soul is present and lives more intensely in all parts of the body, and it is inwardly affected by that which happens to the body; whereas, with men, the body has more pronouncedly the character of an instrument which serves them in their work and which is accompanied by a certain detachment. This is closely related to the vocation of motherhood. The task of assimilating in oneself a living being which is evolving and growing, of containing and nourishing it, signifies a definite end in itself. Moreover, the mysterious process of the formation of a new creature in the maternal organism represents such an intimate unity of the physical and spiritual that one is well able to understand that this unity imposes itself on the entire nature of woman. But a certain danger is involved here [...] The more intimate the relationship of the soul and body is, just so will the danger of the spiritual decline be greater.[40]

For those men whom she had been with, the encounters had been a pursuit of pleasure. We can think that this woman had felt this way too, many times throughout her life. She was accustomed to men not loving her, to being used, as the Pope pointed out. She was not treated as an end, but as a means, and the sense of her diminished value, of her lack of dignity had grown in her. She was a woman wounded by life, by circumstances, by other people, by the lack of a true love in her heart. At the end of the story, Jesus says: *"her many sins have been forgiven"* (v. 47). That is, she was a woman fully aware of her many sins, and the state in which she had been left by those sins. She was at the end of a very dark road: she was a dead and hopeless woman.

She has obviously heard about Jesus. It is very probable that she had even heard Jesus speak. At the beginning of Chapter 15 of St. Luke, just before Jesus teaches the parable of the lost coin, of the lost sheep, and the prodigal son, the Evangelist says: "The tax collectors and sinners were drawing near to listen to him, but the Pharisees and scribes began to complain, saying, "This man welcomes sinners and eats with them" (Lk 15:1-2). Sinners were all drawing near Jesus. In the part of the film that we saw yesterday, there is a nice detail: among the people who listen to Jesus tell the parable of the prodigal son, we see this woman. And there is a moment, while Jesus speaks, that she looks at Jesus with an expression showing that she is being touched by the words of the Lord. Jesus attracted sinners. How beautiful is this! Sinners did not feel fear for his holiness; they were attracted by it.

I think she had personally heard Jesus speak because of a detail of this story that is very feminine - the carrying of an "alabaster flask of ointment" to offer to the Lord. A man does not act like that. No male sinner in the Gospel does anything similar. It is a woman's reaction; it is as if she wanted to win the heart of Jesus by expressing her respect for him with that detail of acknowledgment. It is a gesture of love, a gift that expresses her love and esteem for Jesus, just as her tears will express her tremendous sorrow for the sins she has committed. That would not occur with a stranger—she surely already had some *emotional connection* with the Lord.

He was someone who awakened her affection, tenderness, and understanding. She knows that he will not treat her like those other men in her life. She knows that Jesus is someone special and different, someone who welcomes sinners and gives her the hope of a new life. She is a woman who is drowning in her sins and recognizes in Jesus an open door to salvation. She needed healing, and that is what she will look for in this encounter with Christ.

At the end of this story, Jesus tells her: "Your faith has saved you" (v. 50). That further reinforces the fact that she somehow knew Jesus. She believed. She believed that Jesus could forgive her and give her the peace that she did not have. Maybe she would have heard him say, or someone had told her that he said, "Those who are healthy do not need a physician, but the sick do. I have not come to call the righteous to repentance but sinners" (Lk 5:31-32). Perhaps she saw Jesus in the house of some sinner, like Zacchaeus; perhaps she would have seen him forgive others, like the paralytic.

The important thing is that she trusts in the goodness of Jesus' Heart. She knows that only Jesus can heal her.

Think that *this woman*, again, *is you.* I invite you, in your prayer, to trace your personal history of infidelities to the love of God: to think about the actions of which you are most ashamed in your life. The many sins of omission, the bitterness that you keep within, the things you have failed to do, the most serious sins or those that have left a particular wound in your soul. Think well about all of those because those sins are going to be the gift that you are going to put at the feet of Jesus today. If this woman took him a flask of ointment, you are going to offer something that has much more value to Jesus: your broken pieces. It is the only gift he wants from you today. Try to feel empathy with this poor sinner in the Gospel because, I am sure that you, as a woman, will be able to understand her much better than I.

I invite you, in remembering of the sins of your life, to think of your *lack of gratitude for the love of God.* He has given you everything and you have used what he gave you to offend him. Along these lines, I want to invite you to read a little-known page of Scripture. It is not used in the readings of Holy Mass, perhaps because it can scandalize some people, but it tells the story of a woman who is ungrateful to God. It is an image that God uses to show his people Israel their betrayal of the Covenant. It is found in Chapter 16 of the prophet Ezekiel. God uses the image of a man who meets a poor woman and loves her: *"I entered into a covenant with you"* (Ez. 16:8). He loves her and brings her out of poverty by giving her his own riches and dressing her in beauty: "You were renowned among the nations for your beauty, perfected by the splendor I showered on you" (v. 14). However, that woman betrays God and is unfaithful. The description of this woman's infidelities is perhaps the most graphic and most explicit that is found throughout Sacred Scripture. One finds expressions like this: "At every intersection you built yourself a dais so that you could degrade your beauty by spreading your legs for every passerby, multiplying your prostitutions" (v. 25). It is a powerful story, especially when you think, "That is the story of my life. I am that woman who is unfaithful to God. I have been equally ungrateful to my Lord and my Savior." God feels hurt like a husband who suffers the infidelity of his wife. And yet, God forgives: "For I will re-establish my covenant with you, that you may

93

know that I am the LORD, that you may remember and be ashamed, and never again open your mouth because of your disgrace, when I pardon you for all you have done" (v. 62-63). God always forgives, because he loves us more than we can imagine.

6. *"Bringing an alabaster flask of ointment, she stood behind him at his feet weeping and began to bathe his feet with her tears. Then she wiped them with her hair, kissed them, and anointed them with the ointment"* (V. 37-38).

With a heart that is broken, on the verge of despair, this woman comes to the room where Jesus is. This creates an unpleasant situation because she knows she—a prostitute who was known in the city—is not welcome in the house of a Pharisee. She comes to a place where she knows she is despised and she has to overcome that barrier to place herself at the feet of Jesus. *Omnia vincit amor*, love overcomes all.

Let's look at the *attitude of the woman.* Her sins are what lead her to Jesus. She cares little about the reaction and contempt of others. She seeks Christ, not thinking about anything else, not even about herself. She has all her attention on Jesus. She just thinks of Him. She only sees Him. And Jesus sees her.

See her fall to the feet of Jesus and begin to cry. Her heart is the true flask of ointment at this point. She regrets her whole life: her sins return to her mind and her heart and she cries for every one of them. She begins to feel the sweetness of the Holy Spirit who, with each tear she sheds, purifies that heart. She does not dare to look up. She only sees, between tears, the feet of the Lord, and never stops kissing, caressing, and anointing. Love, pain, faith—and inner comfort—as she weeps.

This woman is now in the attitude that Saint Ignatius invites you to ask for: she is full of confusion and shame, full of intense sorrow and tears for her sins. This is the grace of this day for you. I ask you to become one with this woman and to weep in your prayers for your sins. It would be a good prayer if you only contemplated the feet of the Lord and kissed them, covered them with the tears of your heart and anointed them with the ointment of your repentance. And, while you are doing it, tell Jesus that you love him. Ask for forgiveness. Promise him a new life.

This is a scene that scandalizes the others attending the banquet. The Pharisees feel repugnance, disgust, revulsion. *That woman is a prostitute! Those lips... where had those lips been before? What had those hands touched before? How many men had she kissed before?* When I was preparing this talk, I read something that impressed me: the Pharisees would not even let the shadow of these women touch them because they would be stained by their sin. For those men who were with Jesus, the scene itself was obscene, disgusting, impure.

It's amazing that Jesus allows this woman to touch Him. He does not prevent it. His body is the medicine that God has given us to heal. God became man to give us salvation. The body of Jesus communicates life and grace. The Lord feels the touch of this woman's lips kissing him. He feels the freshness of her tears that are cleaning the dust off of his feet. He feels the softness of this woman's hair and He receives it with gratitude. He feels her hands smooth the ointment on his feet and in all those physical sensations, *the Lord receives the enormous love of this woman.* He knows the story of this woman, knows the history of those lips and those hands. He has seen her brokenness and, in letting himself be touched, he is healing the wounds of this sinful woman.

It is the mystery of the Incarnation, the scandal of a God who has let himself be touched by us. A God whose Body we can touch, receive every day in our mouths in Holy Communion. We are as sinful as this woman. For us too, the Body of the Lord is healing.

7. *"When the Pharisee who had invited him saw this he said to himself, "If this man were a prophet, he would know who and what sort of woman this is who is touching him, that she is a sinner"* (v. 39).

Here we see the attitude of the Pharisee, which contrasts with that of this poor woman: an attitude of pride, of purism, of segregation, of disdain. Let's look at whom he is judging, *first Jesus,* and then the woman. The condemnation first addresses Jesus: "if this man were a prophet..." He cannot be a prophet, because a prophet would know who *this* woman is.

How much care we should have when it comes to judging! Do not judge even what seems most obvious: "Stop judging, that you may not be judged. For as you judge, so will you be judged, and the measure with which you will measure will be measured out to you" (Mt 7:1-2). We cannot expect forgiveness if we are so quick to condemn.

But it is when it comes to judging God, as Simon does here, that we should exercise the utmost caution. It really takes a lot of pride to think that we can make judgments about the Lord based on our poor, limited, and deficient human condition. We are worms and we dare to judge the one who is unfathomable and infinite in his wisdom, omnipotence, and love?

8. *"Jesus said to him in reply, 'Simon, I have something to say to you.' 'Tell me, teacher,' he said. 'Two people were in debt to a certain creditor; one owed five hundred days' wages and the other owed fifty. Since they were unable to repay the debt, he forgave it for both. Which of them will love him more?' Simon said in reply, 'The one, I suppose, whose larger debt was forgiven.' He said to him, 'You have judged rightly"* (Lk. 7:40-43).

We have already seen the attitude of the woman and the Pharisee. Now, let's see *the attitude of the Heart of Jesus.*

Jesus wants to make Simon understand *how much he owes to God.* Simon is not aware of the debt he owes to God. He does not think he owes him much. He does not think he has offended him much. He does not think that he is like that woman who is at the feet of Jesus. The worst thing about Simon is not that he judges and condemns the woman. The worst thing is that he thinks he's a righteous man! Here we have a sinful woman who is aware of her sin and a man who is not aware of his own. And this happens to us: deep down, we think that we are not so bad, that there are people worse than us. Be honest. If you are honest, is it not true that you think like this? We are much more like Simon than the woman who is at the feet of Jesus!

I'm going to say something that may sound scandalous: maybe it would be better if we did something terrible so that we could go to Jesus like this woman. Surely, we would be more humble. Because, as Jesus highlights in this parable, if we do not sin, or if we do not sin gravely, deep down we do not think that we are so bad. Jesus says at the end of this story some impressive words: "Her many sins have been forgiven; hence, she has shown great love. But the one to whom little is forgiven, loves little" (v. 47). It has always seemed to me that here is a syllogism that is badly done, from a strictly logical point of view. The conclusion reached by Jesus is poorly deduced, at first sight. It seems that Jesus should have said: "Her many sins have been forgiven; hence, she has shown great love. But the one who loves little, little is forgiven to him." That is a deduction made correctly. However, the Lord says: "But the one to whom little is forgiven, loves little." In this way, Jesus places even more emphasis on the need to experience forgiveness in order to love. Our sins are a great gift for Jesus, but they are also a great gift for us because they allow us humility and a love that, otherwise, perhaps we would never achieve. Ask God to help you experience the enormous debt you have with Him, a debt so great that you will never be able to repay it.

Obviously, I am not encouraging anyone to sin, but from serious sin can be born an enormous holiness and the other way around, a life without great sins, in many cases, is followed by a spiritually mediocre life.

9. *"He turned to the woman"* (v. 44). In this story, the Evangelist gives us two views. The first was Simon's: "When he saw this, he said to himself: 'If this man was a prophet ... '" It was an arrogant and merciless gaze. Now, Jesus turns to this woman and his eyes are full of admiration and love for her. We could use the words of the Gospel of St. Mark: "Jesus, looking at her, loved her" (Mk. 10:21).

Cry out your sins like this woman, and Jesus will look at you as he looked at her. And he will defend you as he defended her before those who accuse you.

10. *"Then he turned to the woman and said to Simon, "Do you see this woman? When I entered your house, you did not give me water for my feet, but she has bathed them with her tears and wiped them with her hair. You did not give me a kiss, but she has not ceased kissing my feet since I entered. You did not anoint my head with oil, but she anointed my feet with ointment. So I tell you, her many sins have been forgiven; hence, she has shown great love. But the one to whom little is forgiven, loves little."* (v. 44-47)

To Simon, these words of Jesus must have seemed like a slap in the face. Jesus was comparing him to the woman, to *that woman*, and he was telling him that he had felt more loved and better received by her than by him. "You think you're better than her, but she has treated me better than you," Jesus says. "She has loved me more than you have loved me."

Here Jesus takes the side of the woman. It is impressive to see how Jesus defends a woman who had little means to defend herself. Jesus is won over by this woman's love. *"If anyone does sin, we have an Advocate with the Father, Jesus Christ the righteous one. If we acknowledge our sins, he is faithful and just and will forgive our sins and cleanse us from every wrongdoing"* (1 Jn 1:9-2:1).

Imagine what consolation it is for this poor woman to hear these words of Jesus! Jesus speaks to Simon, but he knows that his words are also fall upon the ears and heart of this woman who is at his feet. A woman, who, perhaps for the first time in her life, is publicly recognized, respected, defended, and loved.

Think about her joy when Jesus lifted her from the ground and looked into her eyes, as if they were the only two people in the world, and he said: "Your sins are forgiven" (v. 48). It is difficult, indeed it is impossible, to express in words what only God can make us understand in the heart.

11. *"The others at table said to themselves, 'Who is this who even forgives sins?' But he said to the woman, 'your faith has saved you; go in peace'"* (v. 49-50).

Jesus has scandalized his hosts, as they were scandalized by the presence of that woman in their house. But Jesus and the woman do not care. Both are happy: he, for having forgiven her, and she, for receiving that forgiveness.

It is beautiful to think that, sometimes, an act can redeem a whole life. The word of Jesus is life-giving. It is the word of God. He says: *your faith has saved you, and that woman is saved forever.*

I invite you to think about this woman as she returned home: silent, transformed, touched by divine grace, pierced through and through with peace and joy.

How do you want to return home the day after tomorrow?

Let me tell you something in confidence: the best you can do for your families, your friends, and for your parish and for your country and for the Church, is to convert and live your Christian life with fidelity. I say this in the conviction of what Saint John of the Cross writes in his *Spiritual Canticle*, a truly amazing passage: "A little of this pure love is more precious to God and the soul and more beneficial to the Church, even though it seems one is doing nothing, than all these other works put together."[41]

Here today, at the feet of the Lord, meditating on the reality of our sins and on the debt we owe to the infinite mercy of the Heart of Christ, may God grant us that "pure love" that can transform our lives and our families forever.

7

THE CONSEQUENSES OF SIN

DAY II - HOMILY (Gn 15:1-12. 17-18; Mt 7:15-20)

As I said before, the intention of this Mass is reparation for your sins, for all of our sins.

I invite you to give this celebration a marked sense of remorse and that you offer yourself with Jesus in his sacrifice, especially today, in atonement for the sins of your whole life.

We are on the third day of the Exercises, and we have said that it is a day of purification. The Lord asks us in today's Gospel to bear good fruit. However, we all know our personal history: we are authors of our own decisions and witnesses of the paths we choose. How many times have we been like those rotten trees the Lord speaks of and rejected God's love instead of loving Him as He deserves!

Somehow, this page of the Gospel invites us to consider two themes that Saint Ignatius brought up in the meditations of the first week: I speak of death and hell. I must confess that I cannot understand why we are reluctant to talk about this. It is as if we think that if we were to stop talking about these realities they would cease to exist. We live once, and at an hour that we do not know, we die. If we reject God's mercy, renounce communion with Christ, and cast the supernatural life out of us, we will not live with Him in heaven. "Every tree that does not bear good fruit will be cut down and thrown into the fire."

You may have heard the words of Saint Francis of Assisi: *"Praised be You, my Lord through Sister Death, from whom no one living can escape. Woe to those who die in mortal sin! Blessed are they She finds doing Your Will."* The Christian faith has transformed death in such a way that we can expect it with joy and call it sister. Death awaits us to take us to the union of love with the Holy Trinity. Thomas a Kempis writes: *"How happy and prudent is he who tries now in life to be what he wants to be found in death."*[42] As a priest, I have seen people die smiling. Not many, I must say. They are beautiful deaths, because you see that the person is at peace and leaves that peace in his family when he leaves. He who has spent his life working for God, sees in death the moment of entering into the joy of his Lord. To rest in the heart of Jesus. To see the faces of Christ and Mary. The holy soul cannot wait to be with the saints in heaven.

In these Exercises, we do not have time to meditate on all the subjects that Saint Ignatius invites us to consider, and this homily must be necessarily brief. For this reason, I am going to give you two texts, one on each of these topics, so that you can read them when you have the opportunity. The first of these is a vision of Hell from Saint Teresa of Jesus. It is an impressive text we find in her *Book of My Life*. She writes, "This vision was one of the great mercies of God." and at the end of the story, she speaks about the fruits that vision produced in her. Meditating on Hell does us a lot of good, allows us to turn that terrible mystery into love, helps us grow in zeal for the salvation of souls, and makes us stronger in the face of the difficulties of life.[43]

The second text is a wonderful piece by a Spanish priest who died when I was twelve years old, José Luis Martín Descalzo. He was well known in Spain as a journalist. What I offer you here is the last article he wrote, shortly before his death at fifty-five years ol d. It's a letter to Go d: *The Letter to God from a Dying Priest.* It is a truly beautiful letter, a love letter, a song to the mercies of God throughout his life, which expresses a way of living and a way of dying.[44] Read both texts and let your heart draw from these readings the resolution "to sin no more," to live the Christian life with joy, and to give yourselves to the service of God for the salvation of the world.

8

THE WOMAN CAUGHT IN ADULTERY

"Be near, O Lord, to those who plead before you, and look kindly on those who place their hope in your mercy, that, cleansed from the stain of their sins, they may persevere in holy living and be made full heirs of your promise. Through our Lord Jesus Christ. Amen." (Thursday of the Fifth Week of Lent).

Good afternoon. I hope that on this day you are feeling the peace of God in your hearts. Jesus has taught us to look at and recognize our sins with peace. The sadness or discouragement into which we fall after sinning is the fruit of our pride and not the love of God. As we saw before, the Lord can always bring good out of our sins. I encourage you, when you fall into any fault, to ask God to experience two feelings

107

simultaneously: deep pain for having hurt the Heart of Jesus and, at the same time, joy and gratitude for the good that, in his infinite mercy, he will draw from what was lacking.

It is important that you learn to have a *peaceful relationship with your sins.* I have met people who, after an experience like this one, return to the world believing that they are not going to sin anymore, or that at least a particular sin into which they used to fall may be gone forever. Then they return to their lives, fall back into the same traps, and become discouraged. *"Again? I thought that I had left that behind! I have no remedy."* These are reactions that show how imperfect and proud we are.

1. The test of spiritual progress is not so much failing to fall, but of being able to rise quickly from the falls, joyful in the Mercy of God. This does not mean that our sins do not hurt: it means that they hurt us *for the right reasons.* The pain of sin that is born of the Holy Spirit does not sink us, but raises us up; It does not discourage us, but it impels us to a greater union with God.

Allow me to offer here an excerpt from St. Francis de Sales's extraordinary work, *Introduction to the Devout Life,* which exudes serenity:

> *One important direction in which to exercise gen-*
> *tleness is with respect to ourselves, never growing*
> *irritated with one's self or one's imperfections; for*
> *although it is but reasonable that we should be dis-*
> *pleased and grieved at our own faults, yet ought we*
> *to guard against a bitter, angry, or peevish feeling*
> *about them. Many people fall into the error of being*

angry because they have been angry, vexed because they have given way to vexation, thus keeping up a chronic state of irritation, which adds to the evil of what is past, and prepares the way for a fresh fall on the first occasion. Moreover, all this anger and irritation against one's self fosters pride, and springs entirely from self-love, which is disturbed and fretted by its own imperfection. (...).

Believe me, my daughter, as a parent's tender affectionate remonstrance has far more weight with his child than anger and sternness, so, when we judge our own heart guilty, if we treat it gently, rather in a spirit of pity than anger, encouraging it to amendment, its repentance will be much deeper and more lasting than if stirred up in vehemence and wrath.

For instance: Let me suppose that I am specifically seeking to conquer vanity, and yet that I have fallen conspicuously into that sin. Instead of taking myself to task as abominable and wretched, for breaking so many resolutions, calling myself unfit to lift up my eyes to Heaven, as disloyal, faithless, and the like, I would deal pitifully and quietly with myself. "Poor heart! so soon fallen again into the snare! Well now, rise up again bravely and fall no more. Seek God's Mercy, hope in Him, ask Him to keep you from falling again, and begin to tread the pathway of humility afresh. We must be more on our guard henceforth." Such a course will be the surest way to making a stedfast substantial resolution against the special fault (...)

So then, when you have fallen, lift up your heart in quietness, humbling yourself deeply before God by reason of your frailty, without marvelling that you fell;—there is no cause to marvel because weakness is weak, or infirmity infirm. Heartily lament that you should have offended God, and begin anew to cultivate the lacking grace, with a very deep trust in His Mercy, and with a bold, brave heart.[45]

The saints have learned and always teach us this great balance. Their way of living the faith is already in itself a source of peace, because they know how to judge sin in its seriousness without it leading to irascibility or discouragement. Their humility allows them to have God's perspective and so they can use their falls to climb higher in their journey of love and union with the Most Holy Trinity.

In this sense, I want to remind you of some very beautiful expressions that we find in the *Catechism of the Catholic Church*:

The human heart is heavy and hardened. God must give man a new heart. Conversion is first of all a work of the grace of God who makes our hearts return to him: "Restore us to thyself, O LORD, that we may be restored!" God gives us the strength to begin anew. It is in discovering the greatness of God's love that our heart is shaken by the horror and weight of sin and begins to fear offending God by sin and being separated from him. The human heart is converted by looking upon him whom our sins have pierced.

God gives us the strength to begin anew. There is always hope. God loves us! Everything we are contemplating in these days invites us to trust in the Lord, who loves us so much. *"The human heart is converted by looking upon him whom our sins have pierced."* Look at Jesus crucified, with great confidence in his love, and he will give you a very deep sorrow for your sins and, at the same time, a very great love for him.

2.   Allow me a side remark that I believe is important. Sometimes we hear news that moves us to despair. Despair, as an attitude, is not a Christian position. This last year has been particularly difficult, in this sense. In Spiritual Exercises, we are not to look at the sins of others, but to our own personal sins, for which we cannot put the blame on others.

For this, I find a luminous example in Saint Teresa of Jesus (Teresa of Avila). She was born in the sixteenth century, while Martin Luther was splitting the Church in half in Europe—a major crisis. Let's look at Santa Teresa's way of thinking:

> *At that time news reached me of the harm being done in France and of the havoc the Lutherans had caused and how much this miserable sect was growing. The news distressed me greatly, and, as though I could do something or were something, I cried to the Lord and begged Him that I might remedy so much evil. It seemed to me that I would have given a thousand lives to save one soul out of the many that were being lost there. I realized I was a woman and wretched and*

incapable of doing any of the useful things I desired
to do in the service of the Lord. All my longing was
and still is that since He has so many enemies and
so few friends that these few friends be good ones.
As a result I resolved to do the little that was in my
power; that is, to follow the evangelical counsels as
perfectly as I could and strive that these few persons
who live here do the same. I did this trusting in the
great goodness of God, who never fails to help anyone
who is determined to give up everything for Him.[46]

In my humble opinion, I believe that this is the evangelical position. She recognizes, first of all, that the solution to the problem was out of her hands. All her longing was to give Jesus good friends who will love him. And she says: "I resolved to do the little that was in my power; That is, to follow the evangelical counseling as perfectly as I could and to strive that these few persons who live here do the same." The solution was in following the Gospel teachings as perfectly as she could. She understood that this was the best way to help.

I believe that this perspective is a source of great peace and distances us from many dangers.

3. This second meditation today brings an end to the meditations of the first week of the Exercises. We have dedicated most of this retreat to them because they are really the foundation upon which the whole structure of the Christian life rises. In an experience like this one, it is very important *to feel redeemed by Christ*, to feel deeply loved and forgiven by the Lord. This goes beyond making a

good confession. There are many people who have confessed their whole lives and have never had this experience that I am talking about now. If we are in sin or need the grace of the Sacrament, we can go to receive it whenever we want. Now, however, I am talking about something different.

I mean you have to ask the Lord for the grace to *feel forgiven* in the deepest part of your being. It is to let the action of the Holy Spirit, his anointing, soak all the fibers of your being. It is to contemplate yourself in the infinite love of God who loves you personally. It also means accepting your life as it was. Accept your past life and love it as Jesus loved it. Sometimes you know that God has forgiven your sins but there is bitterness in your heart, the feeling that your heart has been stained. There are people who seem to carry a huge stone in their conscience for their faults from the past life and, although they know that God forgave them when they made their confession, they continue to feel that burden in their hearts. *Jesus also wants to free you from that feeling* that is like an anchor that does not allow you to advance in the Christian life.

We have a hard time forgiving, and it is harder still for us to forget what has been done to us. It takes a very special grace, for example, to look at your husband or your wife if he or she has been unfaithful with the same look of love you had for him in your first love. Sometimes, as a priest, I have met people who say to me, "I have forgiven him, but I cannot love him as before." That is very difficult to heal; it takes a lot of grace from God, a lot of humility, and a lot of mutual love.

When we think about God, we know that he loves us and forgives us, but somehow we believe that when he looks at us, he is also contemplating all our infidelities. We do not feel comfortable under that gaze that truly sees us and scrutinizes everything. It happens to us as it did to Adam in Eden and we hide.

4. I know that the example I am going to give you is very superficial, but bear with me. Imagine the most handsome man in the world. He is good-looking, attractive, strong—one of those men that every woman would sigh over. Imagine that man, a man that any woman would want to have in her life because he is also good, understanding, friendly, funny, and kind. He sets his eyes on you and you are an ugly woman. Not just ugly: imagine that your face is deformed, that it does not even look like a person's face. One that makes people stare and then be afraid. And it is not only your face, but your whole body that is deformed. Imagine also that you live in the greatest of material poverty and this man is wealthy. You live in dirt and he lives in the grandest mansion. You have nothing and He has everything. Well, that man who is so handsome and irresistible, and so wealthy, loves you. He wants to give you his heart and his life. You cannot believe it! When he looks at you, you ask yourself: "Why *me*? Do you not see who I am and how I am? You could have any woman you want, the most beautiful, and you are choosing *me*! I am the ugliest and most deformed woman alive. I look like a monster, even to myself. Why? Why do you look at me with so much love? How can you love someone like me? Don't you see what others see?" In stories like those of Cinderella, she is poor, but at least she is beautiful and smiling. But you are poor and full of physical and spiritual imperfections.

In that situation, you would feel almost humiliated before

others. When other people saw you with him, you would feel humiliated. When you were with him, maybe you would be spending more time thinking about your ugliness than in his love for you.

This example, which seems inappropriate for the Exercises, is in fact very appropriate at this time. When Saint Ignatius speaks of sin in us, and speaks of the "composition of place" for this meditation, he says the following:

> *[I have to] look at who I am, lessening myself by examples: first, how much I am in comparison to all men; second, what men are in comparison to all the Angels and Saints of Paradise; third, what all Creation is in comparison to God: (—Then I alone, what can I be?) fourth, to see all my bodily corruption and foulness; fifth, to look at myself as a sore and ulcer, from which I have sprung so many sins and so many iniquities and so very vile poison. (SE 58)*

And in his *Ascent to Mount Carmel*, Saint John of the Cross writes:

> *So great is the harm that if we try to express how ugly and dirty is the imprint the appetites leave in the soul, we find nothing comparable to it—neither a place full of cobwebs and lizards nor the unsightliness of a dead body nor the filthiest thing imaginable in this life [...] The variety of filth caused in the soul is both inexplicable and unintelligible!*[47]

The story above is not, therefore, a bad example. Basically, in the supernatural order, we see ourselves like this. We see ourselves as deformed, ugly, corrupt, and we cannot put that putrefaction before Jesus. Then there comes a priest or someone, and he tells us that Jesus loves us, and inwardly we say to ourselves: "God cannot love someone like me. How is God going to love a woman like me?" When in prayer we experience his love and we realize that he is watching us with love, instead of enjoying that love, we are so aware of our ugliness that we turn to ourselves and we say: "Lord, why *me*? Your love, cannot be so great that it comes to love the darkest corners of my being, the parts that I hate of myself, the parts of me that I cover because I do not even want to see them. It cannot be!"

I invite you to spiritually "undress" before God in these Exercises. In the presence of the Lord, take off your "clothes" and stand before him in your ugliness. The Lord invites you, when you do that, not think about your ugliness, but only to look at Him, so that you can see how He is loving every part of your being, and in that look He is healing you. Remove all the layers until your soul is left naked before Jesus Christ. I know that you will be afraid to open your eyes because any other person, even yourself, would be disgusted to see what Saint John of the Cross says is inexplicable. In the silence of your prayer, open your eyes and see how Jesus looks at you. He loves you *as you are*, with your history *as it has been.* When you discover yourself and undress like that before Him, He will cover you with His love, He will embrace you and He will love you as no one has ever loved you.

5. All this, which I have just expressed with my words and with the words of Saint Ignatius and Saint John of the Cross,

we see beautifully represented in the passage of forgiveness to the adulterous woman, in Chapter 8 of Saint John. This is the passage for today's meditation and composition of place that I offer for your next meditation.

> *Jesus went to the Mount of Olives. But early in the morning he arrived again in the temple area, and all the people started coming to him, and he sat down and taught them. Then the scribes and the Pharisees brought a woman who had been caught in adultery and made her stand in the middle. They said to him, "Teacher, this woman was caught in the very act of committing adultery. Now in the law, Moses commanded us to stone such women. So what do you say?" They said this to test him, so that they could have some charge to bring against him. Jesus bent down and began to write on the ground with his finger. But when they continued asking him, he straightened up and said to them, "Let the one among you who is without sin be the first to throw a stone at her." Again he bent down and wrote on the ground. And in response, they went away one by one, beginning with the elders. So he was left alone with the woman before him. Then Jesus straightened up and said to her, "Woman, where are they? Has no one condemned you?" She replied, "No one, sir." Then Jesus said, "Neither do I condemn you. Go, (and) from now on do not sin anymore (v. 1-11).*

We are not, as in the case of the woman this morning,

encountering a public sinner. This is an adulterous woman. I think there is also a special message here for you as a woman. In Spain, there is a very good Catholic psychiatrist named Enrique Rojas. My father met him on a retreat, although I do not know him personally. He is the author of numerous books (translated into seven languages) and has been recognized throughout his professional life with many awards. Here in the United States, I have a book of his that I read when I need light on some psychological issues.

Doctor Rojas has written many articles about sex, marital crises, and the will. I remember when I was in Spain, I read an interview with him in a newspaper in which he spoke precisely about infidelities in marriage. In that interview, he said something that I never have forgotten. I must say that, as a priest, I have used it many times when I had to help couples who were going through the problem of infidelity. The phrase of Dr. Rojas was more or less this: "Many men say they are looking for love, but in reality, they are looking for sex. Many women say they are looking for sex, but what they are really looking for is love."

In most of the adultery by women, I think there is something of this. The woman is unfaithful because *she does not feel loved.* For her, sexual expression is a way of feeling loved, rather than a search for physical satisfaction. I want to add to this something that Edith Stein says about women:

> *The deepest feminine yearning is to achieve a loving union which, in its development, validates this maturation and simultaneously stimulates and furthers the desire for perfection in others; this yearning can express itself in the most diverse forms, and*

some of these forms may appear distorted, even
degenerate. Such yearning is an essential aspect of the
eternal destiny of woman. It is not simply a human
longing but is specifically feminine and opposed to
the specifically masculine nature.[48]

We are going to apply this to the woman caught in adultery because, if, as Edith Stein says, this trait is "specifically feminine", it must be present in the heart of this poor woman as well as in yours. This woman (this is my assumption) does not feel loved. She has been caught in an adulterous sexual relationship, but she has not gone to that relationship because she sought physical satisfaction (which, most likely, has been the motivation for the man with whom she was caught), but because she was searching, like the Samaritan woman, for a love that had failed her in her marriage.

6. Maybe they had set a trap for her, maybe the man she was committing adultery with had set that trap with the Pharisees. The Gospel does not give us those details. However, when they present her before Jesus, she feels twice as hurt—both by the fear of being tossed aside and of having given her body to a man who has not truly loved her.

For the enemies of Jesus, all of this is secondary, but for Christ, that is the fundamental thing. The Pharisees have brought the woman into the presence of Christ to test the Lord: they know that Jesus is compassionate and merciful, "slow to anger, abounding in love" (Psalm 103:8). They want to place him in the dilemma of choosing between obedience to the law of Moses (for he had said: "Do not think that I have come to abolish the law or the prophets. I have come not to abolish but to fulfill" (Mt 5: 17).) and the way of mercy.

For the Pharisees, there was opposition between the two. But the Lord is not like us: *God does justice by forgiving.* The act of greater justice in history, which is the crucifixion and death of Jesus in atonement for our sins, is also the moment of the greatest mercy.

I think Saint Therese of the Child Jesus (Therese of Lisieux) expresses it best:

> *Indeed, I hope as much from the justice of God as from His mercy. It is because He is just that He is com-passionate and merciful, long-suffering, plenteous in mercy. "For He knows our frame, he remembers that we are but dust. As the Father has compassion for his children, so has the Lord compassion for us." (...) What joy to think that our Lord is just, that He takes into account all our weaknesses and He knows perfectly all the frailty of our nature. How, then, can I be afraid?*[49]

He knows perfectly the frailty of this woman's feminine nature. He knows that she has sinned, that her yearning for a loving union has taken her to the wrong place, but in that yearning, there's something that He can redeem. And that is why He is going to protect her.

Are not you reflected in that woman? Are you not, in fact, that woman? Do you also identify with that search that has taken you to the wrong places?

7. In this meditation today, I will not go verse by verse, as we have done so far. I invite you, as a composition of place,

to take the words of this verse: *"He was left alone with the woman before him"* (v. 9). St. Augustine says at this moment: *"Relicti sunt duo misera et misericordia.* (They have been left alone misery and mercy.)"[50]

I invite you to have the same experience and to be alone with the One whom Mercy is. As I said at the beginning, in that "being alone" with Jesus, let Him see you. Show yourself before Him as you are. And, while you are in that "being alone", think about these words of Saint Therese:

> *I am certain that, even if I had on my conscience every imaginable sin, I should lose nothing of my confidence, but would throw myself, heartbroken with sorrow, into the arms of my Savior. I remember His love for the Prodigal Son; I have heard His words to Mary Magdalene, to the woman taken in adultery, and to the woman of Samaria. No, there is no one who could frighten me, for I know too well what to believe concerning His mercy and His love.*[51]

Saint Ignatius asks that this meditation on our sins end with what he calls a "colloquy of mercy" with Jesus, "pondering and giving thanks to God our Lord that He has given me life up to now, proposing amendment, with His grace, for the future" (SE 61). After compline, we're going to leave the Blessed Sacrament exposed all night long. There will be shifts of one hour in duration, so that each of you, who wish, can spend some time alone with Jesus. With the number of people we have here, there may be two or three people on each shift, but it will be in any case a moment of intimacy with the Lord. When you arrive at the chapel and you sit before the monstrance, read this passage of the Gospel and think that what you are doing is the same thing that happened to this woman. Listen to Jesus tell you: "Neither do I condemn you." In the presence of Jesus, in that look of Christ Eucharist, leave your life as it has been and ask the Lord for the grace to experience that He has forgiven you *entirely.* Leave your sins there and do not return to them anymore.

You have to trust Jesus and his love. Totally. In that absolute confidence is the secret and, in the end, that is the grace that you must beg for.

8. God has never looked at you badly. Your sin has not caught him by surprise. It is hard to believe this, but God knows you. He knows you very well. He does not reproach you. He does not want you to look back, he wants you to look forward: "*From now on,* do not sin any more" (v. 11). Think that this word of Jesus to you is not simply the expression of a wish, like: "Try to make it better from now on." As we have already said, the word of Jesus is life-giving: when he says to a dead person rise, he comes back to life. Therefore, if he, in your prayer, says to you: "*Do not sin any more*" think that in that word he is giving you the grace of a new life, a life of holiness.

So yes, look at the future and ask the Lord for the grace of being able to say with Saint Paul, "*Just one thing: forgetting what lies behind but straining forward to what lies ahead, I continue my pursuit toward the goal, the prize of God's upward calling, in Christ Jesus*" (Phil 3:13-14).

We ask the Lord that these Exercises are truly the moment to leave our past life, with confidence, in the Heart of Jesus and his infinite mercy and, *from now on*, to live a life of holiness in union with him and for the salvation of the world.

9

MARY AT THE ANNUNCIATION

DAY 3 (MORNING) – SIXTH MEDITATION – CONFORMITY WITH THE WILL OF GOD

"O God, who willed that your Word should take on the reality of human flesh in the womb of the Virgin Mary, grant, we pray, that we, who confess our Redeemer to be God and man, may merit to become partakers even on his divine nature. Who lives and reigns for ever and ever." (On the Annunciation of the Lord)

Good Morning. We have reached our fourth day of retreat and are in what would be the second week of meditations. The first week of the Spiritual Exercises of St. Ignatius is dedicated to the purification of the soul for the contemplation of the mystery of Christ in the second, third, and fourth weeks. I guess at this point I can lay my cards on the table. In a very harmonic way, we have done the meditations of the first two weeks simultaneously, for among other reasons because we have only four days and not thirty. We have meditated on what Saint Ignatius proposes for us in the first week, but we have done it contemplating the life of the Lord, which is typical of the second week.

The life of Jesus is the most perfect norm of life. Saint John of the Cross writes in the *Ascent to Mount Carmel* that we must "have habitual desire to imitate Christ in all your deeds by bringing your life into conformity with his. You must then study his life in order to know how to imitate him and behave in all events as he would."[52]

We already know the words of Saint Ignatius. Precisely at this moment of the journey, he invites us "to ask for what I desire. Here it will be to ask for an intimate knowledge of our Lord, who has become man for me, that I may love Him more and follow Him more closely" (SE 104).

One of the four pillars of devotion to the Sacred Heart of Jesus, whose solemnity we will celebrate tomorrow, is *imitation.* "Learn from me for I am meek and humble of heart," Jesus tells us in the Gospel (Mt 11:29).As we said two days ago, our main objective must be progressively closer union with Christ. In fact, all the different schools of spirituality agree on this: Christ is the way and the culmination of the Christian life.

Therefore, although we have been contemplating the life of Jesus from the first day and, thus, we have been advancing in the meditations of this part of the Exercises, this morning I would like to focus on the most important moment of history in my opinion: the moment in which God became man in the body of the Virgin Mary. I invite you to spend this morning with Mary in Nazareth.

You are making this retreat to know the Will of God in your

life and to have an intense experience of the Lord. I also indicated to you the first day that we want to know God's plan for you as women. Well, all that you are looking for is reflected in the episode of the Annunciation to Mary by the angel.

Edith Stein has a wonderful phrase for you: "Every woman who wants to fulfill her destiny must look to Mary as ideal."[53] She explains that Mary is *"the prototype of pure womanhood"* and that, therefore, women should look for imitation of Mary as the goal of their Christian life:

> *"The imitation of Mary is not fundamentally different from the imitation of Christ. The imitation of Mary includes the imitation of Christ because Mary is the first Christian to follow Christ, and she is the first and most perfect model of Christ. Indeed, that is why the imitation of Mary is not only relevant to women but to all Christians. But she has a special significance for women, one in accord with their nature, for she leads them to the feminine form of the Christian image."*[54]

Edith Stein also invites women like you to cultivate the relationship with Mary:

> *Since the dispensing of graces is entrusted to the hands of the Queen of Heaven, we will find our way to the goal not only by keeping our eyes raised to her but by maintaining a personal trusting association with her (...)*
>
> *That is why an intimate bond exists between Mary*

and us. She loves us, she knows us, she exerts herself to bring each one of us into the closest possible relationship with the Lord—that which we are above all supposed to be. Of course, this is true for all humanity, but most particularly for women (...) And just as the heart sustains the other organs of woman's body and makes it possible for them to function, so we may genuinely believe there is just such a collaboration of Mary with every woman wherever that woman is fulfilling her vocation as woman; just so, there is a collaboration of Mary with us in all works of the Church. But just as grace cannot achieve its work in souls unless they open themselves to it in free decision, so also Mary cannot function fully as a mother if people do not entrust themselves to her. Those women who wish to fulfill their feminine vocations in one of several ways will most surely succeed in their goals if they not only keep the ideal of the Virgo-Mater before their eyes and strive to form themselves according to her image but if they also entrust themselves to her guidance and place themselves completely under her care. She herself can form in her own image those who belong to her.[55]

Therefore, beyond what we can say here in a few minutes, I would like you all to leave this retreat with the purpose of living very close to the Mother of God. We all need Mary, but women need her in a special way because she is one of you. With this outlook, that of a woman who wants to learn Christ from another woman, I invite you to contemplate the mystery of the Annunciation.

What can we say about this scene of the Gospel that has not already been said? It is very difficult to talk about this evangelical scene because so much has been written about it, that we can easily get lost in abstract considerations.

And yet, the starting point is this: a girl who says "yes" to God. A God who becomes a man from that moment. The Holy Spirit will take each of you in a different direction in your prayer. Do not stray too far from this evangelical simplicity.

In the sixth month, the angel Gabriel was sent from God to a town of Galilee called Nazareth, to a virgin betrothed to a man named Joseph, of the house of David, and the virgin's name was Mary. And coming to her, he said, "Hail, favored one! The Lord is with you." But she was greatly troubled at what was said and pondered what sort of greeting this might be. Then the angel said to her, "Do not be afraid, Mary, for you have found favor with God. Behold, you will conceive in your womb and bear a son, and you shall name him Jesus. He will be great and will be called Son of the Most High, and the Lord God will give him the throne of David his father, and he will rule over the house of Jacob forever, and of his kingdom there will be no end." But Mary said to the angel, "How can this be, since I have no relations with a man?" And the angel said to her in reply, "The Holy Spirit will come upon you, and the power of the Most High will overshadow you. Therefore the child to be born will be called holy, the Son of God. And behold, Elizabeth, your relative, has also conceived a son in her old age, and this is the sixth month for her who was called barren; for nothing will be impossible for God." Mary said, "Behold, I am the handmaid of the Lord. May it be done to me according to your word." Then the angel departed from her. (Lk 1:26–38)

1. Saint Ignatius of Loyola invites us, in this meditation of the Exercises, to consider the scene *from God's perspective.* What does God see? A disoriented and lost world; a world dominated by sin; a creature of his, man, who has been perverted and condemned for his sins. In the first chapter of his letter to the Romans, St. Paul has a description of this humanity without God:

Although they knew God they did not accord him glory as God or give him thanks. Instead, they became vain in their reasoning, and their senseless minds were darkened. While claiming to be wise, they became fools and exchanged the glory of the immortal God for the likeness of an image of mortal man or of birds or of four-legged animals or of snakes. Therefore, God handed them over to impurity through the lusts of their hearts for the mutual degradation of their bodies. They exchanged the truth of God for a lie and revered and worshiped the creature rather than the creator, who is blessed forever. Amen. Therefore, God handed them over to degrading passions. Their females exchanged natural relations for unnatural, and the males likewise gave up natural relations with females and burned with lust for one another. Males did shameful things with males and thus received in their own persons the due penalty for their perversity. And since they did not see fit to acknowledge God, God handed them over to their undiscerning mind to do what is improper. They are filled with every form of wickedness, evil, greed, and malice, full of envy, murder, rivalry, treachery, and spite. They are gossips and scandalmongers and they hate God. They are insolent, haughty, boastful, ingenious in their wickedness, and rebellious toward their parents. They are senseless, faithless, heartless, ruthless. Although they know the just decree of God that all who practice such things deserve death, they not only do them but give approval to those who practice them. (v. 21-32)

Saint Paul's description is timeless. It does not refer only to the world before the coming of Jesus Christ, but to the world *away from God.* In fact, it is impressive to read the words of Saint Paul in light of what we see in today's world. It seems that he is looking at our 21st Century. It seems he is describing the world we are living in today.

Yesterday and this morning, you have been meditating on the reality of your sin. Your sin, the sin of men, is a darkness that seemed like it could not be defeated. And yet, God responds to that state of fallen humanity by offering salvation.

2. *God's response.* Saint Ignatius places these words in the mouths of the three Persons of the Most Holy Trinity: "*Hagamos redención del género humano* (Let us work the

redemption of the human race)." God "wills everyone to be saved and to come to knowledge of the truth" (1 Tim 2:4).

God loves man and is not satisfied with seeing him lose himself. The lost sheep is Adam, it is all of mankind that needs to be redeemed, and God goes to look for us all. It is the revelation of God's love as merciful love, a love that forgives and that enjoys forgiving.

God works the redemption of the human race *by choosing to be one of us.* St. John Paul II writes in *Redemptor Hominis*: "His is a love that does not draw back before anything that requires justice in him."[56] He becomes a man to fulfill divine justice, and by becoming incarnate, he accepts everything that choice supposes and means: the way of the Cross written in the plan of redemption, the humiliations, the sacrifices, the works, the contempt.

Redemption is a work of God's love and a revelation of God's love, but it is also a work of a human Heart! *One of us* saved us. Our brother, Jesus.

Personally, I find great consolation in this meditation on the words of Saint Ignatius: to think that God has committed himself to us. The day I first arrived in Nazareth was perhaps the deepest experience of my pilgrimage to the Holy Land. On my knees I adored the mystery of *my* Redemption and experienced there, with intensity that I had never known before, something of this mystery. God made man ... *for me*. Truly, you can get lost, like a little salt in the ocean ... The Father, the Son and the Holy Spirit have not abandoned me, they have not let me be condemned, they have rescued me. I spent more than four hours in silent prayer and I felt things that I had never felt before and that, perhaps, I may never experience again. I invite you, as I told you last night, to feel very loved by God. How good is God!

3. After considering the world in sin and God's response to that sin ("let us work the redemption of the human race"), we approach the house of Mary in Nazareth.[57]

It is the most beautiful morning—full of light, like the transparent soul of Mary.

The greatest of the mysteries of God, the most intense act of communication of God with a human person has taken place in an insignificant external environment. John Paul II, in *Redemptoris Mater*, says that the presence of Mary was "so discreet as to pass almost unnoticed by the eyes of her contemporaries."[58] It goes unnoticed by men, but the eyes of God *are fixed on her*, as the angel will say: "You have found grace in the eyes of God." This is very important; it makes an impression: God sets his sights on what goes unnoticed. We see Mary in that simplicity. In the hiding of her life, she has this dialogue of the Annunciation of universal resonance, but goes unnoticed. It is an intimate dialogue, lived in the secret of a life that in the eyes of others has not undergone any change. It has gone totally unnoticed!

The same thing happens with us: our intimate dialogue with Christ has universal resonance, it has resonance in the life of teaching, of family, of work, when that life is the fruit of an intimate dialogue with Christ. We have to learn to love like that. It does not mean to reduce us to this; each one has his mission that he has to fulfill. But one of the great temptations of man is to do everything in a visible way, not wanting to go unnoticed.

God goes to Nazareth, a lost, insignificant village. When Nathanael hears that Jesus is from there, his comment says it all: "Can anything good come from Nazareth?" (Jn. 1:46) Nobody would have guessed this choice of God; really, his ways are not our ways.

I am going to beg you to forgive me here, but I will not go word by word as in the other meditations. I cannot because in every word, I get lost. I say it honestly. I greatly appreciate those who can talk a lot about Mary in that passage of the Annunciation.

I grab only one of the words and my time is lost in them. I have been asked for many years to speak at the Marian Conference that takes place every summer in Phoenix and I have always said no. This year I have agreed at the insistence of some very good people to celebrate Holy Mass there. I'm speechless when I talk about Mary, even in Spanish. After having been there to Nazareth, that feeling has increased: I love to hear about Mary, but I have a hard time talking about her because I have the feeling that nothing of what I say can do justice to the work that God has done in her. And I read what so many saints have written about her (Saint Anselm, Saint Alfonso, Saint Louis Marie, Saint Bernard, Saint Maximilian, Saint Francis, so many others)and I know that I cannot say anything better than what has already been said, and at the same time, what they have said, while being wonderful, is nothing compared to the reality of what Mary is.

Therefore, I am going to ask you to let the Lord speak to you on this page of Sacred Scripture. In the wonderful text from St. Bernard you will read after this meditation, the saint addresses our Mother, precisely, in this moment of the Incarnation. Saint Bernard asks Mary to hurry to answer "yes" to the invitation of the angel because without her yes, we could not save ourselves. I invite you to enter in this conversation that is full of anointing and piety.[59]

4. I want to focus on the heart of what we are contemplating, on the fact that God has asked for the collaboration of his creature. There is the Archangel Gabriel, waiting for a girl's response and, at that moment, the redemption of the world depends as much on the omnipotence and love of God as on the fragility and response of a girl. What a mystery!

Roberto Benigni, a famous Italian film director (who is not Catholic)once said: "That girl was about to have the possibility of God becoming man, so that man could become God. And the same God, the great God who has given us the great gift of being able to say yes or no, awaited her decision, as the lovers wait for the yes from the lips of those they love, with the fear of those who risk their lives in an answer."

God has prepared Mary precisely for that decisive moment for all human history. All the graces granted to Mary derive from her divine Motherhood. When God gives a vocation, he gives the grace to fulfill it. That is to say, that he not only calls, but also *prepares the person* and enriches him internally so that he can fully carry out his mission on earth. It is important to remember this because sometimes you have the impression that you cannot do it anymore, or that you do not know what to do.

Mary has always loved God. She is "full of grace," as the angel said. Mary loves God, she surrenders to Him fully. That surrender to his love becomes a prayer, and that prayer is the desire for the salvation of the world. And God, who has prepared her from the beginning for this moment to be there, at the center point of God's plan for salvation, at the culminating point of history, at this moment of indescribable transcendence, asks Mary for the gift of her motherhood.

There are few more intimate moments in the life of a man and a woman than the moment when they come together in one flesh to be parents. People are understandably reluctant to even talk about it with others because that moment is sacred. If you allow me the expression, Mary had to overcome her modesty to tell Saint Luke this moment, the most intimate moment of her life. She did it because she was aware that, somehow, it belonged to us, too.

She must surrender, now, again. It is not *just* a consent, a "yes", with God acting upon her as a physician would act upon her body. Her collaboration is that of a Mother in the co-creation of the Son. It is a Mother who, in the act of loving, begets. She is a Mother, and not only in a physical sense!

If a woman were to become pregnant, for example, while she was drunk, she would not at that moment be acting as a mother in the fullest sense. The human way of being a mother is love: she loves and, in that act of love for her husband and her future child, she becomes pregnant.

Mary had always loved God as her spouse, as her only love, but now it is not about loving only as a virgin. At this moment, the Holy Spirit is acting in her to create a *maternal* love. God, in the Annunciation, is not only asking permission of Mary to enter the world: *he is forming in her a mother's heart*, which she did not have. We could put into the mouth of God these words, addressed to Mary: "Until now you have loved me with a spousal love, but now you must learn to love me *as a Mother*. I want to give you that love of a Mother. In order for me to give you this gift, you must accept it. Do you?"

136

God transforms the Heart of the Virgin also into the Heart of Mother. He asks her to be his Mother, by the surrender of herself to God. She understands that she is asked to be the Mother of God Himself, but God does not want only her womb, as if he needed a woman to be born. He wants to beget himself *with an act of love.* He wants the Heart of Mary. We are witnessing the generating act of the Word!

Mary has to answer. In this moment, it is the grace of God that comes upon her, the love of God that floods her, asks for her. He will respect the decision of this little Virgin. It is admirable, in a decision of such transcendence, Mary realizes that at this moment the salvation of the world depends as much on her yes, as on the Will of the Father. Mary's response is her surrender of love.

In Mary, *the first thing is her surrender*, not the action. In the account of the Annunciation, Mary's response does not begin with "Yes, I collaborate;" it begins with "Behold." I am yours, I place my will in accord to your will. You can do with me what you want, "according to your word." This is a very feminine trait. We must check our own level of surrender because we may not often fully give of ourselves; we lack generosity.

Mary's yes makes her a Mother. As I pointed out earlier, before she loved God as a virgin, in spousal love, but from that moment on, she added the dimension of Motherhood to that love. Her yes is the first time that she has loved God as a mother. This intervention of God has changed the Heart of Mary, the way in which she loves Him.

Mary teaches us to give ourselves completely. All of our activity must be the expression of an offer.

5. In the following passage, Edith Stein compares Mary with Eve in a lovely contemplation of this wonderful scene:

> *"The most pure virgin is the only one safeguarded from every stain of sin. Except for her, no one embodies feminine nature in its original purity. Every other woman has something in herself inherited from Eve, and she must search for the way from Eve to Mary. There is a bit of defiance in each woman which does not want to humble itself under any sovereignty. In each, there is something of that desire which reaches for forbidden fruit. And she is hindered by both these tendencies in what we clearly recognize as woman's work."*[60]

"Every other woman has something in her inherited from Eve, and she must search for the way from Eve to Mary." In the Garden of Eden, the demon causes the woman to fall into the trap, demonstrating an extraordinary knowledge of her nature. It is the enemy who initiates the conversation: "Did God really tell you not to eat from any of the trees in the garden?" (Gen. 3:1) Jesus calls him "father of lies" (Jn. 8:44) and here we have the first of the examples. God had not asked Adam and Eve not to eat from any of the trees. He had only forbidden that they eat from one tree. Why does the demon pose the conversation in these terms? I think that Eve's answer makes it perfectly clear to us: "We may eat the fruit in the garden; it is only about the fruit of the tree in the middle of the garden that God said, 'You shall not eat it or even touch it, lest you die.'"

The purpose of the demon was to focus Eve's attention on

that tree. A woman usually grasps affectively to reality, to her experiences, with much more intensity than a man. I remember that a professor of mine in Moral Theology used to say that 95% of the arguments between a husband and a wife could be reduced to the following: the man, while arguing with his wife, is usually thinking: "What a stubborn woman my wife is! I'm giving her a thousand reasons to listen to me and she is not convinced by any of them." Meanwhile, the wife is thinking: "What a fool my husband is! It turns out that I have the only reason that is important in this matter, and he is here bombarding me with reasons that are not worth anything in this situation."

I think there is some truth in the example. The woman can hold onto something—a judgment, a person, a situation in her life—and never let go. As the years go by, she remembers a word that hurt her as though it was yesterday. Men are simpler, I think, in that sense, we "forget" more easily.

I use this example because I think it helps us better understand the conversation between the serpent and Eve. Eve's response seems correct: she defends God from the lie that the snake just told, but without realizing it, *has already fallen into the trap.* The trick was to start the conversation and to look at *that* tree, which perhaps before she had not paid much attention to, but now it is fixed in her mind and desire. "The woman saw that the tree was good for food, pleasing to the eye, and desirable" (v. 6).The best response would have been to not engage, turn her back, and walk away.

How does the devil make the woman want to eat the fruit of the tree? "God knows well that the moment you eat of it your eyes will be opened and you will be like gods" (v. 5).*You will be like gods.* Eve's sin was *wanting to be like God without*

God. She wanted to ignore God, become independent of him. The devil put God before man, as if he were an enemy that did not want our happiness.

Mary has the opposite attitude: "Behold the handmaid of the Lord. Let it be done to me according to your word." In these words is found the most important lesson of our entire Christian life. The New Eve, as I said at the beginning, says yes to God with full freedom. She accepts with joy and peace the sudden change of plans and responds with a serenity that impresses. She understands the responsibility of being a mother and, although the details of how this new mission that God has manifested to her will not be revealed, *she relies on God.* She believes in his word, begets Jesus Christ by faith, and simply puts herself in the hands of God. How much greatness in that simple answer!

6. *"Then the angel departed from her"* (v. 38).You can, at the end of your prayer, accompany Mary in the moments that followed the Annunciation. The Angel Gabriel returns to heaven with the mission accomplished, with the great *Yes* of Mary, and she is once again alone. On the surface, nothing has changed, everything seems to continue as before and yet, in her belly lies hidden the life of her Son, a baby whose name she even knows, because that, too, has been revealed.

I imagine her placing her hand on her belly and saying that name in a low voice, *"the name that is above every name"* (Phil. 2:9):*Jesus* ... the name that expresses in its meaning the identity of the second Person of the Holy Trinity: "God saves." In his *Confessions*, St. Augustine has this expression: *"Ego eram ipse mihi magna questio* (I had become a great question to myself).*[61]* Mary could use those same words:

she knew that she was the bearer of a great mystery. She knew the God of Israel, who had created the world and who had brought his people out of Egypt, who had accompanied them for forty years in the desert, who had carried forward the whole history of salvation, who had manifested Himself in his prophets and had moved the threads of history, now he had chosen her to be his gateway into this world. That boundless God had become tiny in her womb and already dwelt in her body.

The angel's appearance must have seemed almost like a dream, especially in the beginning. What happened is not yet apparent: Mary must continue to believe in that Word that has been revealed to her. The angel has not resolved all her doubts; he has not even shown her how to do what has been communicated to her. She does not know what she should do. It is curious because, although the Revelation of God is always luminous, Mary has been left in great darkness. Sometimes, we believe that the intervention of God offers us all the answers, but that is not reality, and it was not so for Mary either. God elevates, but it is always a way *in faith.* To Mary, this intervention of God has completely upset her plans, as it often does. The Lord usually asks us what we do not expect: through a disease, or an unforeseen circumstance, or a decision that someone makes that affects us. We have to ask Mary to teach us to let ourselves be led by God, to trust in his plans that are always better than ours, to know that God, when a good work begins, carries it to completion (cf. Phil. 1:6).

We are going to ask Mary to teach us to receive the Word of God as she did. May we always trust in the action of the Holy Spirit. May we let Christ dwell in our hearts. May we allow ourselves to be led by God wherever He wishes to take us in these Exercises. May she grant us the charity and faith that she had and the knowledge of how to be faithful to the mission that the Lord reveals to us throughout our lives. And if, as the Archangel Gabriel said, "nothing is impossible for God," let us ask the Lord to help us believe that the impossible can really happen in our lives and that holiness is not an unattainable dream for us but the reality of a life in constant union with Jesus Christ.

10

MARY AT THE VISITATION I

"O God, eternal majesty, whose ineffable Word the immaculate Virgin received through the message of an Angel and so became the dwelling-place of divinity, filled with the light of the Holy Spirit, grant, we pray, that by her example we may in humility hold fast to your will" (Collect of the Mass on December 20th)

If there is a charmingly feminine scene in the New Testament, it is the one that takes us to the mountains of Judea with Mary and Elizabeth. It is an encounter between two women who, in very different but extraordinary ways, received from God the news that they have been chosen to give life to two exceptional children. Everything on this page of the Gospel of St. Luke lifts our hearts as we read

143

it. Everything emanates hope, joy, expectation.

Let us consider this Gospel scene in detail, dividing it into a triptych that will help us to walk and feel with our Mother. In the first part, we will consider the decision to go to visit Elizabeth, reflecting on the reasons that moved Mary to the service of her cousin. I think it offers a great insight into the motivations for this visit and teaches us to face the difficult moments of our life with peace. The second part will be the contemplation of Mary's journey from Nazareth to Ein-Karem, during which we will ask the Holy Spirit for the grace to enter into Our Lady's Heart to consider some of her feelings and attitudes on her journey, which is an analogy of our own pilgrimage through this life. Finally, we will arrive at the scene of the Visitation, a song of joy for the gift of life and definitive salvation in Jesus Christ.

1. *Introduction.* "And the angel left her" (Lk. 1:38).After those first moments of astonishment, which we considered in the preceding meditation, I imagine that Mary would begin to realize, little by little, what had happened to her. Most likely, we can all relate to her based on our own experience when we have received surprising news and have needed a few minutes to digest the information. My mother once told me that when the doctor first informed my father that he had stomach cancer, he lost consciousness and fell to the ground from fear and shock. News sometimes reaches our hearts gently and at other times strikes our souls like a slap in the face.

Mary has remained in the peace that transpired during the conversation with the angel. However, very soon she begins to understand that there are some aspects that have not been revealed to her in the angel's message and that she must discern what to do next. She has seen a ray of heavenly light, but there are many areas that remain in shadow, that have not been clarified, and that she must now examine.

Most likely the first one has to do with her dear Joseph, a good man, who loves her and with whom she has dreamed of a home and a family totally dedicated to the service of God. Both have decided to sacrifice the joy of children in order to surrender with greater devotion to the Lord. Mary's question to the angel leaves no room for doubt: "How can this be, since I have no relations with a man?" (Lk. 1:34)In all the manifestations of the Old Testament in which God, directly or through one of his emissaries, announces the birth of a son, it is understood that this will be possible by the subsequent conjugal union of the spouses. Mary's objection, as a woman already married to Joseph, as the prologue of this passage points out, can only be understood as an avowal to the angel of her intention *of not having relations with a man*, that is, of her resolution to refrain from those relationships from which the conception of a human life could be derived. Actually, it would have been a foolish question if Mary had simply wanted to reveal to the angel that she had not had an intimate life with Joseph *until that moment.* To such a simple question, the angel could have answered her with something like "You are married to Joseph and behold you shall conceive and bear a child."

However, here our Lady demurs because, as the sacred text says, she was troubled inwardly. It seemed a contradiction, since she has given herself virginally to God because in the sanctuary of her heart, *she understood that was what he claimed of her.* Now, that same God who had inspired her to a life of virginity seems to be asking her to sacrifice that very desire that He himself had placed in her woman's heart. That is to say, Mary is a virgin not only because she had never had a relationship in the flesh with any man, but because she had already offered herself to her Lord with the whole of her body and her heart.

The question that she asks at this decisive moment for herself and for the fate of fallen mankind is not simply pointing to her life as it has been until then, but is projected into the future since her offer is that of her whole person, body and soul, to the Lord.

In that desire to give herself totally to God, Mary had found in Joseph a man who understood that desire for virginal surrender to God and accepted her in this way, realizing that this was God's plan for his wife.

The purity of Joseph and his desire to surrender to that same lifestyle was probably born of Mary herself. She had seen in this man a heart of extraordinary spiritual quality. From the beginning she had felt understood and loved by him concerning her plan of virginity and Joseph, for the love of Mary, had embraced the vocation of his wife. But he had also renounced having descendants for the love of Mary, because he would rather be in a marriage with her dedicated to God without children than being a father with, perhaps, another woman. She had ignited in him her own desire for virginity and had helped Joseph to offer himself, too, to God in a virginal surrender.

I remember my dear Fr. Valverde saying that, if the vocation of man is to *lead*, the woman has the special task from God to *elevate* the people around her. This may simplify things too much, but I think that it is right to point out an irrevocable aspect of the mission of women as the Lord has created them. When a woman knows how to be a woman, she lifts spirits, inspires strength in the weak, opens visions of new life, aspires to more noble ideals, brings out the best in man's heart. In the case of the Holy Family, we can imagine that something like this has happened: Mary has raised Joseph, a wonderful man with whom she knows that she can share a supernatural and divine way of life, to desire of a life of virginity for love of Mary and, of course, for love of God. Mary has modeled virginity for Joseph's heart and he has allowed himself be molded in the hands of his wife. He has been the first, in the words of St. Louis-Marie Grignion de Monfort, to live true devotion to the Virgin Mary.

Women have this immense power and it is good in the context of these Spiritual Exercises that you wonder how you are exercising it in your families and with others. Because if the woman is called to *elevate*, there is no doubt also the possibility that, with her words and her attitudes, she could *sink* all those around her. Her presence can also have a demoralizing, even devasting, effect, since she knows what to say to cause harm or what to do to reopen wounds. If the center of the home is the wife and mother, when the woman chooses to oppose or become stubborn on an idea or in a trial, she can wreak havoc, divide a family, or bar the doors of hope.

I want to bring in this context the famous praise of the virtuous woman we read in the book of Proverbs. It serves to portray Mary and to express the biblical ideal of the feminine soul. Honestly, I think that if I were a woman, I would try to learn this page of the Scripture by heart so that I could make my daily examination of conscience based on these words.

Who can find a woman of worth? Far beyond jewels is her value. Her husband trusts her judgment; he does not lack income. She brings him profit, not loss, all the days of her life. She seeks out wool and flax and weaves with skillful hands. Like a merchant fleet, she secures her provisions from afar. She rises while it is still night, and distributes food to her household, a portion to her maidservants. She picks out a field and acquires it; from her earnings she plants a vineyard. She girds herself with strength; she exerts her arms with vigor. She enjoys the profit from her dealings; her lamp is never extinguished at night. She puts her hands to the distaff, and her fingers ply the spindle. She reaches out her hands to the poor, and extends her arms to the needy. She is not concerned for her household when it snows—all her charges are doubly clothed. She makes her own coverlets; fine linen and purple are her clothing. Her husband is prominent at the city gates as he sits with the elders of the land. She makes garments and sells them, and stocks the merchants with belts. She is clothed with strength and dignity, and laughs at the days to come. She opens her mouth in wisdom; kindly instruction is on her tongue. She watches over the affairs of her household, and does not eat the bread of idleness. Her children rise up and call her blessed; her husband, too, praises her: "Many are the women of proven worth, but you have excelled them all. Charm is deceptive and beauty fleeting; the woman who fears the LORD is to be praised. Acclaim her for the work of her hands, and let her deeds praise her at the city gates (31:10-

31).

But now, Mary is a mother and Joseph is not the father of the child. Poor Mary! What will Joseph's reaction be? How does she tell him something that is humanly impossible to accept? How can he process such an extraordinarily unforeseen event? What should she do in regard to him?

2. *St. Joseph's doubt and the decision to visit Elizabeth.* We know the most classic version of what is usually called "St. Joseph's doubt." According to this interpretation, Mary basically decides to hide the news of the angel from her husband, who comes to discover the pregnancy due to the natural development of the pregnancy and the effects that inevitably manifest themselves in his wife's body. His inner struggle, which we discover at least partially in the Gospel of St. Matthew, consists in his certainty that Mary is a holy woman who has not betrayed him, yet, she is pregnant and he is not the father of that child. This is what another Jesuit priest, Father Jorge de la Cueva, described as "evidence against evidence" and consists of being situated between two facts that are equally apparent but contradictory.

Finally, Joseph's doubts are resolved with the announcement of the angel, who tells Joseph in his dreams what Mary had not: that the Child was of divine origin (Mt. 1:20).

The truth is that, if we think about it, this explanation, which is no doubt in line with the sacred text, tries to fill the silences by presenting us with an image of Mary and Joseph that is at least somewhat dissonant with what might be expected. It is a legitimate version, but everything appears blurry and results in the impression that Mary either does not trust her husband, thinks that he would not understand the situation, or simply chooses the path of silence for fear of his reaction. In any of these cases—and I beg that you forgive my boldness—the figure of the Virgin appears to be tarnished. She is represented almost as an immature woman who lacks courage, who waits for St. Joseph to discover her pregnancy by himself without opening her heart to him, a man who without a doubt was her soulmate.

St. Joseph, on the other hand, is no better off. If he did not doubt his wife's innocence, why opt for the path of repudiation? St. Matthew has described this descendant of David as a "righteous" man (Mt. 1:19) bearer of a justice that has permeated all stages of his heart doing good in God's eyes. Is it fair, then, to repudiate someone he considers innocent? I do not know; there is something that, as we say in Spanish, "is screeching." Something seems to be out of place, it does not reflect in either of the spouses a decision that is responsible and worthy of praise.

The interpretation that I find spiritually deeper and more profitable, more harmonious with what we know of Mary and Joseph, that will lead us along other paths. It will help us to understand the scene of the Visitation in a context that, I hope, will be very fruitful for you.

3. Mary has listened carefully to the words of the angel and—as noted in other moments of her life by the evangelist St. Luke (2:19; 2:51)—we can imagine that in the most decisive moment of her life, she reflected on this message in her heart. As we know, the first chapter of this Gospel includes two apparitions of the angel St. Gabriel. The first has Zacharias receiving the announcement of the birth of

the Precursor, John the Baptist. In the face of this good news, he doubts and, as a result of that, loses the power to speak: "Now you will be speechless and unable to talk—the celestial emissary tells him—until the day these things take place, because you did not believe my words, which will be fulfilled at their proper time" (1:20).In contrast to the doubt of this great biblical figure, Mary stands out for her faith in the power of God, "Blessed are you who have believed," Elizabeth will say later (1:45).Our Mother trusts what has been communicated to her and, when she is left alone after the Annunciation, with a faith that does not falter but at the same time does not understand well the mystery of what has happened, examines carefully, word by word, the content of that divine message. She does so because, for her, every expression, every thought is a revelation that God directs, personally, to her woman's soul.

After clarifying the extraordinary and unique way in which her son Jesus will be born (only she will be at the same time virgin and mother),the angel has dropped this phrase into the good soil of her spirit: "The Lord God will give him the throne of David, his father, he will reign over Jacob's house forever and his kingdom will have no end" (1:32-33).Beyond expressing the fullness of Israel's messianic hopes that have finally been realized in her virginal womb, here Mary finds an indication of what to do next.

"He will give him the throne of David, his father..." Mary understands that these words refer to Joseph! If her son is to be the Son of David, it is because of Joseph (cf. Mt. 13:55).Therefore, in this mystery Joseph has a role to play! Mary understands the angel's words as addressed to her husband because in them there is an indication, a clue, that

God suggests in this moment of trial: *Yes, your husband Joseph has a mission in this story. He is not separated from you by my plan of salvation. On the contrary, Jesus is David's son because of his relationship with your husband, the carpenter of Nazareth, a descendant of the king of Israel.* Why would Mary, who is characterized by an open and expansive spirit, withhold this message, *which internally affects her husband*, without saying anything to him? If the Virgin was born for the moment of the Annunciation, Joseph was born to be the "father" of Jesus, as Mary herself calls him (Lk 2:48).Is it permissible to think that our Mother was going to hide from Joseph the words from God that concerned him as much as they concerned her?

On the path of our spiritual lives, we find ourselves many times in the position that Mary went through at this time: the Lord manifests some aspect of our life in the Spirit and, nevertheless, chooses not to unfold the entire story before our eyes. Maybe we would like God to tell us more or tell us everything, to clear away our doubts and dispel the fog that obscures our sight. I believe that, deep down, there is some pride in this attitude because, in reality, what we would like to do is not have to depend on the Lord every step of the way. And God, who is charmed with souls who trust him, reveals Himself to us little by little, step by step. Faith is a dark light, or a luminous darkness, if I am allowed the paradox. It reveals the true meaning of things, but by its very nature, requires us to rely on the Lord in what we cannot see of our life. And, like Mary, we have to learn to receive with gratitude what God is communicating to us, which is enough to take a step forward along the path of faith, and trust that the Lord will reveal to us, at every step, the part of the path that he asks us today, now, to travel.

Therefore, Mary goes to her husband, Joseph, and opens up her heart. She tells him because she *needs* to share with him what has happened to her, because she sees in this man, the support that God has given her through marriage to help her in difficult times. Let's say it simply: She speaks with him because she loves and trusts him! She cannot leave out her husband—he to whom, through the words of the angel, God has also given an important mission to fulfill. This is what St. Edith Stein affirms about her:

> *The integral feminine nature lives in Mary as wife and mother: she never asserts a proprietary right toward her son; as wife, she has a limitless trust and practices compliant submission suitable to her conviction that her husband was given to her by God.*[62]

How would this admirable man receive his wife's confidence? I want to think that we men have a greater affinity with Joseph and we can sense, even a little, what would have gripped his heart. Sure enough, as you say in English, it wouldn't be an "easy pill to swallow." Still—and here is Joseph's greatness of soul—*he trusts Mary.* Joseph, "who was a righteous man," believes his wife's word. This is admirable! St. Joseph's doubts cannot be interpreted as a questioning of Mary, as a kind of suspicion directed against her. His doubts cannot be directed against his wife, whom he loves with all his heart and that he knows is innocent. *St. Joseph does not doubt Mary, but himself!*

In these Exercises, it would be good if we imagined that conversation between the holiest of spouses, that we try to look at their faces, the expressions of both, the seriousness, the tears, the feeling of fragility that these two holy souls would experience. As a priest, I've seen so many people like that! People who sincerely wish to do the will of God *but who do not know what to do.* Nazareth is the place where that dialogue took place: maybe it was in the carpentry shop, where Mary knew she could find her husband w orking. I remember spending a lot of time there, in what is now called the Church of St. Joseph, during my pilgrimage on foot through the Holy Land. It is moving to think that it was in this place that the Holy Family lived these moments of trial!

4. *Joseph needs to think.* The news not only catches him by surprise: he doesn't even see clearly how they should move forward. What do you think our good Joseph would do at this point? He is a servant of the Word of God; he listens to it in the synagogue, celebrates it, and meditates on it in his heart. It may be impossible for us to understand what that Word represented to a devout Jew, who seeks in the Torah the meaning of his life and who lives totally committed to Yahweh.

Therefore, St. Joseph scrutinizes the Word of God, trying to find in it the light he needs in these moments of darkness and finds a passage that has David as the protagonist. It is a text from the Holy Scripture that sheds much light and I want to think that, because of the affinities and parallels it presents with the story of the Visitation, it is much more than pure coincidence. *It answers Joseph's prayer in those difficult moments.* Undoubtedly, he recognizes himself in this story not only because his ancestor is present in him (it almost seems that the words of St. Gabriel were directing him to trace the answer to his doubts in David's stories and life), but because in the feelings of the great King of Israel he now sees his own reflected. The fact appears in the second book of Samuel, chapter six, and refers to the transfer of the Ark of the Covenant to the city of Jerusalem.

For the Jews, the Ark represented the presence of God in the midst of his people. A God, who had chosen them in Abraham, freed them from Egypt by the hand of Moses and accompanied them in the desert until he established them in the Promised Land. Yahweh is not a distant God. He also had his Tent, called the Tent of Meeting, to which he came down to speak with Moses "face to face, as a friend speaks with a friend" (Ex. 33:11-13).In the most sacred part of that tent, the "Holy of Holies," was the Ark that Bezalel had built under the direction of Moses at the beginning of the desert exodus. In the Ark were kept the Tablets of the Law that God had given to Moses on Mount Sinai that established God's Covenant with his people. Later, manna, with which God had fed Israel during their 40 years of pilgrimage, and Aaron's rod, which represented the priesthood of the Old Covenant, were added.

The Ark always represented the presence of God. In it, Yahweh was present and spoke to, accompanied, and illuminated Israel. Sacred Scripture scrupulously presents absolutely everything related to how the Tent of Meeting and the Ark were regulated: who could touch and transport them, the minimum distance that the Israelites could approach, the proper way to act when the glory of Yahweh was manifested in the sight of all in the form of a column of fire. All these details were intended to safeguard the sacredness and the infinite respect due to God, because the proximity of the Lord, if not properly protected, could create a sense of undue familiarity with the Lord, a loss of the reverence due to the Invisible, and thus lower their respect and esteem for the gift they had received.

Precisely the awareness of this reverence is evidenced in the passage of the second book of Samuel (2 Sm. 6:2-9):

> *Then David and all the people who were with him set out for Baala of Judah to bring up from there the ark of God, which bears the name "the LORD of hosts enthroned above the cherubim." They transported the ark of God on a new cart and took it away from the house of Abinadab on the hill. Uzzah and Ahio, sons of Abinadab, were guiding the cart, with Ahio walking before it, while David and all the house of Israel danced before the LORD with all their might, with singing, and with lyres, harps, tambourines, sistrums, and cymbals. As they reached the threshing floor of Nodan, Uzzah stretched out his hand to the ark of God and steadied it, for the oxen were tipping it. Then the LORD became angry with Uzzah; God struck him on that spot, and he died there in God's presence. David was angry because the LORD's wrath had broken out against Uzzah. Therefore that place has been called Perez-uzzah even to this day. David became frightened of the LORD that day, and he said, "How can the ark of the LORD come to me?"*

5. David is afraid to see that Uzzah, with good intention, dies

from having dared to touch the Ark in order to prevent it from falling. Actually, it had to be surprising for all the witnesses to see that good man die on the spot. However, they had not weighed the consequences of touching the holiness of God with sinful hands like ours. Sometimes, good intention is not enough because we can make wrong decisions even when we intend to do good. David wonders: "How can the ark of the Lord come to me?" Fear suddenly assaults the king of Israel he suddenly feels infinite distance between his condition as a creature and the immensity and holiness of the Lord.

The ark was a sign of God's presence but the child that Mary carries in her womb is God Himself! If David felt unworthy to lodge the ark in his house, how would Joseph, a just and good man, feel upon hearing from Mary what the angel had told her? Mary is the true Ark of the Covenant! She carries in her womb the new Covenant between God and man. She is now the custodian of that God who had previously manifested himself in diverse ways but who, in the fullness of time, had decided to become one of us. If we understand David's reverential fear after Uzzah's death, how much more can we understand Joseph's fear in discovering himself standing before the mystery of a God who has become man? If David was terrified of taking the ark home, how could we not understand Joseph's fright of taking Mary, the ark of the New Covenant, into his home?

Therefore, Joseph's doubts do not stem from suspicion towards Mary, but from his humility, of being a righteous man who experiences the holiness of God in its most extraordinary manifestation in history. I imagine him, while listening to Mary, looking with indescribable astonishment at her still flat belly, within which the whole fullness of Deity bodily dwells (Col. 2:9).There, in the womb of his young wife, the One who is Infinite is hidden, and he begins to feel the presence of the Almighty in the fragility of that unborn Child, of the Creator of the Universe concealed in his wife's womb. That is why Joseph doubts and fears—he is acutely aware that the God "who inhabits an inaccessible light" (1 Tim. 6:16)and whom "no one can see" (Jn. 1:18)now rocks silently in Mary of Nazareth's lap.

He feels unworthy! He feels unworthy, in the first place, in relation to Mary: it is as if, upon knowing the story of the Annunciation, his wife's mystery is suddenly revealed to him in all its amazing magnitude. In gentle and absolute respect for his wife, he has always admired Mary's purity, virtue, and charity, but it is now the reality of that young woman, who is still almost a child, is manifested to him: she is the Mother of God! Our good Joseph would think, "My wife is the mother of the Messiah! Yahweh has chosen my wife to become one of us! " That God whom Joseph knew so well, having learned of him since childhood in the traditions of his people, the history of salvation; that God to whom he felt very close because he had a personal, endearing and respectful relationship towards him; that God who had modeled Adam from the dust of Eden and had hung the stars in the night sky; that God who had opened the floodgates of the Red Sea so that Israel could reach the Promised Land; that God who had worked countless wonders and who had been the Savior of his people, accompanying them during all stages of his history; that God *now* was hidden in his wife's body.

The fear of Joseph is the fear of the saint in the presence of God that is revealed to him, multiplied now to extremes that we cannot imagine, both because of Joseph's extraordinary holiness and humility (which made him extremely sensitive to the manifestations of his Lord)and also because here we are at the peak of God's revelations, at the moment of greatest intensity and communication of the divine mystery to men. If Mary is the Ark of the New Covenant, at which he dares not even look (like the publican in the parable of Luke 18:9-14, who could not lift his eyes from the ground), the Child whose presence he already feels in the womb of his wife is the incarnation of God infinitely superior to man; of the God who, in the madness of love, has become one of us.

Thus is Joseph's reaction the same as King David's: "How can the ark of the Lord come to me?" (2 Sam. 6: 9)*How can I live with the ark of the Lord, which is Mary? How can I, the poor carpenter of Nazareth, most unworthy of anyone, become the human father and the teacher of the Son of God? What am I doing in this mystery? What is my role in it? What do I do amidst such holiness? This is far superior to what I can do or I can be asked to do.*

6. The confusion of Joseph finds a certain light in the words of the Angel Gabriel and in the passage of Scripture that we are using now, because what does David do upon feeling unworthy of receiving the ark of the covenant in his house? "So David was unwilling to take the ark of the LORD with him into the City of David. David deposited it instead at the house of Obed-edom the Gittite" (2 Sam. 6:10).The king decides to move the ark to the house of the priest, Obededom. Obviously, David's choice does not mean that he is rejecting the gift of God or the presence of the Lord: it is a reflection of the same feeling of wonder that pervades him for what has happened before. David, thus, gives himself time to consider

what he should do and what Yahweh wants him to do.

And, at this point, Mary and Joseph *understand the words of the angel in the Annunciation as an indication as to what they should do next*: "And behold, Elizabeth, your relative, has also conceived a son in her old age, and this is the sixth month for her who was called barren" (Lk. 1:36). Both understand here that this is a call for Mary to go to Elizabeth's house. It is not an improvised decision: it is likely that the plan was born of Joseph himself, the head of the family, who prays, thinks, discerns, and finds in the Word of God a clue, a suggestion for the immediate future. Joseph's response is perfectly reflected in the feelings of David, his forefather. He recognizes in Mary the Ark that bears the presence of God. Remember that Zacharias, Elizabeth's husband, is a priest, as was Obededom. Everything seems to fit, make sense, within the darkness in which they find themselves. He talks to Mary, and she leaves "without delay" to the mountains of Judah (Lk. 1:39).

I cannot be sure, but it seems to me that this vision of the events is more in line with the spirit of the whole Gospel. As I said before, I find it hard to think that in the most common interpretation of this passage, Mary chooses not to talk to Joseph and escapes on her own to see Elizabeth without telling her husband the cause of that decision. It is hard for me to think that Mary has deliberately chosen to leave her beloved husband aside and that she has chosen to let others know about the pregnancy before Joseph. Above all, it is hard for me to believe because, honestly, it seems unworthy behavior for Mary: I find it irresponsible and almost childish. She, who in all Scripture exudes serenity, balance, admirable maturity, here seems to act almost with haste. I don't know, as I say, but there is a note of that song that does not sound right, that is out of place.

And as I said before, Joseph in this interpretation fares no better. I apologize in advance for the expression, but he seems almost a fool who does not know what is happening around him; indeed, he is the last to notice the problem. In addition, when he finally decides to repudiate Mary in secret, he does so because of feelings or conclusions that not even in the most benign of interpretations seem to be very noble. We do not know if it is because of distrust of his wife, or because of a certain disappointment about how events have developed, or because he doubts the version he has received from Mary.

This other vision of the facts that we have briefly pointed out here is more serene, more harmonious with what we know of Mary and Joseph in Scripture, and, above all, more in line with the spirit of the Gospel in which Mary and Joseph are exemplars of the Christian way of life. It is an understanding that is richer spiritually, that conveys a greater serenity and, thus, seems to convey something of what this admirable marriage experienced in this great test of faith and trust in God.

7. In summary: after the Annunciation, Mary goes to Joseph. She tells him what has happened and what her response to the angel was. Thus, the husband is the first, after Mary, to know the news. Joseph, who is a righteous man, believes his wife and, as a result of that trust, experiences feelings of unworthiness, of uncertainty as to what his mission is in this great mystery. In the reference to Elizabeth that the Angel Gabriel had mentioned and in his humble

listening to the Word of God—particularly in the passage we have reflected on from the second Book of Samuel, in which there are obvious parallels to the situation he is going through—Joseph agrees with Mary and she goes to the house of Zacharias in the mountains, so that both of them can know better from God the next steps they are to take on this surprising new path.

We have to look, to try to understand as much as possible, the feelings that these spouses could have experienced. It is important that we do so because, in these Spiritual Exercises, we must ask for the grace of a new heart. That is, basically, the great work of the Redemption, a work in which we are as engaged just as Mary and Joseph were. Let's not forget that we are all united in that vision of *God who wants to save the world.* In his commentary on Song 27 of the Spiritual Canticle, St. John of the Cross writes that, "God is pleased with nothing but love." Now that you have heard these words, you—just as the Holy Family—are involved in that love with which God does everything. Through that love that you feel and that is given to you in these days, you can trace the path and *touch* and *live in the first person* the experience of Mary and Joseph.

For Mary—who is the first object of our attention—Joseph's response must have been moving, greatly comforting, and deeply troubling. If earlier, Joseph had been astonished to discover a side of his wife that he did not previously know and that the apparition of the angel had revealed to him—Mary is so holy that she has been chosen to be the Mother of God—it is now she who discovers the depth of her husband's soul in a way she had not contemplated before. With this, she would also experience a great admiration for

Joseph's unfathomable faith and holiness.

Let's be honest: anyone else would have reacted to the news in disbelief. We may have felt offended, thinking we were being taken for dummies who are naïve and easy to deceive. *There was only one man on the entire face of the Earth with enough simplicity and humility of heart to receive that news, and that man was her husband.* Joseph was unique. He was not like the other men. He was a "righteous man," as there was not before nor will there be after. Mary needed understanding and finds it in J oseph. Her husband is a man who has the soul of a child and, precisely because of that, welcomes that confidence, humanly implausible, without questioning in the least, the honesty of Mary. That attitude of Joseph must have been an unimaginable comfort for the Virgin. As a woman, she must have felt respected, affirmed, and lo ved. Mo reover, at that time she surely believed herself to be the luckiest and most blessed woman in the world because, although they were poor and lacked even the necessities, what other woman had a man like Joseph by her side?

And yet, to her credit, the pain upon realizing the suffering she had caused her husband immediately followed. Mary sees her husband consumed in pain. Joseph has lost his balance, because the jolt he has just been subjected to has shaken him to the core. It's all so unexpected, so impossible to predict! Such are the pathways of God. Providence will lead us, if we let him take the reins, toward an attitude in which only trust in the Lord really matters. Now Joseph and Mary have to believe in the light, despite the fact that they find themselves in the darkest and thickest night.

Edith Stein has reflected with marvelous delicacy on

Mary's relationship with Joseph, and what she writes corresponds well with the version of the facts offered here. This is what the holy German philosopher says:

> *Should we consider the Mother of God as spouse, we find a quiet, limitless trust which in turn depends on limitless trust, silent obedience, and an obviously faithful communion in suffering. She does all this in surrender to the will of God who has bestowed her husband upon her as human protector and visible guide. The image of the Mother of God demon-strates the basic spiritual attitude which corresponds to woman's natural vocation; her relation to her husband is one of obedience, trust, and participation in his life as she furthers his objective tasks and personality development; to the child she gives true care, encouragement, and formation of his God-given talents; she offers both selfless surrender and a quiet withdrawal when unneeded. All is based on the concept of marriage and motherhood as a vocation from God; it is carried out for God's sake and under His guidance.*"[63]

The attitudes that Edith Stein mentions in this paragraph are all manifested in the explanation that we have offered: unspoken and unlimited trust toward her husband; faithful and natural co-participation in his suffering, sharing in his life in obedience and trust. Selfless giving defines Mary's response and attitude toward St. Joseph in her quiet withdrawal and departure to Ein-Karem at her husband's suggestion. As Edith points out, everything springs from this living awareness that her maternity and her marriage are a vocation that she lives in obedience to God. Exactly the same attitude we saw in the mystery of the Incarnation of the Word: "Behold, I am the handmaid of the Lord. May it be done to me according to your word." (Lk. 1:38)

* * *

We will leave the second part of this episode, so rich in teachings, for the next meditation. Now you can slowly contemplate Mary and Joseph in that suffering through which they have participated in the history of salvation. There are so many lessons of Christian life here that I prefer to let the Holy Spirit suggest in the soul of each one of you what you should reflect on deeply: the greatness of the soul of this marriage, their faith, their quiet pain and patience, their confidence in God who turns our lives upside down in a matter of seconds and whose ways always exceed our ways (Is. 55:8). Ask yourself if, like Mary, you have always raised the lives of your family and closest ones. If the relationship with your husband, if you are married, is involved in the same feelings of Mary in relation to Joseph: admiration, veneration, respect, affection, humble love, and trust.

Above all, I invite you not to lose sight of that Child who already lives in this woman's womb. Ask for that "interior knowledge of Jesus Christ, who for me has become man, so that I may more love and follow him" of which St. Ignatius speaks (SE 104). How much the Lord would be loving Mary and Joseph in those difficult times! He had chosen well who his parents were to be on Earth: simple and poor people who were the two most beautiful creatures of the Creator's hand. Let us, too, let ourselves be modeled by that same loving hand, as Mary and Joseph did, through all the events of our lives.

11

MARY AT THE VISITATION II

DAY 4 (MORNING) – EIGHTH MEDITATION – CHRISTIAN JOY

"Almighty ever-living God, who, while the Blessed Virgin Mary was carrying your Son in her womb, inspired her to visit Elizabeth, grant us, we pray, that, faithful to the promptings of the Spirit, we may magnify your greatness with the Virgin Mary at all times." (Collect Prayer on the Feast of the Visitation)

We return to the story that takes Mary into the heart of the mountains of Judah. We are in these Exercises to encounter Christ. He has given himself to us, God has come to seek us, and this offer demands a journey that we must make. We must go out to meet him, just as he "went out" of himself by becoming one of us. This contemplation of Mary, who travels and leaves her home to serve her cousin, expresses a trait of our Mother that we must imitate and make our own. In the Gospels, Mary is always "on the way:" the Visitation, the journey to Bethlehem, the flight to Egypt, the return to Jerusalem when her Son is lost in the temple, the following of Christ from village to village during his public ministry... She journeys from one place to another, *and the pace is always set by the Lord.*

This aspect is very important. St. Ignatius presents the Exercises as a "conquering of oneself" with the purpose of allowing oneself to be led in everything by God. This appears in an eminent way in Mary, who now moves toward Elizabeth, her cousin in need.

1. *Letting oneself be led by God.* In the Spiritual Exercises, there are many lessons on the Christian life to which we should pay close attention. Above all is the great lesson of accepting changes in our plans when God manifests himself to us in the most diverse ways. A Spanish saint of the twentieth century, the Jesuit St. José María Rubio, summarizes holiness in this fitting expression: "to do what God wants, to will what God does." The first part—to do the Will of God—we usually understand and it does not cost us too much to accept it. But the second part, that of consenting the work of God in our life when he intervenes unexpectedly, without warning, without asking for permission... this hurts us more. We often rebel, and in this attitude, the depth of our pride is revealed to us. Yet, it is necessary *to want what God does,* to accept events as God wants them or allows them for our good. To trust especially in the face of unexpected setbacks in our life, which are many and will not cease to be present along the way.

This is how we see Mary on the morning she sets out on her journey. We said earlier that the decision to visit Elizabeth is shared with Joseph. We can imagine her leaving very early, with the first light of dawn, for the region of Judah, which is so familiar to her. She is leaving her husband behind in Nazareth, and we can see the farewell between them in the circumstances we have briefly described in the preceding meditation.

What a great trial for the Heart of Mary! Suddenly she has become a problem for her beloved husband. She has said yes to God's plan and it is now that she begins to experience the cross that is also part of that salvific d esign. For Joseph, the news that should cause the greatest joy in the heart of any Jew—the conception of the promised Messiah, the definitive salvation offered by God—has left him stunned, perplexed, desolate. His wife is leaving the village where they had both dreamed of a peaceful life, aware that what has just happened has not only turned their lives and their plans upside down—it has overturned the entire history of mankind.

In the last look she has of her husband as she is setting off, Mary sees reflected on his face worry and suffering, his concern for everything that has happened.

2. *The darkness of the Christian experience.* The account of these events should also help us to understand that the manifestation of God in our lives does not mean, as we tend to believe, that everything will suddenly be filled with light and happiness and that we will be able to move forward without darkness or difficulties. Here we have the ultimate revelation of God to mankind, and paradoxically, Joseph and

Mary have been left in the deepest darkness. The same will happen to Christ in the days of his Passion. It is beautiful to learn from these two spouses the lesson of seeking with peace, of advancing without distrust, of suffering without despairing. We can only admire the greatness of the souls of Joseph and Mary, who are united to each other in suffering and in love of God!

3. *Mary's recollection on the way to Ein-Karem.* Let's accompany Mary to this pleasant village near Jerusalem. In his meditation on the birth of the Lord in Bethlehem, St. Ignatius says that in imagining the journey of the Holy Family, the person making the Spiritual Exercises should accompany them to help them in whatever they might need: "making myself a poor little unworthy little slave, looking upon them, contemplating them, and serving them in their needs with all possible homage and reverence." (SE 114)This is an attitude that we can now apply to our contemplation of Mary on her journey to Elizabeth's house. Slowly, without haste, accompany Mary as she makes her way to the mountains. Become a "little slave" and with reverence serve this mother who carries in her womb the Son of God.

On my pilgrimage to the Holy Land, I had the immense grace to walk, albeit from the opposite direction, the same route. For two weeks, from the sixth to the twentieth of April of 2018, I went down from Ein-Karem to Nazareth along the Mediterranean coast.

I remember very well those quiet days. I can well imagine the landscape that Mary saw and passed through to reach her destination. These were the first days of her pregnancy, and we should try to fill in the silences of the Gospel and ask the Lord in prayer to help us to "walk with Mary" and to participate in her thoughts and feelings. Surely these were days of great intimacy for her, days of reflection and intense prayer. That young expectant mother who seemed to be just another Jewish woman on the roads of Palestine; who mixed with other travelers and merchants as they came and went, passing villages looking for water to drink and shade for shelter, crossing paths with troops of soldiers and caravans of strangers, was the Mother of the Savior. She carried in her womb the living Presence of the Creator of the Universe. We can contemplate her in an attitude of *great recollection*: she is oriented toward the Mystery within her, she is "hidden" in her own soul.

> *We must remember that the Word, the Son of God, together with the Father and the Holy Spirit, is hidden in essence and in presence, in the inmost being of the soul. That soul, therefore, that will find Him, must go out from all things in will and affection, and enter into the profoundest self-recollection, and all things must be to it as if they existed not. Hence, St. Augustine says: "I found You not without, O Lord; I sought You without in vain, for You are within." God is therefore hidden within the soul, and the true contemplative will seek Him there in love, saying, "Where have You hidden Yourself?"*[64]

These words of St. John of the Cross in his *Spiritual Canticle* take on an overwhelming meaning when we think of Mary on her way to Zacharias's house. Not only was God hidden in

Mary's soul, but in her own body. At this moment in her life, Mary represents all the persons who have passed through history bringing the hidden presence of God to the people of her time. At the same time, she invites us to think about the mystery of a God who wants to live within us: "Whoever loves me will keep my word, and my Father will love him, and we will come to him and make our dwelling with him." (Jn. 14:23)Mary is the best "guardian of the Word." She has taken it into her body and soul, and for this reason she is particularly loved by the Father and has become the physical dwelling place of the Son of God.

St. Ignatius of Antioch, in his Letter to the Ephesians, chapter XV, writes: "Let us therefore do all things as those who have Him dwelling in us." As you contemplate Mary in this scene, I invite you to meditate on the Church's teaching on the indwelling of the Holy Trinity in the souls of the just. We have alluded to this mystery in the meditation of Bethany, which we can now see fully realized in our Holy Mother: if you are in the grace of God, the Father, the Son, and the Holy Spirit dwell in you in the most intimate and personal way. God is no more present in Paradise than he is in your heart! Mary would live enveloped in that Presence, she would breathe it continuously, she would feel it move in her belly. In a different way, you also can carry it within you, since "he who abides in love abides in God and God abides in him." (1Jn. 4:16).If, moreover, you have been a mother, or if as you read or listen to these letters, you find yourself with child as Mary was, the profound and indescribable experience of motherhood can help you to live this reality in a qualitatively new way. God is more present in you than the child you carry in your womb! As St. Augustine wrote, "*Deus interior intimo meo* (More inward than my innermost self).[5]

You can imagine Mary on her swift journey to the mountains. The handmaid of the Lord comes quickly to serve her cousin. She also goes to discern and find light. She comes wrapped in the love of God, whose Son is present in her body and soul. Mary has only to be seen to be loved.

What were her feelings in these most intense moments of her life? Fortunately, we do not have to imagine them *because she herself wanted to share them with us.* I want to consider here the words of the *Magnificat* that Our Lady proclaims at the conclusion of this journey (Lk. 1:46-55). They reflect her heart, expressing what she is living in her soul as a woman, a mother, and a handmaid of the Lord. The *Magnificat* is not the product of a simple spontaneous inspiration at the moment she greets Elizabeth. This prayer crystallizes *all that Mary carries within, all that she has been pondering along the way, and all that she has been feeling since she received the gift of her son Jesus.* The *Magnificat* is a photograph of her interiority. It is burning lava spewing forth from an erupting volcano. If the Beatitudes are the self-portrait of the soul of Jesus Christ, the *Magnificat* is Mary's self-portrait.

From this prayer full of quotations from the Old Testament that reveal to us the prayerful attitude of one who is a servant of the Divine Word, I would like to highlight three aspects: praise, joy, and humility.

4. *Praise. The Magnificat* is an explosion of praise to God, to whom glory is given for his limitless power and for his plan of salvation. "My soul proclaims the greatness of the Lord!" Mary's canticle thus begins with this exuberant exaltation

to God. That is not all: the overflowing expressions of jubilation follow one after the other, uncontainable and irrepressible from her inebriated soul: "The Mighty One has done great things for me, and holy is his name. His mercy is from age to age. He has shown might with his arm, dispersed the arrogant of mind and heart. He has thrown down the rulers from their thrones but lifted up the lowly." Everything is a source of glory for God in this intermediation that has taken place in Mary's life. What has happened to her is a *great thing* for which the Most High deserves infinite adoration, recognition, and gratitude.

I believe that our degree of intimacy with the Lord is measured especially by the consideration with which we treat this element, which is present in the depths of our condition as creatures. As we have had the opportunity to reflect previously, St. Ignatius told us in the meditation on *Principle and Foundation* that "man was created to *praise, reverence, and serve*" God.

Mary understands her life within the divine plan of Redemption. She understands that she is an eminent part of that whole which we call Salvation History. Her last words in the *Magnificat*—"He has helped Israel his servant, remembering his mercy, according to his promise to our fathers, to Abraham and to his descendants forever"—place her in the course of the history of her people and of plans that are projected into eternity ("forever").She is aware that the Lord is carrying out his plan, that God has not abandoned this world that he loves so much, and that he wants to save it through his Son, Jesus, with the collaboration of people like her. Mary's praise has as its foundation, in its origin, this joyful recognition that the Lord is coming; indeed, he has already come and will fulfill his mission to establish everything in him (Eph 1:10).

Praising God is not only and above all a prayer, but a *life*. It is also to enter into the Lord's salvific plan as Mary did, consciously and willingly. It is to reflect the light of God, which comes to dispel our darkness in this ruined and crumbling world.

In these Exercises, we seek God's grace to highlight the areas of our lives where His light does not rule and to illuminate that darkness so that whatever we do, "whether you eat or drink, or whatever you do, do everything for the glory of God" (1 Cor. 10:31).Is your whole life praise to God?

In order to imitate Mary's spirit of praise, it is imperative that we consider the importance of our little lives in God's great plan. At this moment in Mary's heart, there are two attitudes that seem opposed to each other: a feeling of greatness, and at the same time, a great awareness of her littleness. We will speak later of her humility, but here I would like to dwell on this awareness of being immersed in God's plan. Mary knows that, in this "plot" of which God is both the author and the main protagonist, she has just been given the second most important role.

The Redemption is truly "the most extraordinary story ever told" and I think it is important to feel a part, like Mary did, of something great. In this drama we can all be protagonists because we are all called to redeem the world with Christ. That life of yours that seems insignificant in the eyes of the world, those struggles you face daily that perhaps no one but you will see, and those ordinary acts that will never be written about or recognized are all something *very big in the eyes of God.* The greatest thing because that life,

175

those struggles, those acts complete what is "lacking in the afflictions of Christ" (Col. 1:24).In the Exercises, I invite you to see your existence in the light that faith gives us. I invite you to feel that you are part of the greatest enterprise—the salvation of the world! In that enterprise, just like Mary, God asks you to collaborate with a role of extraordinary importance. It is so important that what you do not do will remain undone. In other words, there will be souls that will be lost, that will be condemned, if you do not "praise" the Lord with a holy life.

In his Encyclical Letter *Mystici Corporis Christi*, Pius XII wrote these impressive words: "This is a deep mystery, and an inexhaustible subject of meditation, that the salvation of many depends on the prayers and voluntary penances which the members of the Mystical Body of Jesus Christ offer for this intention."[66] Yes, the salvation of many depends on your prayers and sacrifices, on the simple works of your daily life carried out with love and the desire to redeem the world with Christ. As the Holy Father writes, we cannot meditate enough on this particular point.

5. *Joy.* We have been talking about the trial to which Joseph and Mary are subjected with the virginal conception of Jesus Christ. We have said that there is an inner darkness that plunges them into uncertainty. However, Mary's Heart is at the same time overflowing with joy! "My spirit rejoices in God my Savior (...)behold, from now on will all ages call me blessed." This points us toward a trait that is very important in the Christian life. I anticipate that it will not be easy to express it in words, but I think that most of us have had experiences that bring us a little closer to what I intend to

say.

Christian joy coexists with pain, the cross, pressure, and suffering of any kind. It does so because it is on *another level*, and is experienced in the depths of the soul as a gift from God that is directly poured out upon us. It is what St. Ignatius describes in his *Rules of Discernment of Spirits* for the second week as "*consolation without precedent cause.*" I do not want to enter now into a lengthy explanation of this beautiful reality, but the important thing here is to see how these two extremes, which at first sight may seem opposed and even irreconcilable, coexist. Mary has suffered much, and at the same time, she has been the most blessed of women. This cross has allowed her to participate more intimately in the joy of God, and at the same time, this joy has prepared her for the great crosses of her life.

In one of his sermons, St. Augustine offers a passage that may help us better understand this paradox in our Blessed Mother. Speaking of the difference between the happiness of paradise and that which we can live in this world, the Bishop of Hippo says with great insight:

> God's praises sung there, sung here – here, by the anxious; there, by the carefree – here, by those who will die; there, by those who will live forever – here, in hope; there, in reality – here, on our journey; there, in our homeland. So now, my brethren, let us sing, not to delight our leisure, but to ease our toil. In the way that travelers are in the habit of singing, sing, but keep on walking. What does it mean, "keep on walking"? Go onward always – but go onward in goodness, for there are, according to the Apostle, some people who

*go ever onward from bad to worse. If you are going
onward, you are walking; but always go onward in
goodness, onward in the right faith, onward in good
habits and behavior. Sing, and walk onwards.*[67]

Mary "sings and walks." She sings in her heart and walks
toward the meeting with Elizabeth.

It is a great lesson, perhaps one of the most important, that
we must learn from our Mother, from Jesus, and from the
saints. Many times we meet people who, when faced with
a major setback or a difficult situation, let circumstances
disturb their inner world. They lose their joy—worry takes
over their soul and smiles are almost permanently erased
from their faces. It is as if they live under a gray cloud that has
darkened and chilled their hearts and pursues them wherever
they go. Mary in this scene lives immersed in the joy of her
divine maternity and at the same time in pain because of
the adverse circumstances and the suffering she is causing
her husband. She lives between the unknown and a great
certainty. She sings and cries.

I have always regarded this as a sign of great holiness.
When a person approaches God and unites himself to him
through love, he makes the divine properties his own. St.
John of the Cross affirms that the soul transformed by love
"seems more like God than like a soul."[68] St. Thomas
Aquinas expresses the same teaching in his commentary
on the verse of John 3:8: "The wind blows where it wills, and
you can hear the sound it makes, but you do not know where
it comes from or where it goes; so it is with everyone who
is born of the Spirit." The Angelic Doctor affirms that the
spiritual man acquires the very features of the Holy Spirit

by transformation in Him: "So it is with everyone who is born of the Spirit; i.e., they are like the Holy Spirit. And no wonder: for as he had said before, 'What is born of Spirit is itself spirit,' because the qualities of the Holy Spirit are present in the spiritual man, just as the qualities of fire are present in burning coal."[69]

Well, one of the qualities of God is what the medieval theologian Nicholas of Cusa called "*coincidentia oppositorum* (coincidence of opposites)":qualities that seem contrary are united in God.

For the subject of holiness, let us take the example of someone who is introverted in character. This type of temperament orients the person to certain qualities for which he or she is naturally inclined. A shy person is normally good at listening, at transmitting serenity, at being a refuge and a shoulder to cry on when we are looking for someone to understand us, at keeping and living in silence, at developing inner worlds, and so on. If an introverted person is kind, it does not usually attract our attention because we consider this a kind of "extension" of their usual way of being. Someone who is shy does not usually contradict people and prefers to keep quiet rather than displease the person in front of them. This quietness may be a virtue or it might be actually a sign of weakness if, out of fear, one does not dare to contradict others even when he must do so.

Well, I said before that I have always thought that it is a sign of sanctity when someone presents in himself this "co-incidence of opposites." When an introverted and shy person is at the same time courageous, capable of going against the mainstream, strong in adverse circumstances, etc., then one has to think of God's action because *his nature does not incline him to that,* and so there is "something else" there, which is probably divine grace. Being timid and determined is a coincidence of opposites that usually indicates progress in the spiritual life—an ever greater union with that God in whom this "*coincidentia oppositorum*" occurs, a God who is eternal and temporal, great and humble, one and triune, powerful and defenseless, Creator and creature.

What has been said can be applied to the question of joy and sorrow experienced simultaneously: it is usually a sign of holiness, of union with God. I would like to bring the words of St. John Paul II in his Apostolic Letter *Novo Millennio Ineunte*, which made a great impression on me when I read them in 2001. The older generation will remember that it was the "programmatic" document with which the Pope wanted to face, as the title of the letter indicates, the new millennium that was beginning to dawn. The Holy Father offered a kind of path on which he invited the Church to walk in this new epoch that was opening up for her and for the world. An important part of the text is dedicated to the contemplation of the face of Christ, and in one section he dwells on the suffering face of Jesus in his Passion. These words are always timely, profound, and fruitful.

I was most powerfully struck by the fact that, speaking of Christ in his agony, John Paul II stopped to speak of the *joy of Jesus even in his torments.* Perhaps this statement is striking or even scandalous to some, but it is a truth that Catholic theology has peacefully possessed for centuries and that is a natural consequence of the hypostatic union in the Person of Christ. Allow me to quote at length, so we might carefully recall here the Pope's considerations:

Jesus' cry on the Cross, dear Brothers and Sisters, is not the cry of anguish of a man without hope, but the prayer of the Son who offers his life to the Father in love, for the salvation of all. At the very moment when he identifies with our sin, "abandoned" by the Father, he "abandons" himself into the hands of the Father. His eyes remain fixed on the Father. Precisely because of the knowledge and experience of the Father which he alone has, even at this moment of darkness he sees clearly the gravity of sin and suffers because of it. He alone, who sees the Father and rejoices fully in him, can understand completely what it means to resist the Father's love by sin. More than an experience of physical pain, his Passion is an agonizing suffering of the soul. Theological tradition has not failed to ask how Jesus could possibly experience at one and the same time his profound unity with the Father, by its very nature a source of joy and happiness, and an agony that goes all the way to his final cry of abandonment. The simultaneous presence of these two seemingly irreconcilable aspects is rooted in the fathomless depths of the hypostatic union.

Faced with this mystery, we are greatly helped not only by theological investigation but also by that great heritage which is the "lived theology" of the saints. The saints offer us precious insights which enable us to understand more easily the intuition of faith, thanks to the special enlightenment which some of them have received from the Holy Spirit, or even through their personal experience of those terrible states of trial which the mystical tradition describes *as the "dark night". Not infrequently the saints have undergone something akin to Jesus' experience on the Cross in the paradoxical blending of bliss and pain. In the Dialogue of Divine Providence, God the Father shows Catherine of Siena how joy and suffering can be present together in holy souls: "Thus the soul is blissful and afflicted: afflicted on account of the sins of its neighbor, blissful on account of the union and the affection of charity which it has inwardly received. These souls imitate the spotless Lamb, my Only-begotten Son, who on the Cross was both blissful and afflicted". In the same way, Thérèse of Lisieux lived her agony in communion with the agony of Jesus, "experiencing" in herself the very paradox of Jesus's own bliss and anguish: "In the Garden of Olives our Lord was blessed with all the joys of the Trinity, yet his dying was no less harsh. It is a mystery, but I assure you that, on the basis of what I myself am feeling, I can understand something of it". What an illuminating testimony! Moreover, the accounts given by the Evangelists themselves provide a basis for this intuition on the part of the Church of Christ's consciousness when they record that, even in the depths of his pain, he died imploring forgiveness for his executioners (cf. Lk 23:34) and expressing to the Father his ultimate filial abandonment: "Father, into your hands I commend my spirit." (Lk 23:46)*[70]

What the Polish Pope said describes Mary's soul at this moment of her life. She rejoices unspeakably and suffers much. And so she goes forward, she walks along the path of life to Ein-Karem. I hope that the contemplation of this scene will also help you to be women like Mary: not to lose your joy in suffering precisely because of your union with God, because of the strength of your hope. In standing here with Mary, we claim a great part of our spiritual life.

6. *Humility.* St. John of the Cross writes that "To be taken with love for a soul, God does not look on its greatness, but the greatness of its humility." What a bold and daring statement! God falls in love! God, who is love (1Jn. 4:8), is capable of "falling in love." Truly, one could spend a lifetime pondering this unfathomable mystery. Now, with whom can God fall in love? Is he not the most perfect Being who contains by essence all perfections? How can he who is fullness and happiness itself fall in love with one of his creatures? St. Augustine himself writes that God is "*superior summo meo* (superior to the highest part of me).["]71

The words of St. John of the Cross above contain two aspects that are surprising at first s ight: the first is that God falls in love; the second is that he can only fall in love with one who is humble enough to receive his love.

In the *Magnificat,* Mary not only rejoices, but rejoices in the fact *that she is little.* She knows that she has not been chosen because she is extraordinary. It is precisely the other way around: she is extraordinary because she has been chosen. It is God's choice that preceded all the graces that Mary received throughout her life. God has set his eyes on her, as St. John of the Cross boldly points out, because she is small: Yahweh "has looked upon the humility of his handmaid." This is also expressed by St. Paul: "God chose the foolish of the world to shame the wise, and God chose the weak of the world to shame the strong, and God chose the lowly and despised of the world, those who count for nothing, to reduce to nothing those who are something." (1 Cor. 1:27-28).

This joy in being little is at the heart of the spiritual childhood of which St. Therese of the Child Jesus is (after Mary)undoubtedly the best exponent. The words that the Little Flower wrote to her sister, Soeur Marie du Sacre Coeur, on September 17, 1896 are well known:

> *Dear Sister, how can you say after this that my desires are the sign of my love? Ah! I really feel that it is not this at all that pleases God in my little soul; what pleases Him is that He sees me loving my littleness and my poverty, the blind hope that I have in His mercy. That is my only treasure, dear Godmother, why would this treasure not be yours? (...) Ah! let us remain then very far from all that sparkles, let us love our littleness, let us love to feel nothing, then we shall be poor in spirit, and Jesus will come to look for us, and however far we may be, He will transform us in flames of love (...) Oh! how I would like to be able to make you understand what I feel! (...) It is confidence and nothing but confidence that must lead us to Love.*[72]

In the Spiritual Exercises, we are all invited to make choices regarding this beautiful virtue. in one of the most transcendental moments of the whole experience of the Exercises, St. Ignatius discusses the three kinds of humility at the end of the meditations of the second week, when the retreatant must proceed to the "choices" of state of life. I want to pick up here the third type of humility that describes the most perfect souls, souls like Mary:

> *The most perfect kind of humility consists in this. If we suppose the first and second kind attained, then whenever the praise and glory of the Divine Majesty would be equally served, in order to imitate and be in reality more like Christ our Lord, I desire and choose poverty with Christ poor, rather than riches; insults with Christ loaded with them, rather than honors; I desire to be accounted as worthless and a fool for Christ, rather than to be esteemed as wise and prudent in this world. So Christ was treated before me.* (SE 167)

"*I desire and choose…*" I have always been impressed by these words, especially because they express a love for Christ that reaches the point of madness. In the second kind of humility there is a kind of resignation, as St. Ignatius describes it: "I *neither desire nor am I inclined* to have riches rather than poverty, to seek honor rather than dishonor, to desire a long life rather than a short life." However, the soul that has reached the third and last degree of humility, a "most perfect" humility, *wants and chooses* the way of Christ, which was a way of reproach, poverty, and the desire to be humiliated. Not only does he accept this, but he asks for it and desires it. He wants it actively and seeks it to the extent that it is the Will of God.

In Mary's words, such humility is translated insofar as she has not, so to speak, stumbled into a humble life, but in becoming "the handmaid of the Lord" *she has consciously chosen it.* She chose to be small and to occupy the place of the least. Mary desired and sought to be poor because she knew that "God fills the hungry with good things."

Humility is, therefore, the result of an active attitude and not simply the fruit of resignation or passive submission. We must choose it! We must seek it! And in the Exercises, we must ask God for the grace, if he wills it, of humiliation, of opprobrium, of poverty, of sickness, of limitation.

How much this costs us! It is terrifying for us to ask for this, isn't it? What if God heeds us? What if we ask for humiliations and the Lord sends them to us? Let me ask you point blank: are you willing to lose the recognition of men and follow Christ, from now on, along the path of self-abasement? It is not just a matter of being small but of *choosing* to be small. It is not a matter of stoically accepting the crosses of life but of rejoicing in them because Christ passed through them. At the very least, you can ask for the grace to be granted to come to desire it as the goal of your walk with the Lord. You know its reward: God will set his eyes on you and fall in love with your tiny soul.

Mary is aware that "the Mighty One has done great works" for her. She is not blind to God's action in her life, and she confesses and proclaims it with a heart filled with praise, as we have said. Her humility is not a pretense—it is neither artificial nor c osmetic. It is not a virtue that leads her to close her eyes when the Lord wants to carry out his plan of love through her. She knows that "God has looked upon the lowliness of his handmaid" and that it was this condition of "humble handmaid" that made possible the greatest work of Redemption: the Incarnation of the Word.

To conclude this section on humility, I would like to share

an anecdote I read about St. Teresa of Jesus—after Mary, my favorite saintly woman. St. Teresa was reputed to be very beautiful. They say that on one occasion someone dared to make that remark in front of her. They pointed out to the Carmelite nun that people went around saying that she was beautiful, intelligent, and holy. To these comments, St. Teresa replied something like this: "God alone knows about being holy; about being intelligent, I have never considered myself a fool; and about being beautiful... it is obvious." *This is humility*: simplicity does not consist in hiding one's qualities, nor in falling into the opposite extreme of proudly attributing them to oneself. Humility is giving God all the credit he deserves for the good things he has done in us. This is what Mary does in the *Magnificat*: her humility consists in recognizing the admirable works of God and attributing to the Lord all the glory, without appropriating anything to herself.

I invite you to walk with Mary in the silence of your reflection. As I mentioned at the beginning of this retreat, all of the above must come from contemplation of Mary, from accompanying her on her pilgrim journey to Ein-Karem, from listening to her, looking at her and living with her. I learned the joy of my parents not as the fruit of a reflection on their way of being, but as the result of living with them, of absorbing their traits and characteristics almost by osmosis, by the community of life, by assimilating, assiduously and joyfully, their way of being and reacting. The same happens in the Exercises. We learn by contact, by vision, by absorption, and for that it is necessary to look, to be silent and to love. I trust that you will discover the essence of the feminine soul in Mary and that, beginning with her and together with her, you will be able to live humbly and joyfully for the glory and praise of God alone.

12

MARY AT THE VISITATION III

"Unworthy servants that we are, O Lord, grieved by the guilt of our deeds, we pray that you may gladden us by the saving advent of your Only Begotten Son." (Collect prayer for Thursday of the Third Week of Advent).

Here we conclude this triptych of meditations on the Visitation with Mary's arrival at Elizabeth's house. We have dwelt so much on this biblical scene because it usually remains in the background. When we have just a few days of retreat, this encounter which is so deep and rich, is usually overlooked in favor of the stories of the Annunciation and the Nativity. It seems to me that this is an example of how the prayerful soul must "coexist" with the scenes we find in Sacred Scripture: the Holy Spirit invites us to stop the rhythm of our reading, which is often so hurried. He illuminates for us the more obscure areas of the biblical text and allows us to contemplate peacefully what the Word of God is telling us. Obviously, in Spiritual Exercises for women, Mary should take precedence because she is not "just one of many" among the myriad of feminine figures that come to our attention in Sacred Scripture. The Mother of Jesus is, in fact, the archetype of the Christian woman and your continuous effort must consist in walking the path that goes from Eve to Mary, as Edith Stein pointed out with great insight.

1. *Composition of place.* Finally, after days of sun and dust, Mary arrives at the threshold of Zechariah's house. She is returning to a region she knows well. Indeed, the memory of the Christian people of the Holy Land has always linked the Mother of God with Jerusalem and the priestly environs of this city.

During my pilgrimage to the Holy Land, I was powerfully struck by the profusion of memories related to the Blessed Virgin in the Holy City and its environs, both in the Catholic tradition and in the Orthodox and Muslim traditions. Many memories of Mary are preserved there, or stories are told about where she was born, who her parents were and where they lived; of her childhood and her relationship with the Temple in which she was educated. If Jerusalem is rightly called the City of David, Mary—who from time immemorial has been venerated as the "Daughter of Zion"—is also one of those figures whose presence can almost be breathed and felt, walking the labyrinthine and ancient streets of the capital of the Kingdom of Israel. The Liturgy of the Church dares to take an even bolder step: on many Marian feasts—especially on the feast of her nativity, September 8—those passages of Scripture that speak of Jerusalem as the depository of the promises of Yahweh are applied to the Mother of Christ, thus identifying Mary with the Holy City.

I am thinking especially of Psalm 87:1-2: "His foundation is on holy mountains, the LORD loves the gates of Zion more than any dwelling in Jacob." and Psalm 121:1-2: "I rejoiced when they said to me, 'Let us go to the house of the LORD.' And now our feet are standing within your gates, Jerusalem." What is affirmed of the latter, indeed, is also said of the former. Can there be any greater connection between the two?

All these testimonies and sources converge in one important point already mentioned: Mary is linked to the priestly environment and to the city of Jerusalem. The episode of the adolescent Jesus lost in the Temple, which St. Luke recounts in his Gospel (2:41-49),also reveals features of Mary's own biography. The Holy Family went on pilgrimage "every year" to Jerusalem from Nazareth. In this biblical scene, Mary finds her Son precisely in the Temple. That is to say, Mary *looked for* Jesus there, a place that was familiar to her as well. This is affirmed by another implication in the episode of the Presentation of Jesus, in the same Gospel (Lk. 2:25-38):*Simeon seems to know Mary.* It is true that this is not explicitly said, but this elderly man, who had always lived in and around the House of God, addresses Mary with great familiarity and closeness using words and expressions more typical of people who have met before than of strangers meeting for the first t ime. S he even hands the Child to Simeon with great naturalness, as one who trusts this grandfatherly figure because she already has a relationship with him prior to this encounter. Who would place their newborn child in the hands of a complete stranger?

The scene of the Visitation that concerns us now also connects Mary with the Jewish priesthood in the very persons of Zechariah and Elizabeth. Of Zechariah we are told that he was a priest of the priestly class of Abijah and that the Angel Gabriel's announcement to him of the birth of John the Baptist took place when he was making the temple offering during his ritual service in the sanctuary of the Lord. Of Elizabeth, St. Luke specifically states that she was "a descendant of Aaron" (1:5)brother of Moses and the first in the line of the Old Testament priesthood. As we find these details by reading between the lines, in harmony with the whole of the oral and liturgical traditions that refer to our Mother and allow us to glimpse her relationship with that priestly world.

However, the truth is that to find Mary, the angel had to go to Nazareth, a remote forgotten village in Galilee (Lk. 1:26). Mary's earliest years revolved around Jerusalem. Joseph and Mary had most likely met in or near there—let us remember that Joseph was a native of Bethlehem, barely 5 kilometers from the Holy City—and yet both decided to "move away from the spotlight" and retire far from the capital. In this move we can discern a real-life plan to which Joseph and Mary feel called and which asks them to withdraw from the religious center of Israel.

Judea and Galilee, Jerusalem and Nazareth, the hustle and bustle of the city and the peace and calm of the village, the ritualism of the Jewish priesthood in the Temple and the religious simplicity of the synagogue, walls built with heavy stones and views of open fields: the contrasts are not random but *intentional*. Joseph and Mary sought a different life—humble, hidden, solitary, silent. Most likely this exodus has to do with the project of a virginal and secluded life. In some way these two geographical points already represent the transition between the old way of living the faith and the newness that Christ will bring, anticipated in the lifestyle of Joseph and Mary, which will make possible the coming in the flesh of the Son of God.

Personally, I find it very fruitful to meditate on these evangelical "silences" because they help me to understand that these people, like us, also had their lives and their troubles. They had to make decisions that were sometimes misunderstood by family and friends. The thought of what they suffered, what they endured, what they felt, brings me closer to them. I see them close to me, full of humanity, close to my own daily struggles. And now, having been able to walk the road that Mary walked, I can now slowly savor the experience of the Virgin Mary, and through the action of the Holy Spirit in my soul, participate in what she experienced during those days.

2. *Mary's love.* Joseph and Mary had withdrawn to Galilee, and now Mary must return, urged by love, to the region of Judah. She sees again the landscapes of her childhood: the blue of the sea gives way to the green of the pine trees on the mountains and her path is an ascent through places she knows well. She walks through her memories crossing places that were part of her own story and that become more

and more familiar to her as she approaches her destination. The tranquility of her beloved Nazareth—"*How is my dear Joseph?*—is left behind as she approaches the geographical heart of Israel, the place that God himself has chosen as the dwelling place of his people (2 Chr. 6:6; Ps. 132:13-14).

Ein-Karem is today just another neighborhood in a Jerusalem that has engulfed this charming area. In Gospel times, however, it was one of the villages near the city where the priests and Levites who performed their ritual service in the Temple resided. I was there for two days and remember those days as a time of grace and quiet joy. Without a doubt, there is something special about Ein-Karem. A place with charm and with a *something* that immediately captures the visitor who goes there with faith: Jesus, Mary, John the Baptist, Elizabeth, Zechariah... something of them still remains in those places.

Mary traveled in haste (Lk. 1:39).Here, as at Cana, we see her attentive to the needs of others. It is an exceptionally feminine trait, about which Edith Stein makes marvelous observations:

> *A glance toward the Mother of God becomes indicative for us again. For example, Mary at the wedding of Cana in her quiet observing look surveys everything and discovers what is lacking. Before anything is noticed, even before embarrassment sets in, she has procured already the remedy. She finds ways and means, she gives necessary directives, doing all quietly. She draws no attention to herself. Let her be the prototype of woman in professional life. Wherever situated, let her always perform her work*

quietly and dutifully, without claiming attention and appreciation. And at the same time, she should survey the conditions with a vigilant eye. Let her be conscious of where there is a want and where help is needed, intervening and regulating as far as it is possible in her power in a discreet way. Then will she, like a good spirit, spread blessing everywhere.[73]

In the angel's message and in the conversation with her husband, Mary has recognized a concrete need and understands that her help is needed here. She is going to intervene "inadvertently," spreading "her blessings everywhere, like a good spirit." What an admirable model for the woman who wishes to respond to God's plan in her daily life!

Mary of the Visitation. Mary of the Way. Mary, who carries Jesus within her. Mary, who lives united in trial with her spouse. Mary, who runs to the aid of Elizabeth. Mary, who finally arrives at her destination, carrying with her the blessings of the Lord and the presence of God in her Heart and in her womb. How beautiful is Mary!

3. *Faith of Mary.* In your personal prayer, you can see the arrival of the Virgin Mother at Ein-Karem. Her soul is filled with emotion, as one who senses that something important is about to happen. "*Behold your kinswoman, Elizabeth,*" St. Gabriel had said to her. Mary believed the angel's word, but her pregnancy is still in the first days of gestation and, so we can presume that there have not yet been physical signs of the presence of the Word in her womb. She does not doubt that what was announced to her has happened, and it is Mary's faith that gives warmth to Jesus from the very

moment of his conception. She will gradually experience the progress of her maternity and her virginal body will adapt itself to the Mystery of her Son, conceived by the Holy Spirit. Her hips will widen, her breasts will enlarge, the form of her womanly body will progressively change, like that of any mother, according to the rhythms that the gestation of her Son will impose on her. All this will happen, but when Mary arrives in that "*mountain town of Judah*" (Lk 1:39) just a few days after her encounter with the angel, this chain of events and physical transformations have not yet taken place—at least not in such a way or with such intensity that they are perceptible to her. Elizabeth's words, "Blessed are you who believed that what was spoken to you by the Lord would be fulfilled." (v. 45) can be understood on the first level as words of assurance in the light of this more immediate perspective: *Mary, you do not now physically feel any sign of your motherhood, but thanks to your faith, you will be happy because you are already a mother. You will see what the Lord has said to you will begin to be "fulfilled" when the changes in your body and in your heart begin.* All that Mary has had so far is faith ... only faith ... nothing but faith. Here, in Ein-Karem, she will receive an inner confirmation that will add firmness to the trust that she has placed totally in the Lord.

In *Lumen Gentium* 58, the Second Vatican Council referred to Mary as a "pilgrim of faith." St. John Paul II developed this thread superbly in his Encyclical Letter *Redemptoris Mater.* I personally find the image of Mary as a "pilgrim of faith" very helpful and rich in teachings for us. Let us say something about it in this prayerful attitude in which we now find ourselves.

The Pope writes that Mary "advanced in the pilgrimage

of faith."[74] This progression should be understood not in the sense of someone who passes from unbelief to faith. But as someone who has had to *progressively assimilate the Mystery of Christ,* a Mystery in which she believed from the beginning. How beautiful it is to think that Mary was the first to believe in Jesus,[75] and how beautiful it is to consider that as it happens with us, the path of faith was also arduous for Mary. She had to progress by taking crucial steps, just as we also must do!

This path is full of days of light and days of darkness, and for Mary, Ein-Karem represents a moment of consolation. According to the teaching of the great masters of the spiritual life, particularly St. Ignatius of Loyola, consolations prepare us for desolations, and these in turn prepare us to receive even greater graces. "May the joy of God be your strength" (Neh. 8:10).It is beautiful to see how Mary exemplifies in this scene of the Visitation what St. Ignatius affirms of souls in the state of consolation:

> *X. When one enjoys consolation, let him consider how he will conduct himself during the time of ensuing desolation, and store up a supply of strength as defense against that day. (SE 323)*
>
> *XI. He who enjoys consolation should take care to humble himself and lower himself as much as possible. Let him recall how little he is able to do in time of desolation, when he is left without such grace or consolation. (SE 324)*

As we saw in the previous meditation on the Magnificat, Mary lowers herself ("For he has looked upon his handmaid's lowliness" [v. 48]),giving God all the glory and placing herself in the shadows. She now allows herself to be filled with the joy that this scene brings her, aware that it is another way station on a continuing journey at which she pauses to provide herself with what she will need later when the days of struggle come.

Until now, all Mary has had is faith, without any sign after Gabriel on which to rely. In the house of Zechariah she will find a great confirmation that will fill her soul with light, joy, and grace. *"Blessed are you who have believed"*: in these words, Elizabeth recognizes that the root of Mary's joy is her faith. Faith is the cause of joy! The world often sees faith as something burdensome, tedious, heavy, dark, boring... but we know that when experienced as an encounter, as a friendship, as a life that grows, faith is the source of the most extraordinary joy. It is "a spring of water welling up to eternal life" (Jn. 4:14)in the words of the Lord himself. It is the cause of complete joy (Jn. 15:11),which neither the world nor death can take from us. Mary's joy, rooted in an immeasurable faith, is entirely supernatural. Her joy consists in the recognition that God's plan is being carried out; the realization that the words of the divine emissary were not a daydream, as her cousin's swollen belly that six-month pregnancy clearly reveals; the surprise of witnessing how her son Jesus—whom she does not yet feel physically—makes John the Baptist leap with joy and lift the belly and soul of his mother Elizabeth in exhilaration. Mary rejoices to see that her hope has not been disappointed and that the Lord *is fulfilling* what He had told her.

How can we not feel close to Mary's experience? Probably, many times we have placed our trust in God without any kind of hand to hold onto. The Lord has invited us to faith, and we have taken that leap into the void with confidence, without receiving an immediate confirming sign from God. Later, when we have needed it and the Lord in his Providence has considered it opportune, He has shown us a ray of light, a sign of his presence, an affirmation that it is the right path. How difficult at the beginning and how joyful to receive the consolation of the Lord afterwards! In the scene of the Visitation, Mary teaches us to persevere, to receive the caresses of God with gratitude and an open heart and to seek the joy of our life in the plan of the Lord that is realized with, in, and through us.

4. *Mary and Zechariah.* Most likely a servant opened the door at Mary's arrival, and possibly also—let us imagine it this way—Zechariah was the first of the spouses to see Mary.[76] Luke's verse seems to allude to this interpretation—"...she entered the house of Zechariah and greeted Elizabeth" (Lk 1:40)—givingthe impression that she *had to enter* the house to see her cousin rather than greeting her at the door.

We fix our eyes on the encounter that the Gospel text places before our eyes - that of Mary and Elizabeth. However, in light of the preceding consideration of the Virgin's faith, I would like to invite you to first contemplate in your personal prayer the moment when the young Mary meets Zechariah, her cousin's husband.

The image is very powerful in its contrasts! Youth and old age. The majesty of the venerable priest and the simplicity of the little village girl from Nazareth. The silence of the mute man and the joyful greeting that pours forth from this blessed girl. The unbelief of the one who has doubted and the faith of the one who is blessed because she has believed.

Try in your composition of place to contemplate this encounter. Zechariah is a good man—a very good man. This is how St. Luke presents the father of the Forerunner and his wife: "Both were righteous in the eyes of God, observing all the commandments and ordinances of the Lord blamelessly." (1:6) We can see in the wrinkled face of this old priest the wisdom of the years and of the Jewish tradition that he treasures, the goodness of a man obedient to God, the faith—in spite of his hesitation with the angel—of a Jew who lives by and for God. These people who in their later years emit holiness from all sides have always impressed me deeply. They are people who are existentially in a different place, outside of this rushed world with its frenetic pace and its inevitable laws. They reflect eternity on this side of existence. Zechariah must have been compelling in his patriarchal, virtuous, honorable, and holy presence.

As Mary stands before him, on the threshold of his house, his gaze rests on her. A simple, beautiful, joyful woman in the youthfulness of her days, almost childlike, but at the same time, mature and sensible. A special light emanates from Mary's body: a virginal countenance that neither Jesus nor Joseph ever tired of looking at and admiring.

"What a beautiful child!" the elderly Zechariah might have thought with purity of heart. Yes, Mary was so beautiful that the Lord, looking at his Mother, never felt banished from Paradise. The Mother of God... a kind of heavenly vision that Zechariah contemplates framed in the doorway of his home. Beautiful, indeed, this child who uplifts and sanctifies just by looking at her.

In the *Spiritual Canticle*, commenting on the verses of the thirtieth stanza,[77] St. John of the Cross writes that *"the flowers are the virtues of the soul; the emeralds are the gifts it has received from God."* As "fresh mornings" the saint understands the days of youth, and says that the virtues that are acquired at the beginning of life are especially beautiful before God: "This time of our life is the early morning; for as the freshness of the spring morning is more agreeable than any other part of the day, so also are the virtues acquired in our youth more pleasing in the sight of God."

Mary is in those "fresh mornings" of youth, and her soul is full of "flowers and emeralds." Her Immaculate Heart is a garden full of grace and life, of purity and light, beside which Eden itself would seem an arid and barren land. God says of her: "All my springs are in you" (Ps. 87:7).Zechariah, on the other hand, is someone in the twilight of his life, perhaps already weary and tired, "undone from hard work."

When he recovers the ability to speak, after the birth of his son, he will call Christ *"the daybreak from on high"* (Lk. 1:78).Here we have the third element that completes this analogy: Mary is the morning that brings the first rays of a star that is about to dawn—her son, Jesus. The radiance emanating from the Virgin is that of the sun which, in her, is already beginning to be seen. Zechariah, however, will not see this new day because his life is inexorably fading away. His time was yesterday: he will not see the light of this star rise, but when Mary arrives at his door, he sees in the face of this young girl the first rays of dawn.

There is no exchange of greetings because the silent and venerable priest chokes on the words as they form in his mouth. It is a meeting between the woman who believed and the man who doubted, between the girl who said yes to the word of the angel and the old man who lost his voice because he did not dare to accept it. Mary's faith and Zechariah's unbelief: two attitudes by which we must measure ourselves and which we must choose in our lives and in this retreat.

The difference in age probably explains, at least in part, the opposite responses of these two individuals before the Mystery of God. Let's face it, as time goes by and we grow older, we lose the candor of childhood and the belief that anything can happen.

An old man carries too much experience in his saddlebags. He knows well the codes that govern the course of things and those experiences strangle his distant childhood naiveté. As the years go by, the same happens with us: the innocence and openness of the child who dared to believe in the impossible get lost in some corner of our story and are never again found. Only the grace of God can make us be born again (Jn. 3:3-7).

To Zechariah, the news that the dry womb of his old wife could give him a child presents as an absolute impasse, even though "nothing is impossible for God" (Lk. 1:37).Reality imposes itself: two elderly people can no longer be parents. Mary, on the other hand, is asked to accept something even more incomprehensible: that God would become man and be born of her without the help of a man. This too is "impossible" and yet the *child believes*. Only the heart of a child could have responded to such an announcement with the intensity of faith as Mary did.

Mary and Zechariah, on the threshold of the house of Ein-Karem, represent two eras in God's salvific plan. They also represent two attitudes. Contemplation of the Mother of God in the quiet of this retreat should lead us to bold trust, to courageous faith, to the certainty that "everything is possible to one who has faith" (Mk. 9:23). Holiness can only arise in the waiting for a great miracle to take place in our souls. In these spiritual exercises the Lord asks you as he asked Martha, "*Do you believe this?*" (Jn. 11:26)

I do not want to conclude this section without mentioning a very tender fact about Zechariah. Various ancient sources agree that this man gave his life in resisting Herod's slaughter of the innocent children by refusing to reveal the whereabouts of his own son, St. John the Baptist. If it happened in this way, somehow his death is connected with the Mystery of Christ and with the fate of those children killed by the delusions of Herod the Great. The words of his son, John, "He must increase; I must decrease" (Jn. 3:30) were first practiced by his father in his last and most eminent testimony of fidelity. The man who doubted before the angel was also the one who sealed his faith in the promises of God with martyrdom.

5. *Encounter between Mary and Elizabeth.* Elizabeth is usually called Mary's "cousin." This word has the transferred biblical meaning of "relative." In this sense, we can take for certain the information gathered by the Byzantine chronicles when they affirm that Sobe, Elizabeth's mother, would be the half-sister of Anne, whose daughter would be Mary.

Allow me here a short digression. The day I left Ein-Karem, April 6, 2018, I chose to visit a Franciscan friary that was to some extent unknown and inaccessible and not too far from the house of St. John the Baptist. I can still bring to mind much of the route in my memory: partially paved roads, few and poor directions to get there, and the feeling that I was heading to an abandoned and uninteresting place. Even I, who had spent almost two years in the preparation for that trip, did not know of the existence of that place until, once there, I realized it. I don't even remember how.

It was about twenty past six in the morning when I said a grateful goodbye to Father Severyn, a Polish Franciscan of extraordinary cordiality who has been running the pilgrim reception in Ein-Karem for years. The friar's dog, always friendly and playful with visitors to the house, delayed my departure. It was a clear day that I expected to be long and demanding. My first stop that day was the Monastery of St. John in the Desert. It took me an hour and a half to cross the small moshav of Even Sapir and reach that little village where, according to tradition, Elizabeth hid her son during the slaughter of the Holy Innocents. Later it would be the refuge where that child would grow to manhood, becoming strong in spirit until the day he finally manifested himself to Israel. (Lk 1:80)

On my arrival, I met no one but Sister Josephine, a little Indian nun who smiled with a beautiful expression of inner peace while sweeping the chapel of the hermitage with a coarse broom made of branches. It was she who recommended that I should continue through the thicket until I found the place where the tomb of Saint Elizabeth is venerated. I was unaware of this information and the news filled me with equal parts surprise and joy. The sun, which had barely risen, had not yet painted the slopes of the valley of Soreq with its light. My walk was truly delightful: the coolness of the morning, the silence of that quiet and still-sleeping wood, the solitude in that small church. I lived a moment of greatest intimacy before the relics of this holy woman, who received me as benevolently in that tiny crypt as in her day she welcomed the visit of the Mother of God that we are considering here.

We have already meditated on much of what St. Luke tells us in this episode: we have entered into the Heart of Mary as she walked, pondering the words of the Magnificat. We have also considered some of Elizabeth's expressions when she sees her cousin arrive. Perhaps the best thing to do at this moment is to contemplate, with the gaze of a soul that sees in the light of the Spirit, the intense joy of this encounter.

Elizabeth raises her eyes and recognizes Mary. The Virgin greets the older woman with a smile and gazes in wonder at the silhouette of a pregnant woman. The gaze of the young woman that rests gently on the rounded belly of her cousin and her sweet voice are conductors of an almost electric grace that shakes and penetrates the body and soul of the one who was called barren. Elizabeth is intoxicated with this anointing and is filled with the Holy Spirit (Lk 1:41).This young woman is all grace and it pours out uncontrollably wherever she goes!

It would seem that this is the natural succession of events, and yet, in his commentary on the Gospel of Luke, St. Ambrose gives us the most accurate perspective of this most delightful episode. In reality, it is not Elizabeth who first experiences grace, but the child, John. "The mother was not enriched before the son," the holy Bishop of Milan perceptively notes, "but after the son was filled, the mother was filled as w ell."[78] Grace begins with the children, and flows from them to their m others. Jesus, who preserved Mary from the first moment of her immaculate conception, now sanctifies the Baptist in the womb before his birth. John, for his part, feels the presence of the Word Incarnate in the young woman who approaches him and leaps with joy as a result of the divine life that has just permeated him completely. It is then that Elizabeth experiences the sudden and energetic movement of her child in the womb, and that energy, which has already saturated the child, is such that it spills out inside his mother like an internal font of grace that cannot be contained.

6. *Consolations of God.* "Blessed art thou among women, and blessed is the fruit of thy womb! Who am I, that the mother of my Lord should come to visit me? As soon as I heard your greeting, the child leaped for joy in my womb. Blessed are you for having believed that what was spoken to you from the Lord would be fulfilled" (Lk. 1:42–45).Elizabeth's words give us cause to reflect briefly on an aspect that in the *Spiritual Exercises* of St. Ignatius and in our Christian life, in general, is of central importance: the consolations of God.

The scene of the Visitation is undoubtedly one of the most consoling moments for Mary that we can find in the Holy Scriptures. The supernatural joy that emanates from this Gospel episode leaps off of the page and splashes the reader in the face every time we reread it in faith. As we pointed out in the introduction to this passage, on a surface level that is too basic and therefore insufficient, we encounter the joy of two women who for different reasons had given up the idea of motherhood. However, God's intervention in history has fulfilled in them this desire that is rooted in the depths of the feminine heart. It is unquestionable that Mary's Visitation is a hymn to the beauty, sacredness, and joy of being a mother. Although motherhood in its mere biological consideration is not the main cause that fills the soul of these women with joy, it is undoubtedly at the origin of their happiness.

Pope St. Paul VI wrote a document called *Gaudete in Domino,* an Apostolic Exhortation on Christian joy that I highly recommend and whose reading is an uplifting source of hope. I would like to quote here a short excerpt:

> *There is also needed a patient effort to teach people, or teach them once more, how to savor in a simple way the many human joys that the Creator places in our path: the elating joy of existence and of life; the joy of chaste and sanctified love; the peaceful joy of nature and silence; the sometimes austere joy of work well done; the joy and satisfaction of duty performed; the transparent joy of purity, service and sharing; the demanding joy of sacrifice. The Christian will be able to purify, complete and sublimate these joys; he will not be able to disdain them. Christian joy presupposes a person capable of natural joy. These natural joys were often used by Christ as a starting point when He proclaimed the kingdom of God.*[79]

These are words to meditate on slowly. It is not a Christian attitude to despise these "natural joys," of which mother-hood is undoubtedly one of the greatest. As the Pope points out, Christ himself has taken this experience to announce all that he has heard from his Father and made known to us (Jn. 15:15).

In relation to the joy of being a mother, Jesus expressed himself in these terms:

> *Amen, amen, I say to you, you will weep and mourn,*

while the world rejoices; you will grieve, but your grief
will become joy. When a woman is in labor, she is in
anguish because her hour has arrived; but when she
has given birth to a child, she no longer remembers
the pain because of her joy that a child has been born
into the world. So you also are now in anguish. But I
will see you again, and your hearts will rejoice, and no
one will take your joy away from you (Jn. 16:20-22).

In these words of Christ, the Lord establishes an analogy
between the joy of motherhood and the joy that is the fruit of
the Holy Spirit and "which no one will take away from you."

In a way, these words of the Lord complete what we said
earlier about consolation: if in moments of consolation the
soul must prepare itself for future desolation, in moments
of trial it must also fill itself with hope, thinking that if it is
faithful, as St. Ignatius affirms in the eighth rule of the First
Week of the Exercises, "*it will soon be consoled*" (SE 321).

These women rejoice in being mothers, in seeing and
hearing each other again. In experiencing the warmth of
friendship, in being able to share what has miraculously
happened to them, and thus teach us to enjoy simply, sponta-
neously and intensely the joys that God offers us in our daily
lives. As a priest, I am never far from some very miserable
people who could be much happier if they *would gratefully*
receive the gifts that the Lord never ceases to bestow on us. At
times, we have such a disordered desire for goods we do
not have that we fail to appreciate and savor the plethora of
ordered, simple, and good joys that God always places within
our reach. In most cases, bitterness is not solved by seeking
a life different from the one we have, but by seeking to find

light and beauty in the existence that the Most Holy Trinity, in its infinite love, has seen fit to give us.

Having said this, it is evident that the great lesson of the Visitation sublimates, as St. Paul VI said, this set of human experiences. The true joy of the Christian is in God! Mary is happy because she was blessed among all women (Lk. 1:42); because she believed that what the Lord told her would be fulfilled (Lk. 1:45);because God her Savior looked upon her lowliness as a handmaid (Lk. 1:48);because the Mighty One accomplished great works in and for her (Lk. 1:49);because the Lord raises up the lowly among whom she herself is numbered (Lk. 1:59).Elizabeth, for her part, rejoices because she recognizes in the visit of her cousin the arrival of "her" Lord who brings definitive salvation (Lk. 1:43);because the Holy Spirit has filled her soul (Lk. 1:41b);because her son has leaped for joy in her womb (Lk. 1:41a).In short, as can be seen, it is a cluster of surging and exultant expressions that are impulsively joined and interwoven, conveying the sensation of a supernatural and overflowing joy because of the *extraordinary action of God.* We can recall here the well-known expressions of St. Augustine:

> *For, you see, as Scripture says, whoever wishes to be a friend of this world will be counted as God's enemy. Just as a man cannot serve two masters, so too no-one can rejoice both in the world and in the Lord.*
>
> *Let joy in the Lord win and go on winning, until people take no more joy in the world. Let joy in the Lord always go on growing, and joy in the world always go on shrinking until it is reduced to nothing. I do not mean that we should not rejoice as long as*

we are in this world, but that even while we do find
ourselves in this world, we should already be rejoicing
in the Lord.[80]

7. *Conclusion: May Mary place us with her Son.* We have
dwelled at some length on this passage which is so rich in
teaching for our spiritual life. It is a moment of increase and
our souls expand simply by seeing Mary.

You also are blessed because you have heard and
believed. A soul that believes both conceives and
brings forth the Word of God and acknowledges his
works.
 Let Mary's soul be in each of you to proclaim the
greatness of the Lord. Let her spirit be in each to
rejoice in the Lord. Christ has only one mother
in the flesh, but we all bring forth Christ in faith.
Every soul receives the Word of God if only it keeps
chaste, remaining pure and free from sin, its modesty
undefiled. The soul that succeeds in this proclaims the
greatness of the Lord, just as Mary's soul magnified
the Lord and her spirit rejoiced in God her Savior.[81]

"May the soul of Mary dwell in everyone." As often happens
to me, the saints succeed in expressing with a few brush-
strokes what I am only able to convey poorly, with a trickle
of words. St. Ambrose comes to synthesize the grace that we
seek in the consideration of this episode: basically, we are all
called to "give birth to the Word of God in us," to let Christ
be formed in our souls (Gal. 4:19), to clothe ourselves with

our Lord (Rom. 13:14) and for this, we must believe, believe that the Blessed Trinity can work wonders in our lives. For this we need the Heart of Mary to reside in us. Anything less will be a poor substitute for the Christian experience. It will be insufficient, ineffective, and sterile.

Beyond what we have considered, the passage in question offers many other life lessons that in a particular way should attract your attention as women: trust in the Bridegroom and the search for light in the Word of God; the need to create silence when we do not see the way forward; the understanding of our life as a song of praise to God; the search for happiness that is capable of living with pain; the living of true humility as the only way to identify fully with Christ; the charity that knows how to act discreetly in the face of the concrete need of our neighbor; the pilgrimage of faith in which we are all called to advance; the blind trust that God can work the impossible, especially when it is a question of our own conversion; the apostolate understood as a simple carrying of Christ in us and sharing his grace with the people we meet on our way; finally, the joy that is born of God, grows in dialogue with him, and finds its fulfillment in the communion of life with the divine Persons and in his saving work.

I encourage you to conclude your prayer by addressing Mary as Elizabeth did—with closeness, with respect, and with trust. She continues to visit those who wish to receive her; she continues to speak to the hearts of those who allow her to enter their inner room; she tirelessly continues to bring the presence of Christ to people of every age.

St. Ignatius of Loyola has a unique expression in his Marian devotion that is not easy to translate into other languages. He used to ask Our Lady "to put him with her Son" or "to place him near her Son."[82] In Spanish it is such an unusual choice of terms that it is not used in any other way or in other contexts.

With St. Ignatius, we can ask Mary to place us with her Son. That is, to unite us to Christ in intimate and life-giving contact. Mary, who in the Visitation takes Jesus and shares him with her family in Ein-Karem, wishes to make the same gift to us today. The Church believes that she continues to come to us when we need her. All over the world there are shrines where our Mother has come to visit us: Saragossa, Guadalupe, Paris, La Salette, Fatima, Lourdes, and others. It seems that the scene we have meditated on does not refer only to a specific event that happened a long time ago: Mary, in fact, never ceases to visit her family. We should invoke her with familiarity, asking her to visit us at dawn, so that we may live a beautiful day in the eyes of her Son; at dusk, so that her light may illuminate our approaching night; in the warmth of the home, so that family life may be a source of peace, rest and joy; in the hustle and bustle of work, so that we may know how to carry it out in such a way that, through it, we may better serve the Lord and our brothers and sisters; at rest, so that it may be a time of human and spiritual growth. In this way, we will be able to achieve the purpose of this retreat and of our Christian life as a whole: to attain the perfection of charity "to the measure of the stature of the fullness of Christ" (Eph. 4:13).

As a complementary reading in one of the moments of rest, I invite you to remember the words that Pope Benedict XVI pronounced at the Shrine of Lourdes in 2008 regarding the "smile of Mary," to which we alluded earlier in the greeting to her cousin Elizabeth. It is truly a reflection full of depth and spiritual sensitivity, which will help us to better receive the grace of the present meditation.[83]

13

MARY IN THE NATIVITY I

DAY 5 (MORNING) - TENTH MEDITATION - PREPARATION FOR THE BIRTH OF JESUS

"Oh, God, who willed that your Word should take on the reality of human flesh in the womb of the Virgin Mary, grant, we pray, that we who confess our Redeemer to be God and man, may merit to become partakers even in his divine nature." (Collect prayer of the Annunciation of the Lord)

We begin this beautiful day feeling all the peace that God is giving us during this special time. It is the peace of those who have withdrawn from the noise that constantly threatens us in today's world. It is also the peace that the Gospel instills in us with its restful meditation and familial intimacy with biblical characters. It is, finally, the peace that has penetrated our hearts while contemplating Mary, especially in the story of the Visitation that we heard yesterday.

Here you are today, determined to continue on the journey of the spiritual exercises and eager to know the new direction that God wishes to show you. Each of you has come here to make a great discovery. To that end, a week ago you decided to leave your daily life—your family and your work—and steer your little boat in the direction of the unknown. The first consideration was that of the *principle and foundation* which gave us the basic orientation of this journey. We saw then that our goal should be praise, reverence, and service of God in Christ. Friendship with the Lord is the new continent where we must land and on which we must build the edifice of our lives.

In the meditations of the first week, you faced a rough and stormy sea. You confronted what Saint Paul calls *mysterium iniquitatis* (2 Thes. 2:3-12), the mystery of sin and its consequences: concupiscence, death, and eternal damnation. We must measure ourselves with these realities because they are obstacles that we must face and because it is imperative that we consider them from God's perspective. Only in this way can we preserve the inner peace that comes from knowing that although we are poor sinners, we have been loved by our Father with an immense and endearing mercy.

From the meditations of the second week—continuing with the nautical analogy—your boat has found much calmer waters, and the winds of the Holy Spirit have blown you into the depths of the Mystery of Christ. You have traveled quickly, as Mary did on her way to Ein-Karem, and she has gifted you with some of the most crucial teachings of the Christian life. The Virgin is the Star that guides us on our nocturnal journey. When we are lost or disoriented, we can always look up at our Mother, because she will always be there to help us, heal us, and lead us to the safe harbor of eternal salvation. That is our final destination: the union of love with the Most Holy Trinity and the final rest in the undying joys of Paradise.

1. On this undoubtedly exciting journey, I have the impression that today the Lord is going to give you a delightful and peaceful sailing since we are going to focus on the mystery of the birth of Jesus in Bethlehem. Many of you have experienced in your own flesh what it means to be mothers. There are many aspects of this mystery that we men will never be able to unravel. Simply put, the Lord has not given us that experience and we can only participate in it when you allow us.

Whether you have been mothers or not, you all have a unique relationship with that extraordinary mystery due to the fact that it is a natural feature of your feminine identity. With Edith Stein, we have seen that in every woman there is a "vocation to motherhood." I want to let the German saint take the floor here so that she herself can explain with her usual clarity and insight this aspect of your deepest mystery.

> *Only the person blinded by the passion of controversy could deny that woman in soul and body is formed for a particular purpose. The clear and irrevocable word of Scripture declares what daily experience teaches from the beginning of the world: woman is destined to be wife and mother. Both physically and spiritually she is endowed for this purpose, as is seen clearly from*

practical experience. However, it follows also from the Thomistic principle of anima forma corporis that such a spiritual characteristic does exist. Of course, woman shares a basic human nature, but basically her faculties are different from men; therefore, a differing type of soul must exist as well. Since the fundamentals of the typically feminine spiritual attitude are quite familiar to us, we will trace it only very briefly.

Woman naturally seeks to embrace that which is living, personal, and whole. To cherish, guard, protect, nourish and advance growth is her natural, maternal yearning. Lifeless matter, the fact, can hold primary interest for her only insofar as it serves the living and the personal, not ordinarily for its own sake. Relevant to this is another matter: abstraction in every sense is alien to the feminine nature. The living and personal to which her care extends is a concrete whole and is protected and encouraged as a totality; this does not mean that one part is sacrificed to another, not the mind to the body or one spiritual faculty at the expense of the others. She aspires to this totality in herself and in others. Her theoretical and her practical views correspond; her natural line of thought is not so much conceptual and analytical as it is directed intuitively and emotionally to the concrete. This natural endowment enables woman to guard and teach her own children. But this basic attitude is not intended just for them; she should behave in this way also to her husband and to all those in contact with her.[84]

What Saint Teresa Benedicta says here is particularly beautiful: God has prepared your body and your soul for the vocation to which he has called you from all eternity as wives, mothers and custodians of what is truly human. Specifically, since motherhood defines your identity in its most intimate aspects, this dimension must always be realized or the meaning of your existence would be irretrievably compromised. That is to say: not all women are called to be biological mothers of new human beings, but all of you must be and feel like mothers in the development of those qualities that the Lord has given you for that purpose.

Edith Stein specifically mentions an aspect that reveals an enormous insight: the natural inclination of women towards the personal is born from this orientation to motherhood and extends to all those who come into contact with her and not only towards her own children. We really need women who always feel like mothers: when they take care of their children; when they teach in school classrooms or in catechesis; when they treat the sick in hospitals; when they pray in the cloisters of convents; when they serve the person in need wherever they may be. Precisely for this reason, I believe that in a special way, women should carefully contemplate the birth of Christ because in Mary you are called to participate in the feelings of a woman who is the Mother of God incarnate and who in Bethlehem changed her way of relating to the world forever. She wants you to participate in this transformation today, if in docility you allow the grace of the Holy Spirit to work in your souls.

2. As usual, in all exercise meditations we ask for the grace already known: "that all my intentions, actions, and

operations be directed in the service and praise of his Divine Majesty" (SE 46),meaning that we come to order our whole life according to the loving Will of the Lord. That is the universal request in these days of retreat. As a particular request, we ask for the "internal knowledge of Christ who has become man for me, so that I love him more and follow him" (SE 104).In this context, let us ask for the grace to "know Christ internally" as Mary, our Mother—a complete and unsurpassed model of femininity according to God's plan—did.

To contemplate the Christmas scene, let us revert to the discussion of events where we left them in the preceding meditation. Mary is in Ein-Karem attending to the needs of Elizabeth, who requires more help as the final phase of her pregnancy approaches. These are days of light and consolation for the young Nazarene, in which she would begin to experience in herself the first changes and signs of her own motherhood. Surely her cousin would guide her in this process, explaining the different stages in the development of pregnancy. Can we imagine the joy of our Mother the first time she felt the movement of her Son in her womb or noticed the changes in her own body caused by the growing Child?

It was in this village where the Heart of Christ began to beat, always in and out of love for men. Today we know that the heart begins to form shortly after the fourth week of gestation and that its first beats can already be heard about a month and a half after conception. So it was here where the Eternal Father heard for the first time the breath of life of that most Sacred Heart. In the silence of your prayer, you too hear those palpitations and think that *since that moment Christ has been loving you,* that this child is yours from the beginning and that God chose to love you with human affections like yours. Truly, we could get lost in this alone...

The Holy Spirit formed in the womb of Mary the Heart of Christ, and also through Mary, the Holy Spirit wants to form the Heart of Jesus in you. One must enter the sanctuary of the soul of this Mother to find the love of the Son there. As John Paul II wrote in his Apostolic Letter on the rosary —*Rosarium Virginis Mariae*— in the school of the Virgin we learn the Lord and configure ourselves to Him. Who can best help us to unite our wills and hearts with Jesus ("have in yourselves the same attitude of Christ" (Phil. 2:5) than she who shaped the Heart of the Lord in her womb and in the journey of her hidden life in Nazareth?

We can also suppose that Mary, at some point in the three months that she spent in the house of Zacharias, would go to the temple in Jerusalem so close to where she was. On April 4, 2018 I walked the same route. I left the pilgrim house owned by the Sisters of the Congrégation de Notre-Dame de Sion on Via Dolorosa—a few meters from the esplanade where the Temple used to stand—and arrived at Ein-Karem an hour and a half later. It is just six miles away. Probably, then, the first pilgrimage that Jesus made to Jerusalem was within his Mother during these days of consolation. Would the Virgin meet old Simeon? We can only guess.

Those days were not a time of rest for the Virgin: the handmaid of the Lord came to help Elizabeth, to *serve her.* As we have seen, she is trying to discern, together with Joseph, the way forward. We can see her in our contemplation like this, always attentive to the needs of her cousin, reserved and collected in her moments of prayer, reflecting the light that her Son communicates to her from within her body and soul.

An anecdote from the life of St. Bernard of Clairvaux relates here. Humbeline, his only sister, had insistently asked him to send her some written recommendations showing her the path to holiness. The Mellifluous Doctor was a man acclaimed even during his lifetime for his eminent knowledge and holiness, and she hoped that someday her brother would send her a most elaborate treatise, beautiful and full of wisdom, in which the Abbot of Citeaux would reveal to her in a higher form, hidden wonders never before seen. Instead, Bernard sent her by letter a phrase with just two words: "Love serves." Perhaps Humbeline was initially somewhat disappointed with her brother's concise message, but as time went by, she understood that what she had asked of Bernard was wholly contained in those two words. Holiness consists precisely in simplifying life in the Spirit and going to the fundamentals. At the core of the Christian vocation, inevitably one always finds love that is placed at the service of others.

That is what Mary does in Ein-Karem: she serves because she loves. She loves to serve. In this way, she quietly teaches us the most intimate character of our mission as disciples of Christ: "the Son of Man did not come to be served but to serve and give his life as a ransom for many" (Mt 20:28). This is how life is in the house of Zachariah and Elizabeth: mornings full of light and days that follow each other in the hope of what is to come.

3. All of this happens in the mountains of Judah, but in

Galilee, Joseph does not see any light and is living the darkest days of his existence. He is a man lost in gloomy thoughts—despondent and on the verge of the most excruciating anguish. He can't sleep. He does not speak to anyone. He takes refuge in his workshop, but only with difficulty is he able to finish his tasks. We already know the cause of these inner torments. Overnight the life of the poor carpenter of Nazareth has been completely turned upside down. Yahweh has intervened and has "turned the sock inside out," as we say in Spanish. He has upset everything. He has ruined all their plans for the future. Let's note that when God acts in our life, He frequently forces us to change our plans. He doesn't do it to sweep away our heartfelt desires, but to *transform and elevate* them, to always give us something greater, something better. However, this divine intervention is usually preceded by the darkness of the trial and that is the situation our Joseph finds himself in now.

The Gospel of Saint Matthew tells us that in the depth of his pain Saint Joseph has resolved to secretly repudiate Mary (Mt 1:19). This decision alone reveals to us the magnitude and depth of his agony. He is willing, like Abraham, to sacrifice what he loves most. How many times he would think about this passage of Scripture! This scene is often referred to as "the sacrifice of Isaac," but in reality, the immolation that God asks, as is seen in the conclusion of the story, is not that of the son's body but that of the father's soul. It was Abraham and not his child who was dying on the way, as they climbed to the top of Mount Moria. And Joseph is like this: dying inside. Later, speaking of Jesus, the letter to the Hebrews picks up these words that have always overwhelmed me: "In the days when he was in the flesh, he offered prayers

223

and supplications with loud cries and tears to the one who was able to save him from death, and he was heard because of his reverence. Son though he was, he learned obedience from what he suffered" (Heb. 5:7-8). We can project these words onto the person of Joseph during these moments that he is going through: "supplications with loud cries and tears." The carpenter cries in his workshop without possible consolation and every time he sees more clearly the course he must follow. If Abraham had to offer his first-born in sacrifice, Joseph gradually comes to the conviction that the victim that he must place on altar of the holocaust is his love for his wife, Mary.

But what would become of her, then? In what situation would this decision leave his wife? Was this in fact the will of the Most High? And, from now on, what?

We have said before that this decision reveals the depth of his anguish. It also reveals what kind of man this extraordinary Jew was. Joseph resolves to repudiate his wife "in secret." This is the chivalry of great souls. The discretion of this resolution, avoiding any kind of disclosure of motives, made him, in full view, the culprit of the resulting situation. In other words, Joseph was a husband who, for no apparent or known reason, was abandoning his pregnant wife. In order to protect Mary's good name, he exposes himself to be irreparably tainted. We can imagine what others might think: *What irresponsibility! He has just taken Mary as his wife and, barely pregnant, he leaves her without her having done anything to deserve this!* Thus Joseph would bear dishonor and shame instead of Mary. As we can see, Jesus was not the first lamb to be taken to the slaughterhouse. "Like a sheep silent before shearers, he did not open his mouth" (Is. 53:7).

Just as Christ took upon himself the sin of the world, Joseph assumes full responsibility for his decision and with this he exonerates Mary from any kind of shame. How could you not love a man of this inner quality?

4. Let us remember that at the root of this torment is the *humility* of Joseph, his astonishment at knowing the divine origin of the Child and the realization that his wife is the Mother of the Son of God. There is too much holiness in all of this for him to be asked to be at the head of this family. Saint Bernard, whom we mentioned earlier, admirably collects this experience of Saint Joseph in one of his homilies:

> *Since, then, he was just and unwilling to expose her, why had he a mind to put her away? (Mt. 1:19) I give you on this point not my own opinion, but that of the Fathers. Joseph's reason was the same as Peter s when he said, "Depart from me, for I am a sinful man, O Lord," (Lk. 5:8) and that of the centurion when he exclaimed, "I am not worthy that thou shouldst enter under my roof." (Mt. 8:8) Joseph looked on himself as a sinner and as unworthy to entertain one in whom he beheld a superhuman dignity. He beheld with awe in the Virgin-Mother a certain sign of the Divine Presence, and as he could not penetrate the mystery, he wished to put her away. Peter was struck with awe at the greatness of Christ's power; the centurion by the majesty of His presence; and Joseph was naturally afraid at the novelty and splendor of the miracle and the depth of the mystery. We need not wonder that he thought himself unworthy of the society of such a*

virgin when we hear the holy Elizabeth exclaim with
fear and trembling: "Whence is this to me that the
mother of my Lord should come to me? " (Lk. 1:43)[85]

Saint Bernard refers here to the Church Fathers, specifically to the interpretation of Saint Ephrem, a Syrian deacon from the fourth century. I especially like the mention of Simon Peter and the Roman centurion, who experience their unworthiness in relation to the Person of Christ. The reference to Elizabeth's words, in turn, is addressed directly to amazement at the holiness of Mary. Joseph has both of these sensations in his heart, *Mary and her Son, the mother of my Lord and God made Man, have been entrusted … to me?*

As we previously noted, underlying this humility is the Jewish awareness of *God's infinite transcendence.* In a world as desacralized as ours, it may be difficult for us to understand this particularity. Yahweh could not be seen and yet continued to live (Ex. 33:20). Reverential fear forbade even pronouncing his name (Dt. 5:11). Furthermore, the representation of the divine mystery through images was severely forbidden (Ex. 20: 4) and we have already considered what happened to Uzá when touching the Ark of the Covenant in an attempt to protect it from falling (2 Sam. 6, 6-7). All of the above helps to understand the insurmountable distance between the Eternal and we who are his handiwork (Eph. 2:10). Certainly, the Most High inhabits an inaccessible light (1 Tm. 6:16). In one of her ecstasies, Saint Catherine of Siena heard from the Father's lips this same truth: "You are she who is not. I am He who is."

Note that the greater the holiness of a person, the greater the *experience* of the majesty and transcendence of God. That is to say, it is not just about *knowing*, but about having an *experience* of what is already known. Joseph's intimate communion with God makes him aware of the abyss that exists between his poor self and the Son that Mary carries in her womb, an abyss that he does not see a way to bridge.

Along with this experience of the infinity of God, Joseph is also convinced of his *inadequacy* for such a mission. Vertigo. Fear. Inability. Let's take the case of someone who is unexpectedly given a responsibility for which he is not prepared. Let's imagine that as we are boarding an airplane, instead of our expected seats, we are taken to the pilot's cabin! We are told to take this plane filled with passengers to its destination and bring it to a happy landing. We lack the slightest knowledge of how to do this. We have never piloted an airplane and we have no idea what all those devices and lights blinking in front of us are for. We buckle up, grip the controller tightly, and are left alone in the nose of the airplane with the lives of nearly three hundred people in our hands. Most likely, we would have a panic attack. Saint Joseph does not lose his peace—the thought of Mary could never disturb anyone—but he is a simple carpenter and feels incapable of educating the Son of God.

I have seen this same experience reflected many times in so many good souls: ordinary persons subjected to extraordinary pressure; normal people beset by completely abnormal circumstances. I believe that, sooner or later, we must all go through something like this and it is precisely in those times of trial, when the one that is straw, burns and the one that is gold, is refined and perfected.

5. The decision, then, is made. With a broken heart and

227

JESUS AND YOU, WOMAN

his life in shreds, Joseph has chosen the route of secretly disowning his wife. It is then when the manifestation of the angel in a dream takes place, showing him the way out. One might think: *But if in the end God was going to show him what he should do, why didn't he tell him before? Why put him through all that anguish if the Lord had already planned to enlighten him?* The answer, up to a point, is simple: basically, because God's ways are different from ours (Is. 55:8-9) and because *it is good for us for it to be that way.* In his book *Inner Peace*, Father Jacques Philippe talks about our attitude when we have to make important decisions:

> *This desire to know what God wants sometimes hides a difficulty in enduring a situation of incertitude. We want to be released from having to decide by ourselves. But, frequently, the will of the Lord is that we do decide for ourselves, even if we are not absolutely sure that this decision would be the best. In effect, in this capacity to decide in incertitude, in doing that which seems to us best without spending hours equivocating, there is an attitude of confidence and abandonment: "Lord, I have thought about it and prayed to know Your will. I do not see it clearly, but I am not going to trouble myself any further. I am not going to spend hours racking my brain. I am deciding such and such a thing because, all things carefully considered, it seems to me the best thing to do. And I leave everything in Your hands. I know well that, even if I am mistaken, You will not be displeased with me, for I have acted with good intentions. And if I have made a mistake, I know that You are able to draw good from this error.*

It will be for me a source of humility and I will learn
something from it! And I remain at peace.[86]

This uncertainty that Father Philippe writes about is an
opportunity to grow in humility and trust. Experiencing
one's own vulnerability, the congenital fragility of our
humble human condition, is a source of great wisdom for
those who let themselves be carried away by the Spirit.
The Lord wants Joseph to understand this more concretely
because he will need it from now on in his dealings with
Mary and Jesus. He is the father of the Holy Family and
after the Incarnation, he will often have to be guided by the
communications he receives from on high, as we see in the
episode of their flight to Egypt. In his mission as head of the
home, he will have to follow what God is showing him, even
if it may be impossible to understand on human terms. He
will live this uncertainty many times from now on and it is
good that this change in plan teaches him this new way of
relating to God that Joseph will need from now on.

The angel finally comes to the aid of the servant of God.
As we have already mentioned, and it is a fully faithful
interpretation of the evangelical text, the angel's embassy
is not intended to reveal to Joseph the divine origin of the
Child—something that he had known from the beginning
from Mary herself—but to manifest the mission that God
Himself has entrusted him in the work of Redemption. The
resemblance to Abraham is shown here again. How beautiful!
When the Holy Patriarch has made the offer of Isaac inwardly
and has already sacrificed him in his heart; when the hand
is in the air about to strike the final blow, God stops the
sacrifice because the test of confidence has been happily

passed. Often times, the Lord does not ask us to give what we love, but He does want us to be willing to interiorly surrender it for love of him, who first emptied himself out of love for us (Phil. 2:7). Here, Joseph has reached the same extreme: in his heart, he has also raised the knife to surrender, out of love for God, his love for Mary—who can peer into this torment?—and that is when the Lord comes to stop the holocaust before it occurs. "All is well, dear Joseph. *Do not be afraid.*"

"Do not be afraid"—the same words spoken to Mary! God's presence is always reassuring; it is always comforting. Saint Ignatius of Loyola notes in the first rule for discerning spirits of the second week of Exercises (SE 329), "It is proper to God and his angels in their motions to give true joy and spiritual joy, removing all sadness and embarrassment." And later the founder of the Society of Jesus adds: "To those who proceed from good to better, the good angel touches the soul sweetly, lightly and gently, like a drop of water that enters a sponge and the bad angel touches sharply and with noise and restlessness, as when a drop of water falls on a stone" (SE 335).

Joseph feels the refreshment of this water that enters the fertile soil of his heart, "removing all sadness and embarrassment." You have probably heard or read about these opening words: "Do not be afraid." They are words that God uses frequently when he reveals a special, demanding vocation, superior to the natural forces of man left to himself. He does this with Moses (Num. 21:34), with Gideon (Judges 6:23), with Jeremiah (Jer. 1:8), and with Mary herself (Lk. 1:30), among many others. What the Lord wants these servants of his to understand is that *he is with them*, by their side, that he knows well that they are poor earthen vessels (Ps. 103:14; 2 Cor. 4:7), that he is very aware of the fact that they cannot by themselves carry out the mission with confidence, but there is no reason for fear because he will personally take care of resolving the dangers and making their endeavors conclude happily.

In the Exercises—engagement with which is a time of special openness to God's motions—the Lord may ask for commitments or difficult decisions that are inherent to the inner movement of love. You can receive here an illumination of the Holy Spirit that invites you to sacrifice something very dear to you. The paschal mystery is a mystery of death and resurrection: first, we must go through the destruction of that which is contrary to divine love and only after that will the doors of full realization in Christ be opened to us. It is the dynamic of our own baptism: "Or are you unaware that we who were baptized into Christ Jesus were baptized into his death? We were indeed buried with him through baptism into death, so that, just as Christ was raised from the dead by the glory of the Father, we too might live in newness of life" (Rom. 6:3-4). In these days of retreat, the interior motions should lead us to "immerse ourselves" in the death of Christ, offering aspects, relationships, projects that are dear to us but that are blocking the way to a greater intimacy with the Most Holy Trinity on the altar of sacrifice.

For this reason, it is important to listen with Mary and Joseph to these words of God, spoken *personally* to you today: "Do not be afraid. I am with you. Everything will be fine. You are under the shadow of my wings. I will take the necessary steps with you. We are fighting together. You will see how much light and how much peace there is at the end of the road."

Somewhere I read that in the Bible this expression is used 365 times and that this number reminds us of the days of the year, as if every day we all need to read or hear these words. I have not personally counted the frequency with which Sacred Scripture records this affirmation, but it would make sense. We are invited to respond to the fears that haunt us throughout each of the days of our pilgrimage through this life with the certainty that the Lord does not abandon us and that He takes charge of our struggles. Or perhaps the frequency with which we read these words in the sacred texts does not relate so much to the number of days per year, but to the many fears that we carry in our hearts. Truly, how many fears we carry inside! In this retreat, we must be able to remove those fears and put them before the Lord, give ourselves time to do that work of introspection in order to hear, for each one of them, the same words that Joseph receives here from the Lord's emissary, "Do not worry."

6. The angel calls Joseph "son of David," a very frequent name in the Gospels for Jesus himself. As we can see, in some way this message is a replica of the one that Mary received earlier, in which the Angel Gabriel had assured the young woman that her Son would inherit "the throne of David, his father" (Lk. 1:32). Saint Joseph then receives a task: "She will bear a son and you are to name him Jesus, because he will save his people from their sins" (Mt. 1:21).

The role of Saint Joseph in this plan is not to be a mere spectator of the events that are unfolding. *He has a responsibility* toward the Child who has been conceived by the work of the Holy Spirit (Mt. 1:20). His job is to "name him." We find ourselves, as they say, before a "story of vocation": the manifestation to man of the mission that God entrusts to him in a personal and non-transferable way, his *raison d'être*. Saint Joseph, in the dream of a night's slumber, receives the revelation of the reason for his existence. If his wife was molded by the Most High to receive the gift of Christ in her virginal womb, this man has been prepared to "name him Jesus," to be the father of this Child in the home of Nazareth.

The expression used by the angel here shows the authority over Jesus that Joseph will have as head of the family of Nazareth. We all remember the moment when in Eden Adam gave names to all creation: "So the LORD God formed out of the ground all the wild animals and all the birds of the air, and he brought them to the man to see what he would call them; whatever the man called each living creature was then its name. The man gave names to all the tame animals, all the birds of the air, and all the wild animals" (Gen. 2:19-20).

Giving the name, then, is much more than a specific assignment at the beginning of life in the flesh of the eternal Word: it is the declaration and recognition, by heaven, of the authority that this simple carpenter was called to exercise over the incarnate Son of God as the father of his little family. The doubts that gripped him are finally resolved, "Yes, Joseph, this mystery surpasses you infinitely, but I will give you the grace to serve and protect it as head in the home of Nazareth."

In one of his homilies, Saint John Chrysostom has the boldness to put these words in God's mouth as he speaks to Saint Joseph:

Do not think that, since the conception of Christ was

233

*the work of the Holy Spirit, you are apart from this
divine work. For even though it is true that you had
no part in the generation, and that the Virgin remains
intact; nevertheless, all that is related to fatherhood
without adversely affecting the dignity of her virginity,
I give all of this to you, just as I ask you to give him his
name. For though the offspring be not yours, yet shall
you exhibit a father's care towards Him. Wherefore
I do straightway, even from the giving of the name,
connect you with Him that is born.*[87]

7. "When Joseph awoke, he did as the angel of the Lord
had commanded him and took his wife into his home" (Mt.
1:24). Upon awakening... Joseph's heart would sing for joy,
like Abraham's when he knew that Isaac did not have to
be sacrificed. He recovers that love for Mary that he had
surrendered in his soul, and God now returns it to him
refined, increased, intensified, warmer, and more alive.
Thus, Saint John Paul II comments on this verse of Scripture
in his Apostolic Exhortation *Redemptoris Custos*:

*"When Joseph woke from sleep, he did as the angel
of the Lord commanded him and took Mary as his
wife." (cf. Mt 1:24) He took her in all the mystery of
her motherhood. He took her together with the Son
who had come into the world by the power of the Holy
Spirit. In this way he showed a readiness of will like
Mary's with regard to what God asked of him through
the angel.*[88]

These words of John Paul II, which admirably express the

greatness of Joseph, direct our gaze once again to Mary, and thus we conclude this meditation, which I hope will be of benefit to you. Think of Mary as she tends to her cousin in Ein-Karem. Take Joseph's silence and make it yours in prayer. Consider how the attitudes of these two spouses prepare for the advent of the Son of God on Earth and ask the Lord to help you live them yourself so that you can be, like Mary and Joseph, the good soil in which God can be born again.

14

MARY IN THE NATIVITY II

DAY 5 (AFTERNOON) - ELEVENTH MEDITATION - THE ROAD TO BETHLEHEM

"Come quickly, we pray, Lord Jesus, and do not delay, that those who trust in your compassion may find solace and relief in your coming." (From the Morning Mass on December 24)

In his meditation on the Nativity from the Spiritual Exercises, Saint Ignatius invites us to consider the journey of the Holy Family from Nazareth to Bethlehem. Here, we want to focus on Ignatius's prelude on the scene of the birth of Christ. Our first composition of place will therefore be the little house of Nazareth and then the path that crosses Palestine until it reaches the small town where the Son of God will finally be born. We are going step by step, asking the Holy Spirit that as a fruit of your peaceful accompaniment of the Holy

Family during these tranquil days of retreat, He may form in you the attitudes of Joseph and Mary in relation to the Mystery of the Incarnate Word. In the method of the Ignatian Spiritual Exercises, the dispositions, feelings, behaviors, and responses of the Heart of Christ are absorbed by assimilation, and that requires living the biblical scenes as though we were present in them. Let us see, then, how that holy couple lived the days that preceded the birth in the flesh of the Eternal Word. This will help us to receive Christ in our lives as they did.

1. *"Mary remained with her about three months and then returned to her home"* (Lk. 1:56). In the scene that serves as a scriptural framework for understanding the decisions of Joseph and his wife in the difficult situation they faced after the Annunciation, note that Mary's stay in Ein-Karem corresponds precisely with a precedent in the second book of Samuel:

> *The ark of the LORD remained in the house of Obed-edom the Gittite for three months, and the LORD blessed Obed-edom and all his household. When it was reported to King David that the LORD had blessed the household of Obed-edom and all that he possessed because of the ark of God, David went to bring up the ark of God from the house of Obed-edom into the City of David with joy (2 Sm. 6:11-12).*

David finally makes up his mind to bring the Ark to Jerusalem when he hears about the blessings that Yahweh has poured out on Obed-Edom and his family during that time. The sacred text tells us that the bearers of the Ark had only gone six steps when the king offered an ox and a calf in sacrifice and then he himself took the lead of the procession, dancing and singing with "shouts of joy and sound of horn." We can draw parallels here with New Testament scene: Mary's presence has flooded the house of Zacharias with copious blessings, sanctifying John the Baptist before he was born, filling her cousin Elizabeth with the Holy Spirit, and finally unleashing the tongue of Zacharias, who returns to praise God with the well-learned lesson that God's faithfulness to his promises should never be doubted.

Joseph "took his wife into his home" (Mt. 1:24).He has probably gone to pick up his wife himself. Upon arrival, he listens in wonder to the marvels that have happened, and it is now he who shares with Mary the story of his experience with the angel. We can imagine the joy of their reunion and conversation, as they tell each other everything and praise the Lord because He has made them better understand what He is doing in their lives and in the history of Israel for the salvation of the world. At last, they can return home: their little house in Nazareth awaits them and their first days of living together.

The Gospel is silent in regard to those six months in which the holy couple lived—out of sight—in their village in Galilee. We can recreate that domestic life in its most everyday aspects. Mary drawing water at the well, Joseph laboring in his workshop, the talks at home, the shared prayers, the infinite respect of two souls who are of one heart, and all the while, a God Child develops silently in the womb of his Mother.

2. *Jesus in the womb of Mary.* In one of his Advent meditations, Saint Alphonsus Liguori correctly points out that unlike other children, Jesus had in his two natures, divine and human, knowledge of his situation in the womb of Mary. He called the Child Jesus during the time of his gestation a "prisoner of love" in the "dark cell" of the maternal womb. "*Prisoner*", because he had chosen to enclosed himself there, and "of love" because the reason for that voluntary imprisonment in the darkness of the Virgin's womb was love: her love for the Father and for men. This is how Pope Pius XII expressed it in his Encyclical on the Sacred Heart of Jesus, *Haurietis Aquas*:

> *The mystery of the divine redemption is primarily and by its very nature a mystery of love, that is, of the perfect love of Christ for His heavenly Father, to Whom the sacrifice of the Cross, offered in a spirit of love and obedience, presents the most abundant and infinite satisfaction due for the sins of the human race; "By suffering out of love and obedience, Christ gave more to God than was required to compensate for the offense of the whole human race."*
>
> *It is also a mystery of the love of the Most Holy Trinity and of the divine Redeemer towards all men. Because they were entirely unable to make adequate satisfaction for their sins, Christ, through the infinite treasure of His merits acquired for us by the shedding of His precious Blood, was able to restore completely that pact of friendship between God and man which had been broken, first by the grievous fall of Adam in the earthly paradise and then by the countless sins of*

the chosen people.[89]

In this contemplation, therefore, we can consider the scene "from outside," seeing the daily life of Joseph and Mary in Nazareth, or more deeply "from within" the Heart of Jesus who silently loves, gives of himself and experiences day by day how his human nature is gradually forming through the miracle of the generation and development of life. What a lesson in humility, silence, and patience Christ gives us from his "dark cell!" What a way God has of doing things! How surprising, how unsearchable are his ways! Such difficulty we have in understanding a God who moves for reasons unfathomable to us! Oh, wisdom of God, which is always madness in the eyes of the world...! Oh, the madness of God, which has caused him to be despised by those whom he has come to save!

3. "In those days a decree went out from Caesar Augustus that the whole world should be enrolled. This was the first enrollment, when Quirinius was governor of Syria. So all went to be enrolled, each to his own town" (Lk. 2:1-3).

It has now been approximately six months since Mary returned from Elizabeth's house. A long enough period of time has passed from their initial joy that Joseph and Mary are experiencing some uncertainty. What was the next step they should take? Should they wait for a private revelation like the previous ones? Surely they were looking for answers, as they always had, in God's Word. What do they find?

They both knew Micah's prophecy that pointed to Bethlehem as the birthplace of the Messiah: "But you, Bethlehem-Ephrathaha, least among the clans of Judah, from you shall come forth for me one who is to be ruler in Israel; whose origin is from of old, from ancient times" (Mic. 5:2; Mt 2:6)

It would have been totally artificial for them to have made the preparations for that trip *with the intention of* fulfilling a passage of Scripture. These are not the ways of God or the way in which we are to live life in the Spirit. It seems to me that many of us tend to do this. We make decisions to suit us based on what we consider to be the Lord's plan. There is in this attitude a lack of docility to divine movements, which can also translate into a certain lack of trust in divine Providence. If we accept that God is guiding us, what is the point of trying to "force" that realization "ahead of" God's timing?

Perhaps the latter is closest to what I intend: *God's timing...* As part of our surrender to the will of the Lord, we must accept that he usually carries out his plans in a time frame that does not correspond to ours. Many times, Divine Patience unnerves us because we do not have all eternity—not even many years—and we tend to hasten the natural unfolding of events. In the supernatural life, one must know how to wait patiently, which is very pleasing to the Lord.

Therefore, Mary and Joseph know *where* Jesus must be born, but they do not know *when* God is going to ask them to make the journey there or *how* the divine plan will be carried out. They will discover it gradually. Like ours, theirs is a walk *in trust.* But the time for the birth of the Child is approaching and they have not received the hoped-for sign from heaven. As you can see, everything is an opportunity to trust the Lord, even in the most human and ordinary circumstances.

In this prayerful waiting, they hear the news from Rome that Emperor Augustus has decreed a census of all of his far-flung Empire, and so Joseph must leave for Bethlehem. How easily would they see the hand of God in this! Surely, they would have marveled at this circumstance. Until that moment, everything has been happening "behind closed doors," quietly, in the context of their tiny world, their family, and those closest to them. Now the Emperor's decision takes the unfolding of events to another level. If the appearance of the angels to the shepherds will later indicate the ordering of the celestial world towards the Child Jesus (Lk. 2:8-20);if the adoration of the Magi will reveal, in the star, the orientation of the universe and of all creation towards Christ (Mt. 2:1-12),as pointed out by the Fathers of the Church and by Pope Benedict XVI; then in the census decreed by Augustus, Mary and Joseph understand that human history as a whole—not only that of the people of Israel—is directed towards that Baby who silently awaits the moment foreseen by God to be born and make "his dwelling among us" (Jn. 1:14).

Regarding this detail about the census, I would like to draw your attention to two teachings of vital importance for us. The first consists in assuming that Providence governs absolutely everything, from the number of hairs on our heads (Lk. 12:7)to the great events of history. Throughout all time God weaves his threads in and through everything, *He leads us.* One of the Advent prefaces of the Holy Mass presents this marvelous expression: "the same Lord who will then show himself to us full of glory, *now comes to meet us in each man and in each event,* so let us receive him in faith and, through love, bear witness to the happy expectation of his kingdom."

Paraphrasing this expression, we can say that in this

event—a political decision!—the holy couple now receives the Lord in faith. The thought that God is willing to do *whatever is necessary* for us to carry on his work of salvation—even great wonders—is beautiful.

It takes faith to see in the decisions of the powerful, who may at times attack the Kingdom of Christ in the world, the mysterious design of the Lord. Nothing escapes God. Nothing happens outside of his redemptive plan. Everything is under the dominion of his omniscience and everything is a vehicle and an occasion of grace for those who love God (Rom. 8:28).

The Most Holy Trinity made use of that apparently capricious and untimely decision so that what was written was fulfilled. We can imagine many of those men protesting against this measure that forced them to leave their homes to register in their places of origin, which were perhaps very far away. How many complaints would Mary and Joseph hear both in Nazareth and on their way to Bethlehem, and yet with what different attitude would they face this circumstance! They were the only ones who could understand God's design in what was happening!

The second teaching makes us look at the attitude with which Mary and Joseph receive this announcement. *"Blessed are the pure in heart for they will see God,"* Jesus will say later in the Sermon on the Mount (Mt. 5:8). Pure souls *know how to see God in all things.* They will see it without a doubt in the joys of Paradise, but that vision of God *already begins in this life.* The pure in heart see God *wherever they set their eyes*: in the works of the created universe, in people, and also in events apparently less related to His mystery. God manifests himself in everything, but only these souls manage to discover His loving and quiet presence in reality.

Saint John of the Cross can help us on this occasion with a beautiful analogy: the heart transformed by the Holy Spirit is like a clean window that lets the sunlight pass through.

> *A ray of sunlight is striking a window. If the window is in any way stained or misty, the sun's ray will be unable to illumine it and transform it into its own light, totally, as it would if it were clean of all these things, and pure; but it will illumine it to a lesser degree, in proportion as it is less free from those mists and stains; and will do so to a greater degree, in proportion as it is cleaner from them, and this will not be because of the sun's ray, but because of itself; so much so that, if it be wholly pure and clean, the ray of sunlight will transform it and illumine it in such wise that it will itself seem to be a ray and will give the same light as the ray. Although in reality the window has a nature distinct from that of the ray itself, however much it may resemble it, yet we may say that that window is a ray of the sun or is light by participation. And the soul is like this window, whereupon is ever beating (or, to express it better, wherein is ever dwelling) this Divine light of the Being of God according to nature, which we have described.*[90]

Mary and Joseph are like that—clean of heart. They have that purity that makes them translucent, and with the light of the Holy Spirit, they see the world *according to* God. That is why, when the Roman soldiers arrive in Nazareth to announce the news of the census, unlike their neighbors, *Joseph and Mary see God* in that decision. In this way, they teach us to have that same clarity when it comes to seeing and evaluating the events of the world. All of them are, in fact, *theophanies* for those who know how to recognize them, and so we do not have to accept the worldly interpretation of the great and small events of history because in everything we can see the hand of the Lord if we are pure of heart. This would be a beautiful request as you proceed in these Spiritual Exercises: "Lord, like Mary and Joseph, may I always see you in everything."

It is evident that, in the current context of the Church and the world, we need to reflect deeply on Augustus' edict in the provident plan of God. In recent years we have experienced scandals, pandemics, political decisions that are more than questionable—when not openly contrary to God's law—as well as turmoil within the Church. On a personal level, too, each one of us can look back on our own story—illnesses, setbacks, losses, misfortunes—have we been able to see the Lord in all this? Have we been pure in heart, or have we acted like the fellow citizens of Joseph and Mary, and spent our time complaining, heads down and pouting about what was happening?

Of all the written works of Saint John Paul II, probably the book that has impressed me the most is seldom cited: *Memory and Identity*. It was published in the same year as his death. I encourage you to read it, or reread it. It is always very helpful. The reader is amazed at both the profound knowledge the Polish Pope had of European history and the interpretations he made of it from the perspective of the Catholic faith and realist philosophy. Much of this work is devoted to providing an "answer" — as much as an answer to the mystery of evil can be given — to the question of totalitarian movements and atheistic thought that were the cause of so much pain in the twentieth century. John Paul II writes from reflection, yes, but also from the memories of those devastating years that he personally lived. In my opinion, the most admirable thing about this work is the vantage point from which the author looks out to consider the events that took place in the Old World. Wojtyla contemplates the suffering of the innocent and the evolution of history *from the vantage point of Divine Mercy.* From that privileged perspective, evil is allowed by God, mysteriously, in order that one may obtain from it an incomparably greater good. At the same time, God places a limit on that evil, so that it cannot do more harm than has been foreseen by Him for the redemption of the world in Christ. We cannot spend too much time on this lengthy teaching, but I cannot resist citing here a passage in which the Polish pope speaks of the first coming of Christ, (which, in the present moment of this retreat, we are considering)the mystery of evil, and of our dear Edith Stein, who is walking with you on this spiritual journey.

It is impossible, then, to speak of the "limit imposed upon evil" without considering the ideas contained in the passage just quoted. God himself came to save us and to deliver us from evil, and this coming of God, this "Advent" which we celebrate in such a joyful way in the weeks preceding the Nativity of the Lord, is truly redemptive. It is impossible to think of the limit placed by God himself upon the various forms of evil without reference to the mystery of Redemption.

Could the mystery of Redemption be the response to that historical evil which, in different forms, continually recurs in human affairs? Is it also the response to the evil of our own day? It can seem that the evil of concentration camps, of gas chambers, of police cruelty, of total war, and of oppressive regimes – evil which, among other things, systematically contradicts the message of the Cross - it can seem, I say, that such evil is more powerful than any good. Yet if we look more closely at the history of those peoples and nations who have endured the trial of totalitarian systems and persecutions on account of faith, we discover that this is precisely where the victorious presence of Christ's Cross is most clearly revealed. Against such a dramatic background, that presence may be even more striking. To those who are subjected to systematic evil, there remains only Christ and his Cross as a source of spiritual self-defense, as a promise of victory. Did not the sacrifice of Maximillian Kolbe in the extermination camp at Auschwitz become a sign of victory over evil? And could not the same be said of Edith Stein – that great thinker from the school of Husserl – who perished in the gas chamber of [Auschwitz-]Birkenau, thus sharing the destiny of many other sons and daughters of Israel?[91]

There is a relationship here between the plot line developed by the Pope and what we are now considering regarding the census decreed by Augustus. Human history as a whole—even in its most mundane or dark avatars—is led by the Most Holy Trinity toward Christ's redemption and his ultimate and final fullness. The obedience of Mary and Joseph teaches us this same purity of soul, which knows how to see God even in the darkest corners of history and instills the hope of knowing that we are always in good hands, for "although we walk through dark valleys, He walks with us and leads us to the green pastures of his kingdom" (Ps. 23:1-4).Perhaps you can draw from this reflection extraordinary reasons for consolation and trust in the Lord.

4. "And Joseph too went up from Galilee from the town of Nazareth to Judea, to the city of David that is called Bethlehem, because he was of the house and family of David, to be enrolled with Mary, his betrothed, who was with child" (Lk. 2:4-5).

The moment has come—let us see the Holy Family leave Nazareth. So far, everything has happened inside the little house, which has been our first composition of the place. Now, Saint Ignatius invites us to look at the path they took, which will culminate in the manger where the Virgin will lay her newborn Son on the first Christmas night, "to see with the sight of our imagination the road from Nazareth to Bethlehem considering its length and width, and if that road is flat, or if it passes through valleys or hills" (SE 112).

I write these words with great emotion. God granted me the grace to be able to walk that same route, between March 16 and 25 of 2018, crossing all of Palestine in ten days until I reached Bethlehem. I will never forget those days, during which I saw Joseph and Mary walk by my side. For that part of the trip, I made the decision to carry the Most Blessed Sacrament with me in a pyx (small round container designed to hold our Eucharistic Lord)that I always carried against my chest. Palestine is a Muslim country today and I knew that I would hardly be able to find a church where I could pray. I also wanted to take the Lord back to those places that He himself traveled with his parents on the way to Bethlehem and that he would cross so many times as an adult. Finally, I thought that, in this way, I could live the experience of Mary in the most vivid way possible, physically carrying—as she did—the presence of her Son Jesus to Bethlehem. How many have been the mercies of the Lord toward this sinner and so many graces received!

The Gospel obviously does not detail the exact itinerary of the Holy Family. However, the route that is sometimes called "the Way of the Patriarchs"—crossing Samaria from north to south—is generally accepted as the most likely option. The reason for this has to do with Mary's physical condition. Since the Virgin was in the last days of her pregnancy, it is reasonable to think that Joseph decided on the shortest and fastest way to get to his city, although this meant having to face unpleasant encounters with some of the residents of that region.

In your prayer, you must "see the people", as Saint Ignatius says (SE 114)."Consider, observe, and contemplate what they are saying" (SE 115). "Look and consider what they do, such as walking and laboring that our Lord might be born in extreme poverty" (SE 116).This meditation must be a contemplation of Mary pregnant, sitting on the donkey, of Joseph pulling on the reins of the reluctant animal, of the conversations they would have had between themselves, with other travelers, and with the natives of those barren lands.

There is a detail in a passage from Saint Ignatius that I want to present for your consideration: *"laboring that our Lord might be born in extreme poverty,"* he writes. This is impressive. For Christ, the simple little house of Joseph and Mary in Nazareth seemed "too much" as the place of his birth. The Most Holy Trinity has chosen the path of humiliation to reveal itself and the poverty of the cave of Bethlehem as the birthplace of the Son of God. The expression of Saint Ignatius calls my attention powerfully: *"laboring* to be born in extreme poverty." God *labors.* That is, he *actively* chooses to go from the extreme simplicity of Nazareth to the maximum poverty of Bethlehem. Here again, we find the opposition between evangelical wisdom and the mindset of the world. What does the world labor for? To get rich! We labor to earn, to save, to fill our coffers. What does God labor for? *To be born in extreme poverty!* In this retreat we must ask ourselves: in what attitude do we see ourselves best reflected? Do we work to live simply? Do we love poverty? Do we actively seek it out, or do we just accept it with resignation when it comes to us?

Christ, from the womb of his Mother, *wants and chooses* the poverty of Bethlehem. It is not something that randomly happens: it is *intentional, sought after, premeditated.* The correlate of this attitude of the Heart of Jesus is the absolute *abandonment* of Mary and Joseph to divine Providence. They leave behind what little they have in their house and go out into the unknown. Brave souls who willingly risk everything at the word of God, souls who go to the unknown with all their trust in the Lord. Look at yourself, as you see the Holy Family approaching Bethlehem, see if you discover those same virtues in yourself. If not, know that God wants to give them to you in these days, if you ask it of him in faith.

5. There is one last aspect of this reflection that I must ask you to meditate on. It seems very important to me that in the peace that the Holy Spirit is giving you these days, you consider it slowly and peacefully. In advance, I must add, that it is a totally countercultural aspect, and perhaps for that reason, it deserves a particularly composed consideration from you. I am referring to Mary's relationship with Joseph. I'm going to have to be a little more "speculative" in this part, but I beg you not to lose sight of the Holy Family on their way to Bethlehem. Deep down, everything springs from this meditation.

Mary lets herself be carried away by Joseph. This is how we see her now, united to her husband's destinies. Perhaps on this path from Nazareth to Bethlehem we see the role of Joseph at the head of his family illustrated more clearly than ever. Mary follows Joseph. Joseph marks the path and the direction, and his wife follows him. She follows him and lets herself be guided by him.

How should the relationship of women and men be? The current environment is so distorted that it is difficult to have a peaceful vision of what God has revealed in this regard. Our inner springs immediately coil—after all, we are children of our time and we have grown up with very specific cultural categories—and we rebel against anything that sounds like women's dependency on men. Let's face it: we have a hard time explaining this extreme because what we read in Scripture and what we tend to think—in line with modern trends—seem to be in open contradiction. We shake off this part of revelation by reacting quickly, almost instinctively, pointing out that the doctrine of the man as head of the family is the result of a very particular historical time in which woman was not fully recognized, and as a result, we must read the Gospel more in line with the current recognition of the rights of women.

In modern-day thinking, there is a streak that runs contrary to the Christian worldview and that goes back to a great extent to the revolutionary doctrines of the Enlightenment and to the philosophies of Hegel's German Idealism and Marx's later Communism. There is an element common to these systems of thought, expressed in different ways according to the schools and the accents of each one: the necessity of the dialectical movement for the progress of society. According to Hegel's teaching, later adopted—with many nuances—by Marx, conflict is at the base of personal and social development. In other words, there is an opposition between the thesis and the antithesis that is necessary because without the belligerent tension between both extremes, the new situation of synthesis could not be reached, which sublimates the preceding steps. In Communism, this antagonism is expressed by the concept of the "class struggle." From this premise, revolution is not only desirable but also essential for society to advance toward better and fairer stages. The interests of the proletarians and the bourgeoisie are *necessarily* opposed, and the outcasts of the earth must rise up against the rich classes to achieve the final harmony of social justice.

Without intending now to analyze this phenomenon in great detail, it seems to me that we see in today's society a kind of mutation that through the sexual revolution of the fifties, sixties, and seventies has largely transferred the "class struggle" to the "struggle of the sexes." The man and the woman are confronted with a dialectical relationship that has blown up the family peace. Women must claim their rights against men, who have denied them for centuries. The most preeminent feminist movement has a marked militant aspect and despises the Judeo-Christian vision of the family as alienating and deeply *macho*. From this perspective, women must also "free themselves" from the yoke that motherhood and the family have imposed on them throughout history. Have we not known women for whom their children are a burden, their husband an impediment to happiness, and their families an environment in which they feel unhappily subjugated?

In the dialectical scheme outlined, one hostile to the Christian conception of the family, "gender ideology" has made its way into the consciousness of many brothers and sisters. This is presented as the *synthesis* that sublimates and perfects the tension between the masculine (thesis)and feminine (antithesis)poles and when this point is reached, there is no longer conflict because *each one chooses what they want to be*. The human being is asexual until, in the exercise of his freedom, he chooses what today's society calls "sexual orientation." Here, sexuality and the way of living it are *exclusively* the fruit of a decision that does not accept limitations of any kind.

In the Christian view, on the other hand, sexuality is a gift that is gratefully received, not the fruit of a decision that can be made regardless of nature itself. The fact that it is a gift inevitably refers to a giver. Since postmodern thought has renounced the idea of creation and of creatures, it cannot refer to a Maker of everything, who is love. In today's world, and paraphrasing Feuerbach, man has no God other than himself (*homo homini Deus*).

Your condition as women, what is sometimes called "femininity," is a gift from God to you, your families, the Church, and the world. Your first step should be the *recognition of that gift received and the gratitude for who you are*. Your femininity is not something you "have," *it is something that you are*, that is knit into the fiber of your being.

No woman should feel ashamed of what she has received *because of the fact* that she is a woman. On the contrary, the development of your "feminine genius" should be your joy and your goal. For this, it is necessary that you understand yourself well, listening to what the Lord has manifested to you through your feminine condition and revelation. Don't let other voices confuse you or cloud your understanding of who you are as a woman. In these Spiritual Exercises, we are trying to reveal what it means in the eyes of God to fulfill the feminine vocation not in an abstract way, but by contemplating the interaction between Christ and some of the women presented to us in the Gospels. In these encounters, Jesus not only reveals his divine mystery, but also the deepest reality of your femininity. We must especially consider the life and manner of Mary as a model and the fulfillment of what it means to be a woman.

At this moment of your Spiritual Exercises, and while we contemplate Mary letting herself be carried by Joseph through the roads of Palestine, I encourage you to trust Edith Stein, who has been accompanying you since the beginning of this experience. She offers you a different model of woman—so different from the disfigured image that the current culture usually presents—and depicts another type of relationship between man and woman, a relationship directed by love and mutual respect rather than confrontation and conflict between the sexes.

Edith Stein meets several conditions that make her an ideal guide for your mission. She lived in the modern world, in cultural and religious climates similar to ours. She is one of the most perceptive philosophers of the twentieth century, and has also dealt with this matter in detail. Throughout her academic life, she suffered unfairness as a woman, yet she always acted with serenity and firmness. Edith joins her knowledge of philosophy with deep theological knowledge. She sealed her life with the supreme act of love: she died in the gas chambers of the Auschwitz concentration camp, thus sharing the destiny of her own Jewish people, of which she always considered herself a part even after her conversion. By canonizing her, the Church offers us her as a model of Christian life and her words as a sure path to holiness. Finally, she is a woman like you—a woman who, by the way, was brave, unconventional, discreet, and at the same time, endowed with an iron will when it came to following the dictates of her own conscience. For these and many other qualities, it seems to me that she is worthy of your total confidence.

Edith Stein represents one of the most prominent minds of the philosophical school of Phenomenology, which was founded by Edmund Husserl. For almost two years, she was Husserl's disciple and personal assistant, and it was he who directed her doctoral thesis on empathy. Let us remember that Edith was one of the first women to obtain a Ph.D. in Philosophy from a German university, graduating with honors (*summa cum laude*)in 1916. Despite this, as a woman she was disqualified from becoming a professor in the universities of Germany.

The great effort of Phenomenology is summed up in Husserl's expression, "to return to things themselves" (*zurück zu den Sachen selbst*). His school was, to a large extent, a colossal effort that reacts to Kant's philosophy and Hegelian Idealism, seeking to recover reality as it manifests itself in the consciousness of man. At the fulcrum of Phenomenology there is a deliberate and tenacious attempt to put aside systems or theoretical explanations and let reality itself speak. For this, Husserl uses the Greek term ἐποχή or the German word *Einklammerung* that literally means, "to put in parentheses", and with them he describes the attitude of the phenomenologist who wants to get to the essence of things. The philosopher cannot get lost in an ocean of ideas. He must reach things and make them manifest to the intellect of the man who wishes to find them. As for Kant, the *phenomenon* blocked access to reality itself (called, with nuances, *noumenon* by the philosopher of Könisberg),for Husserl the phenomenon reveals the essence of things in their singularity.

The same attitude manifests itself in the teachings of Edith Stein, whether she writes about philosophy, psychology, or theology. In fact, her conversion to the Catholic Church is largely explained by this indefatigable search for reality. The study of Phenomenology kindled in Edith the irrepressible desire for truth, which found its fulfillment in the encounter with the Lord. The German saint even said, "My yearning for the truth was already a prayer." After a long and difficult road, that personal Truth that is Christ came to her through Saint Teresa of Jesus. In the summer of 1921, while at the home of her admired friend Hedwig Conrad-Martius, she found the Carmelite saint's *Book of Life* in the family library. Eager to satisfy those longings that philosophy could not fully reach, she read the autobiography in a single night. When she finished it, exultant as a sailor who arrives in port after great storms and omens of shipwreck, she declared, "This is the truth." She had finally come home.

For the subject at hand, this attitude translates into not being carried away by the prevailing currents of thought, but allowing the truth itself to speak. To do this, Edith Stein reflects on the nature and psychological experiences of women as she lived them herself, before the filters of ideologies, fashions, or ephemeral opinions passed through. In her reflection on the soul of women, her sources are the female *ethos* itself and revelation. In this sense, Edith is mind-bogglingly honest. She writes with no other claim than to be faithful to the truth as she receives it in her faith-illuminated intelligence. She knew the words of Saint Thomas Aquinas—several of whose works she translated into German—in which the Angelic Doctor specifies the object of philosophical reflection: "The study of philosophy does not consist in knowing what the men have said, but what is the truth of things. "[92]

We cannot explore Edith Stein's work in any detail now—this is not the place or the context for it. However, I would like to strongly encourage you to read and meditate slowly on *The Collected Works of Edith Stein, Essays on Women* (Washington DC: ICS Publications 2017).This book, published by the Institute of Carmelite Studies Publications, contains her essays on womanhood. I read it for the first time when I was studying at seminary and have read it again in preparation for these meditations. I have very much enjoyed reading it again, and I think you will enjoy it even more. In particular, I recommend the essay *"The Separate Vocations of Man and Woman According to Nature and Grace."* I refer to it so that whoever wishes to do so can delve into this very important topic that determines the fate of many women and families.

* * *

Let us return to Mary and Joseph. Mary participates in her husband's life as head of the Holy Family, and so, they are making their way. They talk with each other; they love each other; they help each other with that union of hearts that is possible between two people who love each other and surrender themselves in marriage. They cross the plains of Palestine, the desert of Judah, and finally, in the distance, they see the city of Bethlehem. I well remember that moment when I too was able to see on the horizon—on a really unpleasant windy day that made the journey difficult and constantly spat sand in my eyes—the place where the Son of God was born. An indescribable emotion seized me at the moment in which George, an Arab Catholic who served as our guide, pointed his finger at the town and told us, "That's Bethlehem." I felt my heart leap in my chest. A few miles further north, the barren desert landscape abruptly ceased and gave way to rolling green hills, among which loomed a modest city. Somewhere amidst those neglected houses, *precisely there*, the Unseen was revealed as a light to the world.

Saint Joseph is hurrying to reach his town. Mary feels that the Child is about to be born and tells her husband. There, in the distance, the sun is dropping behind the mountains and very soon darkness will cover everything with its cloak. Let us accompany the Holy Family on this last leg of their journey. Something without comparison is going to happen, and with God's favor, we will silently contemplate it in the next meditation.

May the Holy Spirit lead you to intimate union with these events in your personal prayer so that you will be truly transformed by them.

15

MARY IN THE NATIVITY III

"Grant us, Lord, as we honor with joyful devotion the Nativity of your Son, that we may come to know with fullness of faith the hidden depths of this mystery and to love them ever more and more." (from the Mass at Dawn on Christmas Day).

We have been approaching, step by step, the Christmas scene. For many saints, this contemplation has been the beginning of a new way of relating to God, full of tenderness, of closeness, and of deep intimacy with him. How can we forget Saint Francis of Assisi in Greccio, creating the first creche scene—a living representation of this mystery of which he himself wanted to be a part? Or the verses of Saint John of the Cross about the birth of Jesus in Bethlehem? Or the Christmas carols of Saint Alphonsus Liguori that are still sung, and his meditations on the mystery of Christmas that are still contemplated in the world today? Or the writings of Saint Therese of the Child Jesus? Or the last thirty-five years of Saint Jerome's life in Bethlehem, doing prayer and penance, dedicated to the study of Sacred Scripture? And so many faithful who, throughout history, have learned to love in the contemplation of God made a child?

Without a doubt, one of those saints especially sensitive to the mystery of Christmas was our dear Saint Ignatius of Loyola. Some of the most tender and endearing pages of his Spiritual Exercises are dedicated to the pious observation of this gospel scene. On his pilgrimage to the Holy Land in 1523, he had the opportunity to visit the Church of the Nativity. He was so captivated by the place and the mystery that came about there, that although already ordained as a priest, he delayed celebrating Holy Mass for a whole year in the hope of being able to celebrate for the first time in Bethlehem. Since the political situation of the time did not make the voyage possible, he finally chose to celebrate his first Mass in the Roman Basilica of St. Mary Major, where the manger in which our Mother laid her newborn Son, as we read in the Gospel of Saint Luke (2:7) is preserved.

As we begin this meditation, we want to ask for the intercession of these and all the saints so that we can enter into that mystery and live these events in proximity and familiarity with the persons who were their protagonists, aware that the Holy Spirit undoes the distance that separates us from them and allows us to live these salvific events and not be simply passive spectators.

In the preceding meditation, we left Joseph and Mary

gazing at Bethlehem from the horizon. The Virgin Mother is feeling in her body the signs that indicate the imminent arrival of her Son, and Joseph quickens his pace. Finally, the time has come. But where will he find a place for his wife? No one in his family lives there anymore and he has no acquaintances who can help him. I can't imagine the feeling of helplessness Joseph experienced at that moment. A man who cannot provide for his family, particularly in times of greatest need, experiences immense pain, because he is acutely aware of being responsible for those he loves the most.

1. *God is rejected.* Until then, Christ has only received affection from men through his parents. First Mary, and then Joseph, gratefully welcomed the coming of the incarnate Son of God and have been loving him ardently during her pregnancy. From his birth, the Lord is going to be exposed to the world of men, to the response of every human being that comes into existence.

As Christian tradition has done since the beginning, it is important to contemplate the mystery of the birth of Christ with an eye on his Passion and Death on the Cross. In fact, the child who is about to be born has come to be offered on the altar of sacrifice. It is his destiny, his mission, and the goal of his life on earth. The Father, through the work of the Holy Spirit, has given the Word a body in order to be the victim of expiation for our sins. The Lord has lovingly embraced, as we have seen, that saving will, for he loves his Father and those whom he already considers his brethren. The Word is not just one like us. He is truly one of us.

On the nights of Christmas and Holy Thursday, the light

of God's love shines with a special intensity. Both nights are also, however, moments of man's greatest rejection of the divine Gift. This is how the Lord himself expresses it with sadness, "light came into the world and men preferred darkness to light" (Jn. 3:19).Faced with these great signs of God's redemptive love, our reply is a resounding "We don't want you with us."

This aspect is expressly mentioned in the three Gospels that tell us about the childhood of Jesus. Therefore, it is an emphasis that we cannot ignore: this is an important teaching. Saint Matthew tells us that when the Magi from the East announced the news of the Messiah's birth, "King Herod was troubled and all Jerusalem with him" (Mt. 2:3). Days later, the monarch will order the slaughter of the Holy Innocents to end the life of that Messiah who has just been born and whose coming threatens—this poor devil believes—his power in the world.

For his part, in his very brief prologue, Saint John mentions—not once or twice, but three times—this rejection of the Person of Jesus Christ. He does it using a more poetic language, moving away from the historical, concrete details to make statements of a more general and, therefore, perhaps more forceful nature:

- "The light shines in the darkness, but the darkness did not welcome it" (1:5).
- "The Word was in the world, and the world was made by it, but the world did not know it" (1:10).
- "He came to his own, and his own received him not" (1:11).

Finally, Saint Luke describes the particular circumstance of that first Christmas night: the moment in which Mary and Joseph had the need to seek refuge in a stable of animals "because there was no room for them in the inn" (Lk. 2:7). God comes to save us and give us eternal life, and we have no place for Him.

This relationship between Bethlehem and Calvary is also pointed out by Saint Ignatius in this meditation of the Exercises: "Look and consider what they are doing, as going on a journey and laboring, that the Lord may be born in the greatest poverty, and as a termination of so many labors – of hunger, of thirst, of heat and of cold, of injuries and affronts – that He may die on the cross; and all this for me" (SE 116). All this, for me... *For me...*

Aren't the evangelists talking here too, on another level of meaning, about your own story? Do you not recognize yourself in some of these verses? Have you, too, not been Herod and have you not feared that God's plan would come to ruin your personal projects? Has not the Lord tried so many times to enter your life and you have not let him in? How many times have you chosen darkness instead of divine light? Before the love of the God that is to be born for us, we should be shaken by our own ingratitude and meanness. How many wasted graces! How many times has God knocked on our hearts (Rev. 3:20)and found the doors closed! So much light the Most Holy Trinity wanted to shed on our souls, and so much have we loved our darkness! How much love has the Lord shown us and what a mediocre response we have given Him!

When thinking about Christmas, we must always bear in mind this contrast between divine mercy and sin, life and death, light and darkness, the gift that is the Child Jesus and the contempt for that gift whose acceptance would oblige us to change our life. We must keep this contrast in mind because it will help us enter more deeply into God's love for us. "God so loved the world ..." (Jn. 3:16).

2. *The experience of the Heart of Mary.* Joseph and Mary enter Bethlehem. Joseph knocks on so many doors, but no one receives them. Many people have come on those days to register and everything is full. From the street, you can hear the revelry of those who celebrate the arrival of visitors and guests. Songs can be heard, the laughter of men animated by the wine, conversations inside the houses and lodgings. There is a crowd around the many tables that are set up to receive strangers and guests; food and drink flow generously; families celebrate reunions and happy gatherings.

"I was a stranger, and you did not welcome me" (Mt. 25:43). This is how the Lord speaks later in the Gospel, with words that he perhaps uttered in reference to his first coming. Can we blame those people for not welcoming the young couple who begged for lodging at the doors of their homes? It would have been different if they had known who the unborn child was, but they did not know. Only faith can help us discover the presence of Christ in those who ask us for help. Indeed, if the same Jesus who lived in the womb of Mary considers as done to himself what we do to others (Mt. 25:45), then every time we have turned our back on a person in need who has asked for help, we have acted in the same way as those people long ago in Bethlehem. In some sense, we are even more guilty than they, because in their case they acted out of ignorance, but we, who have already

266

been warned by the Master's teaching, dare to act as they did then.

"My wife is with child... For charity... Wouldn't you have something for us, just for tonight?"

"No, Joseph: there is nothing for you. You are poor strangers that nobody cares about."

We have deprived this scene of all its rawness, but each door that was closed that night is the cause of unspeakable pain for Mary: "My son, are you not going to have a corner to be born in? Why did you take us out of Nazareth to bring us into this situation? What will become of us today? What are you looking for with this? Where is the house where they will let us stay the night?" There is a weight in the Heart of Mary, an enormous suffering, in these moments. As we have already mentioned, she is a pilgrim in faith and answers are not given to her beforehand. She, like us, often does not understand God's plan and must adapt to it step by step, in the darkness of faith, which is a night of the spirit.

This weight in the Heart of Mary is expressly revealed to us in the subsequent episode of the loss of Jesus in the Temple (Lk. 2: 41-52). There, the Virgin confesses that they had been searching for her Son for three days "in anguish." The situation in Bethlehem is no better. Mary feels that her Son is no longer waiting, and they do not have even a shadow in which to take shelter. Let's take a good look: it is the darkness that precedes the most beautiful light! Of course, God has a plan—which they do not understand now—and this suffering is already the prelude to the joy that is about to come.

3. *Composition of place: the stable of Bethlehem.* In a last

attempt to find accommodations, someone must have told Joseph about a shed where the animals are watered. "You have to get away a bit," they would say, "but the cave will at least give you shelter and protect you from the cold. No one will bother you there." Imagine the moment when Saint Joseph realized that Jesus was going to have to be born *there*. He could no longer continue searching. The time has come for Mary (Lk. 2:6)and they must prepare for the child to be born. Exhausted—I can almost see tears of helplessness creeping from his eyes—he pulls on the reins of the animal carrying Mary and heads for the stable, following the directions he has received. "I could not find anything, my son... Forgive me, Jesus."

A short distance away, Mary and Joseph *see* the stable. The cave that we picture today with a smiling ox and mule, duly illuminated and pleasant—but that, in reality, was a cold, shabby, and smelly stable. The holy couple must have experienced in the first contemplation of the stable, an interior storm impossible to verbalize. Now, visualize the place where your Savior will be born.

This is the place that men have left for God to be born, but there is an even more overwhelming thought than this: *this is the place that God has chosen to be born among us.* Let us remember what Saint Ignatius told us in the preceding meditation: the Lord has "labored" to be born in the greatest poverty. His birth in the stable is not an unforeseen last-minute circumstance, a loose end that, unexpectedly, has come out the opposite of what he had designed in his Providence. No, of all the places and times on Earth, God wanted to be born *precisely here.*

For Mary, the contemplation of the stable has the tenor of

a true revelation, as it happens in those stories in which the plot is resolved only at the very end. *There* she understands everything. "*This* is precisely what my Son has come looking for. *This* has been the desire of his Heart. He took us out of Nazareth to bring us *here*. And for me... He has taken everything from me... and has left me *with Him alone*." We must first arrive at that stripping away of everything before Christ is born in our life. As we have already said, the abandonment and humiliation of the manger is also the abandonment and humiliation of the Cross. The misery of Bethlehem is the poverty of Golgotha. The nakedness of the Child Jesus is also the exposition and derision of the crucified Christ.

The nativity scene in Bethlehem wonderfully represents the Heart of Mary and the end of a spiritual journey that we too are called to travel. Christ is born *only* in the soul that renounces and sacrifices *everything* for him (Phil. 3:8). The stable is absolute simplicity; the stripping of what we love most; the poverty of those who have *nothing* and in that detachment find *everything*. It is the field where a treasure is hidden that is only obtained when we sell what we have to acquire it (Mt. 13:44).For you who are in these exercises, it is the representation of the emptiness that you must reach for Christ to be born in your lives. Jesus is waiting for you to let go of *everything* before entering your heart. He doesn't want you to save anything for him. He wants you to have no other wealth than Him. Are you willing to do that? Are you willing *now* to lose everything in exchange for Jesus being born in you? Do you or do you not trust Him?

Mary, we said, in that gaze pierced by faith, receives the revelation and the meaning of what has happened and embraces it as Jesus does. Joseph also welcomes this mystery from his wife. They both accept that will and the darkness ends for them.

The teaching of this path could be summarized with the well-known expression of Saint Rafael María Arnaiz Barón: "God alone!"

4. *The poverty and simplicity of Bethlehem.* The whole mystery of Christmas is a sublime lesson in gospel simplicity and austerity. "Christ, being rich, became poor for you, to enrich you with his poverty" (2 Cor. 8:9). We meet again with Nicholas of Cusa's "coincidence of opposites": the rich God is born poor. The Eternal enters time. The Invisible is seen in this child. The Mighty One assumes the weakness of a newborn. He who cannot be contained by any creature is enclosed in the tiny body of a newborn baby.

In this tapestry of paradox, God has chosen the most suitable sign to show and express the richness of his love for man. If we think about it, any other form that had been chosen, any adornment prepared for the occasion, would have been misguided and insufficient. On the contrary, in that absolute helplessness the infinity of divine love, the commitment that the Lord has assumed with us by becoming man is best understood.

It would not hurt if, in the Exercises, we take a few moments to consider how we relate to the world around us, and particularly to our property. Poverty is the availability, speed, and readiness to put oneself at the service of God. Perhaps a simple anecdote will illustrate what I want to say: Saint Ignatius informed Saint Francis Xavier of his departure for the Indies on the eve of his departure. As is known, Loyola had not chosen the Navarrese to be one of the first Jesuit missionaries that John III, King of Portugal, had requested for his territories in Asia. However, one of the two chosen priests, Nicolás Bobadilla, fell ill unexpectedly and could not reach Rome in time—oh, God's inscrutable Providence!—so Saint Ignatius could only advise Francis the day before departure, at the last moment. It was March 14, 1540. Saint Francis Xavier's answer is wonderful in its simplicity, "Here I am, Father, I am ready." And so, Francis left carrying only his cassock, a crucifix, and a couple of books, one of them his breviary. Light luggage for one who would never return!

In Bethlehem the Christian sense of poverty is learned. Voluntary poverty is an expression of love. So it was in the case of Christ. It is also an expression of love for men. Saint John Bosco had as his apostolic motto and a reflection of his priestly zeal this maxim: *"Da mihi animas, Domine, caetera tolle* (Give me souls, Lord, and take away the rest)."Jesus must have said something similar when he entered the world and was born in Bethlehem: "Give me souls, Father, and take away the rest." The poverty of the stable expresses the thirst of the Heart of Christ to save the world. May God grant us, in today's Church, a handful of people whose sole objective, in imitation of Jesus Christ, is the salvation of their brethren! Is that also your objective?

5. *The silence of Bethlehem.* "For when peaceful stillness encompassed everything and the night in its swift course was half spent, your all-powerful word from heaven's royal throne leapt into the doomed land" (Wis. 18:14).During the second Sunday of Christmas, the Church boldly applies this

verse from the Book of Wisdom to the birth in the flesh of the Son of God in her liturgy. In the Old Testament, these words refer directly to the deliverance of Israel from Egypt. We know, however, that this was a prefiguring of what was yet to come. It is at Christmas that true hope for man is born, when the only Life that can save those who receive it by faith comes down to earth.

In the houses of the City of David, the clamoring and the noise of men can be heard. In the cave of Bethlehem … there only dwells silence. As we have already spoken about this topic at the beginning of our retreat, I will not elaborate on it further here. What was then a reflection in Bethlehem becomes a *contemplation*. The Nativity finds its possibility in silence. Jesus flees from noise and commotion to be born in that stillness. This continues to be his *modus operandi*: He is neither born nor found in the clamor, but rather in recollection. Saints and spiritual people of all ages have perfectly understood and assimilated this great lesson, perhaps the most important in our life of faith.

Do you love silence? Do you find it in your daily living? Do you withdraw like Joseph and Mary so that the Word can be born and dwell in your heart?

6. *The birth of Christ.* "*Caro cardo salutis* (The flesh is the hinge of salvation)." (Tertullian)The time has come to see Jesus born. I will not even attempt a description of the scene because that is your task, moved by the grace of the Holy Spirit. Nor did the evangelists find a way to relate this extraordinary moment. What pen would have found the right words to describe the birth of God among men? If we had been asked to narrate this unique event, what

would we humans have done? We would most certainly have called upon the best writers in history and given incredible and exuberant descriptions of the Bethlehem scene. In fact, we would have arranged everything for God differently: we would not have chosen a stable, nor would the subdued style of the gospel narrative have been our preference.

With the following simplicity—insulting and almost of-fensive to our way of doing things—God himself has chosen the way to tell us about his birth: "While they were there, the time came for her to have her child, and she gave birth to her firstborn son. She wrapped him in swaddling clothes and laid him in a manger, because there was no room for them in the inn" (Lk. 2:6-7).Can the event be described more simply?

Saint Ignatius writes at this moment of his Exercises that we must become a poor creature and a wretch of an unworthy slave, "looking at them, contemplating them, and serving them in their needs, as if I found myself present, with all possible respect and reverence" (SE 114).Yes, let us make ourselves present at this moment because, really, in the Heart of the Child Jesus, *we were there*, in that cave. Jesus sees you and loves you in Bethlehem. Live with Him, and with Joseph and Mary; let your eyes and soul be filled with the tenderness, love, and beauty of that moment in which God, for the first time, could be contemplated, felt, heard, even smelled, by men.

*What was from the beginning, what we have heard,
what we have seen with our eyes, what we looked
upon and touched with our hands concerns the Word
of life for the life was made visible; we have seen it*

*and testify to it and proclaim to you the eternal life
that was with the Father and was made visible to
us—what we have seen and heard we proclaim now
to you, so that you too may have fellowship with us;
for our fellowship is with the Father and with his Son,
Jesus Christ. We are writing this so that our joy may
be complete (1 Jn. 1:1-4).*

I remember a professor at the Seminary, Father Julián Carrón, insisting on this aspect of the mystery of Christmas and warning us to be on guard against other well-intentioned explanations: be very careful not to stay with *ideas* and lose sight of the *concreteness* of this mystery. One can make many reflections about the birth of Jesus: love, poverty, joy, innocence, to name a few. The attention, however, must be fixed on the matter, on the tangibility, on the tender body of that child who looks out into the world on this precious night. "The *flesh*. What matters here is the *flesh*," said this priest, striking the palm of one hand with the back of the other so that the sound was amplified throughout the university classroom. That perspective seems totally necessary to me.

Tertullian wrote that "the flesh is the hinge of salvation."[93] It is the most important word in Catholic theology and spirituality! Because at the center of everything is Christ, and when we say Christ, we mean "the *Incarnate* Word." That flesh says it all: love, fidelity, commitment, redemption, life, exaltation, humanity, sacrifice, joy, eternity. And, in the exercises, I have to experience that materiality in my hands, in my ears, in my eyes, in my heart. The body of that Child is the remedy for all my ills. The body of that Child is the solution to all my problems. The body of that Child is the path that God has traced for me to find eternal life.

God has become flesh. He has become a child *for me*. What ought I to do for Him?

7. *Bethlehem and the Eucharist*. All of the above would be somewhat contradictory if, in some way, we did not have access today to that materiality that is at the center of all redemptive work and, specifically, of this mystery of Christmas. Because if we become strong in the centrality of the *flesh* and then resign ourselves to having to look at it nostalgically from afar, the time that has elapsed since then would block our possibility of coming into contact with the humanity of the Son of God. Let's say it bluntly: the two millennia that separate us from the night of Bethlehem are too long a distance, and that distance ends up erasing the traces of Jesus Christ like the ocean erases the footprints that someone has left on the beach. So how can we go back to Him?

I will put it another way: God has become flesh *for me to touch*. I—this person who lives here, two thousand years after He did—need to touch Christ *today* in the concrete reality of his flesh. God has become man *so that I can embrace him, contemplate him, listen to him*. That is to say, either the flesh of Christ makes sense for my real life—the only one I have, this one, at this moment—or it is not the true meaning of my existence at all.

It is here that we must direct our gaze towards the Eucharist, because the Lord has given us *that flesh* in the Blessed Sacrament of the Altar. He has given it to us as a vehicle of grace and as the culmination of our deepest longings. We eat it, we swallow it, we consume it because the Lord has wished it to be so: "I say to you, unless you eat the flesh of the Son of Man and drink his blood, you do not have life within you" (Jn. 6:53).

Bethlehem and the Eucharist are the same mystery: the Child who is born in the manger is the same one who awaits us in the tabernacle. The poverty of the manger where Jesus was born is reflected in the simplicity of the Eucharistic species under which the Lord is born at each Holy Mass. The defenselessness of the Child Jesus is the same to which he has voluntarily exposed himself in the Blessed Sacrament of the Altar.

The gospel accounts suggest this relationship with the Eucharist. Already the name of Bethlehem evokes this mystery: as we know, etymologically the word means "house of bread." In the story of the Epiphany, the Magi, prostrating themselves, worship Christ. It is a gesture and an expression that the people of God have repeated since then in Holy Mass, before all the tabernacles of all the churches on Earth.

Above all, we have the gesture of Mary in Bethlehem placing her Son in the manger. I remember Father Mendizábal calling attention to this detail.[94] It is as if by doing this she were giving us her Son, who is certainly hers, but who also belongs to every man who comes to this world. The Virgin offers him from the first moment, as she offered herself to the will of the heavenly Father. She gives him to you generously, without any stain of possessiveness, without wanting to monopolize Jesus exclusively for herself. She lays him down in the manger and, there, Mary becomes the first person to adore the Mystery of the Incarnate Word. Thus, with that humble spirit of openness, of generosity, of awe, marveling at the Mystery that she can finally see with her own eyes, *Mary adores Christ.* In the following considerations we will try to accompany this silent and fervent adoration of our Mother on the first night of Christmas, but first I would like to take a few words from Saint Alphonsus Liguori, linking this scene with the sacramental presence of Jesus in the Most Holy Eucharist.

> *St. Augustine says that it was precisely for this reason that when he was born Jesus Christ wanted to be placed in a manger where animals find food. He did this to make us understand that He had become man also to become our food. "In the manger, where the animals find pasture, he allowed his body to be placed to manifest that his own body would be the eternal food of mortals." He is born daily in the Blessed Sacrament through the priests and in the Consecration. The altar is the manger and there we go to feed on his flesh. Maybe some would like to hold the Holy Child in their arms, as did St. Simeon, but when we receive communion, faith teaches us that not only in our arms, but in our hearts, is the same Jesus who lay in the manger of Bethlehem. He was born to give himself completely to us: "for a child is born to us, a son is given to us (Is. 9:5)."*[95]

8. *Flesh of Jesus, flesh of Mary.* Our path ends within the soul of the Virgin. However, as part of God's own pedagogy, in faith we must first move from the visible to the invisible, from the outer to the inner, from the sign to the deepest reality.

The first thing that Mary contemplates in Bethlehem is the flesh of that little body that we are also seeing in our meditation of this mystery. She wraps her Son in swaddling clothes, but even more closely, *Jesus is wrapped in the flesh that Mary has given him.* In his treatise *On the Mysteries*, speaking of the Eucharist, the great Saint Ambrose of Milan has these words: "what we make present is that body born of a virgin."[96] That flesh that surrounds the Word of God is Mary's flesh! That connects mother and child with ties that we will never be able to unravel.

In the Spiritual Diary of Saint Ignatius, this experience is recollected: the holy founder saw in the Body of Christ during Holy Mass the flesh of Our Lady. The text says:

> *"While preparing the altar, after I had vested, and during Mass, I experienced great interior impulses and wept very copiously and intensely, sobbing violently. Often I could not speak. The same continued after Mass. During much of this time, before, during and after Mass, I felt and saw clearly that Our Lady was very propitious, pleading before the Father. Indeed, during the prayers to the Father and the Son, and at His consecration, I could not but feel or see her, as though she were part or rather portal of the great grace that I could feel in my spirit. At the consecration she showed that her own flesh was in that of her Son with so many intuitions that they could not be written."*[97]

These words from his private diary allow us to take a glimpse in the way a saint *enters* Holy Mass. Sometimes we wonder why we do not leave the Eucharistic celebration transformed by the fire of the Holy Spirit, who is given to us in Holy Communion. I don't know, it is probably because we are not generous in our offering to the Lord and we do not live the mystery with the hearts of the saints. Saint Ignatius is sometimes described as a cold, serious, rigid, inflexible soldier. The portrait that his diary gives us, tells us exactly the opposite: emotion pierced him at each Mass; he crumbled into tears every time he prepared to celebrate it. He did not stop sobbing throughout the Holy Sacrifice. He lost his speech due to the experience that he had in the Eucharistic presence. He was silent for hours after having received the Body of his Lord sacramentally. Thus, God gave him a very special insight into this reality: the flesh of Mary was "in that of her Son." The expression, in old Castilian Spanish, has a special force: her flesh *in* the flesh of Jesus.

Therefore, in Bethlehem Mary sees *her* flesh for the first time "in that of her Son." No child has physically resembled his mother more than Jesus resembled Mary. Children are always the result of the fusion of genetic material from a man and a woman. In all of us there is a singular and unique blend received from our parents and yet, how much children sometimes resemble *one* of their parents! I, for example, have come out more physically similar to my mother. The differences are more apparent now, but when I was little, the resemblance was truly uncanny. When I was about eight or ten years old, I was looking around my grandparents' house and found a black and white photograph of two girls playing on the floor. The photo was hanging on a dark wall and I had never noticed it before. I was impressed to see it because one of those girls was the same age as I was—year above, year below—and her face... it was the same as mine! At first, in my surprise, I was dumbfounded, thinking something along these lines: "What am I doing in an old photograph that was taken before I was born?" The face was *exactly* like mine! It was me! Obviously, I didn't need anyone to tell me who that girl was because her image was written on my face.

In the case of Jesus Christ, his generation took place by the work of the Holy Spirit. Therefore, there was no male intervention. We cannot understand the *how* of this miracle, but all the genetic contribution that the Lord received from a human person, He received from his Most Blessed Mother. Exceptionally, in the DNA of Jesus Christ there is no "mixture" of a human father and mother who each contributed an equal genetic endowment for the gestation of this child. Saint Joseph is not the biological father of Jesus. For this reason, if a son resembles one of his parents even having received genetic mixture from both, how much more would he, who became a man through the intervention of the Holy Spirit and the exclusive biological contribution of his mother, resemble Mary! Joseph probably said to her at some point: "Mary, he's just like you..."

Mary sees "her flesh in that of Jesus" and prostrates herself before the mystery of a God who, in his madness of love for men, has reached this abasement. Because, let's not forget, Mary and Joseph understand who it is that they hold in their arms. Yet He is so... so human! The Incarnation is a mystery that, even in its slightest details, leads us to unconditional and irreversible surrender to the Lord. The humility of God!

If Mary was the first to adore her Son, Joseph was the first to contemplate the face of Jesus, while helping his wife in labor. If Saint Ignatius saw the flesh of Mary in that of Jesus, what can we say here of Saint Joseph? The carpenter of Nazareth immediately fell in love with that Child, the most beautiful, the most holy, the most innocent. He fell in love with that Child, too, because he saw his wife in the physical features of the baby. I imagine him contemplating both, one next to the other, while they slept and rested: the eyes are those of Mary; the mouth, outlined like that of his wife; the color of the skin, the hair with which He was born, his gestures, everything in the child is a reflection of his Mother. They almost seem to breathe at the same rate. The Mother made the Son, but the Son first made the Mother in order to be what he already is: the most beautiful of men (Ps. 44:3). As Saint Anselm writes: "Lady, full and overflowing with grace, all creation receives new life from your abundance. Virgin, blessed above all creatures, through your blessing all creation is blessed, not only creation from its Creator, but the Creator himself has been blessed by creation."[98]

9. *In the Heart of Mary.* "Mary kept these things and pondered them in her heart" (Lk. 2:19).Today we want to enter the heart that preserves all those memories and feelings. Our journey concludes in the Heart of Mary, asking her to share with us some of the affections she experienced on that first night when she was able to embrace her Son, Jesus. I invite you to put yourself in the presence of God and search in the silence of your spirit.

Something changed forever in her woman's soul that day. Mary will not love God in the same way from then on: reverence before the infinite majesty of Yahweh will always be utmost, but nevertheless, the proximity and closeness that springs from this night, brings the Lord closer to her Heart with the deepest intimacy that the Creator can ever have with any creature.

We have quoted St. Edith Stein previously to say that the experience of motherhood changes a woman's heart not only in terms of her relationship with her child, but also in dealing with anyone she meets thereafter. The woman who has become a mother will always love everyone as a mother-woman.

When I invited you to enter the Heart of Mary and experience her feelings, I said it fully conscious of taking this affirmation to its final con sequence. Therefore, now I encourage you to *ask Mary to share in her maternal affections towards Jesus.* See the Lord with her mother's eyes. Love him with her motherly heart. Undo the distance that separates you from God with the touch of his skin and the caresses of your soul. Do not settle for loving Jesus *like* Mary: love him *in* Mary. *Be mothers of Jesus in Mary and love him as your son.* Do not be surprised by the audacity of this statement: was it not He who said that it was his mother who listens to the Word of God and practices it (Lk. 8:21)?

What happens to Mary today? Above all, as it happens to all mothers, suddenly *all of her emotional life is focused on her Son*, who is also the Son of God. All the love that she is capable of *is fixed forever* on Jesus. The world becomes a very small place in which there is no one but Joseph, and, mainly, Jesus. The Virgin looks at her baby, and in that contemplation the image of her Son is engraved in the depths of her soul forever. In the young man who will live with her in Nazareth, Mary will always see the face of this Child. In the prophet of Galilee who will be acclaimed by crowds, she will always discover her little one. In the man who will be crushed for our sins and whose face will be disfigured by blows and wounds, Mary will always find her Child of Bethlehem. In the radiance of the risen Christ, the Virgin will recover the light of the star that today illuminates the night of his birth.

In the cave of Bethlehem, Mary discovers God as she has never worshiped him before. On the straw of the manger, she contemplates him in his extreme helplessness. How it would overwhelm her to see her Son and God so vulnerable! He is at the mercy of the cold, the wind, abandonment, and contempt. Had the Lord chosen to appear gloriously, with fanfare, he would have drawn the attention of all and aroused the fear and admiration of men. Instead, he has chosen the most humble and silent entrance. Inscrutable wisdom of God! How much it costs us to learn your ways!

What will become of you, my Jesus? What will happen to you from now on? My son, tonight I want to make only one plea: may you never lack souls who love you. May you never be alone, you who have come to save us all. May you always find hearts full of love for you who loves us so much. May there always be someone who loves you the way I love you. May you never lack arms that receive you, nor hands that caress you, nor eyes that contemplate you with affection. My son, flesh of my flesh, heart of my heart, life of my life: let me be by your side and serve you. Fulfill this wish for your mother: may souls who burn, like fires ablaze, always shine in this world in love for you. May they always give you warmth so that you are never cold.

The echo of these words reach you in this retreat, and like waves that melt on the shore of your souls, the affections of the Heart of Mary also reach out. Love Jesus with her maternal love. Ask God that all your capacity to love be directed, like that of Mary, towards Christ. Love from now on everything and everyone from Jesus, in Jesus and in respect to Jesus. See the face of the Lord, as if he were your Son, in all the men you meet. Let the Heart of Mary and these exercises be the place of your metamorphosis. From here on become a woman made in the image of the Virgin with her way of relating to God and the world.

10. *The joy of Christmas.* I have always said that the image of Mary in the stable of Bethlehem is the most complete image of Christian happiness. No one has ever been as happy as Mary was on that first Christmas night. She had nothing, and, at the same time, she possessed everything. If in Bethlehem we learn the lesson of poverty, of humility, of silence, of the Cross that is transformed by love, here we also find the most complete teaching about joy.

Little by little, this life is going to take away almost everything. It will take away the people we love. We will lose the strength of youth; the beauty of our spring will end in the decrepitude of the winter of our old age; dreams and projects for the future will be replaced by an existence full of memories and increasingly close to its necessary outcome. The iron health of our youth will give way to illnesses, ailments, and hopeless diagnoses; the stable of our body will collapse almost without realizing it, and one day, it will finally fall apart completely. This is not a gloomy or exaggerated prophecy: *all this is going to happen to you.* What will we have in the end? Looking at Mary at the manger we find the answer: *Jesus.* "Neither death, nor life, nor angels, nor principalities, nor present things, nor future things, nor powers, nor height, nor depth, nor any other creature will be able to separate us from the love of God in Christ Jesus our Lord" (Rm. 8:38-39).

Mary holds in her arms all the joy of heaven, all the glory of Paradise, all the bliss of the angels and the saints. And she knows that *no one will be able to separate her from him anymore.*

In Christian life, we have to carry out this *metanoia.* Obviously, as we have already discussed, we can find joy in created realities when we enjoy them according to God's plan. But if we do so, *according to God*, we will never put our hearts into them. This will always belong to the Lord and it will be He who will fill us with a happiness that does not disappoint and never ends. That is the pilgrimage that we all have to make while we live: to pluck and detach the soul from this world in order to place it completely—without fissures, without fragmentation, whole and complete, like that of Mary—in the Lord.

On this path toward our happiness and fullness in Christ, may we never lack the maternal presence of she who first and best welcomed him, received him, and served him with fidelity and dedication.

16

THE HEALING OF THE HEMORRHAGIC WOMAN AND THE RESURRECTION OF THE DAUGHTER OF JAIRUS

DAY 6 (MORNING) - THIRTEENTH MEDITATION - THE GIFT OF A LIVING FAITH

"O God, grant that we may constantly ponder in our hearts the mysteries of your salvation and faithfully express them in what we do." (from the prayer in memory of Saint Peter Chrysologus, July 30)

We are taking steps along the path of these Spiritual Exercises in our gradual assimilation of the mystery of Christ. In these days the Lord wants to draw closer to you and accomplish an authentic transformation that we can call a true miracle—both because it is beyond our own strength and because only God's grace can accomplish it in us.

Understand well what I am going to say. It is more "difficult" for the Lord to work our *metanoia* in this retreat than it was for him to create the world. Bear with me: At the origin of the universe, God did not have to overcome any resistance. Certainly, it is an extraordinary marvel and we are amazed at the magnitude of that portentous work, but for divine Omnipotence, bringing a world into existence does not in fact represent difficulty. Indeed, for One who can do everything, there is no more or less "difficult" for the simple reason that everything is within his power.

However, the work of conversion (which St. Paul describes in 2 Cor 5:17 as "new creation") requires the sinner's acquiescence. In this respect, God "has his hands tied." This is mindboggling! He needs us to *cooperate* so that it can happen. If we do not want to, if we refuse to do so, if we reject the love that the Lord pours out on us, not even with all his omnipotence could God achieve our change of heart. It is the mystery of human freedom, which the Lord—who is always a gentleman—wishes to respect until the very end. "*Qui creavit te sine te, non salvabit te sine te* (He who created you without you will not save you without you)," wrote Saint Augustine.[99]

Therefore, the fruit of this retreat is, on one hand, miraculous, but on the other, uncertain—even disturbing—inasmuch as it is far from assured. *It depends on you as much as on God.* He will certainly do his part. Are you willing to collaborate with Him?

1. The access door to that wonderful world in which miracles can be performed is *faith.* "God is always almighty," the Curé

of Ars once told his sister. "He can at all times work miracles and he would work them now as in the days of old were it not that faith is wanting."

If I asked everyone here if you have faith, perhaps all of you would answer in the affirmative. However, I tell you that, generally speaking, we do not have faith. Obviously, it depends on what we mean by this. Saint Thomas Aquinas speaks of three different dimensions in acts of faith: *credere Deum, credere Deo and credere in Deum.*[100]

With *credere Deum*, God is expressed as the *object* of our belief. Perhaps it could be translated as "belief in God,", or belief that God exists. When people ask, "Do you believe in God?" They are moving at this level, which is at the base of the pyramid of faith. "Do you think there is a God? Do you think God is real?" I will take for granted that we have all reached this stage, otherwise you would not be on this retreat. However, we are still in a stage of very emergent faith, unable to work the miracle that we are seeking. We have to keep pressing forward.

The second of the expressions, *credere Deo,* has God as the *subject* of our belief. We "believe God," and emphasize that God is someone worthy of our trust and that we accept what He communicates to us. When someone asks us, "Do you believe me?" he is obviously not meaning "Do you think I exist?" What is being investigated here is *confidence.* He is really asking, "Do you believe I am worthy of your trust?" I also want to think that all of us here have reached this point. We believe what God has told us in Revelation. We know that He is true and that what He has given us is therefore true. We accept, in the response of faith, the whole of Revelation, by the authority of God that He can neither err nor mislead us.

Finally, there is a meaning more vital and existential: *credere in Deum*. We could translate it as "entrusting ourselves to God," putting ourselves in his hands, surrendering ourselves to him in love. It is the response of the person who leaps into the void and offers himself to the Lord absolutely and unconditionally. It is here that we find "something more" than faith—there is also love. As Saint Augustine writes in one of his sermons: "*Credere in illum [est] diligere illum* (To believe in Christ is to love him)."[101]

These Latin words —*credere in Deum*— express a movement, the preposition *in* followed by an accusative word that indicates the term towards which the subject of the statement is directed. Therefore, it has an eminently personal dimension. The ultimate goal of faith is not to simply accept what the Lord tells us, but a *personal* union with God himself. "*Fidei finis non potest esse nisi Deus.*"[102]

This is where the distances between some believers and others widen, because not all of us advance towards the Lord with the same intensity or speed. We do not all love God with equal passion. Some crawl along the path of Christian life, others fly.

In these Spiritual Exercises, we have to ask to believe again as we once did, in order to go further. We have to become children again so that the doors of the miracles that we have come to seek in this retreat are opened to us. In the Letter to the Romans (1:17), St. Paul says we must pass "from faith to faith." You must progress to the last stage —*credere in Deum*— and, once there, grow more and more in love and trust until you become like trees planted by the stream, always green and bearing fruit in due season (Jer. 17:8; Mt.

7:17).

Let's put it this way. In each of you *there is a little girl that Jesus has come to revive.* He is walking toward you to awaken the little girl that sleeps in your woman's soul. God needs women with the hearts of girls: innocent, happy, simple as doves, bold in a faith that is capable of conquering the world. All the success of this experience depends on you allowing Christ to enter the innermost room of your spirit to work this miracle. Let Jesus give you back the girl that dwells dormant within you!

We are going to see this aspect of faith and spiritual childhood in a very beautiful passage from Sacred Scripture that has two women as its protagonists: one of them, sick and suffering; another, a child in agony who later dies, but comes to life through the action of Christ, who touches her and restores her to the world of the living.

Today we are going to consider three episodes in the public life of Jesus. The last will in fact serve as a hinge between these meditations and the consideration of the Lord's Passion that will occupy us all day tomorrow. Obviously, we do not have time to dwell on each episode of the Lord's ministry: not even those who do a month-long retreat could cover such an extensive subject. This is a lifelong task, and we will never give up the task. The Mystery of Christ is unfathomable. Let's consider these accounts with calm and peace of mind.

2. With Saint Ignatius - I will never tire of repeating it - we ask for the grace that our whole life—"intentions, actions, and operations" (SE 46)—beordered in the service of God and the humble and joyful fulfillment of his will in us. We already know that this God is not distant and disengaged

from us: He is the God who draws near to me in Jesus Christ, who expresses himself to me in the Holy Spirit, who speaks to me and wants to make a journey with me. Moreover, in the contemplation of the public life of Jesus that occupies us now, we ask as a particular grace that "internal knowledge of Jesus Christ, who through me has become man, so that I may love him more and follow him" (SE 104).

External knowledge of someone does not imply a relationship with that person: I can know *things* about someone else's life without there being a friendship between the two of us. I can know someone's name, their physical appearance, what country they come from, what their profession is, and so on. We have *information*, data that helps us to form an image of people. Actually, as far as knowledge of that person is concerned, we are still, so to speak, in the top crust, the upper shell, and if that is all we have, we have practically nothing. It is still a *very superficial and elementary understanding that does not give us access to the heart.*

It is true that a relationship begins from here: it is the starting point of a journey that can take us very far and determine our entire future, or die when it has only begun to be born. Two people meet, and perhaps they are initially attracted by what they see in each other: these are the most superficial qualities, those that are exposed to everyone's view and reveal *something*, but very little, of the mystery that is stored inside. They awaken in us the promise of what could happen, of a future that would be wonderful if he or she were in my own life. It is the prelude to an adventure ... or the early taste of a bitter disappointment.

When that first *attraction* becomes *attuned* and distances are narrowed, something wonderful happens—if both parties so desire: the other freely opens access to their inner world. A new stage begins in which the discovery of what the other likes, or cares about, or makes them suffer, or moves them, takes place. The other person thus becomes *vulnerable* because, at this level, appearances are left behind, masks are removed, and the deepest corners of the soul are discovered. The other shares with me that which he or she does not make available to everyone: his or her most unmentionable secrets, his or her most hidden thoughts. This—and only this way—is how that love is born and grows, because only when two hearts expand and spill into each other is there the possibility of a mutual and total surrender. This is an *inner* knowledge because not everyone can see it nor is it accessible to everyone, but exclusively to those whom we allow to enter. Only we can give the key that opens this door, and we don't give it to just anyone! We know or intuit well the value of who we really are, of that universe that we call *intimacy.*

In our relationship with the Lord, Saint Ignatius invites us to ask for the *gift* of this inner knowledge. Let us look at this closely. It is a grace. I cannot know the interior of Christ *if He does not give me access to his Heart.* I can have a lot of information about Jesus. If we are Christians, if we go to Mass on Sundays, if we have been in catechesis, we know the broad outlines of his life. We know where he was born and died, what family he came from, what his teachings were, what miracles he performed, and so on. *This is not internal knowledge, nor does it lead us to faith that is adherence to the Person of Christ (credere in Deum)*.As St. James writes, "even the demons have faith and tremble" (2:19).

To *enter* into the *inner knowledge* of the Lord, He has to open the door for me *from within.* We tend to take this step for granted: after all, how can God refuse us? But the truth is that if I reach the depths of his Heart, it is because He lets me in and shares with me the deepest secrets of his soul: "I have called you friends, because I have told you everything I have heard from my Father" (Jn. 15:15).

In this heart-to-heart relationship—*cor ad cor loquitur,* in the words of Saint John Henry Newman—a *reciprocity* is necessary which requires me to open myself to divine grace. This reciprocity is dialogue (prayer), contact (sacraments), intimacy (silence), vulnerability (docility), and love (surrender). Saint Ignatius wants to give us the possibility of this intimate encounter with God, which will inevitably bring about change, a new life, a new birth.

Ask the Lord for the grace of inner knowledge of Jesus Christ! May He open His Heart to you. May he share his most hidden intimacies. May he rest his head on your chest so that He can whisper to you the most reserved confidences, those that are only told to the "friend of the soul."

3. With this petition and these attitudes we enter the fifth chapter of the Gospel of Saint Mark (v. 21-43). It has often been said that the second Gospel, because it is the shortest, is also the simplest, almost in a pejorative sense. Yet we find pearls like this episode, which have a narrative complexity that may go unnoticed at first glance. Notice how the evangelist gradually increases the emotion of the story he is telling us. First, he tells us about the father of a family who urgently seeks Jesus, compelled by the impending death of his beloved daughter. The author then suddenly shifts the spotlight to the woman who touches the hem of Christ's robe

to be healed. While listening to this part of the narrative, the listener almost feels the need to address Jesus, urging him: "Lord, do not delay, do not linger too long here, because there is a little girl who is dying waiting for you. "

Indeed, when the woman is cured, his servants come to say to their master, "Jairus, your daughter has just died." It is like the disappointment before the joy at the end of the story, because the story—when the Lord is present in it—never ends in the darkness of man but in the light and glory of God. Many times, as I have been wandering through this Gospel account in my mental prayer, time slips away in the meditation on this passage of Scripture. I get lost here as if the most interesting and moving story had been placed before my eyes.

What we are going to meditate on together is found in approximately the second part of that fifth chapter. What is referred to immediately before this? The Lord had gone on what we could describe as a true "missionary incursion." He went to the eastern bank of Lake Tiberias, which the sacred text calls "of the Gerasenes" (Mk. 5:1). That was Gentile land. The pigs that will appear later in the story attest to the non-Jewish origins of those people, since that animal, as we know, was impure for the Hebrews. When I was wandering through that part of Galilee on my pilgrimage to the Holy Land, I unexpectedly came across the ruins of a fourth century monastery. It was built in the area where, according to tradition, Jesus' encounter with the demon-possessed man took place, and where that legion of demons ended up being expelled into the herd of pigs that roamed the nearby hills (v. 12).

Always so compassionate in the face of the suffering of

others, Jesus effectively liberates that poor man. The people of that region, however, were so frightened by Jesus' power that "they begged him to leave" (v. 17). How we fear that we are not in control of our lives! It seems that we even want to tell God how to proceed. We are disturbed by Jesus' lordship when it affects us. The thought that he might come and suddenly change everything makes us uneasy; it leaves us with our heart in our mouth.

Because of this rejection, the Lord takes a boat and sets sail for the western shore of the Sea of Galilee, which is the Jewish part of the lake (v. 21). This is where the story that concerns us begins. I invite you to accompany Jesus, to watch him sitting in silence on the little boat and feel the pain he experiences because of that rejection. He suffers not because he feels wounded in his pride; after all, he "is meek and humble of heart" (Mt. 11:29). Rather, he suffers because the people he loves so much despise the salvation that he had wanted to bring them. Christ suffers all this "for me."

On finally arriving at the west bank, the Lord encounters a crowd of people waiting for him. They are his beloved people, for whom the Rabbi tirelessly exerts himself and who will later make him weep tears of sadness (Lk. 19:41). People he has healed by taking upon himself their wounds. People among whom he lives and of whom he himself is a part. The evangelist tells us that "they pressed upon him" (v. 24): the poor man could hardly breathe in the midst of a crowd eager to get close to him.

4. When the news arrives that the Lord has finally returned, Jairus, the father of that twelve-year-old girl, rushes out in search of the miracle maker, the prophet of Nazareth,

because his daughter is dying and only Jesus has the power to restore health to the person he loves the most. He meets the Master and gives him the reason for his anguish: "Please come now! My little daughter is in agony. She needs you." Faced with the suffering of that father who approaches him with a heart broken in pain, the Lord—who has a heart of mercy for everyone—decides to accompany him.

There was also another person there who had heard the news of his arrival: a woman who for twelve years had been ill. The evangelist tells us that her illness consisted in having "flows of blood" that she could not control. For us, twenty centuries later, this is undoubtedly a somewhat strange ailment. We must, therefore, try to place ourselves in that time to understand how badly that woman was suffering.

The book of Leviticus (17:11) affirms that the seat of life resides in the blood. The illness of this woman, therefore, acquires a highly symbolic nuance. It is as if her life had been draining away from her and what she had at that moment was—if we can describe it in this way—a dying, decrepit, diminished existence. Saint Mark (v. 26) tells us that she had spent her entire fortune looking for a cure because in the Jewish world, a person who was bleeding was impure and made anything or anyone they touched impure. Even the place where she sat was *ipso facto* contaminated. They were not even allowed to enter the synagogues or the Temple so as not to defile those sacred s paces. So, in addition to the congenital suffering of such a disease and the hardship derived from her efforts to find a cure, she faced social and religious rejection. Truly, the poor woman had lived a miserable existence.

It is beautiful how the evangelist allows us to *enter the heart and mind of this woman.* Indeed, Saint Mark points out that she, at a certain moment, *thinks*, "If I can but touch the cloak of Jesus of Nazareth, I will surely be healed." (v. 28) With that hope and with that faith, she sets out in search of Christ.

As you meditate and pray, recognize yourselves in this hemorrhaging woman and let the Holy Spirit introduce you to the story in the first person. Try to understand her despair. Imagine it as though you were that woman. Don't you need Christ as much as she does?

5. I invite you to try to depict the vivid scene that this page of the Gospel offers us. People are trying to get closer to the Lord, crowding in, pressing him. Jesus walks through the crowd to Jairus' house with effort. I imagine the apostles almost acting as bodyguards so that the crowd would not crush the Lord. When that woman sees Jesus Christ, she thinks, "This is my chance. It's now or never." Inch by inch, she moves forward, slipping through the crowd. She gets closer and closer to him and when the Lord is finally within reach of her hand, she touches his cloak. Instantly, she feels a shudder run through her body. The evangelist tells us that, at that moment, she *felt* healed (v. 29). Her faith had obtained the reward she had sought.

At that precise moment, Jesus stops. I imagine Jairus, anxiously thinking: "Please, Master, we urgently need to get to my house. My daughter is dying, Lord!" How often is God's timing not ours! We often rush, wanting Him to do what we want *when we want.* But Jesus stops. Think, when that happens, what that woman begins to feel, because Jesus, in a loud voice, exclaims: "Who touched me" (v. 30)? And the apostles, astonished, answer him: "Lord, how can you ask who's touching you? We are like fish in a net here and You ask who has touched you" (v. 31)?The text says that the Lord did not move from there: he was intently looking, with his eyes, for the woman who had been healed.

Saint Mark is the evangelist of the gaze of Christ: several times he refers not only the *fact* that Jesus looked, but the *intention* with which he looked. If you recall, when the rich young man comes out on the road, this hagiographer notes: "Jesus looked at him with love" (10:21).Or, when he healed the man with a withered hand in the synagogue, Mark writes that the Lord looked around him with indignation (3:5), because the Pharisees said that it was forbidden to heal on the Sabbath. Well, imagine the Lord now: stopping, he begins to search among the faces of the crowd for the face of the woman who has touched him with faith. Try to see the faces of those people, who are asking themselves, "Who is he looking for?"

I have often wondered: why did Jesus stop? He could have continued on, especially when that little girl was so sick and needed him so urgently, and the woman would have been healed just the same. I think that perhaps there are two possible answers. The first and most obvious is that the Lord wanted all of us to admire and imitate the example of this woman. If he had not said anything, the miracle would have remained between the two of them. There is also, I believe, another reason. The Lord wanted a *personal* encounter with that woman. He wanted to be able to look into her eyes and for her to feel loved, respected, recognized in her dignity. It is what *Christ wants to do with each one of you.*

With fear, she approaches the Lord because of what was mentioned earlier: according to strict Jewish practice, by having touched Jesus, she contaminated him. Perhaps she expected a harsh reprimand from Christ for her audacity. She was probably also a shy person who had tried to pass unnoticed, without drawing the attention of the crowd at all. Now, instead, Jesus' question unwittingly places her center stage. Finally, I think that fear certainly had to do with the fact that the Lord commanded a great deal of respect. How often in the Gospels is there evidence of this presence of mind of Jesus Christ, who when it was necessary, faced the crowds or the Jewish authorities without fear of anything or anyone! No one dared to touch him. Recall, for example, when they took him out of his town, Nazareth, to throw him off the mountain, and the sacred text tells us that Jesus "made his way among them and went away" (Lk. 4:30). Or the expulsion of the merchants from the Temple of Jerusalem, where no one dares to lay hands on him even though he was alone in front of the crowd (Lk. 19:45-48). That gaze, which was that of the incarnate Son of God, the Truth itself made Man, had to be imposing in a portentous, at times even terrifying, way.

There is an attribute of God that Saint Ignatius mentions with some frequency in his *Spiritual Exercises*: majesty. I think that in our time there is little emphasis on this: either the Lord seems so far away that we hardly relate to him, or we make him so familiar that we end up losing the respect we owe him, almost as if he were just a "buddy." True love knows how to unite closeness with respect. In our relationship with God, we must learn to combine closeness to Christ with recognition of his infinite majesty. Yes, he is one of us. Yes, he wants to have with each one of us a relationship of equals. And, at the same time, and with the same force, we affirm: yes, He is the God who holds in his hands the depths of the earth (Ps. 95:4).Yes: He is the one who will come to judge the living and the dead (Mt. 26,64) and to separate the wheat from the chaff (Mt. 13:37-43). In the woman's fear there is an implicit confession of the majesty of Jesus, which is already a sign of the action of grace in her soul.

6. The poor woman—"trembling," says the Gospel, because she was the only one who knew what had really happened—stepped forward, threw herself at Jesus' feet, and "told him the whole truth" (v. 33).It must have been beautiful to contemplate that woman, with that respect, with that veneration, telling the Lord what had afflicted her for so many years. She pours herself out on Jesus, she tells him everything, and that explanation that she gives at the feet of Christ also heals the wounds of her afflicted soul. After that, there is a brief silence, dominated by the eyes of Jesus, who looks at this simple woman with love.

When the Lord finally speaks, what beautiful words He says! The first word is "daughter" (v. 34),as if to convey peace and tranquility to her. It is an affectionate term. Listen to the masculine voice of Jesus who, looking at you, knowing well who you are, how much you have suffered, and all you have done up to this moment in your life, addresses you in the same way, with the same expression, with the same love: "Daughter."

"Your faith has saved you. Go in peace and be free from your evil." Many people touched Jesus that day among the crowd. Only one person was healed. Only one woman had enough faith to be healed. I think of the Holy Mass and

Holy Communion: every Sunday we can touch the Body of the Lord, and not just his cloak. We *eat* Christ in the Eucharist. Why do we continue in our mediocrity? Why don't we overcome our sins? Why do we not obtain what we ask for? Because we are like the people who were crowding around the Lord. We are distracted with our heads and hearts on other things. We don't put our souls into our request. And God cannot transform us—though he most certainly can and he wants to—because we do not let him.

The Lord looks at the healed woman as if saying to her, "You wanted to touch my cloak, and I, with my gaze and my grace, want to touch your heart. You sought healing for your body, and today I want to heal your soul in a personal encounter."

The similarities that we can draw between this woman and each one of you are evident. Like her, you are seeking a better, different life that you can only receive from Jesus Christ. Like her, it is possible that you too have spent time and resources looking for the solution to your unhappiness in other people, other activities, other ways. Like her, you are sick and need healing. Like her, you have come here looking for a miracle not outside, but inside of you. Like her, Christ wants to direct his gaze and his word to you if you bow down before him. He wants to treat you with affection and respect, and tell you that, if you have faith—*credere in Deum*—he can act in your soul; that Christ wants to give you the true peace that springs from union with him; that there is always hope if we touch him with faith.

7. The narration continues saying that, while Jesus was still speaking, his servants arrived to say to poor Jairus — I think

he could see their faces from afar and imagine the sad news—
"We are sorry, your daughter has died. Why trouble the
teacher any longer" (v. 35)?

Notice that here too we can go to another page of the
Gospel. Jairus' faith was not a living, strong faith. He wants
the Lord *to come to his house to touch his daughter.* Do you
remember when the centurion approached the Lord because
his servant was sick? (Mt. 8:5-13)On that occasion, when the
Lord began to rise to follow him, the Roman replied: "Jesus,
I am not asking you to come to my house. I am not worthy
of that. It is enough that you say a word from here, and
my servant will be healed." Jairus *was not at that place.* He
needed something more and the Lord patiently adapts to the
different degrees of faith in which we find ourselves. Christ
not only physically accompanies him to his home, *he also
accompanies him on the path of faith.* And it is precious that,
at that moment in which Jairus collapses in sorrow at the
news of his daughter's death, Saint Mark tells us that, upon
hearing those words, Jesus said to him: "Do not be afraid,
it is enough that you have faith" (v. 36)An interior battle
would be fought within that man, between the certainty of
the news—the grief for his dead daughter—and the words
of Jesus to the contrary: "There is nothing to worry about,
Jairus. It is enough that you have faith." The Lord sustains
the man's faith and does not let him give up.

Let's note that, if on the one hand it is true that Jairus
wanted Christ to come to his house to heal his daughter, on
the other hand, he now needs a faith even more radical than
that of the hemorrhagic woman. The sick woman was asked
to believe that she could be cured of her illness, but from this
desperate father, Jesus asks for faith to accept that He can

resurrect his dead daughter. Jairus had just witnessed the miraculous healing of the hemorrhagic woman and heard Christ say to the sick woman: "Your faith has saved you." Now, the Lord asks this man to learn the lesson he has seen in the woman and take it, so to speak, to its ultimate consequences: he must accept as possible what is beyond his ability to understand. In this way, the episode of the woman's healing, which at first glance might seem like a setback for his plans, has actually been instrumental in bringing him to the faith that he now needs for the healing of his daughter. It was, in fact, an opportunity that the Lord gave him to lead him to a deeper trust in Him, to foresee in some way the fruit of a faith that expects everything from Jesus.

Thus, the Lord comes to the house of this synagogue official. Scripture tells us that Jesus took Peter, James, and John with him. The narration is so well done, I believe, that the writer must have either been an eyewitness to the scene or heard it from someone who was present. We can intuit this from the details: the name of the person —Jairus—, the age of the girl —twelve—, even the words in Aramaic that the Lord spoke that day— "Talitha koum" —, and at the end of the story, the mention that Jesus asked them to give the girl something to eat. We are there with them, witnessing the miracle!

"Why this commotion and weeping?" Jesus asks, "The child is not dead but asleep" (v. 39). The people there laugh at him. How often we don't understand God either! How often he would like to bring us closer to his Heart and his mystery! And for that, he invites us - this is the great lesson of the Word of God in this passage—to trust him even against our own judgment and the certainty we may have of things. "Even though the child seems to be dead, believe what I am telling you—she is asleep. Now you will see how I wake her. "

The Lord enters the room. How exciting it must have been to be there with the three apostles, her parents. He touches her as her father wanted—"he took her by the hand,"writes Saint Mark (v. 41)—andhe says: "Little girl, I say to you, arise!" And the girl stands up.

8. *You could be that girl.* The Lord wants to raise you up to a better life, too. Perhaps you are dead or asleep in your Christian life and you need a miracle like the one in the Gospel. The same Lord who held the hand of that twelve-year-old girl comes to us at every Holy Mass, so that you can tell him, ask him, receive him. I return to my reflection from before: why were these people healed, resurrected, and we aren't? Could it be that we have less faith than we claim to have? "I often think," the Holy Cure of Ars said in one of his catecheses, "that when we come to adore Our Lord, we should obtain all we wish, if we would ask it with very lively faith, and a very pure heart."[103]

For this reason, I believe that this page that we are considering is, above all, an invitation to put our trust in Jesus. No matter how serious the situation in which you find yourself, you must trust in Him. And what Christ said to Jairus, he says to you today: "*Do not be afraid,* for I am with you. *It is enough that you have faith*, to see miracles like this and greater ones if necessary."

I mentioned at the beginning that Christ wants to enter the innermost room of your souls and awaken the girl that you all carry within you. It is necessary to let him do so because the Kingdom of Heaven belongs only to those who are like children (Mt 19:14).

I believe that the desire to recover our childhood is a longing deeply rooted in the human heart. With nostalgia—"these blue days, and this sun of childhood", as a well-known Spanish poet wrote at the end of his life—the adult looks back, especially if the memories of early childhood are full of light and happiness. Life was very simple then, and many of the worries that concern us now were not even on the horizon. Children ignore the complexities and the houses of cards that we adults have built. Perhaps that is what we long for: the absence of problems, the innocence of an untouched soul, the ability to be surprised by the smallest and most ordinary things.

In the spiritual order, however, "becoming children again" is far from a wistful memory. Nor is it presented to us as a devotional practice—more or less attuned to our tastes—that we can disdain or not based on our personal preferences. Christ's words do not admit of any limitations: the Kingdom of Heaven belongs to those who are like children. Therefore, it is an imperative for those who wish to attain eternal life to return to that lost island where our relationship with God was more spontaneous, simpler and, precisely for this reason, more profound.

This is a topic that could take us far afield. Fortunately, we have many ways to access this vein of Catholic spirituality. I would like to recommend, obviously, our dear Saint Therese of the Child Jesus—always admirable and always full of insight when it comes to this subject—and also Saint José María Escrivá de Balaguer, who has deep insights on spiritual childhood. As supplementary reading, I would like recommend to you the chapter of his book, *The Way*, in which the founder of *Opus Dei* speaks precisely about this matter.[104] As you may know, the work in question is written in the form of maxims and short admonitions, which can be meditated on independently of the others. In your personal prayer, or when you have the opportunity, perhaps you can read them all in succession and return later to those that have touched you with the greatest intensity.

At this point of the Exercises, we can contemplate the moment in which Christ revives this little girl who, now, is you. There is a detail of the episode that I wish to bring up here. I have always been struck by the double mention in this chapter of the twelve-year period of time. The first time this appears is in reference to the illness of the woman with the flow of blood: Saint Mark points out that she had suffered from these hemorrhages "for twelve years" (v. 25). The second time in which this same period is spoken of is to describe the age of Jairus' daughter: "the girl, who was already twelve years old, got up and began to walk. They were the filled with astonishment" (v. 42).Why would the Evangelist include this correlation?

Others will come along who will know how to give a more judicious answer than the one that I am now going to share with you, but for me, Saint Mark is putting the girl and the woman in relationship. In a subtle way, he is inviting us to see the two in the same frame: in fact, he wants us to contemplate them simultaneously. Twelve years before the encounter with Jesus, while the birth of one filled the hearts of her parents with joy, the illness of the other marked the beginning of an ordeal that led to the social, economic, and spiritual misery of the poor little woman. Truly, in this life—vanity of vanities—the purest joys and the most excruciating sorrows are intertwined together. In both cases, Christ's action gives life—both were dead, although each in a different way. In both cases, Christ's humanity is the channel of grace through which they receive the desired healing. And in both cases faith has been the means of access that the Lord has used to "save" (v. 34) both of them—whether personal faith or mediated by others, as in the case of Jairus. In both cases, finally, after Christ's redemptive action, both can return to their lives, now restored by what the Lord has accomplished in them.

Let me ask you: how are you going to return to your life after this retreat? Do you have faith that the Lord will change your heart of stone into a heart of flesh (Ez. 36:26-28)? If the work of the Holy Spirit is described by Christ in his conversation with Nicodemus as "being born again" (Jn. 3:3), do you think that these days, or that this moment of prayer, is really the beginning of a transformed life? When you receive Holy Communion and you touch the Body of Christ from which grace and redemption flow, do you believe in its power to give you what you really need and can make you happy?

Together with the inner knowledge of Christ, I invite you to also ask the Lord, in the Holy Spirit, and through the intercession of the Blessed Virgin, for the gift of a living faith so that, the next time you are able to receive Holy Communion and the Sacred Host touches your tongue, you may have the same confidence as that woman, so that you may be healed of all your illnesses, become trusting children before God, and be able to walk in a new life.

17

ENCOUNTER WITH THE CANNANITE WOMAN

**DAY 6 (AFTERNOON) – FOURTEENTH MEDITATION –
ATTITUDE IN MOMENTS OF SPIRITUAL DESOLATION**

*"O God, our refuge in trials, our strength in sickness,
our comfort in sorrow, spare your people, we pray,
that, though rightly chastised now by affliction, they
may find relief at last through your loving mercy."*
(Collect from Mass in Any Need, Roman Missal)

We are nearing the end of this retreat experience, and as
you already know, the last meditations are going to focus
on the Paschal Mystery of Christ: his Passion, Death and
Resurrection. With that prospect before us, I think that the
encounter I offer you now is a good transition between the
public life of the Lord, his agony, its completion, and his
exaltation at the right hand of the Father.

In the meditation on the Visitation, we had the opportunity to briefly reflect on the consolations of God. It is essential, however, to also acknowledge the reality of *spiritual desolation* because it is in those moments that the strength of our character and the intensity of our love for God are put to the test.

1. In Christian life, moments of disappointment are particularly critical since in them we are much more exposed and vulnerable to temptations or weaknesses that can make us fall. We all have had experiences, to a greater or lesser extent, of this "movement of spirits" —as Saint Ignatius aptly describes it—ups and downs, inner joy or discouragement, ease of doing good or heaviness, pleasure or reluctance, light or dark.

People who do spiritual exercises or a few days of retreat in solitude, usually experience abundant consolations from God. But, it does not always happen. Saint Therese of the Child Jesus, for example, lived many exercises in the most complete aridity. But when the retreatant has made the effort of distancing herself from the distractions of her daily life and being magnanimous in her dedication to the Lord, God—who never allows himself to be outdone in generosity—usually communicates within the soul a joy that the world is simply unable to offer. In these experiences, divine love is felt with particular intensity and the experience fills even the darkest and grayest days with vivid color.

In a couple of days you will return to your usual lives, where the wind does not always blow in your favor, and you will have to fight battles that from here can only be vaguely seen. It is easy to fall into the misconception of thinking that you are now stronger than you were last week, before you began this retreat with the Lord. I often repeat a phrase that we should burn into our memories: *we are not what we feel, we are what we do.*

The scholastics said that in the sphere of our affectivity, we have a *political* dominion over our passions, and over our body and its members this control was described as *despotic*—that is, under normal circumstances for example, my arm moves *when I want it to.* It does not resist the rule of my will. If I want to grab something, or if I want to scratch my stomach, or if I choose to put my hands on my head, my will moves my arm so that it carries out what I want it to do. As it were, the will becomes a *despot* (hence the name *despotic)* for my body, in the sense that the will commands without any possibility of rebellion or disobedience.

The same does not happen with our affections. Most often I do not choose when to feel sad or happy, when to experience fear or joy. I cannot wake up one morning and force my heart not to feel any pain: "Sergio, today I forbid you to be sad." "Until evening comes, I will not allow you to feel angry." This is not how things work. Frequently we experience sadness when we want to be happy. We get angry when we wish we were not. We are afraid when we want to be brave.

It is our decisions and our works that define us as the people we are, and through them, with time and a lot of grace from God, the Holy Spirit will gradually shape our affections in such a way that we can come to conform to Christ and share in his same attitude (Phil. 2:5). As Saint John Paul II expressed in *Veritatis Splendor* quoting Saint Gregory of Nisa, we are "in a certain way parents of ourselves."[105]

Many times I have seen the case of someone who has made

a few days of retreat with great consolation of spirit. Indeed, God has manifested himself to her with great intensity and she concludes that experience feeling that something has changed within herself and that from that moment on she will be able to finally walk the path of holiness. Not long after when I see that same person again, I find her totally demoralized, defeated, disappointed, and depressed—her fervor and holy desires are almost completely extinguished. Usually, she is in an even worse state than before the retreat that had left her so comforted.

In most cases, this situation is due to the following deception. At the end of her silent retreat she *felt* the effusion of divine love in her heart. This led her to believe that her love for God had increased to the same extent and that she could experience that closeness to the Lord. It felt stronger, but was it in fact stronger than before doing the spiritual exercises? Evidently not.

There is a very subtle pride that is disguised as love for God and that hides a self-assurance that is usually a sign of the evil spirit. True consolation leads to deep humility, and this makes us *always* mistrust ourselves.

I don't want you to make the same mistake when you leave here. Let me remind you that you are today the same women who came here a few days ago. Saint Ignatius writes, "He who enjoys consolation should take care to humble himself and lower himself as much as possible. Let him recall how little he is able to do in time of desolation, when he is left without such grace or consolation" (SE 324). Certainly "how little" we are in moments of desolation! May the seed that sprouts out of the ground beware thinking that because it is growing so quickly, it will be able to withstand any onslaught of inclement weather! Its inexperience makes it unaware that an impetuous wind, a sudden downpour, or a hungry little animal is enough to cut off the life that has just begun to grow.

Return home with great humility. Your strength is found *exclusively* in the Lord.

2. Am I dismissing with my words the *importance* of consolation? In no way. We actually need those caresses from God to develop us spiritually. I just want to point out the great danger of thinking that we *are* better because we *feel* better.

As we have already noted, consolation should be received with gratitude and should help us prepare for the battles that will come later. Who does not know Aesop's fable about the grasshopper and the ant? On the sunny days of summer (consolations) we must bear in mind what the coming winter will bring us (desolations). Saint Ignatius expresses the same opinion: "When one enjoys consolation, let him consider how he will conduct himself during the time of ensuing desolation, and store up a supply of strength as defense against that day" (SE 323). Let's not be grasshoppers who lie in the sun and enjoy lazing about because if we do this, then we will fail the test. On the contrary, *consolation must be the beginning of a new life.* It should help us to start healthier habits, to reinforce the constancy that costs us so much effort, to incorporate practices that will bring us great benefits in the future in the arsenal of our spiritual life. The consolations of God must be the *beginning of better and more excellent acts,* keeping in mind that it is not about *doing,* but about *being.* Actions must transform the soul and prepare it for more abundant graces from heaven. In other words: we receive consolations *not because* we are good *but* to make ourselves good, not only to do good, but to let God make goodness grow in us.

3. Something similar, on the contrary, can be said of desolations. If we have previously said that the joys of God should not make us fall into the trap of presumption—leading us to the erroneous conclusion that we believe we are stronger than we really are—desolation tends to take us precisely to the opposite pole: to make us feel weaker than we really are. Or rather: desolation reveals our limitations; showing us, with the greatest of evidence, the fragility of our condition. Are we to deduce from this that we are failing the test? By no means! It only means that *without God* we are doomed to defeat.

Likewise, desolation forces us to experience the absence of the Lord. One day, we feel Him so close that it saturates our soul's palate and the next day, without warning, it has simply vanished. It really is that? Has God "moved away" from us? In fact, He is *always* with us: less felt, certainly, but just as present. Loyola reminds us again:

> When one is in desolation, he should be mindful that God has left him to his natural powers to resist the different agitations and temptations of the enemy in order to try him. He can resist with the help of God, which always remains, though he may not clearly perceive it. For though God has taken from him the abundance of fervor and overflowing love and the intensity of His favors, nevertheless, he has sufficient grace for eternal salvation (SE 320).

There are people who as soon as they feel the temptation lurking in their souls give up without putting up a fight. We will now see what attitude the Lord invites us to assume in such cases. We can already anticipate that what we can never do is to drop our arms and lower the flag. We must be grateful that the goodness of God grants us opportunities to "overcome evil with good" (Rom. 12:21), grow in love, and so cooperate in the salvation of the world. We can't curl up and cry in fear at the test as if defeat were nothing short of inevitable. If holiness consists in the practice of love to a heroic degree, there is nothing honorable in stepping out of the ring for fear of receiving some inevitable blow in combat.

4. *What is the cause of our desolations?* The truth is that, all too quickly, we tend to attribute our periods of darkness to God, in the manner of a leaden cloud that heaven sends us and that rains down on us to wash and purify our souls. However, I invite you not to be too hasty in reaching for that explanation. There is usually a different explanation—one more shameful and hard to admit—identified by Saint Ignatius: our sins and our inconsistency when it comes to serving the Lord are often at the base of these aridities of the spirit, "because we have been tepid and slothful or negligent in our exercises of piety, and so through our own fault spiritual consolation has been taken away from us" (SE 322).

The reason for feeling sluggish in the practice of good and as heavy as a sour stomach in the fulfillment of our obligations is usually the fact that, at some point, we have been remiss: perhaps laziness; laxity in the practice of our fidelity to Christ, or the commission of some sin that by making us savor the flesh has made the spirit insipid. Let's be clear: in most cases, the Lord *does not want desolation for us.* If we have voluntarily jumped into the icy waters of sin, it is logical that we feel the cold of death and it will cost us to warm up again.

So I would like to encourage you to leave here with this resolution: *from now on, and with the grace of God, let us never do anything that we think hurts the Heart of Christ.* It is clear that our human condition will make us stumble. It is also foreseeable that life will put us in situations in which we will not be sure of what we should do and we will make a mistake in choosing the path we should take. We count on the unquestionable fact that even "the just fall seven times" a day (Prv. 24:16), but let's endeavor to never choose something that without any shadow of a doubt is sin or does not carry out the will of the Lord in us.

If you take this firm purpose away with you from this retreat, it would already have been worth your effort to come here. We cannot expect deeper communication with the Lord if we have not habitually and peacefully settled on this first level of Christian life. Let's remember that in his encounter with the rich young man (Mk. 10:17-22) the Lord invites him to a more intimate and radical following only after he hears that he keeps the commandments. This is often the case.

5. The cause of desolation on which we wish to dwell more deliberately here, however, is that which, in the words of Saint Ignatius, has the purpose of "testing" us. This is also indicated by Thomas a Kempis in *The Imitation of Christ*: "I am wont to visit My elect in two ways—by temptation and by consolation. To them I read two lessons daily—one reproving their vices, the other exhorting them to progress

in virtue."[106]

The words of Saint Augustine also serve the case, who, speaking of Satan's temptations, considers the following:

> *Our pilgrimage on earth cannot be exempt from trial. We progress by means of trial. No one knows himself except through trial, or receives a crown except after victory, or strives except against an enemy or temptations. (...)*
>
> *We have heard in the gospel how the Lord Jesus Christ was tempted by the devil in the wilderness... In Christ you were tempted, for Christ received his flesh from your nature, but by his own power gained salvation for you; he suffered death in your nature, but by his own power gained glory for you; therefore, he suffered temptation in your nature, but by his own power gained victory for you.*
>
> *If in Christ we have been tempted, in him we overcome the devil. Do you think only of Christ's temptations and fail to think of his victory? See yourself as tempted in him, and see yourself as victorious in him. He could have kept the devil from himself; but if he were not tempted he could not teach you how to triumph over temptation.*[107]

The spiritual combat with the enemies of our soul, or the dryness that the Lord allows us to experience that we are dealing with here, is a path of growth in faith, and assuming it is the first step, to embrace it as part of our itinerary towards Him, conscious that already in this effort there is a hidden joy, like that of someone who finds the treasure buried in the field and sells what they have to obtain it (Mt. 13:44).

I want to suppose that some of you have already been invited by the Lord to "put out into the deep" (Lk. 5:4), rowing toward the unexplored waters of a greater intimacy with Him. Christ's invitation is the call to greater love, and for this reason, it is crucial that we at least know how to recognize when those first movements that alert us to the presence of the Beloved take place—asking us for permission to allow him to act in us, quietly, confidently—in order to surrender ourselves without resistance to his master hands.

To that end, we are going to look at a female figure from the New Testament who has not yet come our way: I am speaking of the Canaanite woman who begs for the healing of her sick daughter. We ask the Lord to open for us the meaning of what he wishes to manifest here.[108]

We are going to listen to the story, asking God for a heart that receives it as the arid land welcomes raindrops on a stormy day.

> Then Jesus went from that place and withdrew to the region of Tyre and Sidon. And behold, a Canaanite woman of that district came and called out, "Have pity on me, Lord, Son of David! My daughter is tormented by a demon." But he did not say a word in answer to her. His disciples came and asked him, "Send her away, for she keeps calling out after us." He said in reply, "I was sent only to the lost sheep of the house of Israel." But the woman came and did him homage, saying, "Lord, help me." He said in reply, "It is not right to take the food of the children and throw it to

the dogs." She said, "Please, Lord, for even the dogs
eat the scraps that fall from the table of their masters."
Then Jesus said to her in reply, "O woman, great is
your faith! Let it be done for you as you wish." And her
daughter was healed from that hour (Mt. 15:21-28).

6. *The perspective of the Heart of Jesus.* This woman whose name we will never know must have been someone of admirable spiritual stature. The treatment she receives from the Lord shows that He knew the worth of this simple soul. Jesus knew that he could push her to the limit, and that in this way she would be able to grow in adversity and achieve a faith and love that she would not have otherwise been able to reach.

It is crucial that we place ourselves in the proper perspective from the beginning, which is that of the *Heart of Jesus.* Our prayer must always be *Christian*: that is, its purpose is union with the Lord. Baptism, in effect, has united us to the Incarnate Word as the branches are united to the vine (Jn. 15:1-8). It is by virtue of this most intimate union that, participating in the Holy Spirit, we can read the facts of the life of Christ, of his own feelings. His life is ours, his experiences are ours too, and from the recollection of contemplation we can have access to the inner world of the Lord and to what He lived then. It is not a retrospective look because—let us not forget the fundamental truth of our faith—the risen Christ *is alive.* We are not called to a relationship with millenary accounts of past events. My relationship is with the living Person of the risen Jesus Christ, whose Heart now beats full of grace and communicates to me—in the *now* of my present life—his feelings and his love, which are the same that dwelt in his soul *then*.

From this perspective, we return to the biblical text and understand something fundamental for the comprehension of this episode: from the beginning, Christ *wanted to heal the daughter of this woman.* If we do not underline this point from the beginning, it can give us the impression that Jesus changes his mind, that he was reluctant at the beginning of the story to give this woman what she asked of him. Christ did not need to be convinced to work the miracle that the Canaanite woman begs of him. Something similar happens in the story of the resurrection of Lazarus that we read in the eleventh chapter of the Gospel of Saint John. The holy author needs to underline in the prologue of the story that "Jesus loved Martha, Mary, and their brother Lazarus" (v. 5). He has to clarify this point because the Lord's way of acting initially seems to contradict this love for them. Indeed, when he receives the news that his friend is sick, Christ decides to stay two more days in the place where he was (v. 6). Didn't he want to help the one he loved so much? Certainly yes, but along the way he also wants to carry on his work in the souls of his disciples, teaching them and leading them to an even greater faith in Him. The same thing happens to us now in this episode.

If the Lord wanted to heal the daughter of this stranger, why does he treat her so harshly at first and *seem* to disregard her pleas? We could answer in a few words: *to bring this woman into a deeper intimacy with Him.* Or we could answer: *so that the life in the Spirit of this woman would grow to a level that she could not have otherwise reached.* In other words, it is the love of the Heart of Jesus that is going to treat this woman with apparent severity. To give her something more than the simple grace that she was looking for, to elevate the spiritual life of this woman, to expand the walls of her soul, the Lord is going to lead her down this path of apparent rejection.

As you can see, we are talking about another type of desolation here: a desolation that is not is born from our indolence or negligence, but from *the action of God in the human heart.* We must understand that the feeling of abandonment by God or dryness, if it comes from the Lord, for that very reason *comes from someone who is love and is working, moved by charity, toward us.* Why should we think that the silence of God is synonymous with the absence of God? Or that not feeling close to him is equivalent to him moving away from us? It is into this quicksand that the world and Satan want to lead us, but we must not fall into such a crude trap as that.

You must learn this well to understand the way God works in the soul. This is how Saint John of the Cross expresses it:

It must be known, then, that the soul, after it has been definitely converted to the service of God, is, as a rule, spiritually nurtured and caressed by God, even as is the tender child by its loving mother, who warms it with the heat of her bosom and nurtures it with sweet milk and soft and pleasant food, and carries it and caresses it in her arms; but, as the child grows bigger, the mother gradually ceases caressing it, and, hiding her tender love, puts bitter aloes upon her sweet breast, sets down the child from her arms and makes it walk upon its feet, so that it may lose the habits of a child and betake itself to more important and substantial occupations. The loving mother is like the grace of

God, for, as soon as the soul is regenerated by its new
warmth and fervor for the service of God, He treats it in
the same way; He makes it to find spiritual milk, sweet
and delectable, in all the things of God, without any
labor of its own, and also great pleasure in spiritual
exercises, for here God is giving to it the breast of His
tender love, even as to a tender child (1 Pet. 2:23).[109]

The Mystic Doctor uses the example of the child to be weaned on various occasions throughout his work. It helps us understand the critical moment in our spiritual life in which God puts us on the ground so that we can begin to take our first steps. Is it that the mother does not love her child when she teaches him to walk? Doesn't she love him when she starts giving him solid food? Isn't it precisely the opposite, love, which moves parents to take the child of the next stage of his growth?

If the Lord puts us in desolation, let us not allow the cold of the night to make us doubt the fire of Jesus' love for us. Rather, let us ask the Holy Spirit for the grace to recognize in this change of attitude on the part of God an expression of his love for us, which invites us—like the Canaanite woman in the Gospel story—to a more confident faith, a more purified hope and a more tried and true love.

7. *Initial faith of the woman and silence of Christ.* Jesus has left Galilee with his disciples and is entering the territories of Tyre and Sidon in present-day Lebanon. It is the north of the Holy Land, a Gentile area, although from the Lord's subsequent comment we can assume that there was a significant

Jewish presence in that region.

A woman enters the scene about whom the Gospel offers us only two pieces of information: she has a daughter tormented by the devil and she was "Canaanite;" that is, not Jewish. She was a foreigner and did not belong "according to the flesh" to the people of Israel.

What moves this woman to draw closer to Christ? As was the case with the hemorrhagic woman that we previously met, she had *faith* in Jesus. She *believed* that He had the power to heal her daughter. She also calls him "Lord, son of David" (v. 22). There is an explicit recognition of the authority of Christ. It is an infantile faith that, however, is amalgamated with another irresistible ingredient: love for her daughter.

That is to say, unlike the hemorrhaging woman, this Canaanite does not ask directly for grace for herself, but for the person she loves most: her poor, sick daughter. *Omnia vincit amor* (love overcomes all obstacles), and if faith explains why she came to Jesus, it will be love that makes her persist until she overcomes the resistance that Jesus manifests towards her on three occasions.

It is from the depths of her motherly heart that this woman's plea to the Lord is born: "Have mercy on me! My daughter is tormented by a demon."

What is Christ's initial response? "He did not say a word in answer to her" (v. 23). Imagine the scene: Sacred Scripture has told us that the woman "keeps calling out." She made her presence known to everyone and probably the other people there would expect some kind of gracious and benign response from the Master. Not a word. The silences of God, again!

It is important that we understand this: God's silence *is*

already an answer. Pope Benedict XVI, in one of his wonderful teachings, expressed it so accurately:

> *Indeed, it is not only our silence that disposes us to listen to the word of God; in our prayers we often find we are confronted by God's silence, we feel, as it were, let down, it seems to us that God neither listens nor responds. Yet God's silence, as happened to Jesus, does not indicate his absence. Christians know well that the Lord is present and listens, even in the darkness of pain, rejection and loneliness. (...) God knows us in our inmost depths, better than we ourselves, and loves us; and knowing this must suffice.*[110]

God's silence is his *invitation not to lose heart.* The Heart of Christ would be inwardly loving that woman who had placed her trust in Him, and precisely because He loved her and knew of her greatness of soul, he is going to accompany her to an incomparably greater maturity. He does not leave her alone, but without a doubt, it is a very delicate moment because, in the face of Christ's apparent indifference, she might be tempted to throw in the towel: "He doesn't care about me. He isn't answering me. It doesn't make sense to keep on begging."

We are at the first step of the apparent insensitivity of the Lord: indifference. It *seems* that God does not care how bad things are. We could say with the psalmist: "Why so far from my call for help, from my cries of anguish? My God, I call by day, but you do not answer; by night, but I have no relief" (Ps. 22:2-3). There is no answer when we plead with the

Lord. Why doesn't he seem to listen to me and others? What have I done to deserve such treatment from you? God almost seems rude: he doesn't even bother to say no to us. It is then sometimes that the devil slyly approaches us, suggesting that perhaps there is no one up there listening to our lament.

8. *From the indifference of Christ to coldness.* However, the Lord's answer doesn't end there. Initially, Jesus did not speak to her. That is to say, he was apathetic to the prayer of this heart broken by anguish. If the Lord's first attitude to the Canaanite woman's request was indifference, the woman's response to his apparent impassiveness has been *constancy.* A very important lesson for us, because it is one of the reasons why, according to Saint Ignatius of Loyola, God allows these desolations:

> *The principal reasons why we suffer from desolation are three:*
>
> *(...) The second reason is because God wishes to try us, to see how much we are worth, and how much we will advance in His service and praise when left without the generous reward of consolations and signal favors (SE 322).*

The Canaanite woman shows that she does not follow Christ because of what he makes her feel. The trial is bringing out, little by little, the extraordinary worth of this foreigner who will not give up or leave his company.

Her persistence also shows us that by some special light that escapes us, *she trusted in the mercy of Jesus.* She insists because she harbors the hope that, if she persists in her efforts, she will end up softening the Heart of the Lord to her request. She has thus shown that she understands *this language of Christ*, which is not always expressed in words or consolations, and has continued the "inner conversation" with him, not abandoning her plea. This perseverance manifests a presence of the Holy Spirit in her to which this woman responds: love moves her, hope strengthens her, faith will give her the desired reward.

The disciples now intervene, interceding for the stranger: "Send her away, for she keeps calling out after us" (v. 23). They are oblivious to the work that Jesus is doing in the heart of the woman. They are bothered by the cries of the Canaanite woman: "Do something so she'll leave us alone." On another level of meaning, however, we can recognize ourselves in this attitude of the apostles. When faced with someone who is in a moment of spiritual dryness, our reaction is usually to wish that the Lord would bring him out of that darkness as soon as possible. We tend to be blind to the action of the Holy Spirit and prefer the conclusion of the trial rather than the desired fruits of holiness that this desolation is called to produce.

Christ answers with a coldness that is startling: "I was sent only to the lost sheep of the house of Israel" (v. 24). How these words must have struck the foreigner's heart! The indifference of others hurts us when we disclose our suffering to them. Here is a reaffirmation of what the first silence implicitly suggested: Christ has *intentionally* turned a deaf ear to the pleas of this woman. It is as if He were saying to his disciples: "I've already heard her, but don't insist: I don't want to help her at the moment." I write "at the moment" because, although the disciples understood the Lord's expression as a negative, it was actually a *delay*. Christ will eventually grant grace to the woman, but now he apparently does not show any kind of empathy for the pain of the Canaanite woman.

We are going to see a progression now in the two main characters of the scene. The Canaanite woman is going to change in her relationship with Jesus and the Lord is going to progressively conform to the increasingly purified attitude of this woman.

9. *Humility of the Canaanite Woman; from the coldness of Christ to rejection.* Now, the woman humbled herself before Jesus: "But the woman came and did him homage, saying, 'Lord, help me'" (v. 25). There is a modulation with respect to her initial attitudes: the one who shouted now prostrates herself; the one who cried out now pleads respectfully. She has inevitably felt the indifference and coldness of Jesus Christ and known how to understand, or at least intuit, what was really happening. She has persisted, she has pled and now she bows down. "If I humbly fall at his feet," she thinks, "perhaps he will give me what I am asking for."

We are accustomed to reading in Sacred Scripture of many biblical characters who fall to the ground as a sign of fear, respect, or adoration. In the modern world we no longer see this gesture very often, but seeing someone prostrate before another, with their forehead to the ground, is deeply overwhelming. You cannot express greater abasement. In the face of such a simple, stunningly humble attitude, even we would have reacted with understanding, kindness, gentleness, or benevolence.

Jesus could have opened his hand at that moment and

given her what she had been asking for along the way. Christ was more willing to give her that grace than she was to receive it. However, Jesus reacts in an almost rude way, which would powerfully draw the attention of his disciples who were so accustomed to seeing their Master welcome the pleas of the suffering. For the third time—unique in the Gospels—this woman receives a negative answer! *No. I have said no. It doesn't seem right to me.* "It is not right to take the food of the children and throw it to the dogs" (v. 26). The answer is emphatic, icy, hurtful, very harsh. It is a humiliation that probably none of the eyewitnesses understood. Someone could have said to Jesus: "Master, if you don't want to grant what she asks, it is enough not give it to her, but don't tell her that, don't treat her like that."

Let us realize this: the harshest answer is also the one that is closest to final grace. It is not a coincidence. Jesus is striking the iron on the anvil, but he is also nearing the completion of his masterpiece. He has been internally encouraging this Gentile with faith, hope, and love, and in the action of continuing the interaction with her now, *Jesus is giving her the true message* that words cannot convey: He wants to lead her to a better spiritual place. This is the test that this woman is going through: it is as if he was discouraging her, but by continuing the conversation, he was encouraging her not to give up.

This is important: I just pointed out that Christ had said "no." In fact, it was not an absolute refusal. If that had been the case, she should have obeyed and withdrawn her request. However, the Lord has said: "It is not right..." Somehow, in the words of Jesus there is *an invitation not to give up her appeal* and to *trust everything to the Lord's mercy,* since she cannot expect anything based on the justice of her cause. Where others understood the words of Christ as a closed door, this stranger has seen a window through which she is going to try to sneak in.

10. *Wonderful final response from the Canaanite Woman.* After the icy words of Jesus, so uncharacteristic of him and so unexpected for those who knew the goodness of his Heart, I imagine a deathly silence and the gazes of all directed toward the woman lying prostrate on the ground. People expected an answer. Christ also awaited the woman's reaction. Let me ask you: what would you have answered? After, not one, not two, but three refusals from the Lord ... we probably would have walked away mortified with humiliation. Isn't it true that we would have misinterpreted Jesus' expression, taking for harshness what, in reality, was the proof of immense love? This woman had advanced in the ways of the spirit more in those few moments than perhaps in all the years of her life.

As a wounded woman a battle would be fought in her heart. She would think about her possessed daughter. She would feel the bitterness of this triple humiliation, and above all, she would process the words of Jesus within her: "It is not right to take the food of the children and throw it to the dogs." Here is a lesson in humility: Christ wants to make her aware of her unworthiness: "The grace you are about to obtain for your daughter is not due to you. You will not be able to take credit for the consolation that she is about to receive." Again, it is Saint Ignatius who comes to give us light by presenting to us the third and final reason why God allows us in his Providence to go through spiritual desolations:

The principal reasons why we suffer from desolation are three: (...)

The third reason is because God wishes to give us a true knowledge and understanding of ourselves, so that we may have an intimate perception of the fact that it is not within our power to acquire and attain great devotion, intense love, tears, or any other spiritual consolation; but that all this is the gift and grace of God our Lord. God does not wish us to build on the property of another, to rise up in spirit in a certain pride and vainglory and attribute to ourselves the devotion and other effects of spiritual consolation (SE 322).

The Lord knows the worth of this stranger and is going to take her to another level in her life of faith. The way to do it so far has been indifference, coldness, apparent rejection, discourtesy, contempt, and denial. This is how God carries out his work in the souls of his best friends, not because he does not love us, but precisely because he wishes to lead us to a better love, which follows Christ not because of the consolations he receives from him, but as we pray in the act of contrition, because he is "all good."

To this woman, who was already prostrate on the ground, the words of Jesus sink her even more. *A dog is not given the food of the children. Are you aware that you ask for something that is far above your status?*

The woman gathers herself inwardly and responds to the Lord with some formidable words, which reveal both her spiritual quality and the work that the Holy Spirit has done in her after the three apparent rejections of Jesus Christ:

"Please, Lord, for even the dogs eat the scraps that fall from the table of their masters" (v. 27).

This Canaanite woman, who has been publicly humiliated by the incomparable gesture of Jesus, does not rebel proudly, does not walk away in fear, does not respond angrily to the Lord's slight. In her reply she expresses an attitude of the most beautiful humility. By accepting Christ's comment, *she places herself in his hands confidently, unconditionally, and absolutely.*

It is possible that initially she had approached the Master because she had heard about the healings that He was doing wherever he went. Perhaps the awareness that Jesus was healing everyone made her feel almost "entitled" to have her request duly received. "If he cares for others, why not help my daughter in her need?" That is, she had a certain confidence in herself, and somehow she anticipated the outcome of her request based on the conviction that her need deserved to be addressed.

If at the beginning there was any sign of that attitude, at this point in the story we see that it has completely disappeared. Above all, this stranger peacefully embraces the humiliation to which Jesus has just subjected her. It is as if she were saying to the Lord: "You are absolutely right, Master. I don't deserve what I'm asking of you. Who am I? You have said it well: a dog that does not deserve to put the food of the children in its mouth." One thing is clear: she no longer makes her request because she considers herself worthy of it.

How easy it is to subtly fall into the temptation to believe that what God gives us somehow corresponds to our efforts! Or that we are not as bad as others; that, somehow, if God gives us consolations, it is because we have "earned" them. The Lord has to put us in a state of desolation so that we recognize that all the good we have comes from Him, and that in our account of having and owning, we have a debt with Christ that we will never be able to pay.

After accepting the humiliation with meekness, this woman answers with a finesse and a spiritual height that reveals the action of the Holy Spirit: "What you have said is true, Lord. I do not raise this request to your Heart because I deserve it, but keep in mind that even a puppy can eat the scraps that fall from his masters' table." Impressive! She does not even ask Him to feed her—that would also be too much—but to allow her to snatch the little that inadvertently falls onto the floor from the children's table. If this is not audacity ...

"Look, Jesus: I'm already on the ground. If something falls from the table of your goodness, won't you let me pick it up so it doesn't get lost?" Her faith in the power and mercy of Jesus has not waned at any of his first three responses: she has responded to each with greater confidence. Certainly, as the Lord will tell her soon, only a very deep and great faith could withstand such a test. At the same time, Christ's actions have made that faith grow even more. Now is the time for it to bear the desired fruit.

There are many admirable traits in this woman. Personally, what amazes me the most is her ability to understand the Lord's responses not as a *rejection* but as a *delay* of the grace she is begging for. She has been in tune with the Heart of Christ from the beginning and has grasped, in the Holy Spirit, that Jesus was "postponing" the moment of granting her grace. Saint Ignatius writes that those who find themselves in desolation must think that "that consolation will soon return" (SE 321) if they remain faithful. In the darkness of this trial, she sees at the end of the tunnel the light that comes from the love of Christ. This woman has penetrated into the intimacy of the Heart of Jesus and has understood it better than the others who were there. The Spirit has conformed the rhythm of her interior life with that of Christ and in that harmony of two hearts that beat in unison, they have found each other.

11. *Outcome of the test. Admiration of Jesus Christ.* "'O woman, great is your faith! Let it be done for you as you wish.' And her daughter was healed from that hour" (v. 28). I must confess that whenever I read this verse I feel a deep envy—which I hope is holy—towards this Canaanite woman. Jesus not only surrenders to the faith of this foreigner, he is amazed! "How great is your faith!" It is an expression of astonishment from Christ that testifies to the enormous faith of this mother: she had asked for a few crumbs and Christ is going to offer her a succulent banquet, curing her demon-possessed daughter.

Yes, a faith that moves mountains is the fruit of the spiritual desolations that we are considering here. A faith that makes us agreeable to Christ because we can then seek him with our intention purified of imperfections, selfishness, defilement, and attachments that do not allow us to take flight toward God. A faith that seeks the Lord for himself, and not for what he makes us feel. A faith that has borne fruit in love.

In some way, the demon-tormented daughter represents a *previous life that the Lord wishes to take you out of during these exercises.* When the mother asks for the grace of healing, she does so by *identifying* with her own daughter: "Have mercy on me!" (v. 22), "Lord, help *me*!" (v. 25) You can borrow these words and direct them to Christ yourself. You can learn from this woman and join with her too. You will find, I am sure, more than one similarity. If you humble yourself before God as this Canaanite woman did, and appropriate her attitudes and responses, you can expect from Jesus, who loves you so much, an equal response for you too. Isn't that, deep down, what you are looking for in this experience of prayer?

In her book, *The Interior Castle*, Saint Teresa of Jesus brilliantly relates humility and truth in Jesus Christ when she writes:

> *"Once, while I was wondering why our Lord so dearly loves the virtue of humility, the thought suddenly struck me, without previous reflection, that it is because God is the supreme Truth and humility is the truth, for it is most true that we have nothing good of ourselves but only misery and nothingness: whoever ignores this, lives a life of falsehood. They that realize this fact most deeply are the most pleasing to God, the supreme Truth, for they walk in the truth. God grant, sisters, that we may have the grace never to lose this self-knowledge! Amen."*[111]

The action of Jesus has allowed this woman to know her most intimate truth: that she is "misery and nothingness," that she has nothing good in and of herself. *Only after having the experience of desolation* can this truth be reached, not in a theoretical or speculative way, but in an experiential, internally felt and existentially welcomed way. That is why we should rejoice in desolation: we are very imperfect and the dust of this world clings to our souls too easily. Christ wants to refine our heart and fill it with his light.

The question is, do we *really* want to go through it? Have we been faithful in the desolations that the Lord has sent us in the past? When we have come to Him and He has responded to us with silence or coldness have we reacted with the humility of this extraordinary woman? It's dizzying to face these questions honestly, right? Many times, I have recalled the words of Saint John of the Cross in his *Spiritual Canticle*:

> *O that men would understand how impossible it is to enter the thicket, the manifold riches of the wisdom of God, without entering into the thicket of manifold suffering making it the desire and consolation of the soul; and how that the soul which really longs for the divine wisdom longs first of all for the sufferings of the Cross, that it may enter in.*
>
> *For this cause it was that St. Paul admonished the Ephesians not to faint in their tribulations, but to take courage: "That being rooted and founded in charity, you may be able to comprehend with all the saints what is the breadth, and length, and height, and depth; to know also the charity of Christ, which surpasses all knowledge, that you may be filled to all the fullness of God."*
>
> *The gate by which we enter into the riches of the knowledge of God is the Cross; and that gate is narrow. They who desire to enter in that way are few, while*

335

those who desire the joys that come by it are many.[112]

Do you want to suffer to enter the thicket of the Cross? Only in this way will we reach the heights for which we have been created and to which God calls us.

But to conform to this mystery of the Cross, just as is suggested in this story of the Canaanite woman, we must fix the gaze of our heart on the Passion of our Lord Jesus Christ, into which we will respectfully and prayerfully enter.

18

MARY IN BETHANY

*"Almighty ever-living God, who as an example of
humility for the human race to follow, caused our
Savior to take flesh and submit to the Cross, graciously
grant that we may heed his lesson of patient suffering
an so merit a share in his Resurrection. Who lives and
reigns with you in the unity of the Holy Spirit, one God,
for ever and ever."* (Palm Sunday Collect Prayer)

We are on the eve of the Solemnity of the Sacred Heart of
Jesus.[113] What a beautiful way to celebrate this day—in the
Spiritual Exercises, listening with greater silence and more
attention to the heartbeat of Jesus.

These words will serve to help you contemplate the Passion
of Jesus. We will have several hours, until tomorrow, to

contemplate the immense love of the Heart of Jesus that on the cross was forever opened for us. His blood purifies us, and his water satisfies us forever. Saint Ignatius invites us to stand before the immense love of our Redeemer. Each one of you is invited to stand next to the cross of Christ and look at him, contemplate him, love him: "They will look upon him who they have pierced" (Jn. 19:37).

I want to explain to you how we are going to contemplate the Passion: I am going to give you suggestions based on the Gospel and the words of Saint Ignatius of Loyola in his Exercises, to help you meditate with fruit on this moment in the life of Jesus. When an entire month of Spiritual Exercises is done, a person spends a whole week focused on the Passion. We do not have that much time, but I want to say something in this regard. The Passion of Christ cannot be covered in a week, a month, a year, or a whole lifetime. Precisely for that reason, it must always be present in our Christian life, since it is a mystery that we must gradually assimilate, step by step, as we move along the path of our life. Wanting to "see everything" in a few days would be reckless.

As these words are simply intended to help you meditate on the Passion, I would like us to look at an episode in the life of Christ that, in the Gospel of St. John, is the prelude to those events. I am referring to the anointing of Mary in Bethany found in Chapter 7. As you know, in the fourth Gospel, the account of the Passion begins from Chapter 8. Therefore, we are on the threshold of the sufferings of Christ that will eventually lead him to his death on a cross.

1. *We return to Bethany*, that place to which we have already been during these Spiritual Exercises and which brings such

pleasant memories. "Six days before Passover Jesus came to Bethany, where Lazarus was, who Jesus had raised from the dead" (Jn. 12:1). St. John gives us the chronological fact: we are six days away from the sacrifice of Christ on Calvary.

It is possible, therefore, to perceive an enormous tension in the air. On the one hand, the enemies of Jesus are preparing to kill him. Jesus is aware of this hostility. In fact, at the end of Chapter 10 we are told that the Pharisees had already tried to arrest him, so he had left Jerusalem. The disciples also saw that something was being prepared against Him. When the Lord finally decides to go up to Jerusalem, Thomas says openly: *"Let us go to die with him"* (Jn. 11:16). On the other hand, more and more people came to Jesus. The Gospel of St. John tells us that especially after the Resurrection of Lazarus, the crowds followed Christ and many believed in Him. The Pharisees even say: *"Look, the whole world has gone after him"* (Jn. 12:19). And the day after this anointing in Bethany, the triumphal entry into the Holy City takes place. The Lord was the great star that Passover and attracted all the attention, as well as the anger of those who wished to see him dead.

Therefore, there was a feeling in the air that something big was going to happen. Maybe that's why the Lord returns to that little corner where he feels at home. In Bethany he had always been comfortable. He was among people who loved him and whom he loved.

To me, these details of the Gospel are charming because they reveal to what extent Jesus was truly human. The divine Person of the Word also had a human psychology, and we see him going to seek refuge, warmth, company, friendship, and understanding.

2. "Jesus came to Bethany, where Lazarus was. They gave a dinner for him there, and Martha served, while Lazarus was one of those reclining at table with him" (v. 1-2). Sitting at the table was Lazarus, whom Jesus had resurrected shortly before. Lazarus represents us, we were dead and Jesus has revived us.

"Our friend Lazarus," Jesus calls him in the preceding chapter (v. 11). It would be wonderful if Jesus could call you friend, too, after these Exercises. It really depends on the grace of God, which you will not be lacking, and on your decision about the life that you choose to take from now on. At the end of this story, the Evangelist will say: "(The) large crowd of the Jews found out that he was there and came, not only because of Jesus, but also to see Lazarus, whom he had raised from the dead. And the chief priests plotted to kill Lazarus too, because many of the Jews were turning away and believing in Jesus because of him" (v. 9-11). It would be equally beautiful if the same happened with you at the conclusion of these Exercises: that people believed in Jesus because of you. May your family and friends desire to draw closer to the Lord when they see the miracle of your resurrection after these days of retreat.

We return to see Martha serving, just as we contemplated her at the beginning of these Exercises, but with an attitude of a totally different heart. She has just experienced the resurrection of her brother and has seen the power of Christ over death itself. Now she does not complain as before. She serves the Lord, but has understood that *"there is need of only one thing"* and, in that service she does for the Lord, she listens to him and loves him.

Where is Mary, the third sibling? It is evident that Mary

also had knowledge of what was being prepared. Did Jesus tell them? Did her woman's intuition perceive it? Did she hear it from someone else, among the many who went to Bethany to see Lazarus in those days? We do not know, but she receives that light. She knows that Jesus has very little time left to live. His end is near and soon her Master, the one she loves, is going to be taken away.

Therefore, there is a contrast between the joy of that banquet that has been prepared in honor of Jesus and the weight that Mary feels in her heart. When two people love each other, there is an attunement that makes you experience what your loved one is feeling. The Lord had announced for the third time to his disciples on this last trip to Jerusalem that suffering and death awaited him before he was resurrected. However, the Gospel notes that "they understood nothing of this; the word remained hidden from them and they failed to comprehend what he said" (Lk. 18:34). The Lord must have experienced a certain loneliness with his disciples. When we try to share with someone something that is important to us, and do not find understanding in the other person, it saddens us. Mary, on the other hand, has that harmony with the Heart of Jesus and in his eyes discovers the drama that is about to be unleashed.

Again, this is a quality to which women seem to be more inclined by nature. Says Edith Stein:

> *Her strength lies in her intuitive grasp of the concrete and the living, especially of the personal. She has the gift of adapting herself to the inner life of others, [52] to their goal orientation and working methods. Feelings are central to her as the faculty which grasps*

341

concrete being in its unique nature and specific value; and it is through feeling that she expresses her attitude.[114]

Mary has adapted herself to the inner life of Jesus. She has discovered in the Heart of Jesus that the sadness of death is about to knock on the door. Maybe they were celebrating that dinner in gratitude for the resurrection of Lazarus, which had happened a few days before. But Mary could not sit down at the table as if nothing was happening, since those would be their last hours in the company of Jesus. Speaking of the death of a friend of his, St. Augustine writes in his *Confessions*:

> *I was astonished that other mortals lived, since he whom I loved, as if he would never die, was dead; and I wondered still more that I, who was to him a second self, could live when he was dead. Well did one say of his friend, Thou half of my soul, for I felt that my soul and his soul were but one soul in two bodies; and, consequently, my life was a horror to me, because I would not live in half. And therefore, perchance, was I afraid to die, lest I should die wholly whom I had so greatly loved.*[115]

Mary, with that delicacy that is so characteristic of her, could have similar thoughts: "How can I be happy when he will soon die, he whom I love? How can I continue living if the Lord dies, who is not half of my soul, but my whole life?" The thought was terrible to her, because she could not live torn in half.

342

Somehow, she was already anticipating the suffering of the Passion; her heart had already begun to suffer with the Lord. This aspect is very important in the meditation of the Passion of Christ. Speaking of the grace that should be asked in each meditation, Saint Ignatius points out:

> *The petition has to be according to the subject matter;*
> *that is, if the contemplation is on the Resurrection,*
> *one is to ask for joy with Christ in joy; if it is on the*
> *Passion, he is to ask for pain, tears and torment with*
> *Christ in torment (SE 48).*

And, more specifically, in the case of the meditations of the third week of the Exercises, Saint Ignatius says that we have "to ask for grief with Christ in grief, anguish with Christ in anguish, tears and interior pain at such great pain which Christ suffered for me" (SE 203).

In the Exercises, we do not simply seek to feel sorry for the sufferings of the Lord, not even to feel pain for what the Lord suffers for us. Grace is to suffer *with Christ.* That is, we ask the Holy Spirit to grant us, through grace and union between us and Christ our Head, to grant that we may experience the same pain suffered by the Heart of Jesus in the days of his Passion, in the measure and with the intensity that He allows for us, according to our faith and our ability to do so.

That must be your request, too. Mary has that attitude. She feels her heart oppressed by the tempest that is about to break loose against her Beloved. In addition, the Lord allows her to participate in that suffering that will have Jesus say five days later, "My soul is sorrowful even to death" (Mt. 26:38). Just as Jesus had suffered with her a few days before and had mourned the death of her brother, Lazarus, now it is Mary who suffers with the sadness that the Heart of Jesus is beginning to feel before his imminent Passion. It is the suffering of two people who love each other and who suffer together because they share the pain, as well as the moments of happiness.

3. "Mary took a liter of costly perfumed oil made from genuine aromatic nard and anointed the feet of Jesus and dried them with her hair" (v. 3).

At the most opportune moment, Mary enters the room with a bottle of perfumed oil. Imagine the scene, the surprised looks of everyone in the house. Some, like Lazarus, look at his sister with eyes of approval and affection, but others do not understand Mary and question her publicly, to the point that Jesus will have to defend her publicly. In the Gospel of St. John, Judas is the only one who expresses his disapproval, but in Mark we are told, "There were some who were indignant (...) They were infuriated with her" (Mk. 14:4,5). They do not understand the gesture because they look at it from outside of love. Jesus is seeing only the heart of Mary who suffers with Him.

We have to see this scene as a mysterious expression of the Passion and Resurrection of Jesus. In the Gospel of Saint Mark, the Lord says: "She has anticipated anointing my body for burial" (Mk. 14:8).

It is a gesture of wonderful tenderness: Mary anoints the body of Jesus before it is taken away from her. She wants to have that tenderness with Jesus as a way to express all of her love for him and to say, "I am with you in this." Mary, with that supernatural finesse of the person she loves, is saying to Jesus: "Lord, you are going to be hated, humiliated, and despised. They are going to do terrible things to you and you are going to die because there are people who do not love you. When you are in that moment, remember that I love you. Smell this fragrance and think of me. I will be here loving you and suffering with you."

This is a symbol of the Resurrection because Mary is doing something that is performed on corpses in the *living* body of the Lord. It is also a mysterious symbol of his Passion, especially with a detail that is not in the story of Saint John, but in that of Saint Mark. John tells us that Mary anointed his feet with the perfumed oil. St. Mark gives us a beautiful detail; "She broke the alabaster jar and poured it on his head" (Mk. 14:3).

That broken alabaster jar is Christ crucified. In the Passion, the body of Jesus will also be "broken," and the perfumed oil of the Holy Spirit will fill the whole world. Mary is also expressing her love for Christ. She offers herself completely, she does not want to keep a drop of love, and she is emptying herself as Jesus empties himself for her in his Passion. Jesus understands the meaning of the gesture that Mary has just made, understands what that broken bottle means. Breaking the jar is the symbol of an irrevocable surrender. She does not want to hold back anything, as Jesus will not withhold anything.

In his letter to the Philippians, St. Paul describes the mystery of the Incarnation and the Passion of Jesus with the Greek word *kenosis* (Phil. 2:7). It has been translated in many ways because the original term has many nuances that cannot be expressed with a single translation. Many times it is translated as "self-emptying." It is also translated as "making oneself nothing," or "self-annihilation."

By becoming a man and, above all, by dying for us, Christ *ekénosen*—he emptied himself. He gave us his all. Saint Ignatius says that in these meditations of the Passion of the Lord we have to consider "how the Divinity hides itself, that is, how it could destroy its enemies but does not do so, and how it leaves the most sacred of Humanity to suffer so very cruelly" (SE 196).

But let's return to the story. When I preside over the Sacrament of Matrimony and I am with the couple before the altar at the moment in which they exchange the consent that makes them husband and wife, I always lower my gaze and never look at them. I have the impression that, although there are many of us present, that moment belongs exclusively to them.

I imagine that when they have the right interior disposition, it's as if everything around them disappears. There is no music, no guests, nothing else, because the world becomes a very small place where there are only two people. They speak to each other as if no one is listening or watching them. This happens now between Jesus and Mary. She anoints Jesus and Jesus lets himself be anointed by her. There is no one else at the table, there is no noise of guests, there is nothing besides the two of them, loving each other and letting themselves be loved. For a moment Jesus no longer suffers; he no longer thinks about what is coming. The world has become a very small place where only Jesus and Mary are. The Word of God says, "Love covers a multitude of sins" (1 Pet. 4:8). Now the love of Mary covers, soothes, the suffering Heart of Jesus for the multitude of our sins.

Mary of Bethany is the first of the repairing souls. Reparation is one of the fundamental aspects of the devotion to the Sacred Heart of Jesus. It is to understand that the Heart of Jesus suffers, and to want to soothe its suffering because the pain of the Heart of Jesus hurts as if it were my own, because it is mine, because I love him, because that suffering has saved me, because I cannot be happy if I do not suffer with the beloved. Mary's double gesture of anointing and wiping Christ's feet expresses the act of loving (anointing) and repairing (wiping).

How beautiful it is to meditate on this Gospel scene on the eve of the Solemnity of the Sacred Heart of Jesus! Mary of Bethany is showing you the way to enter the Heart of Jesus: love him, be sensitive to him, break the jar of your heart and pour your love on Jesus, make him feel loved today as you meditate on his Passion. Empty yourself as Jesus emptied himself for you.

The broken bottle is also a sign of Mary's reparation. It is a sign of an unrequited love, of a love that is going to be taken by death, of a love that is offered to us as a gift, but that is going to be broken, rejected.

Is this not, perhaps, the cause of the greatest suffering for many women in this world? Women who are not loved by their husbands, or by their children, or by their parents, or by other people? How easy it is for these women to sympathize with the Heart of Jesus!

Let us imitate Mary and anoint Jesus ourselves. How can we do it? Through the anointing of the head, which is reparation to Jesus, and the anointing of the feet of Jesus, which is the love of our brothers and sisters. Origen, a Father of the Church, explains this:

347

We too can anoint the Lord's head and feet. We anoint the feet of the Lord when we do works of charity and love in the gift of our brothers, because our brothers are like the feet with which the Lord walks today on earth. And we anoint the head of the Lord when we do works of pure gift of the Lord, without apparent utility, at least, of men. Such are: prayer, virginity, penance. And we can do both: anoint the Lord's head and feet.[116]

4. "The house was filled with the fragrance of the oil" (v. 3).

Mary breaks the bottle and anoints first the head and then the feet of Jesus and, little by little, the perfume of that oil spreads first throughout the room, and then throughout the corridors and throughout the house. I imagine Saint John, already old, writing this memory in his Gospel and breathing deeply to remember again the aromatic smell of that perfume of Mary in Bethany.

This is where we can recall what we said the first day, when we talked about the "application of the senses."[117] You have to try to imagine this smell and let the Holy Spirit work in your senses. These senses are also spiritual senses. What really smells good in this scene is the love of Mary and Jesus. You must smell that love.

I want here to add something, as I understand it, a wonderful detail of this extraordinary woman, because it seems to me that it deepens even more the gesture and tenderness of Mary.

Verse 7 of this passage has always been problematic to understand. The verbal form used by Jesus is very strange.

Indeed, it is so strange that in Max Zerwick's authoritative *A Grammatical Analysis of the Greek New Testament*, the author writes that the text is "not healthy;" that is, the word has been written erroneously in the old copies of the Gospel of St. John.[118]

As we have already said, the version of the synoptic Gospels reads as follows: "She has anticipated anointing my body for burial" (Mk. 14:8). But the Gospel of St. John says something slightly different: "Let her keep this for the day of my burial" (v. 7).

Father Enrique Farfán, an extraordinary professor of Theology who always read the Bible to us directly from Hebrew and Greek, explained that the words of Jesus in this Gospel can be better understood in the original Aramaic spoken by the Lord. Without going into all the details of the explanation, Jesus is seeing and living this moment as that of his true burial on Good Friday. For this reason, the translation of Saint Mark translates better the meaning of the anointing when it says: "She has anticipated anointing my body for burial."

But the question is this: if St. Mark says that Mary broke the alabaster jar and poured the oil, how can Jesus say in Saint John: "Let her keep this for the day of my burial"?

This shows the tenderness of what Mary has done: Mary holds the fragrance of that oil in her hair and on her hands! Saint John has told us that she dried the feet of Jesus with her hair. Let's look at the scene again. She breaks the bottle of oil and anoints, with great love, the head of Jesus with hands that are filled with that extraordinary perfume. She anoints the head of Jesus, gently, with wonderful tenderness. Then she bends down and returns to the feet of Jesus—Mary is always at the feet of Jesus—and anoints his feet with those same hands that were full of the oil that had been poured onto the Lord's head. The feet of Jesus are filled with that "genuine aromatic nard" and Mary dries his feet with her hair. Everyone in the house smells that perfume. Whose perfume is that? The perfume of Jesus and Mary! At that moment, both smell the same, and Mary can say with St. Paul: "We are the aroma of Christ for God among those who are being saved and among those who are perishing" (2 Cor. 2:15).

Mary is saturated with the smell of Christ: she carries it in her hair, she carries it in her hands, she carries it in her heart. And Jesus, defending her from those who had protested that it was a waste, says: "Leave her alone. Let her keep this for the day of my burial." What Jesus means is: let her keep this fragrance in her until the day of my burial.

This is where the gesture acquires a meaning that takes our meditation to another level. The smell of each person is very distinct and personal. Many times, when we smell something that has been in contact with another person, we can smell the person and that smell brings us the memory of that man and that woman. Even when we touch another person, sometimes we pick up their smell and sometimes, even when we are already far apart, we smell the other person on us. Women seem to have a more developed sense of smell than most men. Recently, I had left my alb at the rectory and was at the parish to celebrate the Holy Mass. I took one of the albs that were hung in the vesting room. When I put it on, I suddenly smelled Father Antonio and I remembered, from the smell of the alb, that it was the alb he had worn this Easter at St. Anne. He was already very far away, many weeks had passed, but his smell was still there.

From this perspective, we can enter the depth of that moment of infinite tenderness between Mary and Jesus, when he tells her to keep the oil "for the day of my burial." After that dinner, Jesus leaves Bethany and walks toward his Passion. But something very beautiful happens: Jesus takes with him the smell of Mary, and Mary remains in Bethany with the smell of Jesus. I want to believe that, during the following days, Mary would be wrapped in the presence of Jesus thanks to the smell of that perfumed oil. She would feel embraced and loved by Jesus who, as Saint Ignatius says, "suffers all this for my sins." For her sins. And, when she learned what they were doing to Jesus on Thursday and Good Friday—remember that Bethany is only two miles from Jerusalem—her way of participating in the Passion was the silence and presence of Jesus that she smelled on her own body. That smell and presence is the gift that Jesus wanted to give her.

But it is still more impressive to think of this in the other way: Jesus takes with him the smell of Mary. Christ will suffer the greatest pains that any human being has ever suffered. He suffers them as we say at every Mass, willingly. Saint Ignatius of Loyola says that Jesus *"wants to suffer"* (SE 195). The same Lord says in the Gospel of St. John: "This is why the Father loves me, because I lay down my life in order to take it up again. No one takes it from me, but I lay it down on my own" (Jn. 10:17-18).

The greatest sufferings of Jesus are not the physical ones, although these are terrible. The most excruciating torments of Jesus are interior: betrayal, fear, loneliness, despair, condemnation of souls, ingratitude, rejection, the hardness of men's hearts, feeling unloved by men and abandoned even by his Father. There is no way for us to understand this although these inner sufferings are the ones we have to consider the most and in which we are called to participate.

Jesus, throughout his Passion, in indescribable pain, at certain moments, *smelled of Mary*. He had that smell on his head and on his feet. And he knew there was someone who was loving him. That everything was not sin. That it was worth suffering and dying for souls like his friend Mary, that there, in Bethany, on the other side of the mountain that he could see from the cross, she was suffering with him and loving him with all her heart, as a woman loves.

Therefore, this detail of the smell of the perfume, in the first level of its meaning represents the gift of the Holy Spirit that Jesus pours out when He is broken in his Passion, helps us to understand the depth of Mary's soul and the true meaning that she wanted to give this gesture. It helps us to understand that her intention was to repair, restore *the Heart of Jesus*, saying: "I love you and I will be loving you while you are suffering, and this perfume will remind you." It helps us to understand the tenderness of Mary's heart that wanted Jesus to feel loved in his Passion and in the darkest moments of his life.

It also helps us to give this gesture a dimension of intimacy that we could not understand otherwise. Allow me to use a very bold analogy, with infinite respect for Jesus and with a huge respect for the sacredness of married life. I suppose that when a husband and a wife physically join in conjugal intercourse, something similar happens. I suppose that when one later smells the other, that memory evokes that moment of intimacy. If the physical union has been carried out in a loving way, with tenderness, according to the Will of God, that smell reminds them of the love of the husband and the wife.

The comparison is not irreverent, but in fact allows us to understand the intimacy of this moment between Mary and Jesus. In Sacred Scripture there is only one other book in which the scent of spikenard is mentioned and that is the Song of Songs. Do you see what I am getting at? There, the "bride" anoints her Beloved with the same perfume: "While the king was upon his couch, my spikenard gave forth its fragrance" (1:12). A little further on, the bridegroom goes to his beloved and smells this scent on her. The Lord understands that Mary has this sacred text in her mind and heart, that this is the meaning she is giving to the gesture, that the words of the Song illuminate what she does not dare to say. Is this not the most subtle and beautiful declaration of love in all of Scripture? Mary's anointing with that perfume allows us to enter into her soul and listen to the inner conversation that takes place between her and her Lord. Let us listen to the dialogue that Jesus -also reclining- and Mary now silently say to each other and that only they understand, in this gesture intentionally sought by both of them:

[The Bridegroom:]
   Your lips drip honey, my bride, honey and milk are under your tongue; and the fragrance of your garments is like the fragrance of Lebanon.
   A garden enclosed, my sister, my bride, a garden enclosed, a fountain sealed!
   Your branches are a grove of pomegranates, with

fruits of choicest yield:

Henna with spikenard, spikenard and saffron, sweet cane and cinnamon, with all kinds of frankincense; myrrh and aloes, with all the finest spices;

A garden fountain, a well of living water, streams flowing from Lebanon.

[The Bride:]

Awake, north wind! Come, south wind!

Blow upon my garden that its perfumes may spread abroad.

Let my lover come to his garden and eat its fruits of choicest yield.

(Song of Songs 4:11–16)

This is how these two hearts speak to one another: Jesus finds consolation in the love of his beloved and she asks Jesus to enter into the depths of her soul and to enjoy the love that he gives her. Really, we could get lost in this scene... and never leave again.

Look at the anointing in Bethany as a moment of the greatest intimacy in which you can be called to have the same experience with the Lord. May your love also serve to console the suffering Heart of Christ. Feel his love surround you, as you anoint the Heart that makes you feel deeply and infinitely loved, especially in times of greatest difficulty.

5. "Then Judas the Iscariot, one (of) his disciples, and the one who would betray him, said, 'Why was this oil not sold for three hundred days' wages and given to the poor?' He said this not because he cared about the poor but because

he was a thief and held the money bag and used to steal the contributions" (v. 4-6).

Judas is on another wavelength. It is also important to enter into the inner drama of this disciple. It is striking to think that, although he did not imagine it, he was also six days away from his own death. These are also his last days and he is going to die despairing.

Many things could be said about Judas, but it would be very long and perhaps distract us from the contemplation of Jesus and Mary. The heart of Judas has hardened with the passage of time. He has lived with Jesus, he has heard his words, he has witnessed his miracles—and he has hardened. Judas is the figure that reminds us that we should receive the graces of God and not abuse the goodness of God. The betrayal of Judas has eaten away at his heart. Nobody but Jesus knows about the drama taking place in his disciple's soul. Even at the Last Supper, the other apostles will not suspect him. One thing is clear: in the heart of Judas there is no longer any love for Jesus. He has received more even than Mary, because he has lived closer to the Lord, he has witnessed every step of his public life, but everything has been in vain for him. Let's not be harsh with Judas because, most likely, we are more like him than we are like Mary. We have also betrayed Jesus for thirty pieces of silver many times in our lives, and now we need to repair not only the sins of the world but, above all, our own sins, because, as Saint Ignatius of Loyola says, we have to feel grief and confusion "because for my sins the Lord is going to the Passion."

6. The last point to consider of this passage, as preparation for the meditations on the Passion, has to do with *the value*

of the oil used by Mary.

All four Gospels put the accent on the value of that perfume. It is something that God wants us to notice. Translations usually say that its value was "more than three hundred days' wages" (Mk. 14:5). The word that appears in the Gospel is "*denarii.*" The denarius was a currency that paid the wages of a person working all day. If you remember, for example, in the parable of the men who are invited to work in the vineyard (Mt. 20), that is the wage offered by the owner of the vineyard to the workers.

Therefore, the perfume that Mary uses, made from a plant that is rare and highly prized for its deep, lingering, aromatic scent, is approximately what a person could earn in a whole year working. How much would that be for us, today? $40,000? $50,000? This may be inaccurate, but just imagine what the gift that Mary was giving to Jesus was worth. That price had to do with the scarcity of the plant, the strong and aromatic smell it gave off and how long the fragrance lasted once spilled.

From a human perspective, it is reasonable for those people to qualify that as a "waste" (Mk. 14:4). Moreover, this outrage is so reasonable that we would probably have thought the same thing and described it with the same words. Spending the savings of a whole year of work on oil to anoint a person who was not yet dead is, humanly speaking, a waste.

If you allow me the word, it is "foolishness." I use this word because it gives us the clue to understand something of this mystery, the word that St. Paul uses to speak of the cross and of the crucified Christ: "The message of the cross is foolishness to those who are perishing, but to us who are being saved it is the power of God (...) We proclaim

Christ crucified, a stumbling block to Jews and foolishness to Gentiles, but to those who are called, Jews and Greeks alike, Christ is the power of God and the wisdom of God" (1 Cor. 1:18,23–24).

I must admit that now I am sharing with you an idea over which I've obsessed for a long time. It has been with me since my pilgrimage on foot through the Holy Land. I do not know if I will know how to express it exactly, but it really seems important to me. Although I do not understand it myself, my intuition tells me that here lies the secret of holiness.

Let me express it this way: as Saint Paul says, the wisdom of God is foolishness for the world and for us. It has always struck me that God can sometimes ask for things that make us seem crazy in the eyes of the world, things that even we cannot understand. We are afraid to take those steps because we fear people's opinions, and we are afraid to take risks and lose everything. It's hard for us to trust God totally. God puts us to the test to take our trust in Him to heights that we cannot imagine. Heights that force us to leave our mental schemes and our life plans aside and bet everything on God. For that, we have to be willing to die crucified with Jesus and, most of the believers, lie down or retreat because of fear.

I have always been struck by certain acts of the saints that seem to be real madness. Think, for example, of the sacrifice of Isaac that God asks of Abraham. It is very easy to be wise after the event, but what would you have thought if you were Sara, the wife of Abraham, and your husband told you that God was asking him to sacrifice your only son? Surely you would have attacked Abraham. "Are you crazy? God cannot ask that of you! Didn't God give you Isaac to become the father of a great nation?"

Or think of Saint Francis, that morning when in the Piazza of Assisi and before all the people, he began to completely undress in front of everyone and, especially, before his father. Imagine that you are walking around downtown and you see a man taking off his clothes until he is stark naked like Saint Francis. What would we think of him? I do not think anyone would think, "He is a saint." Even Saint Francis was called "the madman of Assisi."

I have realized that these kinds of things, which seems very strange to us because they are behaviors that we do not see every day, are very common in the lives of the saints. Decisions or behaviors that cannot be understood by people around them, often even good people. I could give you many examples. Take Saint John Bosco, for example: they went to look for him in the oratory where he worked with his orphaned children to take him to the insane asylum. The truck arrived at the oratory sent by his brother priests, who thought he had lost his mind. The last biography I read about a saint a few weeks ago is that of Saint John of God. Saint John of God was admitted to the insane asylum in the city of Granada in Spain because it was evident to everyone that he was crazy.

And Saint Ignatius himself, when he converted, was someone who, they said literally, "had gone mad for the love of God." You can think of many more examples, and you will see how it happens so often in the lives of saints.

In thinking more about this, I realized that deep down the root of these behaviors is in Jesus himself. There is a verse in the Gospel of St. Mark that we do not usually pay much attention to: "When his relatives heard of this they set out to seize him, for they said, 'He is out of his mind'" (Mk.

3:21). See? Is that crazy? In the Passion, when he stands before Herod, as we will see in the movie tonight, Jesus is considered a fool.

And, in thinking about this even more, I realized that, really, the work of man's redemption is the work of a God who, really, is out of his mind. I would be afraid to call Jesus crazy, if it were not that so many saints have already done so. Saint Catherine of Siena writes in her Dialogues: "You placed your dwelling in the beauty of the creature, of which you fell in love like a madman and a drunkard."[119] Another saint, the Italian Carmelite Mary Magdalene of Pazzi, called Jesus "crazy of love." Saint Teresa of the Andes said: "Christ, that crazy man of love, has made me crazy."

The Incarnation is a true madness and the Passion of Christ is the greatest of the madness. The Passion of Jesus, like the perfume of Mary, is a "waste." Because God could have saved us without suffering so much, without having to reach those inconceivable extremes. Jesus understands Mary because in her "waste" he is also contemplating his "waste."

The saints are the ones who have entered into this madness of God's love and have allowed themselves to get drunk on that love. They tell us with the words of St. Paul in his second letter to the Corinthians: "if we are out of our minds, it is for God" (2 Cor. 5:13). The wisdom of the saints is often described as "the folly of the cross." Human reason will always try to set limits within the margins of human prudence, but as Saint Bernard says,

You want to tell me why and in what measure God is to be loved. I reply, the reason for loving God is God himself, and the measure, is to love without measure.[120]

I said before that the secret of holiness is here. Obviously,

I'm not encouraging anyone to make extravagances or perform meaningless acts. It would be an artificial and, therefore, carnal imitation of Christ. What I am saying is that God can ask for things that we cannot understand, that will expose us to the condemnation of good people, that will force us to take a leap of faith in the most absolute vacuum. God can ask for that. He can ask for a share in the mystery of the Passion and lead us to lose everything, as St. Paul says: "For his sake I have accepted the loss of all things and I consider them so much rubbish, that I may gain Christ" (Phil. 3:8).

I want to say that there are people who are very, very good, who will go to heaven because they love God, but who will never be holy because they lack, we lack, this madness of God, this madness of the saints. And I think that in the Exercises we have to ask Jesus for this *metanoia*, which is not just to stop sinning. It is, as we said yesterday and two days ago, to have the mind of Christ. It is breaking the bonds of our mental schemes in which we are confined and opening ourselves totally to the action of God in our souls.

In the account of the anointing at Bethany we find the two mentalities confronted: the mentality of the world, which is prudent according to human prudence; and the mentality of God, who loves without measure and arrives at excess. Where are we?

In the meditations of the Passion, we must be amazed at that crazy love of Christ for us or, as Saint Ignatius says, *"for me."* We must contemplate the folly of God and we have to give an answer to that madness. I finish with the words of Saint Ignatius himself, wishing for you that the contemplation of the Passion of Christ will produce fruits of transformation:

> *Imagining Christ our Lord present and placed on the Cross, let me make a Colloquy, how from Creator He is come to making Himself man, and from life eternal is come to temporal death, and so to die for my sins. Likewise, looking at myself, what I have done for Christ, what I am doing for Christ, what I ought to do for Christ. And so, seeing Him such, and so nailed on the Cross, to go over that which will present itself (SE 53).*

19

THE GRAIN OF WHEAT

DAY 7 (MORNING) – SIXTEENTH MEDITATION – THE PASSION (I)

"Almighty ever-living God, who as an example of humility for the human race to follow caused our Savior to take flesh and submit to the Cross, graciously grant that we may heed his lesson of patient suffering and so merit a share in his Resurrection." (Palm Sunday Collect)

The last meditation has been, in my opinion, the best preparation to dedicate all this day to the calm consideration of the Passion and Death of the Lord. I strongly encourage you to stop the clocks, as if there is nothing beyond this day that you are living. On the other hand, the thought is beautiful that, for your contemplation of the agony of Jesus until his burial, you will have approximately the same period of time in which those events unfolded. In less than twenty-four hours, Christ traveled his painful way from Gethsemane to Calvary. You can almost walk step by step, at the same pace, and accompany Jesus in all that he "suffers in his humanity and wants to suffer" for me (SE 1 95).Ask the Holy Spirit to live it with that same intensity, with a divine love that will definitely render you to your Lord.

1. I would like to remind you of the attitudes we spoke about yesterday following the teaching of Saint Ignatius. He invites you to have true *compassion* for Jesus Christ. It is not just about feeling pity for the Lord, but also about sharing in his pain and *suffering together with him* (*cum-passio*).Loyola also pointed out to us the need *to enter into the Heart of Jesus.* Our consideration cannot be reduced principally to the physical torment and the cruel tortures to which the Son of God is subjected for our sake, we must also reflect on the fact that He does it "for me," wanting to suffer for love of me. We have to *personalize* the Passion. This is how Saint Paul puts it: "I live by faith in the Son of God who has loved me and given himself up for me" (Gal. 2:20).

If you have carried out the preceding meditation fruitfully, the thought that you "were" Mary of Bethany should console you. That is to say, *you have consoled Jesus with your love* and He has taken all that affection with him to the Passion. The scent of your perfumed oil lingers in his hair and when He breathes deeply, Christ inhales your love for Him and he fills his lungs and Heart with it. He will have you continuously present with him, and you too have been anointed by the Holy Spirit with the fragrance of the Lord. A true *impregnation* has taken place by which Christ has covered you with himself

(Gal. 3:27).You can smell him in the consolation that he is giving you; feel him in "those eyes desired which are outlined in my heart" as Saint John of the Cross so beautifully writes.[121]

The Passion of Christ has the inner power to transform our whole existence; to make great sinners into great saints. It is the most sublime meditation and nothing can better help us to take flight than the contemplation of what God has done out of love for us. This is how the Lord himself expresses it in one of his revelations to Saint Faustina Kowalska:

> *There is more merit to one hour of meditation on My sorrowful Passion than there is to a whole year of flagellation that draws blood; the contemplation of My painful wounds is of great profit to you, and it brings Me great joy.*[122]

The reason for this efficacy lies in the fact that here it is definitely revealed how far-gone Jesus is in his love for us. Has God lost his mind in rapture over his creature? Allow me to call Christ mad, as I did yesterday. Love for you has certainly driven him mad, and his sacrifice is the greatest folly imaginable by a God madly in love with his creature. A God out of his mind, unhinged in his salvific will. Oh Lord! What have we done to deserve you as our Redeemer? How can you love us so much when we love you so little?

2. In the same chapter of the fourth Gospel, where we read the account of the anointing at Bethany, we find the moment of his triumphal entry into Jerusalem. Immediately after this, a scene takes place that always seemed to me a little strange

and which we will now briefly consider. Saint John tells us that among those who had come to the Holy City to celebrate the Passover, there was a group of Greeks who approached Philip with the following request: "We would like to see Jesus" (Jn. 12:21).That is what we are also looking for today: we want to see the Lord, and so we are very interested in listening attentively to Christ's response.

Those pilgrims do not exactly approach this disciple by chance. Philip is in fact a Greek name and reveals the very probable Hellenic origin of that apostle. Philip speaks with Andrew and together they present to the Lord the supplication of these foreigners.

What is Jesus' response? "The hour has come for the Son of Man to be glorified. Amen, amen, I say to you, unless a grain of wheat falls to the ground and dies, it remains just a grain of wheat; but if it dies, it produces much fruit. Whoever loves his life loses it, and whoever hates his life in this world will preserve it for eternal life" (v. 23-25).

I have said before that this episode seems "strange" to me and the reason is this: what does the request of those Greeks have to do with the Lord's reply? It seems as if Christ's response had nothing whatsoever to do with what those men had asked of him through his apostles. How would they react when they heard those words? They would probably be perplexed, not understanding its meaning. However, as we are going to see next, Jesus' response goes directly to the heart of what had been asked of him, taking the initial request to a dimension that goes beyond what those people were really asking for. Doesn't the Lord always work in this way? With his words, he lifts us up; with his works, he transforms us.

These people wanted to *see Jesus.* The Lord's answer to them is, basically, "If you really want to see me, that is, if you want to know who I am; if you are interested in me revealing the *mystery of my person* and mission, you must *see me die* like the grain of wheat. You cannot see me now because my love is going to unfold before you in all its magnitude only when I fall to the ground and die. *Then* you will be able to see me."

With his answer, Christ is pointing them to the summit of Calvary, where they will be able to see, in the one "whom they have pierced" (Jn. 19:37), the grain of wheat that dies to give life to the world. It is there where we *contemplate* God's love for us in the most eminent way and where the interior of his Heart, which is all love and mercy for mankind, is revealed to us in all its fullness. At the same time, the fruit of that death will be discovered on the morning of the Resurrection when he springs forth from the earth victorious and immortal.

The same is true for us, two thousand years later. To see who Jesus is and how much he loves us, we must look at his Passion and Death. That is what we want to do today. That is where his mystery is revealed, where Christ unveils himself to us and lets us see him in all the depth of his love for us. At the beginning of this day that lies before you, this passage is also an invitation from the Lord for you to let "your eyes be filled" by the love of Christ for each one of you. He is going to manifest himself to you and he will let you see him in the reality of his openness and intimacy. Do you really want to see Jesus?

3. This last question does not permit a quick answer. What does it really mean to "want to see Jesus?" In his own reply,

the Lord offers us the solution to this question. Indeed, the words of Christ to those Greeks can also be read in reverse, as words referring *to us* and not only to Him. That is, he invites us to die like the grain of wheat to bear fruit. At the same time, He is teaching us that *in order to see Jesus, we must first die because only then will He manifest Himself to us.*

In this way, to the request of the Greeks who ask to see the Lord, Christ responds by saying, "When I die on the altar of the Cross you will really be able to see who I am and how much I love you." On the other hand, and referring to us, the Lord seems to say, "If you want to see me, you must first be willing to fall to the ground and die. Only then can you truly contemplate me."

This is where we battle: in generosity to Jesus. We would like it to be the other way around, right? We want the Lord to reveal himself to us first and for us to deny ourselves completely afterwards. Perhaps that is the reason why our life never really changes. It would be very different if our starting point was that of a *radical and absolute surrender* to Jesus, the attitude of the one who "wants to take advantage of everything," as Saint Ignatius writes (SE 20).It is there that the fruit of these days of retreat and of our Christian life in general is decided: in the *generosity* that we have towards the Lord.

Allow me a very illustrative example. In the eighth speech of the *Glories of Mary*, Saint Alphonsus María de Liguori offers the following anecdote:

> *Father Silvanus Razzi tells of a pious priest who loved our Blessed Lady very much. One day he became inflamed with the desire to see the Blessed Mother.*

He decided to pray for this favor. Mary sent an angel to tell him he could have his wish—but under this condition: that after the vision he would be blind. The man accepted the condition.

One day the Blessed Virgin appeared to him. But the man had become somewhat reluctant to settle for blindness, and so he decided to look at Our Lady with one eye only. However, entranced by her beauty, he could not help opening the other eye. But at that moment Our Lady vanished. The man became sad. He did not regret that his one eye had gone blind, but he was sorry not to have seen Mary with both eyes. So he resumed his prayers and begged to see the Blessed Virgin again, protesting that he would gladly accept total blindness in return for the favor. The man's devotion pleased our Blessed Lady and so she appeared a second time. But this time, instead of allowing him to become totally blind, Mary healed the other eye and restored its sight.

This story is delightful in its simplicity and reveals a very human trait. For you, it is almost a warning at the beginning of this pivotal day of your experience in this retreat. Many times, when we approach the Lord —like the priest in the Alphonsian narrative— we *cover one eye*. What do I mean? We want God to show himself to us, but deep down, we are not willing to *give everything*.

You must ask yourself, before seeing Jesus in his annihilation, in his excruciating agony, if you have come to this retreat with one eye covered. Maybe you want to be better or to live your life of faith more intensely, but do you have the desire to risk your whole life and change *whatever is necessary* for him? The course of these exercises has brought you to this point and now you must measure yourself against a God who has not reserved anything for himself, who has loved "to the end" (Jn. 13:1), who has poured out every last drop for you and *who demands the same response from you in order to transform you.* We cannot enter this day half-heartedly. It is not honest to want to negotiate a cheap and limited surrender on our part with a God who has given everything. Shame on us to dare to enter the sacred ground of the Passion in this way.

So before even opening Sacred Scripture to meditate on the agony of Jesus, pray to the Holy Spirit to place in you the disposition, the desire to die to whatever is necessary, to consider everything as refuse "in order to win Christ" (Phil. 3:8).

Allow me to express it in the words of Saint Bernard: "Learn from Christ how you should love Christ."[123] If He has emptied himself for you, do not expect Him to give Himself to you without first cleansing your heart from everything that prevents union with Him.

4. At the same time that we ask for the grace to be willing to *truly see* Jesus in his pain and death, it is important to implore the grace of a *new look* at the crucified One. It is an idea that has already appeared in our Exercises, but which modulates in a different way depending on the moment in the journey. Allow me, once again, to illustrate it with another example that, in this case, has come to us through Saint Teresa of Jesus.

370

In chapter 22 of the *Book of her Foundations*, the Carmelite saint tells us about the conversion of Catalina Godínez before an image of Christ on the cross. The writer first describes the worldliness of this young woman and her desire not to let herself be ruled by anyone. She belonged to a family "of noble lineage," wealthy, who enjoyed "plenty of temporal goods." Despite the fact that her father had tried to marry her to several suitors, she had always refused because "it seemed a low thing to be subject to anyone." Saint Teresa says of this young woman that "she had a high esteem for herself."

One morning, before her father woke up, while she was in her room, Catalina contemplated the crucifix that hung on the wall. Obviously, she had seen the image many times and knew the account of the Lord's Passion. She discovered nothing new that day, and yet something *happened,* and that *something* changed her life forever. What was different? Obviously, the grace of God, but what changed *was her gaze*: she contemplated that Jesus that she had seen so many times before, but she saw him in a *new and different w ay*. Let's listen to Saint Teresa as she tells the story:

> "*One day while in a room next to the one in which her father was lying down, she happened to read on a crucifix the inscription that is placed over the cross. Suddenly when she read it, the Lord worked a complete change in her: (...) The moment she read the inscription, it seemed to her that just as sunshine enters a dark room, a light came into her soul by which she understood the truth. With this light she set her eyes on the Lord who was on the cross shedding blood,*

371

and she thought about how badly He was treated and of His great humility and about how different the road of pride was that she was following. There must have been some space of time in which the Lord suspended her. There His Majesty gave her a deep knowledge of her own misery, and she desired that all might know of it. He gave her so great a desire to suffer for God that all that the martyrs suffered she desired to suffer with them. She experienced such profound humiliation and self-abhorrence that were it not an offense against God, she would have wanted to be a very dissolute woman so that all might abhor her. Thus she began to despise herself with great desires for penance, which afterward she put into effect. She at once promised chastity and poverty and wanted to see herself so subject that she would have rejoiced to be carried off then to the land of the Moors and remain there. All of these virtues lasted in her in such a way that the experience was clearly seen to be a supernatural favor from our Lord, as will be said later, so that all might praise Him."[124]

If I insist on this aspect, it is because I consider it to be *by far* the most transcendental and decisive. I doubt very much that today God will give you top-secret revelations of his mystery. Do not expect anything like that because pride, always devious, can hide there. What the Lord undoubtedly does want to give you on this journey is the grace of a *new look* that pierces your soul and shakes you interiorly in such a way that nothing is the same from now on. He wishes to grant you this *today*—"today is the day of salvation" (2 Cor. 6:2)—sothat the manifestation of his immense love may be the beginning of a life of holiness.

5. When you conclude this experience of the Exercises, you must transfer this new look to the other areas of your life. Really, love makes all things new and when you return home, you have to see everything with the novelty of a child for whom the spectacle of the world is being unfolded before his eyes for the first t ime. If you are married, you must contemplate your husband as you did the day you fell in love with him. If you live with your parents, you should treat them with tenderness without keeping unpleasant or painful memories of them. If you work, you have to carry out your tasks with the excitement and joy with which you began them on the first day. If you get out of bed in good health tomorrow, you have to face the day full of gratitude, like someone who wakes up in a new universe where everything around them is a source of joy, energy, and grace.

In this way, this week here will have been a true *school of life* for you and you will return rejuvenated, renewed, transformed.

6. As you can see, I do not mind repeating the ideas that are more transcendental.

As a seminarian, I remember visiting on several occasions a venerable Dominican priest, Father Antonio Royo Marín, who was possibly the most dazzling preacher in Spain during the 1950s and 1960s. For nearly thirty years he was a professor of Theology in Salamanca and received from John Paul II the *Pro Ecclesia et Pontifice* medal in recognition of his theological work, his writings, and his unwavering fidelity to the Magisterium of the Church. He passed away in 2005 at the age of ninety-two, after a long life of service to Christ and his bride, the Church. Personally, I consider him a saint and I think that this breed of men no longer exists in the world today. We have lost them, much to our misfortune.

In one of those charming conversations at the Atocha Monastery in Madrid, Father Royo Marín impetuously exhorted us to *insist on the fundamentals.* I still remember the vehemence of his expressions and the force with which he transmitted them to us in that little room warmly illuminated by the tired afternoon sun. I can almost hear him as I write these words even with the distance of more than twenty years that separate me from that moment: "Repeat!" He would tell us. "Repeat! Do not get tired of repeating! Because the important things are few!" That old Dominican man, always wrapped up in his beloved white habit of the Order of Preachers, almost blind, squinting with difficulty through old, dirty, and thick glasses, was quite right. When faced with the temptation to transmit novelties, I prefer to go back to the basics and delve into them, not leaving them until I have properly internalized them. As the old saying goes, *repetitia iuvant,* that things that are repeated are retained more firmly.

The very method of Saint Ignatius is based, to a great extent, on *repetitions.* Due to lack of time, we have not been able to practice this feature of the Exercises, but when they are done for a full month, Loyola insists on repeating the meditations, usually up to five times *each day.* The purpose of this is to help us discover with greater *clarity what the Holy Spirit* is indicating to us in the consideration of the reflection that we are doing at that moment. Perhaps at the beginning we have a lot of "material" to meditate on, but after five hours in the same exercise, the normal thing is that we end by sifting and narrowing everything with which we began prayer, the aspects in which we feel that God is *especially* manifesting his Will over us: this is where we have to focus, avoiding excessive dispersion. As the saint himself notes and we recall, "it is not much knowledge that fills and satisfies the soul, but the intimate understanding and relish of the truth" (SE 2).

So, at the conclusion of this brief introduction, I allow myself to remind you now of what Jesus shares with us in the Gospel of Saint John (10:17-18):"This is why the Father loves me, because I lay down my life in order to take it up again. No one takes it from me, but I lay it down on my own." Christ *gives himself voluntarily.* In the darkest night, He steps forward and allows himself to be bound, tortured, and crucified *for love of you.* It is his desire to save you that pushes and urges him to give his life: "I have come to set the earth on fire, and how I wish it were already blazing" (Lk. 12:49)! That fire is none other than love, a volcano of love that is the Heart of Jesus, and which finally, during the Passion, will begin to bleed with the burning magma of salvation. The wound in his side will be the cleft through which the gift of Redemption for all men will run ardently. We, too, hope to arrive there at the end of this journey. May the Lord grant us that grace.

20

MARY AT THE FOOT OF THE CROSS

"O God, who willed that, when your Son was lifted high on the Cross, his Mother should stand close by and share his suffering, grant that your Church, participating with the Virgin Mary in the Passion of Christ, may merit a share in his Resurrection." (Collect Prayer, Memorial of Our Lady of Sorrows, September 15).

In the second meditation of this day dominated by the overwhelming figure of the suffering Christ, I want to take you to the foot of the cross on which Jesus was raised for our salvation. "The cross," it has been said, "is the book that, in silent eloquence, teaches the science of salvation." St. Thomas Aquinas, for his part, writes that for the Passion

377

of Christ completely suffices to fashion our lives. "Whoever wishes to live perfectly should do nothing but disdain what Christ disdained on the cross and desire what he desired, for the cross exemplifies every virtue."[125] I invite you to pause here on your way and consider if there is anyone who has loved you as he has loved you.

"Near the cross of Jesus stood his mother..." (Jn. 19:25). We cannot leave these Spiritual Exercises without contemplating the image of the sorrowful Virgin. We have seen Mary at the beginning of the human journey of the Word of God. We have walked with her along the paths of Palestine and shared her joy at the birth of her Son, the poorest of the poor. Now, we fulfill our duty as her children by approaching her in the most difficult circumstance of her life, the moment of greatest darkness that precedes the most luminous morning of her existence.

1. *Mary's journey to Golgotha.* For Mary, Calvary represents the culmination of an interior journey that began in Nazareth and Bethlehem. We Catholics usually have an unconfessed problem when it comes to our Mother. We have been taught since we were little children the need to incorporate Mary into our Christian life and one of the reasons for this has to do with the very imitation of Jesus Christ. If the Lord loved his mother, how can we not love her too? We have been told so many times how much Jesus loved and loves Mary: no one has the Sacred Heart loved more than she who is "full of grace." Everything in Our Lady's soul is lovable, all of her is delightful in the eyes of God. There is no corner of her interior dwelling that is not inundated by divine love, and so of all human persons, only in Mary has the Most Holy Trinity

found supreme and perfect satisfaction.

We Catholics carry this in the DNA of our spirituality, regardless of our origin, culture, or state in life. *De Maria numquam satis*: we can never say too much about her.

Precisely because of all of the above, when we scan the pages of Sacred Scripture, we would expect to find a tenderness on the part of Christ towards Mary that would allow us to glimpse traces of the boundless love of the Son of God for his Mother. Instead, it pains us to note the opposite. In the Gospels, Jesus doesn't seem to treat the Virgin with the closeness, or tenderness, or affection of a son for his mother. A review of the various passages in which their paths cross emanates distance, coolness, even harshness on the part of the Lord! Jesus' behavior towards his Mother makes us uncomfortable to an extent. It leaves us somewhat disheartened, perplexed and circumspect because we seem to find a certain tension between what we have been taught about this particular topic and what we read in the Word of God. I want to focus on this aspect, which reaches its culmination in the crucifixion of the Lord and which for us is a very great lesson of Christian life.

Our Lady's model is truly admirable. Reading the Gospels, one has the inevitable impression that *Jesus becomes progressively more separated from her.* We want to offset the harshness of these episodes or smooth out the brusqueness of Jesus toward his Mother with various deflections, but we cannot deny the reality: it is there and we have to recognize it.

Yes, it seems that the life of Christ is a gradual, ever deeper separation from Mary. Let us briefly review this journey because it illuminates the scene before us now, the moment of the maternal presence at the foot of the cross.

This "detachment" begins at the very moment of the birth of Jesus, as we have already seen. The very fact of abandoning the maternal womb already expresses a detachment that is not only physical but also internal: we can contemplate Mary placing her Son in the manger, already, from the beginning giving him to God and to mankind in an attitude of offering, aware that this Child was special, that he belonged to everyone and not only to her.

Eight days later, the presentation in the Temple takes place, when Christ is offered to Yahweh in fulfillment of the prescriptions of the Mosaic law (Lk. 2:21-39). There, moreover, Mary hears Simeon's prediction of a storm on the horizon of her life: "this child is destined for the fall and rise of many in Israel, and to be a sign that will be contradicted... and you yourself a sword will pierce" (v. 34-35). Indescribable pain and suffering at some point in an unknown future are foreseen for her.

Did Mary see this prophecy fulfilled in her anxiety over the loss of the Child Jesus at the age of twelve in Jerusalem? In this passage, our Mother's moving lament escapes her: "Son, why have you done this to us? We were looking for you in *anguish*" (Lk. 2:48). Christ's reply to Mary shows that what happened was *deliberately* intended by Him. Jesus separated himself from his parents, *knowing full well what he was doing.* That is to say, the distance that caused Mary and Joseph to suffer was not the result of an absent-minded Jesus unintentionally wandering through the crowded streets of the Holy City. It was the consequence of a *decision expressly willed* by the Lord. This scene is the only Gospel passage in which Mary calls Jesus *"son."* Christ answers her by telling her that he must occupy himself with the things of *his Father*. That is to say, Jesus answers her by underlining the primacy of His eternal sonship with God. It is as if the Lord was enlightening his Mother as to the priority that his bond with the heavenly Father had over his relationship with her as mother.

The next episode recorded in Sacred Scripture takes us to Cana of Galilee almost twenty years later (Jn. 2:1-11). It seems to me that we do not grasp the harshness of the Lord's response to the Virgin here. With the utmost discretion, she had limited herself to explaining the pressing need of those newlyweds: "they have no wine." Christ's reply is curt, short, apparently excessive in its acrimony: "Woman, how does your concern affect me?" (v. 4) This is a very harsh reply! It is so because the expression refers not only to the situation of the moment, but to *the very relationship of Jesus with Mary.* The Lord does not say to His Mother, "What do you and I have *to do with this matter?*" Instead, Christ says to her, "What do you and I have to do with *each other?*"

In order for us to understand how icy this expression must have sounded, let us think about the following. Grammatically, the same phrase that the Lord employs here with his mother—"τί ἐμοὶ καὶ σοί (what do you and I have to do with each other)?"—is the one that, in the Gospel of St. Mark, Satan addresses to Jesus in the person of a possessed man! In a ferocious manner, the demon says in that passage to Jesus Christ, "τί ἐμοὶ καὶ σοί, (What do you and I have to do with each other)" (Mk. 5:7)? We cannot now consider this most beautiful passage in the detail of all its teachings, but I hope that what has been said will suffice to better grasp in what way Jesus addresses his beloved Mother here.

Finally, during the ministry of his public life, Mary appears on two more occasions, and in both passages we find responses from Jesus that apparently bypass the Virgin. In the first, someone announces to the Lord that his mother and brothers have come to see him and are outside waiting for him. Do we find perhaps some expression of joy on the part of Christ, some explicit indication or recognition of his love for her? Not at all. "Who is my mother, and who are my brothers? And looking around at those seated in the circle he said, "Here are my mother and my brothers" (Mk. 3:33-34). Certainly not the warmest of welcomes. In the second case, to the comment of a woman who "compliments" his mother in a loud voice, "Blessed is the womb that carried you and the breasts at which you nursed" (Lk. 11:27), the Lord redirects this praise by widening and opening it not only to Mary, but to everyone who hears the Word of God and puts it into practice: "Rather, blessed are those who hear the word of God and observe it" (Lk. 11:28).

Thus, the feeling one has reading Scripture is that of a progressive distancing—intentionally sought by Jesus—that reaches its culmination on the cross where, on the one hand, Christ gives himself to the Father—"into your hands I commend my spirit" (Lk. 23:46)—and, on the other hand, he entrusts Mary to the protection of his beloved Disciple: "Behold your mother. And from that day on he took her into his home" (Jn. 19:27). Thus, we arrive at the zenith of this apparent separation that began in the cave of Bethlehem. Let's take a closer look: it is not simply that the Lord distances himself from her because of his death; it is that before dying, as it were, he *transfers his sonship* to John: "Woman, behold your son" (v. 26). In other words,

Christ not only separates himself from Mary by his death, but before that moment arrives, he has already "abandoned" her into the hands of another.

St. Bernard describes in one of his sermons the suffering of the Virgin upon hearing those words from the lips of Jesus:

> *Were those words, 'Woman, behold your Son,' not more than a word to you, truly piercing your heart, cutting through to the division between soul and spirit? What an exchange! John is given to you in place of Jesus, the servant in place of the Lord, the disciple in place of the master; the son of Zebedee replaces the Son of God, a mere man replaces God himself. How could these words not pierce your most loving heart, when the mere remembrance of them breaks ours, hearts of iron and stone though they are!*[126]

I know that all the passages I have just mentioned could be answered by offering the *spiritual* meaning of each of the stories. At this level, what might seem at first sight to be an angry reply from the Lord is in reality an exaltation of his Mother. The fact that this is so cannot lead us, however, to deny the *literal* meaning that is at the basis of the correct interpretation of the sacred text: the proper explanation must consider *both* levels of meaning without detriment to either of them.

What was the Blessed Virgin's reaction to these episodes with her Son? Sacred Scripture spares us from having to suppose an answer: "Mary kept all these things, pondering them in her heart" (Lk. 1:29; 2:19; 2:51). In other words, she not only participated in the mysteries of Christ's life, but she *pondered them attentively.* The handmaid of the Lord learns from Jesus, takes everything with her and reflects on it within herself, digests it slowly, assimilates it little by little. It is an admirable attitude: she never reacts angrily, but *let herself be "done unto" by Christ.* The Lord's responses, so difficult to reconcile with filial love, are in reality the hammer blows on the anvil that give form to a precious metal—the gold of which Mary's immaculate Heart is made—and form a faith that has never wavered, but that has found itself, like us, at a crossroads that have left it confused.

In the episode of the Canaanite woman, we have already seen that the words of Jesus served as a *purification* for a great soul at an extraordinary spiritual height. In the case of Mary, this darkness does not have the purpose of *purification,* but rather of *appraisal* of the work that the Holy Spirit has been doing in her since the very moment of her conception. Therefore, the interior journey to which Mary was invited by Jesus does not lead her to a separation from Him—as could be deceptively deduced from appearances—but to a *gradual union* with her Son in the darkness of faith, and this is in fact very luminous for us because it helps us to see in her the work that the Most Holy Trinity also wishes to accomplish in us. How can we explain this?

2. In the *Spiritual Canticle,*[127] speaking of the supreme degrees of union with God, St. John of the Cross affirms that in them the soul is enlightened about the substantial mysteries of the hypostatic union and the union of men in God. Mary believed from the beginning, but throughout her life the Lord enriched her faith with new insights that illuminated what

she had already accepted—the divinity of her Son—making it progressively more tangible, more vivid. That is to say, as St. John of the Cross indicates, in all those moments of Mary's life to which we have referred, what is revealed little by little to the Virgin is *the mystery of the hypostatic union of her Son*—the divine filiation of Christ, his relationship in the Father, the union of men with Jesus and the vocation of Mary in relation to Him—which she already knew by faith but which is illustrated with special lights. Each step of her journey is like a ray of light that does not reach the depths of the mystery, but which is progressively made manifest to her. It is an "understanding without fully understanding," which reveals as well as conceals, which penetrates her soul to its depths, but which does not prevent her from having to continue to advance in the understanding of the Mystery of Christ, which is "like a rich mine, with many recesses full of treasures, and however deeply we may descend we shall never reach the end, for in every recess new veins of new treasures abound in all directions."[128]

And the Mystic Doctor points out that in Christ are hidden all the treasures of wisdom and knowledge:

> *But the soul cannot reach these hidden treasures unless it first passes through the thicket of interior and exterior suffering: for even such knowledge of the mysteries of Christ as is possible in this life cannot be had without great sufferings, and without many intellectual and moral gifts, and without previous spiritual exercises; for all these gifts are far inferior to this knowledge of the mysteries of Christ, being only a preparation for it.*

This is how Mary is at the foot of the cross, passing through and entering into the "thicket of exterior and interior suffering." This should give us much light and comfort because the work of God in our souls follows a similar itinerary to the extent that we allow the Lord to act in our hearts. Like Mary, we are called to progressively embrace the mystery of Christ, to walk without understanding, to lack all the answers and to be perplexed by the way in which the Lord proceeds in our lives. In short, we have been invited to unite ourselves to Christ crucified because only "if we have died with Christ, we believe that we shall also live with him" (Rom. 6:8; 2 Tim. 2:11).

My dear Father Carlos Valverde, SJ used to repeat this beautiful expression: "Suffering is the price of being." This statement is true on so many levels. Mary's journey with Jesus, which led her to the foot of the cross, represents this embodiment in the order of grace of the same principle: the cornerstone of holiness is conformation to Jesus, who allowed himself out of love to be crucified. At the foot of the cross, Mary gathers that love which pours out of the Heart of Christ in streams, filling the cup of her own Immaculate Heart. Our Lady thus appears before our eyes as the *first disciple of the Crucified One,* faithful where so many have failed, accompanying her Son and receiving from Him, from the precious throne of the cross, the admirable lesson of the greatest love.

On this most important day of these Spiritual Exercises, you too must become a disciple of Christ at the foot of the cross. Jesus gives us much light in the darkness on Calvary! It is not easy to express it in words, but at times, when one is going through a very dark moment, the only thing that gives peace, calm, rest, encouragement, and consolation is to take refuge in the shadow of that crucified God, and to raise our eyes to feel ourselves looked at and loved by Him.

3. "Behold your son" (Jn. 19:26): *the woman's participation in Mary's spiritual motherhood.* The "pilgrim of faith" discovers, then, in her relationship with Christ and throughout her earthly existence, her mission, which is revealed to her every step of the way and which reaches its definitive manifesta-tion next to her crucified Son: to extend her motherhood to all the disciples of Jesus. St. John Paul II expresses it in these words:

> *If through faith Mary became the bearer of the Son given to her by the Father through the power of the Holy Spirit, while preserving her virginity intact, in that same faith she discovered and accepted the other dimension of motherhood revealed by Jesus during his messianic mission. One can say that this dimension of motherhood belonged to Mary from the beginning, that is to say from the moment of the conception and birth of her Son. From that time she was "the one who believed." But as the messianic mission of her Son grew clearer to her eyes and spirit, she herself as a mother became ever more open to that new dimension of motherhood which was to constitute her "part" beside her Son. Had she not said from the very beginning: "Behold, I am the handmaid of the Lord; let it be to me according to your word" (Lk. 1:38)? Through faith Mary continued to hear and to ponder that word, in which there became ever clearer, in a*

way "which surpasses knowledge" (Eph. 3:19), the
self-revelation of the living God.[129]

If by the cross our Mother reached the summit of her union with Jesus in the darkness of faith, Christ's words finally reveal to her the mystery of her own identity, of who she is in God's redemptive plan. By being the mother of the Word Incarnate, Mary has been constituted the source of life for all men. The words of Jesus—"Behold your son"—are not simply an invitation for Mary to recognize herself as the Mother of Christ's disciples from that moment on, but rather they openly manifest to her what she *already was from the beginning* of salvation history. By conceiving the Head in the little house of Nazareth, she generated the rest of the members of the Mystical Body of Christ. Now, Mary had to assimilate this reality as the Revelation of Jesus Christ unfolded, and it is here, in the agony of Good Friday, that she grasps the depth of this mission.

Therefore, when Jesus exclaims "Behold your son," the Lord is not only entrusting his "beloved disciples" to Mary: in fact, he is inviting her, in faith, to *discover Jesus' presence in them.* "There you have your son" is a way of saying to her: "Mother, you have me now in them. Look at me in them. Find me in them. Love me in them. *There you have your son*: there you have me." Christ is a few moments away from dying on the cross, but he remains alive, so to speak, in John and in those to whom he is giving life by his death. If you recall, in the episode of the resurrection of the widow of Naim's son, we are told that Christ, seeing the suffering of that woman, "had mercy on her and said to her, "Do not weep" (Lk. 7:13) and, on raising the young man from the dead, "gave him back to his mother" (v. 15). If the Heart of Jesus was moved by the pain of that widow, how much compassion would he not feel for his own mother in this terrible trance of the crucifixion? As in Naim, the Lord's words bring Mary back, as it were, to her living Son, insofar as Jesus dwells in the hearts of those who believe in him (Eph. 3:17). Thus, what could be interpreted at a first level of meaning as a separation is really the expression of Christ's most tender love for his Mother. Jesus becomes close to Mary in his disciples and thus consoles her as she suffers the inevitable loss of her Son through death.

In some way, Mary's motherhood over the Church, which had begun at the Annunciation, becomes here—with the death of Christ—the moment of a most painful childbirth. Yes: the scene of Calvary is a description of childbirth. Mary unites herself to the redemptive act of her Son, gives herself with him for the salvation of the world, embraces the task that Christ entrusts to her at this decisive moment, and births us in the order of grace at the foot of the Cross. She can exclaim with St. Paul at that moment: "My children, for whom I am in labor until Christ be formed in you" (Gal. 4:19)!

As you can see, Bethlehem and Golgotha overlap again. They are two moments of the same reality, a birth at two different intervals. If the first part of this birth—the birth of the child Jesus in Bethlehem—was painless, as Tradition has handed down to us, now Mary's Heart must "expand" to give birth to all mankind, and this expansion causes her the most terrible birth pains. The "sword" that was prophesied to her is piercing through her soul to unite it totally to the redemptive suffering of her Son Jesus, thus completing in her flesh what is lacking in the Passion of Christ, for the sake of his body, which is the Church (Col. 1:24).

We are not only speaking about the Blessed Virgin: *we are talking about you, too.* The vocation to motherhood is part of the mission that every woman is called to fulfill. To be a mother is to give life and to cultivate it in others. It is a task, an attitude towards others, an effort for the education and development of those who cross your path; it is a willingness to suffer for love so that others may receive the grace of salvation; it is joyfully renouncing whatever is necessary for the good of those entrusted to you. For a Catholic woman, all this is elevated to the transmission of the "true life" that wells up into eternity (Jn. 4:14) and which God has entrusted to you as a mission in a particular way. The Lord is counting on you for this transcendental adventure of the spirit!

All these traits of woman are crystallized at the foot of the cross in Mary, whose traits you are called to reproduce in your "being a woman." This is how our dear Edith Stein expresses it:

> *Filled with the spirit of supernatural maternity, woman has the the mission to win others over as children of God. In a particular way, woman is a symbol of the Church, the Bride of Christ. Supernatural maternity impregnates only women who live and die with Christ, and who awaken through education the same purpose in those entrusted to them. But the Mother of God is among all women the most intimately bound to Christ; she is the heart of the Church of which Christ is the head. Her*

*singular support gladdens all women who want to be
mothers in this supernatural sense. For just as Mary
begat total humanity in Christ through her offspring
—"Be it done unto me according to Thy will"— just so
does she help those who strive to unveil Christ in the
heart of another. Thus, woman's mission is to imitate
Mary. She must further the life of faith by providing
a secure and enduring foundation. As teacher, she
must be the maternal, loving educator for Christ. She
must nourish a rich life of faith in young persons
through their intellectuality and voluntariness. By so
consecrating herself to supernatural maternity, the
Catholic woman becomes an organ of the Church.
And, in this way, she will fulfill this function in the
religious life as in a life united to God in the world.*[130]

If Mary gave birth to her children on Calvary, then in her,
God is entrusting to you the same mission of being "mother
of all the living" (Gen. 3:20). To every woman who comes
into this world, Christ crucified gives a part of humanity—in
your family, in your work, in your circle of friends, in those
whom Providence places in your lives—so that you may be
mothers to all of them, giving them eternal life. To every
woman, Christ crucified says in Mary, with Mary, and as
to Mary: "Behold your son." Therefore, every Christian
woman, particularly every Catholic woman, must discover
her vocation as a mother at the foot of the cross, receiving it
from Christ *who trusts in you.*

I think that in your experience of giving life to those around
you, this glimpse of the suffering of Mary's heart in this
terrible hour is a source of support for you. She suffers for

the death of her beloved Son and for the rejection by her other children of the gift of Redemption that Christ won on the cross. She remains with us and accompanies us silently as she did with Jesus crucified. She intercedes for us and unceasingly invites us to return to God and to do what the Lord tells us (Jn. 2:5). She participates in the mission of the Holy Spirit, her spouse: the third Person of the Most Holy Trinity, who is uncreated Love and unites in the mystery of God the Father, with the Son, and in the economy of salvation insofar as love unites us with God. Mary is so united to the Paraclete that she identifies with his own mission: to unite her children with the Son.

Do we not see this insistence and maternal presence in so many Marian apparitions? She always gives us the hope of a better life, and tirelessly invites us to listen to Jesus and to follow his word with confidence.

May you also be a woman like Mary: strong, tender, discreet, humble, simple, dedicated, silent, beautiful, trans-parent, maternal in all the expressions of your daily life, transformed into love by the action of the Holy Spirit, trans-mitter of grace, full of faith and hope.

4. The woman, called to be an eminent icon of God's compassion in the world. I would like to conclude these considerations about Mary of Sorrows by presenting to you an idea that I read in an article by Pope Benedict XVI before he was elevated to the See of Peter. The year I studied Mariology, our professor invited us to read a book that collected articles by the Swiss theologian Hans Urs von Balthasar and Joseph Ratzinger, then Prefect of the Congregation for the Doctrine of the Faith. These articles have been translated and published by Ignatius Press under the title *"Mary, the Church at the Source."*

There is an idea expressed there by the then Cardinal Ratzinger that more than twenty years later continues to be a source of reflection and contemplation for me. In the appendices, I include the text to which I refer here and which is truly moving.[131] There you will be able to read with great benefit what I am now going to limit myself to outlining.

I said earlier that Mary participates in such a way in the mission of the Holy Spirit that she identifies absolutely with him: just as the Person-Love (in the happy expression of St. John Paul II)[132] unites men with God, our Mother unites her children with the Risen Christ. For my part, in the meditation on the Nativity, I dared to affirm that no son has ever resembled his mother as much as Jesus resembled Mary and that, if I may draw a parallel, the Lord could well have said of the Virgin (although with a substantially different meaning) something similar to what he said to Philip during the Last Supper: "He who sees me, sees my Mother." Well then, on Golgotha Mary becomes, after Jesus, the most perfect visible expression of the merciful love of the eternal Father.

I remember here again, with tears in my eyes, my dear Father Carlos Valverde, SJ. How much I miss him! His favorite part of the whole Bible was undoubtedly the fifteenth chapter of the Gospel of St. Luke. He used to say hyperbolically that if the whole of Scripture were lost and only this biblical narrative could be preserved, we would find in it enough material to form an accurate picture of God and his love for us. Obviously, the heart of this chapter is the parable of the prodigal son, which he called, as did Benedict XVI, St. John

Paul II and other authors, "the parable of the good father." His commentary on this story was so beautiful! Every time I heard it from his lips, it seemed new, uplifting, original, and unprecedented.

This is how the Jesuit used to begin his commentary: "'A father had two sons' (Lk. 15:11). A strange first statement! In this house, was there not a mother?" And he would answer himself: "Yes, there is, and she will appear at the end of the story." What did Father Valverde mean? He meant that when the son returns, and we see the father go out to meet him, kiss him, embrace him effusively, dress him and rejoice with overflowing expressions of affection for the son who has returned alive, we find ourselves with the description of some features that are *eminently maternal*. The Jesuit priest said, "He is a father with a mother's heart." Not only does this seem to me to be a most beautiful statement, but I consider it one of the best and most accurate descriptions of our heavenly Father that I have ever heard. Who is the first Person of the Most Holy Trinity? "He is a Father who has a mother's heart." The truth is that, when God portrayed himself in his Word, he presented himself as one who loves us as the best of mothers: "Can a mother forget her infant, be without tenderness for the child of her womb? Even should she forget, I will never forget you" (Is. 49:15).

In Cardinal Ratzinger's article, he expands on the scriptural basis for this affirmation, indicating that in Hebrew the word that expresses God's compassion is *rahamim*, which literally means "maternal womb." So, in order to speak of his compassion and mercy towards men, God has chosen as the best representation of his love *a feminine and maternal image*. Now we return to the foot of the cross, where this "father who has the heart of a mother" offers us Mary as a reflection of Himself. The truth is that my hands are trembling as I write this... It is now the sorrowful Virgin who can say with her Son: "He who sees me, sees the Father" (Jn. 14:9). Ratzinger writes:

> The Old Testament, with a word taken from the language of the body, tells us how God shelters us in himself, how he bears us in himself with compassionate love. The languages into which the Gospel entered when it came to the pagan world did not have such modes of expression. But the image of the Pieta, the Mother grieving [leidend] for her Son, became the vivid translation of this word: In her, God's maternal affliction [Leiden] is open to view. In her we can behold it and touch it. She is the compassio of God, displayed in a human being who has let herself be drawn wholly into God's mystery. It is because human life is at all times suffering that the image of the suffering Mother, the image of the rahamim of God, is of such importance for Christianity. The Pieta completes the picture of the Cross, because Mary is the accepted Cross, the Cross communicating itself in love, the Cross that now allows us to experience in her compassion the compassion of God.[133]

This is something we could get lost in. Our Lady of Sorrows, the maternal suffering of God, the compassion of the Father, is made "patent," "visible," and "tangible" in such a way that Mary is united to the mystery of God, the Most Holy Trinity, and reflects in the most perfect way imaginable in a creature, the compassion of the Father, the mercy of the Son and the charity of the Holy Spirit.

Therefore, if you want to see how much the eternal Father loves you, after contemplating Jesus, you must look at Mary by the cross. In her you will see reflected all of God's love for you.

If you are afraid of being rejected for your many sins, after contemplating Jesus, you must look at Mary by the cross. She will give you hope.

If you doubt God's love after a life lost in worldliness, superficiality, or vice, after contemplating Jesus, you must look to Mary by the cross. She will inspire you with confidence.

If you think that holiness is not for you because you missed that train a long time ago with a mediocre and lukewarm Christian life, after contemplating Jesus, you must look to Mary by the cross. She will put into your soul the desire for evangelical perfection.

Mary's compassion is the compassion of the Father. In Mary's maternal suffering, God's merciful compassion is made present. Precisely for this reason, in Mary we always find hope, refuge, relief, and rest.

I invite you, then, to contemplate Mary so that you too, a woman of the twenty-first century, may become an *icon* of God's compassion in the world. If the Lord has chosen to express his mercy with an image that refers to the mystery of woman, then each one of you should be a transparency of that divine compassion. Like the *Pietà* at the foot of the cross, people should be able to see in you that trait of God's love, so necessary for those who seek the hope of a better future. Ask yourself to what extent your being a woman reflects

God's compassion for the world, for *your* world. Can people see and find *in you* God's mercy? St. Faustina Kowalska has a prayer that could only have come from that "feminine genius" of which St. John Paul II speaks. It is a prayer that is in the "arsenal" of my particular prayers and to which I have frequent recourse. This is how she composed it:

I want to be completely transformed into Your mercy and to be Your living reflection, O Lord. May the greatest of all divine attributes, that of Your unfath‑ omable mercy, pass through my heart and soul to my neighbor.

Help me, O Lord, that my eyes may be merciful, so that I may never suspect or judge from appearances, but look for what is beautiful in my neighbors' souls and come to their rescue.

Help me, that my ears may be merciful, so that I may give heed to my neighbors' needs and not be indifferent to their pains and moanings.

Help me, O Lord, that my tongue may be merciful, so that I should never speak negatively of my neighbor, but have a word of comfort and forgiveness for all.

Help me, O Lord, that my hands may be merciful and filled with good deeds, so that I may do only good to my neighbors and take upon myself the more difficult and toilsome tasks.

Help me, that my feet may be merciful, so that I may hurry to assist my neighbor, overcoming my own fatigue and weariness. My true rest is in the service of my neighbor.

Help me, O Lord, that my heart may be merciful so

that I myself may feel all the sufferings of my neighbor. I will refuse my heart to no one. I will be sincere even with those who, I know, will abuse my kindness. And I will lock myself up in the most merciful Heart of Jesus. I will bear my own suffering in silence. May Your mercy, O Lord, rest upon me.[134]

In this time of prayer in which you will contemplate the crucifixion of the Lord, may He grant you the grace to find consolation for your sufferings in Mary. May you go forth transformed into images of your sorrowful Mother, and like her, may you become life-giving mothers and presences of God's compassion in your surroundings. Finally, ask the Most Holy Trinity for the grace to unite yourselves with Mary to the offering of Christ crucified for the salvation of the world.

21

THE OPEN HEART OF JESUS

DAY 7 (NIGHT) - EIGHTEENTH MEDITATION - PASSION (III)

"Grant, we pray, almighty God, that we, who glory in the Heart of your beloved Son and recall the wonders of his love for us, may be made worthy to receive an overflowing measure of grace from that fount of heavenly gifts. Through Christ our Lord." (Collect Prayer, Solemnity of the Most Sacred Heart of Jesus).

This day of your Spiritual Exercises inevitably ends in the shadow of the dead Christ who still hangs on the cross. The great decisions of life must be made precisely here at the feet of our crucified Jesus. *Stat crux dum volvitur orbis: the cross stands steady while the world turns.* So it is. In the midst of an ephemeral and passing universe that never ceases turning, filled with transitory beings that are born and die, opinions that come and go, ephemeral fads that shift and change, images that follow one another in rapid succession, the cross affirms itself and stands unmoved, always sure, certain, imperturbable. In this impermanent world, there is something that in fact remains and resists the continuous and silent erosion of time. In the perilous navigation of the agitated and convulsive sea of this life, the cross of Christ is the true mast to which we must tie ourselves—as Ulysses did in Greek mythology—so as not to be trapped by the siren songs that seek our doom. Our arrival at the port of salvation depends on it: "so must the Son of Man be lifted up, so that everyone who believes in him may have eternal life" (Jn. 3:14-15).

Ave crux, spes unica (*O hail the cross, our only hope*). Why does the Church sing these words? Why is the cross our only hope? In the reading from the Office of the Feast of the Exaltation of the Holy Cross, September 14—taken from the sermons of St. Andrew of Crete—we find the answer:

> *Had there been no cross, Christ could not have been crucified. Had there been no cross, life itself could not have been nailed to the tree. And if life had not been nailed to it, there would be no streams of immortality pouring from Christ's side, blood and water for the world's cleansing. The legal bond of our sin would not be cancelled, we should not have attained our freedom, we should not have enjoyed the fruit of the tree of life and the gates of paradise would not stand open. Had there been no cross, death would not have been trodden underfoot, nor hell despoiled.*

The cross represents the synthesis of heaven and earth, of love of God and love of man, of death and life. It is an irresolvable paradox: the high priest who becomes the victim of his own sacrifice. It is the ultimate humiliation and, at the same time, the greatest exaltation. It is simultaneously defeat and victory, affront and triumph, slander, and recognition. It is losing oneself in order to find oneself. In the Spiritual Exercises, this is the place to which St. Ignatius takes us whenever we must make final decisions: before Christ crucified. Here the sinner goes to weep for his betrayals, shed tears of contrition, and beg for the grace of a new life. From the tree of the cross, he gathers the sweet fruit of redemption and learns the lesson of the most sublime love. At the foot of the cross, the pride of the rebellious man dies, and he begins to judge everything in a different light. To this place, to the shelter of this shadow, I bring you now so that you may measure yourselves by the mystery of your salvation.

1. One should always come away from this meditation with a *mature and humbled sense of one's own dignity.* Who am I, really? Someone who has been ransomed by the death of an incarnate God; someone for whom God gave up the last drop of his precious blood. I am someone so loved by God that He saw fit to empty himself so that I would not be eternally lost. Truly, your life must be very important, and as a consequence, you must take it with all the seriousness it deserves. To St. Angela of Foligno, Christ crucified once said: "My love for you has not been a hoax." No, the One who allowed himself to be nailed to a cross for us did not love us frivolously: the Lord loved us *seriously*, and we cannot respond with mediocrity.

Christ dead on the cross is the *most terrible representation of the reality of sin.* The "wisdom of this world" (1 Cor. 3:19) can say whatever it wants and it will deceive us into believing that it is alright to consent to certain imperfections and faults; that this or that is "not so bad;" that today, what has always considered evil is now good. Can you look at Jesus crucified and dare to say these things to a God whose life has been taken away by *your sin?* You were the executioner of this terrible outcome and, if you do not want to reckon with this in the present life, the time will come for you, at your death, to look Christ in the eye and give him your excuses. What cowardice in so many of us who never "reach the end," as St. Teresa of Jesus would say![135] Lord, pardon and mercy! Where is our heart? What are we doing with our lives? Where are we going?

2. "And bowing his head, he handed over the spirit" (Jn. 19:30). Death has just put an end to an unspeakable and excessive agony. Lifeless, unmoving, serene, the corpse of Jesus hangs on the cross with exquisite dignity and majesty. The ordeal has ended for him, and from his quiescent face you must gather the peace of one who has been able to say, "It is finished"(v. 30). These are the words of one who has conquered. Let us make no mistake: Christ crucified is, from the tree on which He still rests, a victorious king. The violence unleashed against Him has been unable to triumph over His will, and love has prevailed over the selfishness of men. "I myself won the victory" (Rev. 3:21): these words of the Rabbi of Galilee now crown the man we see sleeping on the scaffold of the cross.

I invite you to contemplate him slowly and deliberately.

Examine every inch of his body with your eyes. Look at the marks from every one of the blows he received: every wound on his torso, every cut on his back, every bruise on his limbs. See and smell the stinking spittle that still clings to his bleeding skin. Every sign of torment is, in the end, a proof and a declaration of love for you, an "I love you" written in blood on the body of the Lord.

Look especially at his hands, hardened by the silent labor in the workshop of Nazareth. Hands that worked so many miracles, blessed so many sick people, broke bread for so many hungry people, caressed the faces of so many children. Hands that are now broken and stiffened by the nails that mercilessly pierced his nerves and tendons.

Look at his feet with their flayed and bloodied soles. Feet which tirelessly traveled the roads of Palestine in search of countless lost sheep, which were kissed and anointed by women, holy and sinful alike. Feet that now are twisted and battered, rigid and contracted by the iron with which they have been pinioned to the rough wood of the cross.

Contemplate the face of the "the fairest of the sons of men" (Ps. 45:3). The eyes that looked as no one had ever looked before; those lips from which flowed words never heard before; those cheeks, once flushed with life and vigor, now swollen and bruised; the beard that has been brutally cut by the Roman soldiers stained with dirt, sweat, spit, blood, and tears.

How is it possible to reduce a man to so miserable a state? How can anyone be so distorted and deformed? "... so marred were his features, beyond that of mortals his appearance, beyond that of human beings" (Is. 52:14). Is it possible *not* to take the Christian life seriously after witnessing such a sight?

3. In this brief description of the devastation of the Lord, I have not yet spoken about the most important wound, the wound in his open side, to which we want to give all of our attention from now on.

> *Now since it was preparation day, in order that the bodies might not remain on the cross on the sabbath, for the sabbath day of that week was a solemn one, the Jews asked Pilate that their legs be broken and they be taken down.*
>
> *So the soldiers came and broke the legs of the first and then of the other one who was crucified with Jesus. But when they came to Jesus and saw that he was already dead, they did not break his legs, but one soldier thrust his lance into his side, and immediately blood and water flowed out.*
>
> *An eyewitness has testified, and his testimony is true; he knows that he is speaking the truth, so that you also may come to believe.*
>
> *For this happened so that the scripture passage might be fulfilled: "Not a bone of it will be broken." And again another passage says: "They will look upon him whom they have pierced (Jn. 19:31-37).*

The way in which St. John presents this episode is inviting us to notice a meaning that goes beyond what can be learned at first sight. There is a striking disproportion between the solemnity of the wording "an eyewitness has testified, and his testimony is true; he knows that he is speaking the truth," and the event itself that he relates. Was this ardent gravity necessary to tell us about something that could have passed as an anecdotal or even irrelevant detail? Why the witness's emphasis on this particular moment of Christ's Passion? What is there here that makes it so crucial?

This is a well-known feature of the fourth Gospel and is used to indicate a moment of particular transcendence amidst the entire work of salvation. It is a kind of raised flag that invites us not to overlook the deeper significance of what is happening and to pay attention to what Christ is doing, applying the light of faith in order to grasp its full meaning. Let us think, by way of example, of the scene of the washing of the feet. In and of itself, it is a commonplace act, not unusual at the time. However, St. John prefaces that episode as follows:

> Before the feast of Passover, Jesus knew that his hour had come to pass from this world to the Father. He loved his own in the world and he loved them to the end. The devil had already induced Judas, son of Simon the Iscariot, to hand him over. So, during supper, fully aware that the Father had put everything into his power and that he had come from God and was returning to God, he rose from supper and took off his outer garments. He took a towel and tied it around his waist (Jn. 13:1-4).

There is a truly striking break between the lyricism and solemnity of the introduction and the very prosaic act of washing the dirty feet of a group of men. In reality, the evangelist is capturing the attention of the reader, pointing him toward the fact that in what he is about to say there is much more than what can be discovered at first sight. He is saying: "Pay attention! The work of redemption is being done here!"

So then, let's be attentive to this signal from St. John and pause here in the recounting of the piercing of Jesus' side. Let us ask the Holy Spirit to allow us to rise up to the Heart of Jesus so that the reality of what is happening here may be revealed to us.

4. Everything happens in just a few seconds. To be sure that Jesus is really dead, the soldier has pierced his side with a spear. The steel is embedded in the chest of the Crucified, disappears under the languishing skin and slips through his ribs. The whole body of the Lord sways limply. Truly, the torture is over for the poor Nazarene. He no longer lives—he who as God cannot die. The moment arrives to remove the shaft. To pull out the end of the pike, the soldier must now overcome the resistance of the entrance wound with a quick, violent, and forceful movement in the opposite direction.

It is then that the last residue of blood that was lodged in the Heart of Jesus makes its way through the newly opened wound and gushes outward profusely. St. John, standing at the foot of the cross, *sees water*—the serous fluid of the pleura and the pericardium—mingle with red blood and gush forth abundantly. They are two rivers of grace that wash and purify man's filth as they flow.

No, it is not a small and insignificant detail. St. John "has testified, and his testimony is true" (v. 35). He understands that Holy Scripture is fulfilled here. John's "seeing" is more than just looking: it is a *faith penetration* of the fact, which grasps the depths of the meaning of what is happening.

In 2010, while I was studying in my beloved Rome, a group of Spanish priests made a weekend trip to Turin for the Exposition of the Holy Shroud, an event that had not taken place since the Great Jubilee of 2000. As you may know, the Holy Shroud is usually protected in a bulletproof glass structure, and only on very rare occasions is it exposed to public view for veneration by the faithful. It was, therefore, a unique opportunity that we could not miss. Pope Benedict XVI himself was there the week after our pilgrimage and led a beautiful meditation before the relic that I would like to recommend to all of you.[136]

Those were two unforgettable days. The company was undoubtedly most pleasant (Where are my brother priests now?) and Turin left an indelible mark on my soul. Particularly special for me was the visit to the places connected with St. John Bosco, whom I had read about since I was a child and who still holds a special place in my heart. However, the highlight was prayer before the burial cloth that wrapped the lifeless body of the Lord that we are now contemplating. It was displayed very high up and illuminated from behind, so that in the darkness of the small cathedral the silhouette of Christ imprinted on the linen majestically dominated the entire basilica. I am moved now as I recall that unrepeatable experience.

What moved me most was the bloodstain from the side of the Lord, and honestly, I don't think that it could leave anyone indifferent. It is a huge gush of blood, which extends strikingly from the right side of the crucified. It is the largest bloodstain on the entire canvas and captures the eye with the intensity of its scarlet color and the preeminence it acquires in the whole. The face and the blood: undoubtedly, these are the two elements that stand out above all others. In his words before the Shroud a few days later, Benedict XVI invited the Church to look *especially* at the wound of the Heart:

> *This face, these hands and these feet, this side, this whole body speaks. It is itself a word we can hear in the silence. How does the Shroud speak? It speaks with blood, and blood is life! The Shroud is an Icon written in blood; the blood of a man who was scourged, crowned with thorns, crucified and whose right side was pierced. The Image impressed upon the Shroud is that of a dead man, but the blood speaks of his life. Every trace of blood speaks of love and of life. Especially that huge stain near his rib, made by the blood and water that flowed copiously from a great wound inflicted by the tip of a Roman spear. That blood and that water speak of life. It is like a spring that murmurs in the silence, and we can hear it, we can listen to it in the silence of Holy Saturday.*
>
> *Dear friends, let us always praise the Lord for his faithful and merciful love. When we leave this holy place, may we carry in our eyes the image of the Shroud, may we carry in our hearts this word of love and praise God with a life full of faith, hope and charity.*

The day before concluding this retreat, in the silence of this prayer experience, you too are moved by the Spirit to listen to this word that God speaks in the blood of that open Heart. Let me ask you: what is he saying *to you today*?

5. Perhaps we are accustomed to seeing this devotion to the Heart of Christ as "just one more" among many others. It is often described as a "pious practice" (said almost pejoratively) and compared with other expressions of popular faith from bygone eras. Sadly, it is being forgotten by many Christians, who consider it sappy, corny, sentimental, childish, non-scriptural, and the fruit of an immature faith.

In the face of this trend that seeks to displace or even completely bury devotion to the human Heart of God, the Church unceasingly and vigorously protects it, convinced that in it is found the "sum of all religion" and the "pattern of more perfect life."[137] It was Pope Pius XI who, in his Encyclical Letter *Miserentissimus Redemptor*, used these bold expressions which, I confess, gave me a real "spiritual jolt" when I heard them. Pius XII also repeats them in his wonderful *Haurietis Aquas*.[138] I understood that in making such categorical affirmations, the Church is doing nothing more than taking up the testimony of the beloved disciple who at the foot of the cross received this light in order to share it with men and women of all times. In fact, St. John first sees it himself (Jn. 19:35), and only then directs our gaze to the Savior's open chest with the words of the prophet Zechariah: "They will look upon him whom they have pierced" (v. 37).

Why does this devotion synthesize everything? I think one of the keys is to understand this: THE HEART OF JESUS IS **ALIVE**. As you consider these words of mine, at this very moment, Jesus has a Heart that is alive. Be silent and you will even be able to hear his heartbeat there in the background, as a pregnant woman can hear the heartbeat of her baby. By exploring the interior of your soul you have access to the

Heart of Jesus. Hear its murmurs, its rhythm, its beating. "Christ, raised from the dead, dies no more" (Rom. 6:9).

Ask the Holy Spirit to help you with this because I am not referring to reflecting on an idea, but to having a heartfelt, deep, lived experience of Christ, who has a living Heart. This radically changes life. And that is what you came here seeking in these Spiritual Exercises: not a simple "readjustment," but a true rebirth. This was also the experience of St. Paul on the road to Damascus. For him, until that moment, Christ was a dead man. Blinded by the radiance of the Risen One, Saul asked, "Who are you, sir?" to which a voice answered, "I am Jesus the Nazorean whom you are persecuting" (Acts 22:8). The inner light that Saul then receives is this: "He who I thought was dead is alive! What I do *I am doing to him.*" In other words, his life, which he thought had no relationship to Christ, was in fact a one-on-one with the Lord.

Devotion to the Heart of Jesus leads us to the central mystery of our faith: Christ is alive! Notice that in our contemplation of Jesus crucified, this life is expressed in the blood that flows from his side. "Blood is life," Pope Benedict said in the quotation we mentioned earlier. In Scripture (Lev. 17:11), blood is indeed the seat and symbol of life, and Christ communicates it to us as the fruit of redemption at the end of his passion and death. In other words, Jesus dies, but his open Heart gives us a torrent of life.

If the blood that pours from the breast of Jesus is not a symbol of death, it is precisely because of its union with the water that flows with it. As the Belgian Jesuit Father Ignace de La Potterie has masterfully shown, if the blood represents the life of Christ and his love for mankind that reaches "to the end" (Jn. 13:1), then the water is the symbol of the Spirit that the crucified One gives to us with his offering on the cross.[139] We have received this interpretation from Jesus himself who, in the Gospel of St. John, prophesied that the gift of the Spirit would flow from his Heart: "Let anyone who thirsts come to me and drink. Whoever believes in me, as scripture says: 'Rivers of living water will flow from within him.' He said this in reference to the Spirit that those who came to believe in him were to receive. There was, of course, no Spirit yet, because Jesus had not yet been glorified" (Jn. 7:37-39).

On Calvary, St. John sees this *living* water flowing from the breast of Jesus. It is the same water of which the Lord spoke to the Samaritan woman, and which we were able to contemplate a few days ago, and as we said then, to make this connection even clearer, the Beloved Disciple points out that the two episodes take place at the same time of day—noon. (Jn. 4:6; Jn. 19:14)

"Let anyone who thirsts come to me and drink...." Christ invites you now, in these Exercises, to place your lips on his chest and drink... You, a woman thirsting for a love that does not disappoint, can now go to the cross. At other times you have drunk from "broken cisterns" (Jer. 2:13) and have not been satisfied. How many disappointments you have experienced! How many times you have loved and not been loved in return! So many tears those other little "loves" have cost you! Ascend now to the Lord's side: He is all yours. If you drink, you will no longer want to taste other waters. The love of Christ will give you everything that your soul has always been seeking. Drink now, in the intimacy of that bridal chamber which is the cross of Jesus, alone with Him.

6. Perhaps you are asking yourselves why, of all the passages of the Passion of Jesus, we have chosen the episodes of Mary's presence at the cross and of the piercing of Jesus on the cross. It was not a random choice: in them, the two most basic dimensions of the woman's soul are realized. I am referring to motherhood and espousal, attributes that are intertwined in Mary and in each of you in a most singular way. From this point of view, the contemplation of our Mother at the foot of the Cross and of the open side of Christ are not only privileged manifestations of God's love for you, but also revelations that unveil unique aspects of your mystery, that is, of the women you are called to be in the eyes of Jesus.

The Lord gave me a special insight on my pilgrimage to the Holy Land, especially in the days I spent in Cana. It has stayed with me with a strength and a light that I cannot express in words. I am convinced that none of what I am about to say is "new," but as far as I am concerned, I did experience it as such and it continues to be so as I received it not as "knowledge" but as "experience," if you understand what I am trying to express.

I could summarize it this way. At Cana, Christ *manifests himself* as Spouse; at the Last Supper, Jesus *celebrates* his Marriage in the bodily gift of the Eucharist; on Calvary, the Lord *consummates* his nuptials with the Church.

Here, as you find yourself praying, contemplating with deep emotion—as St. Ignatius writes, the love of Jesus *for you*—let's adopt a more intimate consideration of these events. After all, in the word "Church" *you yourself are signified*. Sometimes we take refuge in the plural for fear of the consequences that could result from a *personal* vision of these mysteries. Loyola, on the other hand, moves us away from this approach that buries us in the anonymous multitude and invites us in his Exercises to see our relationship with Christ crucified as a very personal, singular, one on one with Him.

To this end, from now until the end of this meditation, I want you to assume, without misgivings, the consideration of the Church as the bride of Christ. Be bold in your prayer. Think of Jesus as *your spouse* and of his sacrifice on the cross as bodily *union with you*, in that love which is proper to spousal self-giving.

God has made you a woman and has placed in your soul this very strong orientation toward union with a man in the marriage covenant. The male is also naturally directed toward this union, but in the woman it acquires particular traits and intensities. As with the maternal dimension, this is an aspect that *must be realized in every woman* so that she may acquire the "full stature of Christ" (Eph, 4:13), the fullness of love. It cannot be put aside, postponed or disregarded. It is crucial, essential, fundamental, transcendental.

How scary is it to love sometimes! One fears the lack of correspondence and the pain that comes from it. We carry so many wounds inside us for this reason! When we project these experiences onto Jesus, even without being fully aware of them, they block us and prevent us from giving ourselves generously to Him. Today, however, I invite you *not to be afraid.* With Jesus, you need to only have *confidence.*

Let me first introduce you to your spouse. For that, we must now make a brief stop in that lost village in Galilee where one morning the Lord goes with his disciples to the wedding of some acquaintances. There, Christ manifests himself to you as your betrothed. How fortunate you are!

The most beautiful, the best, the most loving of all men: Jesus. In his Gospel, St. John expressly presents Christ to us as the *bridegroom*: he does so on the lips of the Baptist, who affirms with beautiful words—both for the image and for the love and humility they convey: "The one who has the bride is the bridegroom; the best man, who stands and listens to him, rejoices greatly at the bridegroom's voice. So this joy of mine has been made complete. He must increase; I must decrease" (Jn. 3:29-30).

In these nuptials that I invite you to contemplate, Jesus is one of the guests. However, at the deepest level of faith, St. John identifies Christ at the end of the story with the one who is getting married. He does so with such subtlety that we may never have realized it before, but notice that when the headwaiter says to the bridegroom, "but you have kept the good wine until now" (Jn. 2:10), *he is really addressing Jesus*. For who is the one who has *really* kept the good wine and has given it to be distributed to the guests? The Lord, not the material bridegroom at that wedding! Or to put it another way, Jesus and the bridegroom of the wedding—from the typological point of view of reality and symbol—end up being confused in such a way at the end of the story that Christ, who had entered the scene as a guest, is revealed at the end of the narrative as the bridegroom, as *your* bridegroom. And in the miracle he performs, *he is saying to you*: "When I marry you, I will transform your whole life. The best is yet to come when you unite with me, if you choose to marry me." It is a promise, a love that is not imposed but offered for you to embrace *if you want to do so.*

The moment of your betrothal to Christ comes at the Last Supper. The Eucharist is the banquet and the place of celebration. There, every day, your spouse awaits you to bring you to the altar and unite with you. The signs of the water turned into wine, which the Lord used at Cana, are present again in the chalice of this supper, where the same miracle happens again. In the cup of sacrifice, the water is turned into wine and this becomes, now really and not only symbolically, Jesus.

The Holy Mass is *always* the celebration of the marriage of Jesus to you, not because it is repeated over and over again, but because the *yesterday* of the Last Supper is made present again in *today's* history. It is not bound by the rules of time, because he the one for whom "a thousand years are merely a day gone by" (Ps. 90:4). The words of consecration that Jesus pronounces are eminently spousal words: it is a *covenant,* a *bodily self-giving* that expresses in turn an absolute, irrevocable, unconditional offering, until death. "This is my body which is given," "This is my blood of the new covenant, which will be shed." It is a declaration of love, but not just any kind of love, but *conjugal* love: covenant, bodily self-giving, fidelity, fruitfulness. It is all here.

I invite you to feel taken *by the hand* at Holy Mass, and when you hear the words of consecration, I invite you to *inwardly and silently give yourself also to Jesus, just as He is giving Himself to you* in marriage. Again, there is a connection between the Heart of Jesus and the Eucharist, to the point that, *in reality, they are the same mystery.* In all the tabernacles of the world is hidden that living Heart that has loved men so much and *really is* waiting for you, offering you intimacy, silence, and love.

We had to pass through Cana and the Cenacle to better understand the reality of Calvary. The marriage that was prefigured in Galilee and celebrated at the Last Supper is now consummated on the cross. As is well known, the theological and canonical doctrine of the Church considers that the moment of consummation—in which the spouses unite bodily to *become one flesh* —confers on the bond between man and woman the character of absolute indissolubility. It is, so to speak, the final touch that seals the union already realized in the celebration of marriage. A validly celebrated marriage still lacks something, and *that something* is the act toward which it is naturally ordered: the union in the flesh that opens to the transmission of life.

Let us try to remove from the scene on Golgotha everything that deprives this contemplation of its intimacy and silence. In today's world, we have headphones that almost completely reduce so-called "ambient noise:" When you put them over your ears, it is as if the surrounding sounds disappear and a surprising silence is magically created. Let's do a similar exercise now, looking with the eyes of the soul at our crucified Jesus. For a few moments, the cacophony of voices, expletives, insults, and mockery that surround the Lord disappear; the decibels that stunned us with their intensity are suddenly lowered, and even the by-standers who witness the execution vanish from the scene of the crucifixion. Just as in the scene of the woman caught in adultery and left alone before the Lord, only you and He are left. He is about to die, and you are at His feet. And there is no one else there.

What is the Lord doing? He is loving you *corporately,* and in that bodily surrender, he is *giving life.* Behold the consummation. Truly, the cross is the bridal chamber to which today Jesus invites you to ascend with Him. His body is a source of purity, of grace, of redemption. We have already seen in the healing of the hemorrhagic woman how energy released from Him heals and transforms.

7. I would like to draw attention to something that has great significance in this context: on the cross, the most holy body of Jesus is *naked.* In the most horizontal explanation of the facts, this nakedness was the way his enemies found to humiliate the Lord even more. In his infinite modesty, to see himself thus exposed to the gaze of those who did not love him must have been a cause of enormous pain for the Lord. In one of his catecheses on the Theology of the Body, St. John Paul II made the following comment regarding the act of stripping a person of his clothing, as a way of objectifying and denigrating him:

> *Mention should also be made especially of other circumstances, such as those of concentration camps or places of extermination, where the violation of bodily shame is a method used deliberately to destroy personal sensitivity and the sense of human dignity. (...) man does not wish to become an object for others through his own anonymous nakedness. Nor does he wish the other to become an object for him in a similar way.*[140]

Using these words of the Pope, we can say that the Pharisees, with the help of the Roman authority, wanted to *objectify* Christ in order to *destroy* the sense of his dignity. They wanted to publicly humiliate him with his nakedness, knowing that for Jesus, whose heart was so sensitive, this would mean indescribable pain. In turn, Christ *allowed it.* That is to say, he accepted this mockery with humility and did so in order to give his nakedness a *spousal* meaning. The naked body of Christ is expressing to you in these Exercises the offering of his *intimacy.* Please understand that I do not mean this in a sexual way. The invitation to enter into a communion with him that reaches the deepest aspects. John Paul II himself explained that "the body through its own visibility manifests man. In manifesting him, it acts as intermediary, that is, it enables man and woman, right from the beginning, to communicate with each other according to that *communio personarum* willed by the Creator precisely for them."[141]

In the Passion, God *laid bare* all his love for you. He expressed it in that nakedness which is an invitation to unite yourself to Him. You are now alone before him, at his feet, and at the climax of this retreat, in the intimacy of the bridegroom who undresses before his bride, his crucified love invites you to undress before him as well, figuratively speaking.

You probably feel embarrassed to do so, and possibly that embarrassment is born of pride. We do not want to unveil ourselves before Jesus *because we are ashamed of ourselves.* We do not even want to see ourselves. Unveiling ourselves is a painful experience because it forces us to remember aspects of ourselves that we wish did not exist. Have we not felt this way at times when we approach the Sacrament of Confession and feel that it is difficult to bring out what is inside us?

In this composition of place that I propose to you—Jesus crucified and you, alone, with no one else but yourselves on the summit of Calvary—I encourage you to do the same as the Lord has done for you: undress and let Christ look at you — not necessarily literally but allow him to see you as you are. Do not be afraid that his gaze will be cold or disappointed. He will look at you tenderly, with immense love, and in this way, he will heal you and reconcile you with yourself and with God. For his mercy to heal your soul, you must tear off all the layers you wear, the masks with which you appear before others, and place yourself, as you are, before the Lord. This is perhaps the most difficult exercise for us because, like Adam and Eve, we want to hide behind the tree so that the Lord will not see us (Gen. 3:8). Come out of your hiding place and strip yourself of everything. Let the bridegroom love you as *you really are.* Only then will you be able to unite yourself to him and receive his life.

It is crucial in your journey of faith *to know and feel personally and spousally loved by Christ crucified:* "We have come to know and to believe in the love God has for us" (1 Jn. 4:16). Just as the conjugal act should always be a moment to feel loved by the spouse with tenderness, intensity, and delight, union with Christ, the Spouse who agonizes on the cross, should lead you to *feel now* the caress of Jesus in your soul, as he says to you: "with age-old love I have loved you" (Jer. 31:3); "as a bridegroom rejoices in his bride so shall your God rejoice in you" (Is. 62:5); "you are mine" (Is. 43:1).

Stay there as long as you want: perhaps without words, receive into your soul all Christ's love for you and love him because, as he himself reveals to us here, the Lord thirsts (Jn. 19:28). These two words *are spoken to you now.* What Christ thirsts *for is you.* God has a human heart and that heart thirsts to be loved. An ancient hymn in honor of the Sacred Heart of Jesus contained these words, "*Quis non amantem*

419

redamet (Who will not return love to the one who loves)?" Today you are asked to love the one who loves you. Love the one who for love of you has sought for you when you were lost. Love the one who weeps when you leave and rejoices when he finds you. Look at that heart that has loved us so much and ask him to always help you to know how to respond to his love for you.

Today Jesus is begging you to love him with your woman's heart. That complementarity that God has made between the soul of man and the soul of a woman is also realized in your relationship with Christ. He loves you as a man, and you love him as a woman. He loves you with his heart of man, and you are called to respond to his love with your woman's heart. Only in that relationship with Jesus will you feel fully loved, nourished, consoled, strengthened, and enlightened. Only in the wounded Heart of Jesus will you find the door that is always open to you. Only in that fountain will you be able to satisfy your thirst for love completely.

8. Christ's life is coming to an end. In this context in which we are considering the sacrifice of Jesus as the consummation of his spousal love for you, his last words are precisely these: *consummatum est* (It is finished)" (Jn. 19:30). The Greek word used by St. John is "Τετέλεσται," which has as its root the term "τέλος"—finality, end, goal, fulfillment. That word appears in the first verse of the thirteenth chapter of the Gospel, when the holy author tells us that Jesus "loved his own in the world and he loved them to the end (εἰς τέλος ἠγάπησεν αὐτούς)," giving the impression that St.John intends to link the beginning and the conclusion of the Passion of Christ, not only to mark the structure of the

narrative, but also to express the meaning of Jesus' words on the cross. His "It is finished" means, "I have loved you to the end." Therefore, without forcing the meaning of the sacred text, we can interpret his words—*consummatum est*—as the expression of the bridegroom who has *consummated* his union with you, with the one to whom he had betrothed himself. "This is a great mystery, but I speak in reference to Christ and the church" (Eph. 5:32).

Yes, Christ has loved you *to the end.* He consummated his spousal love on the cross and this led him to give his life *for you.* We can return to the Savior's breast and conclude this meditation in this way. If from Adam's rib, God offered the first man the gift of his wife Eve, from the open Heart of Christ, the Father gives his Son the gift of his bride, who is the Church, *which is you.* "Everything that the Father gives me will come to me, and I will not reject anyone who comes to me (...) And this is the will of the one who sent me, that I should not lose anything of what he gave me" (Jn. 6:37-39). Redemption is certainly a gift that Jesus Christ offers to his Father—to whom he presents the gift of a humanity reconciled in love—but it is equally a gift of the Father to his only Son, *to whom he gives a bride who loves him and whom he can love.* The Heart of Jesus reveals to us, therefore, what is the most intimate reality of your being: you are a gift that the Father and the Son, in the Holy Spirit, give to each other and receive from each other. You are a gift, you must be a gift for Jesus, loving him and receiving all his love and mercy.

Speaking of woman, Edith Stein affirms that "It is her gift and happiness to share the life of another human being and, indeed, to take part in all things which come his way, in the greatest and smallest things, in joy as well as in suffering, in work, and in problems."[142] You are all called to realize this experience with Christ and this is one of the fundamental aspects of devotion to the Heart of Jesus: *reparation* is really to participate in the "joys and sufferings" of the Lord. Christ wants to share with you his inner world and the feminine aspiration to unite with the male in the most intimate aspects corresponds totally to this desire of the Heart of the Lord. To be authentic, your communion with Jesus must be capable of reaching these extremes. Remember the expression of St. Ignatius: "sorrow with Christ in sorrow, anguish with Christ in anguish" (SE 203).

On the other hand, you must allow Christ to love you as the spouse of your souls: "Husbands, love your wives, even as Christ loved the church and handed himself over for her to sanctify her, cleansing her by the bath of water with the word" (Eph. 5:25-26). The Heart of Jesus is the source of salvation from which flows the water that purifies us (Is. 12:3): we drink of this water in Baptism, in the Eucharist, in silent prayer, in loving union with the Lord. Here we find the grace to begin a new life, for God "turned the rock into pools of water, flint into a flowing spring" (Ps. 114:8). We can explain it in many different ways, but, in the end, it all boils down to *letting ourselves be loved by Christ, to being recipients of his love* so that it can enrich, without losing anything, the soil of our soul.

* * *

The Lord has died on the cross, but his life has been left

within you, so that you may protect it, receive it, and increase it in your woman's soul. This is also an aspect that can be considered from the perspective of *consummation*: the new life of grace is already growing, like a seed, in your heart. If you welcome it and know how to respond to it with generosity in a life of holiness, that seed will be fruitful not only in you, but in the lives of many others. That is what these Exercises should be: the opportunity that God has given you to fill you with grace so that you can become a diffuser of that supernatural life for others. May it truly be so!

I am going to leave here my words so that each one of you may take from them what you want and let the wind of the Spirit blow on your sails and take you where He wills to lead you (Jn 3:8). Look at the One whom your sins have pierced. The Heart of Jesus is sensitive to your response: give yourselves therefore to Him and love much the one who is loved so little. Be faithful to the love of Christ and do not leave the cross without taking from Jesus the grace that he promised you through the prophet Ezekiel (36:25-28), the great gift of the work of redemption: a new heart.

22

SAINT MARY MAGDALENE

DAY 8 (MORNING) – NINETEENTH MEDITATION – THE RESURRECTION

"Clothe us, Lord God, with the virtues of the Heart of your Son and set us aflame with his love, that, conformed to his image, we may merit a share in eternal redemption. Through our Lord Jesus Christ. Amen." (Votive Mass of the Most Sacred Heart of Jesus).

Good morning to all. We have finally reached the conclusion of this retreat, and we do so on the Solemnity of the Sacred Heart of Jesus.[143] You can see in this coincidence a message of love from the Most Holy Trinity to each one of you. The Lord has been waiting for you at the end of this path that you have traveled to reveal His love for you.

You have reached this goal after meditating on the sufferings of Christ in his Passion. In Mel Gibson's movie, "*The Passion of the Christ,*" I am struck by the moment when the soldier plunges the spear into Jesus' side: not a little water and blood comes out, but a stream of water that bathes Mary, Saint John and that very soldier. It is an experience that invites you to come to the Lord today: let his love bathe you, cleanse you and purify you.

1. The meditations of the fourth week of the Exercises are truly delightful. We contemplate the risen Christ and we travel with him from Jerusalem to Galilee to see the different manifestations of the risen Lord. Beginning with an apparition that does not appear in the Gospel but that St. Ignatius includes in his Exercises: the apparition to the Blessed Virgin Mary.

If in the meditations of the third week, St. Ignatius asked for the grace to suffer with Christ, to participate interiorly in the agony of the Lord, here he says that we must participate in the joy of the risen Jesus. The saint says that I should "ask for what I want, and it will be here to ask for grace to rejoice and be gladly intensely at so great glory and joy of Christ our Lord" (SE 221).

Ask today for this joy of which Saint Ignatius speaks. Not just any joy, not just "being happy" but "to be gladly, intensely so at the great glory and joy of Christ our Lord." That intense joy is the joy of the Risen Lord. Be bold in your prayer and ask to participate in the joy of the Heart of Jesus the morning of the Resurrection. Friends share the difficult moments and suffer together, but they also share the joys together, and the Lord does not want to wait for eternity to make you feel that joy: in your personal prayer, today, this morning, He wants to fill you with that joy that gives meaning to all things.

This is very important. In his *Gaudete in Domino,* Pope Saint Paul VI writes: "It is indeed in the midst of their distress that our fellow men need to know joy, to hear its song."[144] This morning, you yourselves must hear the song of joy, that song of the Holy Spirit that resonates in the hearts of the disciples of Jesus.

If you are sad for any reason, if there is something that afflicts you, I would like you to hear these words: "Woman, why are you weeping" (Jn. 20:13)? Do you recognize them? Have you heard them before? Maybe they ring a bell for you. The woman who heard them for the first time did not know where they came from either. She was a woman saddened by the blows of life, who had lost the cause of her joy a few days before.

2. "Woman, why are you weeping?" In the context of this meditation and these Exercises, these words are spoken to you as well. Listen to them in your heart. That voice that enters the depths of your heart is asking you why you are crying, that is, what is making you sad in life. It is asking you where your heart is. Before turning to see who is speaking to you, take time in your prayer to answer that question.

Yesterday we contemplated with awe the corpse of the Crucified Christ. The "composition of place" to which I invite you today is the contemplation of the resurrected body of Jesus. You can contemplate it with Mary Magdalene, the first woman who heard these words, on the morning of the resurrection, in chapter 20 of the Gospel of Saint John.

Mary Magdalene does not need to be introduced because

we all know her. She was one of the women who had followed Jesus during his public ministry in Galilee. The Gospel of St. Luke indicates that the Lord had expelled seven demons from her (Lk. 8:2). Mary Magdalene had been healed by Christ. He had freed her from the power of Satan. She had experienced the power of Christ deeply. God had touched her life and raised her to a new dignity. Imagine your joy at being healed by Jesus. Tradition tells us that it was she who washed the feet of Jesus with her tears in the scene we meditated on two days ago. Recall everything we said then and how Jesus gave her a new heart with his forgiveness and his mercy.

Mary was so captivated by the Lord that she left her home in the small village of Magdala next to the lake of Tiberias and followed Jesus from town to town, from city to city, to learn from Him. In chapter 8 of the Gospel of St. Luke, we read that she belonged to the group of women who accompanied Jesus and his apostles and "provided for them out of their resources" (Lk. 8:1-3). Immediately following this comment, in the same chapter, Jesus tells the parable of the sower. Mary Magdalene had always been "good soil," where the Word of Jesus had fallen very fruitfully. In the story of the appearance of the Risen One, the Gospel records the original Aramaic word with which she addressed the Lord: "'Rabbouni,' which means Teacher" (v. 16). Yes, Jesus was her teacher and her master, and she was Jesus' disciple.

All these traits of Mary Magdalene also describe the action of God in your own life. Like her, you are also a woman touched by Jesus. You, too, have been forgiven, many times, personally, by Jesus. He has loved you and you have followed him throughout your life: you sat down to listen to his word many times, you have supported Him and provided for Him and his disciples out of your resources. Your heart has been soil into which the Word of God has fallen and you've learned from your "Rabbouni" his words of eternal life (Jn. 6:68).

The Gospels also tell us about the presence of Mary Magdalene with Jesus during his Passion. What heinous suffering she experienced! The attitudes towards the suffering of Jesus were very different in our Mother Mary and in Mary Magdalene. The Mother of God suffered more than anyone, to the point that the tradition considers her a martyr.

As we recall from St. Bernard, the faith of the Mother of God was tested in the crucible of trial and she responded faithfully. In the silence of the first Holy Saturday, she was also the only one who "hoped against all hope" (Rom. 4:18), and, for that reason, we called her Mother of Hope.

Mary Magdalene, however, did not have that hope when Jesus' life was extinguished on the cross. She believed that everything ended with the death of Christ. She was certain that on Mount Calvary the story she had shared with Him had irrevocably reached its final page.

She suffered upon witnessing the Passion and death of him whom she loved so much. She thought she was losing Jesus forever. Nonetheless, how much she loved him!

3. "On the first day of the week, Mary of Magdala came to the tomb early in the morning, while it was still dark, and saw the stone removed from the tomb" (Jn. 20:1).Commenting on this Scripture verse, St. Thomas Aquinas quotes the book of the Song of Songs: "Set me as a seal on your heart, as a seal on your arm; for stern as death is love, relentless as the nether world its devotion; its flames are a blazing fire" (6:2). Mary goes to the tomb while it is still dark, illuminating the

path with the flames of a love that is as stern as death.

Imagine the inner turmoil of this woman when, upon reaching the tomb, she finds the stone removed: surprise, fear, and infinite pain. Her heart would stop. "They have taken my Lord, and I don't know where they laid him." she will say later (Jn. 20:2). Notice that, deep down, the cause of Mary's pain is her lack of faith. Had she believed in Christ's resurrection, she wouldn't have given into desolation and tears. Is that not, deep down, the cause of our sorrows, too?

We should be the happiest of people. How can anyone who knows everything that has been revealed to us be sad? If happiness, as we all perceive, is found in love, how can anyone who knows the love of God be sad? How can a person who knows that he is always and infinitely loved by God be sad? I remember the words of Saint John of the Cross on the second day: "What more do you want, O soul! And what else do you search for outside, when within yourself you possess your riches, delights, satisfaction, fullness, and kingdom—your Beloved whom you desire and seek?"

Saint Francis of Assisi said that sadness is sometimes the worst temptation. A soul that saddens easily is a soul that does not advance lightly along the paths of the Christian life. He always carries a weight in his heart that drains him and makes him drag his feet instead of flying towards union with God.

I would like to read a text from St. Augustine in which he talks about vinegar and honey, and I would like you to understand, in this context, the word "honey" as "joy", and the word "vinegar" as "sadness".

Saint Augustine says:

Holy longing exercises us just so much as we prune off our longings from the love of the world. We have already said, Empty out what is to be filled. With good you are to be filled: pour out the bad. Suppose that God would fill you with honey: if you are full of vinegar, where will you put the honey? That which the vessel bore in it must be poured out: the vessel itself must be cleansed; must be cleansed, albeit with labor, albeit with hard rubbing, that it may become fit for that thing, whatever it be. Let us say honey, say gold, say wine; whatever we say it is, being what cannot be said, whatever we would say, it is called God. And when we say God, what have we said? Is that one syllable the whole of that we look for? So then, whatever we have had power to say is beneath Him: let us stretch ourselves to Him, that when He shall come, He may fill us. For we shall be like Him; because we shall see Him as He is.[145]

The contemplation of the risen Christ must help you remove the "vinegar" from your heart so that He can put in the "honey" of his joy. That is what Christ did with Mary Magdalene. We have to make an effort because there are people who keep a lot of vinegar in their hearts. Maybe because of past experiences, because of the blows that life has caused, perhaps because they have a character that inclines them to sadness and that makes them always see the glass half empty. Saint Teresa of Jesus once said: "From silly devotions and sour-faced saints, good Lord, deliver us." We cannot be happy or sad depending on how well or how badly things are going, depending on whether reality adjusts to what we want. The happiness for a disciple of Christ consists in being united to Him. Therefore, to be always happy is not an unattainable goal. The word of God says it! "Rejoice in the Lord always. I shall say it again: rejoice" (Phil. 4:4)!

I want to insist on this: God wants to make us happy, but we have to get rid of the vinegar first. You have to work on your own character, on your own temperament. We cannot spend our whole lives putting the accent on the bad things in our lives because there will always be something that saddens us and that sadness makes us blind to so many beautiful things that God gives us daily. I honestly believe that one of the greatest obstacles to experiencing the joy of Christ is our way of being. There are people who are very good, but very unhappy; who have very beautiful lives, but are always sad.

My favorite saint, after Saint Joseph, is Saint Phillip Neri. I love him. In an article written by Bishop Thomas Olmsted in 2015, our bishop recalled that the poet Phyllis McGinley called Saint Phillip Neri "the merriest saint alive." How can we not love such a man?

St. Philip Neri seems to never have had a bad day. He was always cheerful, always telling jokes. His heart was always full of the joy of the risen Christ. Of course, he suffered a lot because "it is necessary for us to undergo many hardships to enter the kingdom of God" (Acts 14:22), but he never manifested sadness. Surely the main cause of this constant joy was his union with God and the transparency of his beautiful soul, but undoubtedly one of his secrets was his character. I must admit that many Italians have a natural inclination to this continuous joy: I see Roberto Benigni, for example, the film director who I quoted earlier, and when

I think of that attitude of a life full of positivity, I think of Saint Francis of Assisi or Saint John Bosco, and I see that same quality, supernaturalized by the grace of God.

To describe the character of St. Philip Neri, there is a word in Italian that cannot be translated well in any other language, although those of us who speak Spanish understand it well: "*festività*." This is how a person who knew St. Philip Neri describes this quality, the *festività*, as he saw it reflected in the character of this saint:

> "*The Word signifies an expansive good humor, and above all cordiality and natural bearing. To go farther, it is an attitude which extends to everything, both things and people, and especially to the vicissitudes of life. In the daily affairs of life it is the absence of anxiety... accompanied by the power of treating as a joke what one cannot really enjoy. Its method is pleasantry, a lively and joyous manner, a joke or a witticism, by which one extricates oneself from difficulties.*"[146]

I encourage you to work in this attitude towards life because, whoever possesses it, will better receive the joy of the risen Christ and will advance much farther and much faster in the path of the Christian life than those who live always worried or anguished by things all or almost everything.

4. "*Jesus said to her, 'Woman, why are you weeping? Whom are you looking for'*" (v. 15)?

That is the question that Jesus asks you today, at the close of these Spiritual Exercises. From now on, from this retreat on, who are you going to look for? We return to the teachings of the Principle and Foundation. Jesus comes to meet you, as he went to meet St. Mary Magdalene, to change your heart, to change the goals of your life, so that from now on you no longer seek the living one among the dead (Lk. 24:5) So that you do not seek your joy in an empty grave, but in Him and only in Him.

Ask Jesus to feel the intense gladness that only He can give us: "Jesus said to her, 'Mary!' She turned and said to him in Hebrew, 'Rabbouni,' which means Teacher" (v. 16). How beautiful it is that Jesus called Mary by her name! Only then does she recognize Jesus, in that ring of his voice, in his way of pronouncing her name. Nobody had called her with so much love! Only Jesus had pronounced her name with such affection, with such tenderness.

Try to experience what Mary felt when she heard her name and realize that the man who spoke to her ... was Jesus! We have known cases in which, due to a natural catastrophe, or an attack, the family has been informed that their loved one had passed away. Imagine yourself in that situation. You are told that the person you love the most, your son, your husband, your parent, your boyfriend, your best friend, the person you most respect, has died. And then, days later, you receive a phone call. On the other end, you hear your name spoken, and in that voice, unmistakably, you recognize the person you love the most. He is alive!

Mary recognizes the person she loves the most. He is alive! The voice of Jesus, pronouncing her name, ignites a true inner transformation that we cannot understand. Mary understands everything. It is an enlightening that expels all the darkness of her life. Her life, which had lost all meaning and purpose, suddenly regains all meaning. Fear transforms into awe, sadness into joy, night into day, pain into joy.

In a way, everything that we have been looking for in these Spiritual Exercises is condensed in this encounter, in this wonderful moment. We came looking for an experience of personal and deep encounter with Christ that will change our lives.

Here we have it.

You must hear Jesus call your name, look into your eyes, come out to meet you on this final day of retreat. You must let the presence of Jesus, which is sun without sunset; melt the ice with which you came here a few days ago. "Mary of Magdala went and announced to the disciples, 'I have seen the Lord,' and what he told her" (v. 18).

You have also seen the Lord and you, too, have to go and announce what you have seen. Sometimes, when one has an experience like the one you are about to conclude today, one in which the Lord grants us the experience of so much inner peace, one would want to stay here forever, like the Apostles on Mount Tabor, or like Mary Magdalene, who falls at the feet of Jesus and clings to them. Jesus had to tell her: "Stop holding on to me" (v. 17).It is as if Mary thought: "I do not want you to run away from me again. I have lost you once, I will not lose you again." This is how the wife in the Song of Songs expresses herself: "I had hardly left them when I found him whom my heart loves. I took hold of him and would not let him go till I should bring him to the home of my mother" (3:4).

We do not want to go back to the battlefield, but Jesus says to you, as he said to Mary: "Go. Go to my brothers" (Jn. 20:17).Go back to your family, to your world, to your life, and tell everyone that I am alive, that "I die no more" (Rom. 6: 9). In 2006, on the occasion of the feast of St. Mary Magdalene that we celebrate on July 22, Pope Benedict XVI said the following:

> The story of Mary of Magdala reminds us of the fundamental truth: a disciple of Christ is one who, in the experience of human weakness, has had the humility to ask for his help, has been healed by him and has set out following closely after him, becoming a witness of the power of his merciful love that is stronger than without and death.[147]

5. Today's solemnity is suggesting the same message to you. The following year, Pope Benedict said something that impressed me so much that I wrote them down and I always carry them with me:

> The Lord took his wounds with him to eternity. He is a wounded God; he let himself be injured through his love for us. His wounds are a sign for us that he understands and allows himself to be wounded out of love for us.
>
> These wounds of his: how tangible they are to us in the history of our time! Indeed, time and again he allows himself to be wounded for our sake. What certainty of his mercy, what consolation do his wounds mean for us! And what security they give us regarding his identity: "My Lord and my God!" And what a duty they are for us, the duty to allow ourselves

in turn to be wounded for him![148]

These words of Pope Benedict connect the contemplation of the risen Christ with the Solemnity of the Heart of Jesus. Look at the open side in the body of the Risen One. That wound is the access to the Mystery of his Heart—a Heart that, in the words of the Lord to St. Mary Margaret, has "spared nothing, even to exhausting and consuming itself, in order to testify its love."

We have been talking about the Heart of Jesus from the first day because Saint Ignatius has invited us, every step of the way, to consider the life of Christ *from within*. The imitation of Christ proposed by the Exercises is an imitation of the attitudes and feelings of Jesus. It is evident that we cannot imitate the external aspects of the Lord's life. The Sermon on the Mount, which we have been hearing in the Gospels of the Masses of these past weeks, invites us *to change our heart*. Speaking of this sermon, Fr. Mendizábal used to say that the religion that emerges from it is a religion of the heart.

I have always thought that, in his Providence, the Lord assigned to the Society of Jesus the propagation of devotion to the Sacred Heart of Jesus because the fundamental elements of this spirituality (imitation, reparation, consecration and trust) are all found in the Spiritual Exercises.

The Heart of Jesus is a mystery into which we can peer only from the Resurrection. Again, Father Mendizábal said that the graphic representations of the Heart of Jesus that exist in images, paintings or sculptures, and that we have all seen so many times, fail in the essential aspect: the Heart of Jesus is the heart of a *living* person. Therefore, the beat of that Heart is the fundamental element. The images of the Heart of Jesus are "frozen" images but in the glorified body of the risen Christ, his Heart is *now* beating. What the devotion to the Heart of Jesus wants to teach me is that that Heart loves me *now*, it beats for love of me *now*, that it is sensitive *now*, that it suffers for my sins *now*, that it enjoys my healthy joys *now*. Devotion to the Heart of Christ does not want so much to remind me how much Jesus loved me, but how much he loves me *now*. In the words of Pope Benedict, Jesus "allows himself (present tense) to be wounded out of love for us".

The heartbeat of Jesus is therefore not a detail; it is the most important element! So, the best "place" to contemplate the mystery of the pierced Heart of the Lord is his glorified body. Father Mendizábal repeated many times the expression "Christ is risen and alive with a throbbing heart." I want you not to look away from that Heart that beats in the risen Christ.

As I said yesterday, the Redemption has been possible because the One who carried it to term has been one of us. He who saved us is not simply a divine Person—it is more accurate to say that we have been saved by the human Heart of a divine Person. What a great mystery this is! As the Second Vatican Council affirms, God has loved us with a human heart.[149]

The Church teaches us that in the Person of Christ three different types of love coexist, united harmoniously as three threads that intertwine to form a single cord: a divine love, which is the love of the Holy Trinity, the same love with which he loves the Father and the Holy Spirit; a human love that springs from his human will; and a human love that is sensitive and that refers to the whole dimension of the affections, feelings and emotions that are so characteristic of our human condition. The best place to understand these three loves is in the prayer of Gethsemane, when Jesus says: "My Father, if it is possible, let this cup pass from me; yet, I will not, but as you will" (Mt. 26:39).As one Father of the Church, Saint Maximus the Confessor, points out, in this phrase we find the three loves:[150] the Will of the Father who loves the world and wants to redeem it (and that Will of the Father is the same Will of Jesus as a God);the sensitive love of Jesus that is expressed in the words "not as I will," because to Christ the sufferings of the Passion caused fear and rejection; and the human will of Christ who, so to speak, unites the two previous loves by choosing to submit to the plan of salvation and, on the one hand, embraces the Father's love, and on the other hand directs his human sensitivity towards the fulfillment of Father's plan of redemption.

In the Heart of Jesus we find those three loves united, but the accent is placed on the sensitive love of the Lord, that world of emotions and feelings that is ours: that makes us fall in love, saddens us, frightens us, moves us, desires things that seem impossible; causes us to dream, to sigh, to cry, to enjoy, to laugh, to tremble, to feel alone, to miss those who are not with us. That which is so ours is also part of God, since he became man in Mary.

See your life from the Heart of the risen Christ. Ask God for the grace to understand that you are the joy of Jesus now when you love him and that Jesus hurts from our sin and suffers when we say no to him. The open side of the risen Christ teaches us that our sins, *now*, open his Heart. That God has become vulnerable for love of us. That he experiences the lack of correspondence when we choose the path of our egoism. That He enjoys our company as we enjoy our best friends. That he is sad if he sees us sad and happy if we are happy. In the apparitions of the risen Jesus, we see the humanity of Jesus. They are stories that have a very special flavor precisely because of that. Jesus does not look for his enemies, who had taken his life, but he goes out to meet his friends, comforts them, lifts them, cheers them up, gives them back hope. He really gets on his level, at our level, to raise us.

For this reason, the Church exhorts us to place devotion to the Heart of Christ at the center of our Christian life. That is why I want to encourage you to carry out today your consecration to the Heart of Jesus. At the end of the Spiritual Exercises, Saint Ignatius invites the person to surrender completely to God, in that prayer that I believe we have all heard at some time:

> *Take, Lord, and receive all my liberty, my memory, my intellect, and all my will — all that I have and possess. Thou gavest it to me: to Thee, Lord, I return it! All is Thine, dispose of it according to all Thy will. Give me Thy love and grace, for this is enough for me (SE 234).*

Pope Benedict XVI, speaking of this prayer, said to a group of Jesuits: this is a prayer "which to me always seems too sublime in the sense that I hardly dare to say it, yet we must always be able to return to it."[151]

It is a prayer in which we offer God our whole life, our whole being, so that from this experience we have had, we offer ourselves without reservation to the service of

God. Today we are going to close the Exercises with the consecration to the Heart of Jesus that comes to express the same oblation to the Lord. We will do it after Holy Communion when we have Jesus present within us.

I ask you, in this last hour of meditation of this retreat, to take what God has been manifesting to you and when you consecrate yourselves to the Heart of Jesus, place in his presence the purposes, the hopes of a new life, the feelings that the Holy Spirit has been putting in your heart, and offer them also to *"Jesus Christ risen and alive with a beating heart"* so that He makes them effective in the new stage of your life that begins today.

We ask Mary to teach us to live always in tune with the Heart of her Son and as we conclude these Spiritual Exercises, we also place in her our hopes for a holy life. May she show each of you the woman you are called to be, that you learn from the example of our Mother and that we truly live, like her, only and exclusively for Jesus.

23

"IN ALL THINGS LOVE AND SERVE"

DAY 8 (AFTERNOON) - TWENTIETH MEDITATION - MEDITATION TO ATTAIN LOVE

"Instill in us, Lord, the spirit of wisdom, truth and peace, so that we may know what pleases you and, once known, may we carry it out with one mind and will." (Collect Prayer - Mass at a spiritual or pastoral meeting)

The Spiritual Exercises of St. Ignatius close with a wonderful meditation, which he himself entitles "contemplation to attain love." In reality, since we began this experience more than a week ago, everything has been a "contemplation to attain love:" That is what you came here seeking, and I trust that this is what you have found. St. Ignatius concludes his work with a reflection that crowns this journey of the spirit that you have been laboriously making and that is an introduction to contemplative prayer.

In Catholic spiritual theology, the word contemplation has several meanings. In its proper sense, the term refers to the ultimate degree of prayer—"perfect contemplation" St. Teresa of Jesus calls it in her *Way of Perfection*—attained by those who reach the summit of holiness.[152] This type of prayer is *always* a gift of God that man cannot obtain as the exclusive fruit of his efforts. I believe that it is necessary to call attention to this because frequently one hears expressions that seem to suggest the opposite: if I apply this *method of prayer*, if I do this or that, I will be able to have "contemplative prayer." The best I can say about this approach is that it uses the word "contemplation" in an *ambiguous* sense: we use the same word to refer to *substantially* different realities.

On another level of meaning, we can speak of contemplation as that "application of the senses" to which St. Ignatius of Loyola encourages us in his *Spiritual Exercises* (159, 208, 226): an effort of the *imagination*, in cooperation with divine grace, to represent to ourselves in the most vivid way possible, a Gospel scene or setting in which communication with God is made possible. When, for example, we *contemplate* the episode of the Annunciation, we imagine that event and the setting where it took place in order to interact intimately with it. Note that the use of the word "imagination" in no way intends to oppose what we understand as "reality." God directs the faculties of the soul so that, through these representations—which certainly each one composes according to his or her capacities—the person reaches the core of what *really* happened.

In the context of the present meditation, however, it is

necessary to bring up another meaning of the term contemplation: I am referring to the well-known Ignatian expression that exhorts us to be "contemplatives in action."

Loyola concretized this expression by saying that to be contemplatives in action means "to find the presence of our Lord in all things."[153] I think that sometimes these words are abused, attributing to them a meaning to which St. Ignatius would never agree. At times, it almost seems that the expression "contemplatives in action" is used to justify an almost total absence of prayer because "everything is prayer." The truth is that such a contemplative attitude to life will never be the result of an empty and frivolous existence.

The contemplative gaze is not improvised. It is the fruit of a deliberate choice of the path of silence and a life of prayer assumed with truly martyrial fidelity. In fact, only those who abandon themselves completely to the action of the Holy Spirit and detach themselves from their own will, will be able to see God in all things. This point is sometimes difficult to convey because we often meet people whose prayer life is practically non-existent, yet they are convinced that they already find God in everything they do and therefore do not need to apply themselves or reform in this regard. How can we help those who believe they do not need help?

If we take St. Ignatius himself as a reference point, we will immediately realize that his life of prayer followed paths of uncommon depth. His *Spiritual Diary* remains the privileged witness of his most intimate secrets. Loyola burned his most private writings, but fortunately for us, a few notes were saved from the fire and have come down to us: brief annotations, barely sketched, that give us access to the innermost recesses of an extraordinary heart.

If St. Ignatius had not left us these notes, we would never have been able to imagine the soaring heights of his mystical soul. The man we see portrayed in the *Spiritual Exercises*, in the *Constitutions* of the Society of Jesus, or in the greater part of his letters is that of an impressive organizer, a most prudent counselor, a soldier of the Divine. In the fragments of his incomplete *Diary,* we discover his tender sensibility, his heart in love, his spirit always moved by the mysteries of the faith that he experiences deeply and profoundly. The military man reveals himself to us here as a mystic; the superior, attentive to detail, as a contemplative, engrossed in the union of his soul with God. Reading these pages, one inevitably has the feeling that only the crust of his inner world has been revealed to us. His life in the spirit must have been an unfathomable stream that will always remain forever hidden from our curious gaze.

In the last years of his life, St. Ignatius seemed to be more and more absorbed in his dealings with God. He spent the first hours of his day in absolute recollection: in the chapel adjoining his room—which can still be visited today in Rome—he lost himself in the mystery of the Most Holy Trinity. It was customary for our saint to celebrate Mass amid sobs and tears because on the altar the most unfathomable mysteries of God were revealed to this faithful servant and he received the most intimate effusions of his friend and Lord, Jesus. Only in this way could he "find God in all things." For example, as if he had returned to the longed-for island of his childhood, he would speak to the flowers in the garden to ask them to lower their voices and not speak so loudly about their Maker, "for I already know," he would exclaim, "what you are telling me!" Many nights he would go up to the terrace of the Company's residence and his gaze would be lost among the stars, and he would cry and moan: "*Heu, quam sordet mihi terra, dum caelum aspicio* (Oh, how poor the earth seems to me, when I contemplate the sky)."

Following the teaching of St. Ignatius, we can say that in prayer we accustom our gaze to recognize the presence of God in all things. "When I awake, let me be filled with your presence" (Ps. 17:15). From that morning encounter with Jesus, the disciple plunges into the maelstrom of his daily life able to discover the mark that the Beloved has left on persons, circumstances, and creatures. In work and in action, we are called to strive to remain in love and in the uninterrupted encounter with the Lord.

1. The ideal of the Christian life consists in living habitually in this presence of the Most Holy Trinity, in such a way that nothing distracts us from our union with the Lord. St. Therese of the Child Jesus confessed that she had never been distracted from the presence of God for more than three minutes.[154] I remember an anecdote that Father Valverde told me about the Venerable Manuel García Nieto, whom he knew at the University that the Society of Jesus directed in Comillas (Cantabria). This Jesuit priest was at the train station and went to the ticket office to buy his ticket. A kind young man was there to attend to his request. Father Nieto said to him, "Good morning. Two tickets, please." The answer caught the clerk's attention because the priest was alone and the station was completely empty. Puzzled and curious, he asked, "Father, two tickets?" To these words, the Jesuit reacted quickly: "Excuse me, excuse me! I

meant to say, one ticket." How beautiful it is to have such a relationship with God! Close, affectionate, friendly.

We must take care that our activity is elevated by this presence of the Beloved in the lover. I heard the following anecdote from Father Mendizábal. A group of faithful came to visit a monastery where, years before, an abbot with a reputation for holiness had lived. There they met an elderly monk who was asked if he had known this saintly superior in his youth to which he replied in the affirmative. The reply aroused the curiosity of the visitors, who asked, "Could you please tell us a story about Abbot Godefroi?"

"In fact, what I remember most about him," replied the Benedictine, "and what he repeated to us incessantly, was the following: 'Do not become godless in the cloister!'" The pilgrims, who were expecting something more elevated, more devout, more pious, were somewhat disappointed by the answer. The monk continued: "Yes, that is very important! Because often times, in our activity, even in the holiest places or occupations, we "become atheists." We forget that God is there, and we end up living and carrying out our activities like those who have no faith." The best antidote to avoid falling into this suffocating horizontality is precisely to live in the loving and continuous presence of the Father, through the Son, in the Holy Spirit.

2. Having said this, "contemplation to attain love" wants us to go a step further and discover this divine presence not only in ourselves but *in everything that exists or has happened to us in life*. It is a matter of first finding love in order to be able to respond to it, to *attain* it, according to the title that St. Ignatius himself gave to the present consideration. In

Loyola's second admonition for this meditation, the saint writes the following:

> *Love consists in a mutual sharing of goods, for example, the lover gives and shares with the beloved what he possesses, or something of that which he has or is able to give; and vice versa, the beloved shares with the lover. Hence, if one has knowledge, he shares it with the one who does not possess it; and so also if one has honors, or riches. Thus, one always gives to the other (SE 231).*

With enormous audacity, St. Ignatius applies these words to God in his relationship with his children: if we say that he loves us, and love consists in "giving of that which he has or is able to give," then the Lord must give to us in the measure of his love for us. If he really loves us so much, he must have given us much, for as Loyola also notes, "love ought to manifest itself in deeds rather than in words" (SE 230). As we will see below, everything that is or has been good in our lives comes from the loving hand of God. Let us ask this evening, with the assistance of divine grace, to help us to "contemplate love in our lives."

For this meditation, St. Ignatius invites us, as a composition of place, to place ourselves before God, the angels, and the saints "who intercede for me" (SE 232). It is a beautiful visualization of the dogma of the communion of saints. At the throne of the Most High, they are now imploring graces for you. Your response in these days can be the beginning of a series of incalculable consequences. Let me give you an example. If you place a seed in the palm of your hand, you will see how tiny it is, but in it is hidden an almost infinite potentiality: the germ of a tree which, in turn, contains the life of many other trees. We could say - if we disregard for a moment the factor of time – that an entire forest is virtually hidden in your hand within that small fragile seed which is now at your mercy.

God, in his omniscience, knows the effects of all created causes. Let's imagine that the fate of that seed is to give rise, over hundreds of years and through countless biological processes, to a whole forest of strong and long-lived trees. God *already sees that forest* which, somehow, now "fits" in the palm of your hand. However, for this outpouring of life to spill forth and come to pass, you must initiate the movement: you must push the first piece in this domino effect. How? By simply planting the seed. What a responsibility! That small seed that initially you were going to discard, that seemed so insignificant to you, suddenly takes on an importance that you had not been able to see *before,* considering *now* what could emerge from it *in the future* if only you plant it in good soil.

You may not believe it, but your response to divine love in these exercises is that seed, and the angels and saints *know it because they see it in God.* They know that if you let it grow, these days that have undoubtedly gone unnoticed by the world and will never make newspaper headlines or lead the news on the TV, will start a chain of unforeseeable events that will affect your life and the existence of who knows how many countless others. History will be different, salvation will come your way, if you respond generously. When, in the summer of 1534, a young man from Navarre named Francis accepted the invitation of St. Ignatius to make a month of spiritual exercises on the outskirts of Paris, no one knew what was going to happen thereafter. Few gave importance to the experience that changed the life of Xavier, and was the trigger of an explosion that brought the faith to Japan, founding Christian communities in the Orient, making Christ known to thousands of souls who embraced the faith and then communicated it to countless generations later. The examples could be multiplied *ad infinitum.* The most obvious, however, is not that of St. Francis Xavier, but that of our Mother Mary: from her "seed" sprouted the tree from whose fruit all the other trees of the world come.

Therefore, before you continue, become aware of the responsibility that your generosity has for you, for your family, for your community, for your country, for the Church and for the world. It is not an exaggeration when I write that the salvation of many depends on your surrender to God starting today.

As petitions of this meditation, we find the general one that we should already know by heart— "that all my intentions, actions, and operations may be directed purely to the praise and service of His Divine Majesty" (SE 46)—and the particular one which, in this case, is the following: "intimate knowledge of the many blessings received, that filled with gratitude for all, I may in all things *love and serve* the Divine Majesty" (SE 233). How beautiful! St. Ignatius wants you, recognizing God's gifts, to respond in gratitude by loving him *in everything.* Gratitude becomes generosity; generosity becomes love; love becomes unconditional service.

We ask for an "inner knowledge" as we have already repeated on numerous occasions. it is not a question of revealing to us something we did not know, but of under-standing what we probably already knew, but we *do it in a new, inner, deeper way.*

3. *Contemplation of the goods received from God.* Undoubtedly, the heart of this meditation, and of the Christian life as a whole,- is the consideration of the goods received from the Lord. As always in the Exercises, it is fundamental to *personalize* these reflections. The Most Holy Trinity has *given you* everything you are about to contemplate: he thinks of you, he has made you the recipient of all these gifts, he has loved you in each of the gifts you have enjoyed throughout your life.

During my first year as a priest, I remember having a conversation about this with a woman who did not believe in God, and I was trying to open her up to the possibility of that love that "moves the sun and all the stars."[155] We were talking next to the church of one of the small villages I was pastoring. The church was perched on top of a hill from which we could see, meandering timidly through the bare willows, a stream that irrigated the orchards and fields of that Castilian autumn. The view was certainly marvelous in its simplicity.

Unable to lead that young woman to a greater openness to the mystery of God, I lamented aloud that, with her closed-mindedness, she was missing the most beautiful part of her life: the Lord's love for her. To help her visualize what I wanted to tell her, I commented, "It is a pity that you are not able to see all that is now set before our eyes. You look at the landscape from here and see only beautiful things. I know that all this is a gift that God is *now* giving me. He has put it in front of my eyes this afternoon *so that we can see it right now*, to remind us how much He loves us. You see things, I see gifts. You see objects, I see love."

I believe that blindness is the sin of ungrateful people: they see *things as things, not as gifts,* and that prevents them from contemplating the best and most beautiful things in the world around us. This meditation seeks to *open our eyes* to see the world and our life as a gift and, behind that gift, to discover *the love that makes it possible.* Are you ready to enter into this wonderful adventure?

I am going to indicate below a series of gifts and I would like to ask you to go *very slowly* over each one of them. Take all the time you want and do not rush. Taste them as if they were ice cream melting on your tongue: do not bring the next bite to your mouth until you have finished savoring the one that is now melting inside you. St. Ignatius writes that you should "recall to mind the blessings of creation and redemption, and the special favors I have received" (SE 234). Let us break down, little by little, each of these three groups. Let us begin with the gifts of creation.

3. a. *Created world.* As I pointed out earlier, God created everything for us: "or everything belongs to you... the world or life or death, or the present or the future: all belong to you and you to Christ, and Christ to God" (1 Cor. 3:23). Just as a father hands over to his son his most precious work, the Most Holy Trinity has ordered this marvelous universe that we inhabit *for you,* as if you alone existed. A child of God can never contemplate with indifference the sun that illuminates us, the fertile fields, the millenary mountains, the immense oceans, the wild animals, the rain that falls for us from the

sky, the firmament full of stars: everything belongs to you! Everything has a message: "I am a gift *to you* from a God who *loves you.*"

Am I saying that God made every creature that exists, every bird that sings, every breeze that caresses us, every blade of grass that grows in the field, *for me?* Yes, I affirm it, full of the same amazement that permeates you. Couldn't we get lost in this? In fact, I encourage you from now on to never lose this perspective: *everything is yours...* how can we not take special care of the created world if it is a gift from our good Father God?

Now, reality is not simply a gift from God. It is not only that He is *truly present* in everything that has being. It is also that in creation God is *actively at work for me!* This is how St. Ignatius puts it:

> *Consider how God works and labors for me in all creatures upon the face of the earth, that is, He conducts Himself as one who labors. Thus, in the heavens, the elements, the plants, the fruits, the cattle, etc., He gives being, conserves them, confers life and sensation, etc. Then I will reflect on myself (SE 236).*

God *works and labors for me...* The Most Holy Trinity is not idle within His creatures, nor is He satisfied with giving them only the being that makes them exist: He is working! He intentionally works for you, serving you! Think of the image of a husband who, while his wife still sleeps, rises early to work in the fields and does so with immense love in order to provide for his family. His wife awakens to an empty bed, knowing that her husband has risen early and is already at work for her.

God is always on the clock. He works for you. This is amazing! There is a most beautiful hymn in the Liturgy of the Hours for the recitation of Compline that expresses this idea of a God who does not sleep. "*Precamur, sancte Domine, hac nocte nos custodies, sit nobis in te requies, quietas horas tribune* (We beseech you, Holy Lord, protect us this night. Let us take our rest in you; grant us a tranquil night)." Unbeknownst to me, sleeping, traveling, resting, He is at work *for me.* In every cell of my body, in the air that I breathe, in the movement of the stars that furrow the infinite heavens, the Lord is embracing me, caring for me, loving me. How can I not love such a God?

3. b. *Created goods that are part of you. Your femininity.* In the following consideration, I encourage you to think of all the gifts that are part of the person *that you are.* This is how St. Ignatius expresses it:

> *Reflect how God dwells in creatures: in the elements giving them existence, in the plants giving them life, in the animals conferring upon them sensation, in man bestowing understanding. So He dwells in me and gives me being, life, sensation, intelligence (SE 235).*

We should not overlook the bundle of gifts that make us ourselves. Your life is an immense gift *to you.* In a world where hundreds of thousands of conceived children are prevented from being born, you should not take this great gift for granted. Have you thanked God this morning for your health? Many of our brothers and sisters struggle with physical and mental illness. Think about your physical capabilities: have you thanked the Lord for the fact that you can get out of bed and walk? Many of our brothers and sisters are unable to do so.

There is a touching video on the Internet of a Christian singer-songwriter named Tony Meléndez. As a result of a medication that was prescribed to his mother when she was pregnant, this Nicaraguan by birth came into the world without arms. With great effort and tenacity, he was able to develop an enormous dexterity in the use of his feet and this has allowed him to perform activities that would seem impossible for someone without hands: driving a car, painting, and playing the guitar. He had the opportunity to perform before St. John Paul II in Denver in 1987 during World Youth Day. Since then, he has been dedicated to spreading hope with his testimony and his music. In the video to which I refer, Tony ends with a reflection that awakens us to *the amazement of everyday realities*. He says something similar to this: "Many times I have been asked: 'Tony, in today's world, where can we see miracles?' I see *a hand* and when someone raises his hand, I, who have no arms, think: 'For me, that is a miracle.'"

You have to put yourself in his place: for someone who lives without limbs, the movement of a hand represents an impossibility. For most of us is something simple and commonplace—writing as I am doing now or turning a page of a book while reading or scratching an ear if it itches—for someone like Tony this becomes an unattainable dream or, at least, a real achievement because the distance that separates him from these activities is infinitely greater than for those of us lucky enough to have arms and use them daily without much thought. If we lived in a world where people had no hands, wouldn't you feel privileged to have yours? If it were natural for men to be born without eyes, wouldn't you consider yourself lucky to have those windows to the world around you? If people were born deaf, wouldn't you marvel every morning at being able to hear the extraordinary world of sounds that surrounds us?

Do you realize that *everything you take for granted in your life is a gift?* Your mobility, your body with its senses, your intelligence, your capacity to love, your memory, everything is a gift and for all of this St. Ignatius invites you today to be grateful. Sadly, we humans get used to the extraordinary and only when it is taken away from us do we begin to value it. Health, youth, initiative, resilience, are all qualities that we appreciate when illness, decrepitude, exhaustion, limitation appear. Why can we not appreciate them with gratitude while we possess them? As happened to Job with his possessions, one day we will no longer have them with us and *it is now* that we can offer them to the Lord.

In these Spiritual Exercises we have talked a lot about what it means to be a woman. Your femininity is also a gift *to you*, and I encourage you, in your personal prayer today, to thank God for having made you a woman. There is a cluster of extraordinary qualities that are part of you because *you are a woman*. We men will never possess them and they constitute your most intimate identity. These are attributes that permeate every fiber of your being: your body, your soul, your psyche. Your whole reality *is feminine*, and this is how the One who brought you out of nothingness wanted you from all eternity. Before the creation of the universe, when God alone existed, He already loved you as His daughter: "with age-old love I have loved you" (Jer. 31:3). Therefore, to be who you are, to be as you are, and at this moment of our discourse, to be the woman you are—with the set of traits, characteristics and peculiarities that separate you from any other human being and make you a unique and unrepeatable person—has not been the fruit of a chain of random causes or of chance. It is the fruit of a choice. *Someone wanted you this way and endowed you to be the woman you are.* You must therefore experience infinite gratitude because you exist, because you were loved before you existed, and because you are a gift that contains a marvelous plurality of gifts, not only for others but above all for yourself. How many women lack this grateful gaze towards themselves? How many women do not love themselves as they are and wish to transform their own nature to become what they cannot be? How many women look at themselves with contempt, even hatred, because they judge themselves with criteria other than those that arise from this grateful gaze that comes from faith?

As I have just pointed out, your womanhood is also a gift to others. Allow me an obvious example: my mother's femininity has been and is a gift to me, to the point that, without this gift, I would not be here nor would I be the man who speaks to you today. I don't think I need to explain the reasons for this statement. I am a man, I am a son, I have become the person I am, *thanks to my mother.* Now I invite you to make the leap to yourself and not to circumscribe the example I have just offered to the sphere of *motherhood:* your femininity has been the cause of a cascade of goods that

458

many of us have received *because you are a woman.* Truly, the world would be a much worse place without you and all that good that has come into it through your womanhood.

In this regard, I would like to speak to the words of St. John Paul II in his Apostolic Letter *Mulieris Dignitatem*, and I would like you to listen to the Pope's gratitude to God for the gift that *each one of you* is for the world and for the Church. In his 1995 letter he not only thanks women, he thanks God himself as the source of every gift for having given us each and every one of you. Perhaps the pope's expressions will help you to see areas of yourself that sometimes you are not able to see:

> *"If you knew the gift of God" (Jn. 4:10), Jesus says to the Samaritan woman during one of those remark-able conversations which show his great esteem for the dignity of women and for the vocation which enables them to share in his messianic mission.*
>
> *The present reflections, now at an end, have sought to recognize, within the "gift of God", what he, as Creator and Redeemer, entrusts to women, to every woman. In the Spirit of Christ, in fact, women can discover the entire meaning of their femininity and thus be disposed to making a "sincere gift of self" to others, thereby finding themselves.*
>
> *During the Marian Year the Church desires to give thanks to the Most Holy Trinity for the "mystery of woman" and for every woman - for that which consti-tutes the eternal measure of her feminine dignity, for the "great works of God", which throughout human history have been accomplished in and through her.*

After all, was it not in and through her that the greatest event in human history – the incarnation of God himself – was accomplished?

Therefore the Church gives thanks for each and every woman: for mothers, for sisters, for wives; for women consecrated to God in virginity; for women dedicated to the many human beings who await the gratuitous love of another person; for women who watch over the human persons in the family, which is the fundamental sign of the human community; for women who work professionally, and who at times are burdened by a great social responsibility; for "perfect" women and for "weak" women – for all women as they have come forth from the heart of God in all the beauty and richness of their femininity; as they have been embraced by his eternal love; as, together with men, they are pilgrims on this earth, which is the temporal "homeland" of all people and is transformed sometimes into a "valley of tears"; as they assume, together with men, a common responsibility for the destiny of humanity according to daily necessities and according to that definitive destiny which the human family has in God himself, in the bosom of the ineffable Trinity.

The Church gives thanks for all the manifestations of the feminine "genius" which have appeared in the course of history, in the midst of all peoples and nations; she gives thanks for all the charisms which the Holy Spirit distributes to women in the history of the People of God, for all the victories which she owes to their faith, hope and charity: she gives thanks for all the fruits of feminine holiness.[156]

3. c. *Events in our life. Your personal history.* God's care for you has also been translated into all the circumstances that have been part of your life which have never been random. Everything that has happened on the path of your existence can be transformed into grace, growth and maturity. Even the most adverse situations—sufferings of every kind, illnesses, persecutions, violence, misunderstandings, abandonments—can be transformed into love and serve for the glory of God and the salvation of the world. "Suffering is present in the world in order to release love," St. John Paul II once wrote.[157] Everything has a redemptive value; nothing is to be lost forever.

"Contemplation to attain love," as you are seeing, is a watchtower, a vantage point from which to contemplate the spectacle of our whole life as a *gift of God.* For this reason, it is crucial that you also know how to consider the particular benefits you have received in the account of your own personal story which also shape the reality that has made you the person you are today. Think of your family, your social and cultural environment, your childhood, the country where you were born, the education you received, the places you have visited, the people you have met and who have deeply marked your life. My dear Father Valverde used to say that "two human paths never cross by chance." Your life journey has also been willed by God! Thanks to him, you were able to know him, to advance in the knowledge of the faith, to receive the first sacraments, to have access to the person of Christ and the Church. To have the resources to face this hostile and dangerous world. Much of this is still in your memory, and these experiences and memories form the basis of your identity, have shaped your soul and made you the woman you are.

Perhaps you will tell me that not everything you have had to go through has been exactly pleasant and wonderful. Here, it seems to me, St. Ignatius also invites us to *reconcile ourselves with our own life*. You must accept your history as it has been, including the darkest pages. You must be able to look at the path you have taken with peace, knowing that "for those who love God, all things work together for good" (Rom 8:28). I know that many experiences have been traumatic. Unjust wounds have also been opened in you and some of them still bleed in your heart. Suffering is "sacred ground" before which, like Moses at Sinai, we should all take off our shoes and enter with the utmost respect. When a person has suffered a great deal, our words are often not very helpful in as much as we speak of what we have no experience of, and this often leads to a certain lack of empathy.

I want to repeat what we have shared before in these exercises: evil can be redeemed. Suffering can expand our capacity for understanding and love. The injustices we have suffered can also be sublimated, giving them meaning in Christ crucified. Those terrible experiences can take you to heights you would otherwise never have been able to reach. In this meditation, you should contemplate them all "to attain love." In some cases, the Holy Spirit will lead you to forgive the one who did you so much harm. In others, to take the lesson of life that was hidden in that trauma. Still in others, it will simply consist in leaving what happened in the hands of God without understanding why it happened and continuing to walk with joy. Ask God for the grace that your story will not be a source of bitterness and sadness for you, but a school of life, an occasion for goodness, a blessing for you and for others.

3. d. *Gifts of Redemption. Gift of Jesus Christ.* The weighing of all the benefits previously considered is something truly marvelous, indescribable, and overwhelming. They all have their origin in the Lord, who pours out upon us "as the rays of light descend from the sun, and as the waters flow from their fountain" (SE 237).

However, this takes on a new dimension if we consider the following: because God loves us, he has given us everything we have. Now, all this is a kind of preparation or foretaste, because what He really wants is to *give us is Himself.* St. Ignatius writes: "how much, as far as He can, the same Lord desires to give Himself to me" (SE 234).

It is as if God is offering himself little by little in creation and thus wants to prepare us for the moment when he will be able to give himself completely to us. In his gifts we see a *partial* reflection of his goodness, but the limitation that is proper to the created condition of things does not succeed in *fully* expressing the infinitude of his love for u s. They *progressively* reveal to us, if we know how to appreciate them, the love and tenderness of our Father for us. In this way, he prepares us to receive the greatest gift in which are hidden *all the treasures* of his grace: himself.

In his *Practice of Love for Jesus Christ*, St. Alphonsus Liguori summarizes marvelously what Loyola has shown us so far:

All holiness and perfection of soul lies in our love

for Jesus Christ our God, who is our Redeemer and our supreme good. It is part of the love of God to acquire and to nurture all the virtues which make a man perfect.

Has not God in fact won for himself a claim on all our love? From all eternity he has loved us. And it is in this vein that he speaks to us: "O man, consider carefully that I first loved you. You had not yet appeared in the light of day, nor did the world yet exist, but already I loved you. From all eternity I have loved you."

Since God knew that man is enticed by favors, he wished to bind him to his love by means of his gifts: "I want to catch men with the snares, those chains of love in which they allow themselves to be entrapped, so that they will love me." And all the gifts which he bestowed on man were given to this end. He gave him a soul, made in his likeness, and endowed with memory, intellect and will; he gave him a body equipped with the senses; it was for him that he created heaven and earth and such an abundance of things. He made all these things out of love for man, so that all creation might serve man, and man in turn might love God out of gratitude for so many gifts.

But he did not wish to give us only beautiful crea-tures; the truth is that to win for himself our love, he went so far as to bestow upon us the fullness of himself. The eternal Father went so far as to give us his only Son. When he saw that we were all dead through sin and deprived of his grace, what did he do? Compelled, as the Apostle says, by the superabundance of his love *for us, he sent his beloved Son to make reparation for us and to call us back to a sinless life.*

By giving us his Son, whom he did not spare precisely so that he might spare us, he bestowed on us at once every good: grace, love, and heaven; for all these goods are certainly inferior to the Son: He who did not spare his own Son, but handed him over for all of us: how could he fail to give us along with his Son all good things?[158]

The gift of Jesus Christ! One is at a loss for words... Lord, thank you for loving us so much! How can we be indifferent to so much love? How can we not leap for joy knowing that we are the recipients of *all God's love?*

"He who did not spare even his own Son, but delivered him up to death for us, *how will he not also give us everything else along with him*" (Rom. 8:32)? Starting from Jesus Christ, let us now consider all the gifts that belong to the realm of grace: the gift of Mary, our guardian angel, the Church, the sacraments, faith, Paradise, each of the movements of the Holy Spirit in our soul. In each these gifts we could equally lose ourselves: why have *I* been given the immense, infinite, undeserved grace of being part of the people of God, of the Body of Christ, of being Catholic? I do not write this with the slightest hint of pride or complacency. In a world with so many religions, with so much disorientation, with so many good people who are misguided and who seek without finding, one feels the joy of belonging to the family of the Church.

It is an indescribable joy! As a final additional reading

of this retreat, I would like to invite you to read slowly Pope Benedict XVI's address to the young people during the eleventh World Youth Day in Cologne in 2005. It is a reflection that I am very fond of because I was there. The year after my ordination to the priesthood, I was asked to accompany a Catholic Action youth group from my city, Cuenca, who were going to participate in this event. It was a wonderful trip! That vigil on the esplanade of Marienfield, listening on the radio to the simultaneous translation of the Holy Father's words... Benedict spoke of holiness and sin in the Church, emphasizing, however, the light transmitted to us by the saints and the joy of belonging "to this great family that we see here; we are glad to have brothers and friends all over the world. Here in Cologne, we discover the joy of belonging to a family as vast as the world, including Heaven and earth, the past, the present, the future and every part of the earth. In this great band of pilgrims we walk side by side with Christ, we walk with the star that enlightens our history."[159]

4. *Response to God's gifts: the total surrender of ourselves to the Lord.* Do you remember the title of this meditation? "Contemplation to attain love." Up to now, what we have done has been, basically, to contemplate. We have reviewed our whole life and asked the Holy Spirit to open the eyes of our heart to see the world, our life, all that has passed through us, as a great gift that reveals the infinite and personal love of the Most Holy Trinity. At this point, we should feel overwhelmed by a love that we have not deserved, that has been given to us to savor and to respond to. The way in which the Lord draws us to himself consists in opening

his hand and filling us with innumerable goods. What does he expect of us? Only one thing: *that we love Him.*

"Then I will reflect upon myself, and consider, according to all reason and justice, what I ought to offer the Divine Majesty, that is, all I possess and myself with it. Thus, as one would do who is moved by great feeling, I will make this offering of myself" (SE 234). On love of God, St. Bernard notes the following in his commentary on the book of the Song of Songs,

> *For when God loves, all he desires is to be loved in return; the sole purpose of his love is to be loved, in the knowledge that those who love him are made happy by their love of him.*
>
> *The Bridegroom's love, or rather the love which is the Bridegroom, asks in return nothing but faithful love. Let the beloved, then, love in return. Should not a bride love, and above all, Love's bride? Could it be that Love not be loved? Should not a bride love, and above all, Love's bride? Could it be that Love not be loved?*[160]

Love is adulterated when it is offered in exchange for something other than the loved one. When we love someone as a *means to another end*—wealth, stability, security, even our own happiness—we are really loving ourselves, not the other person. This is using the other person instead of loving him or her. However, there is nothing reprehensible or suspicious in desiring the love of the one we love. On the contrary, as St. Bernard himself points out, *correspondence is in the very nature of love.* In other words, reciprocity is the summit of perfect love. For this reason, friendship is the best love.

Look at your Maker, made a beggar for your love. He is poor because, although he has everything, what he desires he cannot obtain unless *you give it to him.* Love turns the lover into a beggar who pleads for the alms of correspondence. The rich man becomes poor, the sane man loses his mind: one would be willing to leave everything to "attain the love" of the beloved. What is the use of possessing the whole world if we cannot enjoy the only thing our soul longs for? *Mutatis mutandis*, John Paul II's bold and joyful expressions about the human person can be applied to God, since we are his image: "Man cannot live without love. He remains a being that is incomprehensible for himself, his life is senseless, if love is not revealed to him, if he does not encounter love, if he does not experience it and make it his own, if he does not participate intimately in it."[161]

Understand well what I am going to say, God cannot live without love either, because He *is love.* That's why He seeks yours. He begs for it. He implores it. He beseeches it in everything that exists: in the air, in the sun, in the earth, in the water. In the mountains, the fruit, the animals, the trees, the stars. In life and in all its manifestations. In good people. In the readings that have opened vistas of glory for you. In the Paradise we hope to reach, the beautiful landscapes, the happy experiences, the people who have paved the way before you. In the challenges overcome, and the storms that have made you better. In the love you have received, and the body that is your temple and the tent which you inhabit. In the moments of sincere friendship, the times when you have felt fully alive, and the places you have been.

In the sounds of a forest awakening, the pleasure of rest after a day spent in the service of God and mankind. In the tears that have washed your soul, and the silence that has been filled with so many messages. The company of those who have pushed us when we could no longer bear it. The family, the sweet memories, the bitter hours, the peace of that quiet corner where you could pray feeling the closeness of God. The footsteps of your wandering, the hot baths, the penances you did, Christ crucified, the serenity of the Eucharist, Mary's smile, the times you have enjoyed, the difficulties you left behind, the limitations that pushed you to grow and stand on your own feet. The satisfaction of fulfilled duty, living for others, working for others to be saved, savoring simple joys. A ray of light that warms you when you are cold, an ant that tickles you, a shadow that shelters you when the sun burns brightly. Pains that help you appreciate the periods of goodness, advice that illuminated your path, graces that moved you internally, consolations in which you received the visits of the Spirit, desolations that helped you to be humble, experiences that you felt only once, goodness in abundance that is given to us every morning... in *everything* is God asking you to love him. Are you finally going to love him?

The offering to which St. Ignatius invites us is that of an unconditional, absolute surrender, to the measure of the gift we have received in Christ. St. Bernard here continues the passage we have just quoted above:

> Rightly then does she give up all other feelings and give herself wholly to love alone; in giving love back, all she can do is to respond to love. And when she has

poured out her whole being in love, what is that in comparison with the unceasing torrent of that original source? Clearly, lover and Love, soul and Word, bride and Bridegroom, creature and Creator do not flow with the same volume; one might as well equate a thirsty man with the fountain.

What then of the bride's hope, her aching desire, her passionate love, her confident assurance? Is all this to wilt just because she cannot match stride for stride with her giant, any more than she can vie with honey for sweetness, rival the lamb for gentleness, show herself as white as the lily, burn as bright as the sun, be equal in love with him who is Love?

No. It is true that the creature loves less because she is less. But if she loves with her whole being, nothing is lacking where everything is given. To love so ardently then is to share the marriage bond; she cannot love so much and not be totally loved, and it is in the perfect union of two hearts that complete and total marriage consists. Or are we to doubt that the soul is loved by the Word first and with a greater love?

We could summarize the words of St. Bernard by saying that the only way to correspond to a God who loves us absolutely is to give ourselves to him in the *same way.* That is to say, *without reserve.* The prayer that we quoted in the previous meditation, "Take, Lord, and receive all my freedom, my memory, my understanding...", Loyola includes it here, as the crowning of the whole experience of the Exercises. This is the hour of truth.

5. Yes, it is the hour of truth. You have listened much these days and you have received abundant graces from the Most Holy Trinity because you have entered into an intimate dialogue with Him. You have been soft clay, and to the extent that you have let Him, the Father, shaped you into a new woman. Applying his hands—the Son and the Holy Spirit, as St. Irenaeus points out with gentleness and love.[162] In the end, the time comes to answer him: yes or no, all or nothing, newness of life or continuity with the person you were. St. Paul writes: "As God is faithful, our word to you is not 'yes' and 'no.' For the Son of God, Jesus Christ, who was proclaimed to you by us, Silvanus and Timothy and me, *was not 'yes and 'no,' but 'yes' has been in him.* For however many are the promises of God, their 'yes' is in him; therefore, the Amen from us also goes through him to God for glory." (2 Cor. 1:18-20)

In the Lord there is no "today yes, and tomorrow no." Are you willing, from this hour on, to live the Ignatian motto of "in all things love and serve" God, and in Him, mankind? This is the grace you must ask for now.

My mission ends right here. The next page of this book is no longer mine: it is yours to write. It is your life, your freedom, your answer. It is up to you to choose your path from now on, *your* way, *your* decision. I can only pray to the Lord through the intercession of the Blessed Virgin Mary, St. Teresa Benedicta of the Cross (Edith Stein), St. Ignatius of Loyola, and all the angels and saints, that you will not lack generosity. *Be the woman* God created you to be. Live holiness without compromise in your daily life. Become light and let the world see God in you as you see God in the world. Embrace faithfully the faith of the Church, which is beautiful only when it is lived faithfully, without reduction or accommodation. Throw yourself into the work of saving souls and do not grow weary of doing good (2 Thes. 3:13). If we persevere, the hour of rest will come when we reach Paradise. Until then, we must fight.

Let us put the means at our disposal to sanctify ourselves. Let us know how to wait. Let us always have Mary as our Mother and intercessor, and then let us rest in the Heart of Jesus Christ, who is God and who lives and reigns forever and ever. AMEN.

II

APPENDICES

24

APPENDIX I

PIECES OF ADVICE FOR A FRUITFUL RETREAT

I would like to give you some direction about prayer, which I think may be useful for everyone, especially for those who feel a little lost because they have never had an experience like this before. I want to give you some simple guidelines to help you pray during this retreat.

Obviously, one could say a lot about prayer. There are entire bookstores on the subject, and my goal is not to unravel all of their mysteries. I do not have the capacity to do so either. There are many extraordinary books about prayer.

There is a famous phrase of Saint Jane Frances de Chantal, in which she says that the best method for prayer is not to have one. Father Jacques Philippe says that prayer is not a type of yoga exercise in which, in the end, the emphasis is on what we do.[163] Christian prayer is a grace, it is not the fruit of our effort or the result of our activity. It is, as the *Catechism* says, a gift.[164] It is evident that if prayer is a loving conversation with God, the first condition is that God reveals himself to me, and his revelation is a gift to me. I do not deserve it. I do not cause it when I want it. It happens when he wants it.

That said, I think we all need a certain direction because, when a person who has never meditated is invited to dedicate one hour of her day to meditation, it is normal for that person to ask: "And how do I do it?" In fact, what Saint Ignatius of Loyola proposes in the Spiritual Exercises is a method of prayer that sometimes draws attention because it is very regulated. Saint Ignatius knew, however, that a method is only a method—it is a means to an end and, therefore, does not have an absolute value. It can be changed if it does not work, but it should not be despised beforehand because the Holy Spirit also speaks to us through these qualified teachers.

The *Catechism of the Catholic Church* says the following:

> *The witnesses who have preceded us into the kingdom, especially those whom the Church recognizes as saints, share in the living tradition of prayer by the example of their lives, the transmission of their writings, and their prayer today (...).*
>
> *The different schools of Christian spirituality share in the living tradition of prayer and are essential guides for the faithful. In their rich diversity they are refractions of the one pure light of the Holy Spirit.*
>
> *The Spirit is truly the dwelling of the saints and the saints are for the Spirit a place where he dwells in his own home since they offer themselves as a dwelling place for God and they are called his temple.*[165]

The word *method* comes from the Greek. *Meta* is a preposition, meaning beyond or through. The word *odos* means road. It is the word used by Jesus in the Gospel of Saint John when He is described as "the way, the truth and the life" (Jn. 14:6). That is, a method is a path through which an end is reached. The suggestions that I am going to give next will help you to an encounter with God. If, on the other hand, the Holy Spirit in your prayer decides to take you "another way," follow him freely. Do not stick to what I say, not even what you want. If you would allow me an example, this is like sailing in the sea on a small sailboat. I am going to give you directions to begin your journey by sea, how to use the navigation instruments, how to row, and other useful information, but I also ask you to extend your sails and, in doing so, to put yourself at the mercy of the winds. When the Holy Spirit, whom Jesus describes in the Gospel like the wind (Jn. 3:8), blows on the sails of your boat, stop rowing, do not resist him, do not try to change the direction but go where He wants to take you.

1. The first thing I want to tell you is that your prayer in these Exercises has to be very simple. Saint Ignatius says: "It is not knowing much, but realizing and relishing things interiorly, that contents and satisfies the soul" (SE 2).

There are people who, when they meditate, spend more time in the head than in the heart. For them, to meditate is to reflect, to deduce teachings from theoretical principles, to contemplate an abstract truth and to look for their applications in daily life. Think, think, and think. In Spiritual Exercises, everything that we have in our heads must descend to the heart. The *Catechism* is categorical and resounding in this respect: "According to Scripture, it is the heart that prays. If our heart is far from God, the words of prayer are in vain."[166]

2.I encourage you to be very aware of what Saint Ignatius calls "repetitions." It does not refer so much to the repetitions that we do based on meditating on the same things, but on what I feel God is bringing to my attention repeatedly throughout my prayer times. Maybe there is an idea that continually comes to me, or a relationship with someone about whom the Lord is giving me light, or an aspect of my life about which I see that God is asking me to be more careful. Docility to the Holy Spirit is also *that*. That is to *listen* to what the Lord is manifesting to us and, if he is showing it to us, in that light that He gives us he also offers us the grace to make the change that He wants to make in our life and in our heart.

3. During the times of prayer, simplicity consists above all in that "realizing and relishing things interiorly, that contents and satisfies the soul," as Saint Ignatius says. You have to relish things interiorly. When one is relishing food, the secret is not to eat quickly, but to savor the taste in your mouth without hurry. In prayer, this inner relishing consists of looking for where the Holy Spirit is giving me that satisfaction. This is not bad, it is not selfish, it is not to seek joy, but to put oneself in the hands of God and enjoy his action in the soul.

In prayer, sometimes you will read a lot because you do not find anything and you must seek the Lord. Other times, simply feeling the presence of God is a form of interior relishing and, therefore, you should not start reading, worried about covering all the points of meditation. I confess that, for example, at a particular level, many times I do not need to read anything when I do my meditation: I close my eyes and suddenly I feel in the loving presence of God, and I stay there all the time, with Jesus, without hurry. Other times, in an hour I have only read one verse of the Holy Scripture because there the Lord gives me so much that I do not need more. The same goes for you these days: do not run, do not rush, do not want to eat the whole plate at once. Do not seek the satisfactions of God but the God of satisfactions.

Saint John of the Cross speaks of spiritual gluttony in his work *Dark Night of the Soul.* There is no danger of gluttony only when we eat, but also when we pray. Saint John of the Cross says there are souls that "cannot read enough spiritual books, and one minute they are meditating on one subject and the next on another, always hunting for some gratification in the things of God."[167]

4. As I said before, the method of this retreat will be the contemplation of scenes of the Gospels that have as protagonists Jesus and a series of women who are related to him.

I ask that throughout your meditation time, you always have the scene before your eyes. It is what is called in the Spiritual Exercises "composition of place." Everything you ponder must come from contemplation. The more you move away from the Gospel scene, the worse the quality of prayer will be. The scenes that you are going to contemplate are flowers full of pollen. You have to imitate the bees, which do not go to another flower until they have taken from one, all the pollen that is in it. Stay like bees, stuck to the flower.

Do not fly away to another flower if it is not because God is inviting you to move.

Have the gospel scene always before your eyes. A tip can be to read several times throughout your prayer, not to stray too far from it. That rereading will also help you to look at details that perhaps went unnoticed the first time you read it.

5. I want to raise a red flag especially to people who are more intellectual, or speculative nature. The experience of the Exercises is not like theological formation. For example, when I read a beautiful idea in a book of Theology, I enjoy it, I meditate on it, I often get lost there. Moreover, the Lord also wants us to do that in our Christian life. Surely, in these Exercises, I can grab one of those books and find in them beautiful and true ideas that produce a healthy joy. It is the joy of truth. Now, in the Spiritual Exercises we must seek what we feel or reflect is born of the contemplation of the person, life, and humanity of Jesus Christ. I can rejoice in the love of God because, for example, I read the *Treatise on the Love of God* by Saint Francis de Sales and in it, I understand the nature of God's love, its essence, its properties, and from that reading I am joyful and amazed at the love of God. Or I can rejoice in the love of God because I contemplate the crucified Christ and his contemplation awakens love in me, as it happened to Saint Teresa of Jesus when she saw that beautiful image of the flagellated Christ that is preserved in the Monastery of the Incarnation in Ávila. Saint Teresa writes:

It happened to me that one day entering the oratory I

saw a statue they had borrowed for a certain feast to be celebrated in the house. It represented the much wounded Christ and was very devotional so that beholding it I was utterly distressed in seeing Him that way, for it represented well what He suffered for us. I felt so keenly aware of how poorly I thanked Him for those wounds that, it seems to me, my heart broke. Beseeching Him to strengthen me once and for all that I might not offend Him, I threw myself down before Him with the greatest outpouring of tears.

I think I said that I would not rise from there until He had granted what I was begging Him for. I believe certainly this was beneficial to me, because from that time I went on improving.[168]

The second one is the experience that we are looking for in the Exercises. Seeing Christ and feeling that our heart breaks when we see his love for us. And, in the meditations, you must continually have Jesus before you. In the Exercises, we do not go from the principles to the resolutions, from the top down, but from the bottom up, from the contemplation to the change of life. Prayer is an exercise of love. In the words of Saint John of the Cross, "In love with the Beloved alone."

6. I want to explain a little bit about what "composition of place" means. We can understand it wrongly and think that it is simply to imagine the details of the "scenario" in which the fact of the life of Jesus we are meditating happens, like just envisioning the place in which each particular mystery, or event, unfolds.

It is true that, at first, we have to do what Saint Ignatius calls "application of the senses" (SE 159, 208, 226): we have to try to "see" the people who appear in the particular event, observing what they do, hearing what they say, feeling what they did, smelling what they did. In this sense, we have to dedicate some time to "imagine" the place, see the faces, and think about the space in its smallest details.

These senses are spiritual senses: that is why Saint Ignatius says that we must contemplate the ugliness of sin, either smell the sweetness of God's love, or feel touched by the love of God. It is, then a work of the Holy Spirit in us.

Now, after having implored the grace of the Holy Spirit, after having made an act of the presence of God and after having represented in your minds the setting of the scene, you have to jump into it. You have to make yourself present to that event. You are not simply a spectator who sees the facts of Jesus' life in the third person. You have to put yourself in the picture. It is essential that you enter in. Let the Holy Spirit put you into the scenes you are contemplating. Let yourself be absorbed by the mystery and open to its action, following the light and movement of the Spirit of God.

This composition of place simplifies the prayer: Sometimes, the hour of meditation will leave me in the contemplation of a detail, of a look, or of a word. Sometimes, the Holy Spirit will lead me to focus on the reactions of people, or on the interior attitudes of Jesus Christ that manifest in his face. Other times, the scene will move me and make me cry from pain, or joy, or admiration, feelings that provoke the action of the Holy Spirit to grieve my sins, or to increase my hope, so that my love for Christ becomes stronger.

7. This way of praying may seem, if not well explained, somewhat artificial, but it is n ot. It is something very profound, which is at the basis of our identity and our faith.

We never lose sight of the fact that prayer is a gift; prayer is a covenant of love; prayer is being in communion with Christ.

Our first covenant with Christ took place the day of our baptism. On that day, we put on Christ, as St. Paul says. "All of you who were baptized into Christ have clothed yourselves with Christ" (Gal. 3:27). In our baptism, we become children of God through Jesus Christ (Eph. 1:5).

From that moment, we are blessed "with every spiritual blessing in the heavens" (Eph. 1:3). We are united to Jesus in such a way that we belong to Jesus, and Jesus is ours: "All belong to you, and you to Christ, and Christ to God" (1 Cor. 3:22-23).

When I was in Rome, God put in my path a saint who has deeply touched me with his writings. I have his writings in my tablet, so I can say I take this saint everywhere I go and often he is in my prayers. I go back to his writings because they always give me a lot of light. It is Saint John Eudes, who was one of the first promoters of the Devotion to the Sacred Heart of Jesus even before the revelations to Saint Margaret Mary Alacoque in Paray-Le Monial. Saint John Eudes is an author who delves into this spirituality of the mysteries of the life of Christ, to the point that the *Catechism* quotes him precisely speaking on this subject.

I want to read another passage in which he talks about Jesus as our Head. He says:

I beg you to consider that Our Lord Jesus Christ is your

true Head, and that you are one of His members, and that from that fact there are five important results: (a) That He stands to you as the head to its members, so that everything in Him is yours, His spirit, His heart, His body, His mind, and that you must make use of them as your own for the purpose of serving, praising, loving and glorifying God. (b) That you stand to Him as do the members to the head, for which reason He ardently desires to make use of all that is in you for the service and the glory of His Father, as of things that are His own. (c) That not only does he so stand in regard to you, but also He wishes to be in you, to be living and reigning within you, as the head lives and reigns in its members; and that He desires all that is in Him to live and reign in you: that His mind should live and reign in your mind, that His heart should live and reign in your heart, that all the powers of His soul, all His interior and exterior senses and all His passions should live and reign in the faculties of your soul, in your interior and exterior senses, and in your passions, so that. . . the life of Jesus may visibly appear even in your flesh and in your external deportment. (d) That not only do you stand in a particular relationship to the Son of God, but that you must be in Him as the members are in their head, that all that is in you must be incorporated in Him and receive life and direction from Him, that there is no true life for you to save only in Him alone. . . that outside Him there is only death and perdition for you, that He must be the sole principle of all the movements, customs, and functions of your life, and that finally you must live only for Him, in Him and by Him, in accordance with the divine words: 'None of us lives for oneself, and no one dies for oneself. For if we live, we live for the Lord, and if we die, we die for the Lord; so then, if we live or die, we are the Lord's. For this is why Christ died and came to life, that he might be Lord of both the dead and the living. That you are one with this same Jesus, as the members are one with their head, and that consequently you must have but the one mind, the one soul, the one life, the one will, the one sentiment, the one heart . . . and that He Himself must be your mind, your heart, your love, your life, your all.[169]

This is wonderful. God so loved the world, he gave us his only Son. Jesus belongs to you. Jesus is yours. Not just his merits, his graces, his blessings. The very Person of Jesus is your inheritance. His life is also yours.

Therefore, when we meditate on the mysteries of Jesus' life, we have to keep in mind what the *Catechism* says:

All Christ's riches" are for every individual and are everybody's property. "Christ did not live his life for himself but for us, from his Incarnation " for us men and for our salvation" to his death "for our sin " and Resurrection "for our justification."

Christ enables us to live in him all that he himself lived, and he lives it in us. "By his Incarnation, he, the Son of God, has in a certain way united himself with each man." We are called only to become one with him, for he enables us as the members of his

Body to share in what he lived for us in his flesh as our model.[170]

In what Jesus lived, we are present. He is seeing us there, he is loving us there, he takes us into his Heart and he contemplates us in the faces of those people we see in the Gospel. This is not imagination; it is the most beautiful reality. "I live by faith in the Son of God who has loved me and given himself up for me" (Gal. 2:20).

8.This "for me" of Saint Paul is always very important, but more so in the Spiritual Exercises. Saint Ignatius speaks of it throughout the Exercises. Just as I said before, in Exercises it is not about going from ideas to conclusions, but from contemplation to the grace that God is inviting us to ask for. Nor is it about thinking so much about Jesus as the Savior of the world as in my Savior. Remember the experience of Saint Teresa of Jesus to which I referred. Or that of Saint Paul on the road to Damascus "Lord, what do you want me to do" (Acts 22:10)? Or the one of Saint Francis in the church of San Damiano where Jesus calls him by his name: "Francis, rebuild my church."

In one of his most famous statements, Saint Ignatius says: "to ask for what I want: it will be to ask for interior knowledge of the Lord, Who for me has become man, that I may more love and follow Him" (SE 104).

This "for me" has to help you enter the Heart of Jesus during your prayer. It places us in the sphere of "intentionality," in which we see not only what Jesus does but why and for what he does it. We enter into the mystery of his love for us, divine and human love at the same time. He allows us, in the Holy Spirit, to experience what Jesus felt for us in the mysteries we are contemplating. We no longer see it from the outside, but from within. That is why San Ignatius speaks of "interior knowledge," it is the knowledge that is born of love, of intimacy with the other person, of the grace of God that unveils the reality behind the mere factual events.

9. In the last point of this presentation, I want to give you a very simple guide for what could be an hour of meditation. The most important thing is to understand that prayer is an exercise in love. The goal is to be "In love with the Beloved alone."

I limit myself to pointing out the different steps, not for you to do from the first to the last, but to the extent that it can help you:

- Prepare the prayer, looking for the right place, the body position that most helps you to be united with Jesus, having at hand the materials you need.
- Soothe your spirit. Before beginning prayer, seek calm, serenity, clarity of heart and mind. "Attention turned inward" (Saint John of the Cross).
- Place yourself in the Presence of God. This is the most important step, in my opinion. Saint Teresa says that "mental prayer in my opinion is nothing else than an intimate sharing between friends; It means taking time frequently to be alone with Him who we know loves us."[171] To have that conversation of love, we must first feel his presence, in his love, loved and received by him. You can invoke his presence by making the Sign of the Cross. Ask for the grace of knowing how to let yourself

be guided by the Holy Spirit.

- Contemplation / meditation. Here we find the steps of what is usually called *Lectio Divina (lectio, meditatio, oratio et contemplatio)*. Read the Bible passage without hurry, do the composition of place that we talked about before and the application of the senses (without hurry) and from there, let the Spirit take the reins. Sometimes you will slowly contemplate one aspect of the scene, or a single word will give you all the nourishment you need. Or you will discover yourself talking with Jesus or with someone from the Gospel scene.

- Conclusion. It is important to close the hour of meditation by spending a few minutes pleading for the grace that we think God has shown us in prayer. It is not necessarily a purpose; it can be a great feeling of gratitude, or the pain of sins, or a desire to be more generous with God, or to change bad habits. Ask God to give you the help you need to act according to what He has let you see. Offer yourself to Him in a great act of trust. At the Savior's command, you can conclude with the Our Father (which contains everything we can ask of God), a Hail Mary, and a Glory Be.

25

APPENDIX II

Key excerpts from EDITH STEIN, *Essays on Woman*[172]

"In the talk which I gave in November 1930 in Berndorf concerning the foundations of women's education, I tried to draw the picture of woman's soul as it would correspond to the eternal vocation of woman, and I termed its attributes as expansive, quiet, empty of self, warm, and clear. Now I am asked to say something regarding how one might come to possess these qualities.

I believe that it is not a matter of a multiplicity of attributes which we can tackle and acquire individually; it is rather a single total condition of the soul, a condition which is envisaged here in these attributes from various aspects. We are not able to attain this condition by willing it, it must be effected through grace. What we can and must do is open ourselves to grace; that means to renounce our own will completely and to give it captive to the divine will, to lay our whole soul, ready for reception and formation, into God's hands.

Becoming empty and still are closely connected. The soul is replenished by nature in so many ways that one thing always replaces another, and the soul is in constant agitation, often in tumult and uproar.

The duties and cares of the day ahead crowd about us when we awake in the morning (if they have not already dispelled our night's rest). Now arises the uneasy question: How can all this be accommodated in one day? When will I do this, when that? How shall I start on this and that? Thus agitated, we would like to run around and rush forth. We must then take the reins in hand and say, "Take it easy! Not any of this may touch me now. My first morning's hour belongs to the Lord. I will tackle the day's work which He charges me with, and He will give me the power to accomplish it."

So I will go to the altar of God. Here it is not a question of my minute, petty affairs, but of the great offering of reconciliation. I may participate in that, purify myself and be made happy, and lay myself with all my doings and troubles along with the sacrifice on the altar. And when the Lord comes to me then in Holy Communion, then I may ask Him, "Lord, what do you want of me?" (St. Teresa). And after quiet dialogue, I will go to that which I see as my next duty.

I will still be joyful when I enter into my day's work after this morning's celebration: my soul will be empty of that which could assail and burden it, but it will be filled with holy joy, courage, and energy.

Because my soul has left itself and entered into the divine life, it has become great and expansive. Love burns in it like a composed flame which the Lord has enkindled, and which urges my soul to render love and to inflame love in others: *"flammescat igne caritas, accendat ardor proximos."* And it sees clearly the next part of the path before it; it does not see very far, but it knows that when it has arrived at that place where the horizon now intersects, a new vista will then be opened.

Now begins the day's work, perhaps the teaching profession— four or five hours, one after the other. That means giving our concentration there. We cannot achieve in each hour what we want, perhaps in none. We must contend with our own fatigue, unforeseen interruptions, shortcomings of the children, diverse vexations, indignities, anxieties. Or perhaps it is office work: give and take with disagreeable supervisors and colleagues, unfulfilled demands, unjust reproaches, human meanness, perhaps also distress of the most distinct kind.

It is the noon hour. We come home exhausted, shattered. New vexations possibly await there. Now where is the soul's morning freshness? The soul would like to seethe and storm again: indignation, chagrin, regret. And there is still so much to do until evening. Should we not go immediately to it? No, not before calm sets in at least for a moment. Each one must know, or get to know, where and how she can find peace. The best way, when it is possible, is to shed all cares again for a short time before the tabernacle. Whoever cannot do that, whoever also possibly requires bodily rest, should take a breathing space in her own room. And when no outer rest whatever is attainable, when there is no place in which to retreat, if pressing duties prohibit a quiet hour, then at least she must for a moment seal off herself inwardly against all other things and take refuge in the Lord. He is indeed there and can give us in a single moment what we need.

Thus the remainder of the day will continue, perhaps in great fatigue and laboriousness, but in peace. And when night comes, and retrospect shows that everything was patchwork and much which one had planned left undone, when so many things rouse shame and regret, then take all as it is, lay it in God's hands, and offer it up to Him. In this way we will be able to rest in Him, actually to rest, and to begin the new day like a new life.

This is only a small indication how the day could take shape in order to make room for God's grace. Each individual will know best how this can be used in her particular circumstances. It could be further indicated how Sunday must be a great door through which celestial life can enter into everyday life, and strength for the work of the entire week, and how the great feasts, holidays, and the seasons of Lent, lived through in the spirit of the Church, permit the soul to mature the more from year to year to the eternal Sabbath rest.

It will be an essential duty of each individual to consider how she must shape her plan for daily and yearly living, according to her bent and to her respective circumstances of life, in order to make ready the way for the Lord. The exterior allotment must be different for each one, and it must also adjust resiliently to the change of circumstances in the course of time. But the psychic situation varies with individuals and with each individual in different times. As to the means which are suitable for bringing about union with the eternal, keeping it alive or also enlivening it anew—such as contemplation, spiritual reading, participation in the liturgy, popular services, etc.—these are not fruitful for each person and at all times. For example, contemplation cannot be practiced by all and always in the same way.

It is important to each case to find out the most efficacious way and to make it useful for oneself. It would be good to listen to expert advice in order to know what one lacks, and this is especially so before one takes on variations from a tested arrangement."

26

APPENDIX III

Key excerpts from SAINT TERESA OF JESUS, *The Book of Her Life*[173]

"A long time after the Lord had already granted me many of the favors I've mentioned and other very lofty ones, while I was in prayer one day, I suddenly found that, without knowing how, I had seemingly been put in hell. I understood that the Lord wanted me to see the place the devils had prepared there for me and which I merited because of my sins. This experience took place within the shortest space of time, but even were I to live for many years I think it would be impossible for me to forget it.

The entrance it seems to me was similar to a very long and narrow alleyway, like an oven, low and dark and confined; the floor seemed to me to consist of dirty, muddy water emitting foul stench and swarming with putrid vermin. At the end of the alleyway, a hole that looked like a small cupboard was hollowed out in the wall; there I found I was placed in a cramped condition. All of this was delightful to see in comparison with what I felt there. What I have described can hardly be exaggerated.

But as to what I then felt, I do not know where to begin if I were to describe it; it is utterly inexplicable. I felt a fire in my soul but such that I am still unable to describe it. My bodily sufferings were unendurable. I have undergone most painful sufferings in this life, and, as the physicians say, the greatest that can be borne, such as the contraction of my sinews when I was paralyzed, without speaking of other ills of different types – yet, even those of which I have spoken, inflicted on me by Satan; yet all these were as nothing in comparison with what I then felt, especially when I saw that there would be no intermission nor any end to them.

These sufferings were nothing in comparison with the anguish of my soul, a sense of oppression, of stifling, and of pain so acute, accompanied by so hopeless and cruel an infliction, that I know not how to speak of it. If I say that the soul is continually being torn from the body it would be nothing – for that implies the destruction of life by the hands of another – but here it is the soul itself that is tearing itself in pieces. I cannot describe that inward fire or that despair, surpassing all torments and all pain. I did not see who it was that tormented me, but I felt myself on fire, and torn to pieces, as it seemed to me; and I repeat it, this inward fire and despair are the greatest torments of all.

Left in that pestilential place, and utterly without the power to hope for comfort, I could neither sit nor lie down; there was no room. I was placed as it were in a hole in the wall; and those walls, terrible to look on of themselves, hemmed me in on every side. I could not breathe. There was no light, but all was thick darkness. I do not understand how it is;

though there was no light, yet everything that can give pain by being seen was visible.

Our Lord at that time would not let me see more of Hell. Afterwards I had another most fearful vision, in which I saw the punishment of certain sins. They were the most horrible to look at, but because I felt none of the pain, my terror was not so great. In the former vision Our Lord made me really feel those torments and that anguish of spirit, just as if I had been suffering them in the body there. I know not how it was, but I understood distinctly that it was a great mercy that Our Lord would have me see with my own eyes the very place from which His compassion saved me. I have listened to people speaking of these things and I have at other times dwelt on the various torments of Hell, though not often, because my soul made no progress by the way of fear; and I have read of the diverse tortures, and how the devils tear the flesh with red-hot pincers. But all is as nothing before this: It is a wholly different matter. In short, the one is a reality, the other a description; and all burning here in this life is as nothing compared with the fire that is there.

I was so terrified by that vision - and that terror is on me even now as I write - that though it took place nearly six years ago, the natural warmth of my body is chilled by fear even now when I think of it. And so, amid all the pain and suffering which I may have had to bear, I remember no time in which I do not think that all we have to suffer in this world is as nothing. It seems to me that we complain without reason. I repeat it, this vision was one of the grandest mercies of God. It has been to me of the greatest service, because it has destroyed my fear of trouble and of the contradictions of the world, and because it has made me strong enough to bear up against them, and to give thanks to Our Lord who has been my Deliverer, as it now seems to me, from such fearful and everlasting pains.

Ever since that time, as I was saying, everything seems endurable in comparison with one instant of suffering such as those I had then to bear in Hell. I am filled with fear when I see that, after frequently reading books which describe in some manner the pains of Hell, I was not afraid of them, nor made any account of them. Where was I? How could I possibly take any pleasure in those things which led me directly to so dreadful a place? Blessed forever be Thou, O my God! And oh, how manifest is it that Thou didst love me much more than I did love Thee! How often, O Lord, didst Thou save me from that fearful prison! And how I used to get back to it contrary to Thy will.

It was that vision which filled me with very great distress which I felt at the sight of so many lost souls, especially of the Lutherans - for they were once members of the Church by Baptism - and also gave me the most vehement desires for the salvation of souls; for certainly I believe that to save even one from those overwhelming torments, I would willingly endure many deaths. If here on earth we see one whom we especially love in great trouble or pain, our very nature seems to bid us compassionate him; and if those pains be great, we are troubled ourselves. What, then, must it be to see a soul in danger of pain, the most grievous of all pains, forever? It is a thought no heart can bear without great anguish. Here we know that pain at last ends with life, and that there are limits to it, yet the sight of it moves us so greatly to compassion; that other pain has no ending, and I know not how we can be calm when we see Satan carry so many souls daily away.

This also makes me wish that, in a matter which concerns us so much, we did not rest satisfied with doing less than we can do on our part - that we left nothing undone. May Our Lord vouchsafe to give us His grace for that end. I sometimes reflect that even though I was terribly wicked, I had some concern about serving God, that I didn't do certain things I see are done in the world as if they amount to nothing, and, finally, that I suffered great illnesses and with a lot of patience, which the Lord gave me, yet wasn't inclined to criticize or speak evil of anyone — nor does it seem to me I could have wished evil on anyone. Neither was I covetous nor do I ever recall being envious in such way that it would have been a grave offense against the Lord; and there are some other things — for even though I was so wretched, I usually had the fear of God. Yet, in spite of all this, I see the place the devils had already prepared for me. Indeed, on account of my faults, it seems to me I still merited greater punishment. But, nonetheless, I say that it was a terrible torment and that it is a dangerous thing to be satisfied with ourselves, nor should the soul that falls at every step into mortal sin be at rest or content. But for the love of God, we should avoid the occasions; the Lord will help us, as He did me. May it please His Majesty not to let me out of His hand lest I fall again, for I have already seen where I would end up. May the Lord not allow it because of who His Majesty is, amen.

After having seen this and other things and secrets that the Lord because of who He is, desired to show me about the glory He will give to the good and the suffering that will go to the evil, I was anxious to know the manner and way in which I could do penance for so much evil and merit something in order to gain so much good. I was desiring to flee people and withdraw completely from the world. My spirit was not at rest, yet the disquiet was not a disturbing but a delightful one. It was obvious that it was from God and that His Majesty had given the soul heat so as to digest other heavier foods than those it was eating."

27

APPENDIX IV

Key excerpts from JOSÉ LUIS MARTÍN DESCALZO, *Razones para el amor*[174]

Thank you. This word could sum up this card to you God, my love, because that is all that I have to tell you: thank you, thank you. Looking back from the mountain top of my 55 years what do I see except the endless mountains of your love? In my history there is no region which is not illuminated by your mercy to me. There has never existed a time in which I did not experience your loving, fatherly presence caressing my soul.

Even yesterday I received a card from a friend who had just heard about my health problems. She wrote me furiously, "A huge load of rage invaded my whole being, and I rebelled against God for allowing people like you to suffer." Poor thing! Her affection does not let her see the truth. While I am no more important than anybody, my whole life is a testimony to two things, being and faith. In my 55 years I have suffered more than a few times at the hands of people; I have received curses and ingratitude, loneliness and misunderstanding. However, from you I have received nothing but endless gestures of affection, including my latest sickness.

First you gave me being, the marvel of being human. The joy of experiencing the beauty of the world. The joy of being part of the human family. The joy of knowing that, in the end, if I put everything in a balance the cuts and bruises will always be far less than the tremendous love which these same people have put on the other side of the balance in my life. Have I been more fortunate than others? Probably. Now, how could I pretend to be a martyr of humanity knowing for certain that I have had more help and understanding than difficulties?

Furthermore, you accompanied the gift of being with the gift of faith. In my childhood I felt your presence at all hours. You seemed very gentle to me. Your name never frightened me. You planted a fabulous capacity in my soul: the capacity to know that I am loved, to feel that I am loved, to experience your presence daily in the passing of each hour. There are some people, I know, who curse the day of their birth, who scream at you that they did not ask to be born. I did not request it either, because I did not exist prior to that. But knowing what my life has been, I would have implored, begging for existence, this same one which you have given me.

I suppose that it was absolutely necessary to be born in the family you chose for me. Today I would give everything I possess just to have the parents and siblings which I had. All of them were living witnesses to the presence of your love. Through them I learned so easily who you are. Thanks to them loving you, and loving others became so much easier. It would have been absurd not to love you. It would have been difficult to live in bi tterness. Happiness, faith, and trust were like the custard which my mother infallibly served after supper, something which would certainly be provided. If it wasn't served it was simply because eggs weren't available that day, not because love was lacking. I also learned that pain was part of the game. Not a curse but part of the price of living, something which would never be enough to take away our joy.

Thanks to all this, now, I feel ashamed to say it, pain does not hurt me, nor does bitterness make me bitter. Not because I am brave but simply because ever since my childhood I have learned to contemplate the positive aspects of life and to take the dark aspects in stride. It turns out that when they come they aren't so dark but just a little gray. Another friend writes to me these days saying that I will be able to endure dialysis "getting drunk on God". This seems a little excessive and melodramatic to me. Because ever since my childhood, I have "gotten drunk" on your normal presence, God, and in you I always feel ironclad against suffering. Or perhaps it is because true pain has not arrived.

Sometimes I think that I have had "too much good luck". The saints offered y ou g reat t hings. I h ave n ever had anything important to offer you. I fear that, at the hour of my death, I am going to have the same thought that my mother had when she passed. The thought of dying with empty hands because nothing you sent me was unbearable. Not even the loneliness or the desolation which you give to those who are truly yours. I'm sorry, but what do I do if you have never abandoned me? Sometimes I am ashamed thinking that I will die without having been at your side in the Garden of Olives, without having had my agony in Gethsemane. It's just that you, I don't know why, never took me away from Palm Sunday. Sometimes, in my heroic dreams, I have even thought that I would have liked to have a crisis of faith in order to prove myself to you. They say that authentic faith is proved in the crucible. I have never encountered any crucible other than your caressing hands.

It's not that I have been better than others. Sin lurks within me. You and I both know how deeply. The truth is even in the worst times I have not fully experienced the black shadow of evil thanks to your constant light. Even in misery I have still been yours. In fact, your love for me seemed to increase when I made more mistakes.

I also presumed on you during times of persecution and difficulty. You know that even in human things there were always more good people at my side than traitors. For every incomprehension I received ten smiles. I had the good fortune that evil never did me harm. Most importantly it never made me bitter inside. Even bad experiences increased my desire to become better and resulted in unexpected friendships.

Later you gave me my astonishing vocation. To be a priest is impossible, you know that. But it is also marvelous, I know that. Today I certainly don't have the enthusiasm of young love as in the first d ays. But fortunately, the Mass has never become a mere routine, and I still tremble during every confession I still know the unsurpassable joy of being able to help people and the joy of being able to proclaim your name to them. You know, I still weep reading the parable of the prodigal son. Thanks to you, I still am moved every time I recite that portion of the Creed which speaks of your passion and death.

Naturally, the greatest of your gifts was your Son, Jesus. Even if f I had been the most miserable person, if misery had pursued me in every part of my life, I know that I would only have had to remember Jesus to overcome them. Knowing that you have been one of us reconciles me with all of our failures and emptiness. How is it possible to be sad knowing that you have walked upon this planet? How could I want more tenderness than meditating on the face of Mary?

I have certainly been happy. How could I not be? I have been happy here, even outside the glory of Heaven. Look, you know that I am not afraid of death, but I'm not in a hurry to get there either. Will I be able to be any closer to you there than I am now? This is the marvel: we have Heaven from the moment that we are able to love you. My friend Cabodevilla was on to something when he said, "We are going to die without knowing which is the greatest of your gifts, that you love us or that you allow us to love you."

For this reason it pains me greatly to know people who do not value their lives. Indeed, we are doing something infinitely greater than our own nature, loving you, collaborating with you in the construction of a great edifice of love!

It is difficult for me to say that we give you glory here. That's too much! I am content believing that resting my head in your hands gives you the opportunity to love me. It makes me laugh a little that you are going to give us Heaven as a reward. A reward for what? You are clever. You give us Heaven and give us the impression that we deserved it. You know very well that love can only be repaid with love. Happiness is not the consequence or the fruit of love. Love is in itself alone, happiness. Knowing that you are my Father is Heaven. Of course you don't have to give me anything, loving you is itself a gift. You can't give me more.

For all of this, my God, I have wanted to talk about you and with you in this final page of my "Reasons for Love". You are the ultimate and the only reason for my love. I have none others. How could I have any hope without you? What would my joy be founded on if I lacked you? What tasteless wine would my love become if it were not a reflection of your love? You give strength and life to everything. I know very well that my only task as a person is to repeat and repeat your name. With that, I take my leave.

28

APPENDIX V

From SAINT BERNARD[175]

You have heard, O Virgin, that you will conceive and bear a son; you have heard that it will not be by man but by the Holy Spirit. The angel awaits an answer; it is time for him to return to God who sent him. We too are waiting, O Lady, for your word of compassion; the sentence of condemnation weighs heavily upon us.

The price of our salvation is offered to you. We shall be set free at once if you consent. In the eternal Word of God we all came to be, and behold, we die. In your brief response, we are to be remade in order to be recalled to life.

Tearful Adam with his sorrowing family begs this of you, O loving Virgin, in their exile from Paradise. Abraham begs it, David begs it. All the other holy patriarchs, your ancestors, ask it of you, as they dwell in the country of the shadow of death. This is what the whole earth waits for, prostrate at your feet. It is right in doing so, for on your word depends comfort for the wretched, ransom for the captive, freedom for the condemned, indeed, salvation for all the sons of Adam, the whole of your race.

Answer quickly, O Virgin. Reply in haste to the angel, or rather through the angel to the Lord. Answer with a word, receive the Word of God. Speak your own word, conceive the divine Word. Breathe a passing word, embrace the eternal Word.

Why do you delay, why are you afraid? Believe, give praise, and receive. Let humility be bold, let modesty be confident. This is no time for virginal simplicity to forget prudence. In this matter alone, O prudent Virgin, do not fear to be presumptuous. Though modest silence is pleasing, dutiful speech is now more necessary. Open your heart to faith, O blessed Virgin, your lips to praise, your womb to the Creator. See, the desired of all nations is at your door, knocking to enter. If he should pass by because of your delay, in sorrow you would begin to seek him afresh, the One whom your soul loves. Arise, hasten, open. Arise in faith, hasten in devotion, open in praise and thanksgiving. Behold the handmaid of the Lord, she says, be it done to me according to your word.

29

APPENDIX VI

Homily of His Holiness BENEDICT XVI in Lourdes, 15 September 2008[176]

Yesterday we celebrated the Cross of Christ, the instrument of our salvation, which reveals the mercy of our God in all its fullness. The Cross is truly the place where God's compassion for our world is perfectly manifested. Today, as we celebrate the memorial of Our Lady of Sorrows, we contemplate Mary sharing her Son's compassion for sinners. As Saint Bernard declares, the Mother of Christ entered into the Passion of her Son through her compassion (cf. *Homily for Sunday in the Octave of the Assumption*). At the foot of the Cross, the prophecy of Simeon is fulfilled: her mother's heart is pierced through (cf. *Lk* 2:35) by the torment inflicted on the Innocent One born of her flesh. Just as Jesus cried (cf. *Jn* 11:35), so too Mary certainly cried over the tortured body of her Son. Her self-restraint, however, prevents us from plumbing the depths of her grief; the full extent of her suffering is merely suggested by the traditional symbol of the seven swords. As in the case of her Son Jesus, one might say that she too was led to perfection through this suffering (cf. *Heb* 2:10),so as to make her capable of receiving the new spiritual mission that her Son entrusts to her immediately before "giving up his spirit" (cf. *Jn* 19:30):that of becoming the mother of Christ in his members. In that hour, through the figure of the beloved disciple, Jesus presents each of his disciples to his Mother when he says to her: Behold your Son (cf. *Jn* 19:26-27).

Today Mary dwells in the joy and the glory of the Resurrection. The tears shed at the foot of the Cross have been transformed into a smile which nothing can wipe away, even as her maternal compassion towards us remains unchanged. The intervention of the Virgin Mary in offering succour throughout history testifies to this, and does not cease to call forth, in the people of God, an unshakable confidence in her: the *Memorare* prayer expresses this sentiment very well. Mary loves each of her children, giving particular attention to those who, like her Son at the hour of his Passion, are prey to suffering; she loves them quite simply because they are her children, according to the will of Christ on the Cross.

The psalmist, seeing from afar this maternal bond which unites the Mother of Christ with the people of faith, prophesies regarding the Virgin Mary that "the richest of the people ... will seek your smile" (*Ps* 44:13).In this way, prompted by the inspired word of Scripture, Christians have always sought the smile of Our Lady, this smile which medieval artists were able to represent with such marvellous skill and to show to advantage. This smile of Mary is for all; but it is directed quite particularly to those who suffer, so that they can find comfort and solace therein. To seek Mary's smile is not an act of devotional or outmoded sentimentality, but rather the proper expression of the living and profoundly human relationship which binds us to her whom Christ gave us as our Mother.

To wish to contemplate this smile of the Virgin, does not mean letting oneself be led by an uncontrolled imagination. Scripture itself discloses it to us through the lips of Mary when she sings the Magnificat: "My soul glorifies the Lord, my spirit exults in God my Saviour" (Lk 1:46-47). When the Virgin Mary gives thanks to the Lord, she calls us to witness. Mary shares, as if by anticipation, with us, her future children, the joy that dwells in her heart, so that it can become ours. Every time we recite the Magnificat, we become witnesses of her smile. Here in Lourdes, in the course of the apparition of Wednesday 3 March 1858, Bernadette contemplated this smile of Mary in a most particular way. It was the first response that the Beautiful Lady gave to the young visionary who wanted to know who she was. Before introducing herself, some days later, as "the Immaculate Conception", Mary first taught Bernadette to know her smile, this being the most appropriate point of entry into the revelation of her mystery.

In the smile of the most eminent of all creatures, looking down on us, is reflected our dignity as children of God, that dignity which never abandons the sick person. This smile, a true reflection of God's tenderness, is the source of an invincible hope. Unfortunately we know only too well: the endurance of suffering can upset life's most stable equilibrium; it can shake the firmest foundations of confidence, and sometimes even leads people to despair of the meaning and value of life. There are struggles that we cannot sustain alone, without the help of divine grace. When speech can no longer find the right words, the need arises for a loving presence: we seek then the closeness not only of those who share the same blood or are linked to us by friendship, but also the closeness of those who are intimately bound to us by faith. Who could be more intimate to us than Christ and his holy Mother, the Immaculate One? More than any others, they are capable of understanding us and grasping how hard we have to fight against evil and suffering. The Letter to the Hebrews says of Christ that he "is not unable to sympathize with our weaknesses; for in every respect he has been tempted as we are" (cf. *Heb* 4:15). I would like to say, humbly, to those who suffer and to those who struggle and are tempted to turn their backs on life: turn towards Mary! Within the smile of the Virgin lies mysteriously hidden the strength to fight against sickness and for life. With her, equally, is found the grace to accept without fear or bitterness to leave this world at the hour chosen by God.

How true was the insight of that great French spiritual writer, Dom Jean-Baptiste Chautard, who in *L'âme de tout apostolat*, proposed to the devout Christian to gaze frequently "into the eyes of the Virgin Mary"! Yes, to seek the smile of the Virgin Mary is not a pious infantilism, it is the aspiration, as Psalm 44 says, of those who are "the richest of the people" (verse 13). "The richest", that is to say, in the order of faith, those who have attained the highest degree of spiritual maturity and know precisely how to acknowledge their weakness and their poverty before God. In the very simple manifestation of tenderness that we call a smile, we grasp that our sole wealth is the love God bears us, which passes through the heart of her who became our Mother. To seek this smile, is first of all to have grasped the gratuitousness of love; it is also to be able to elicit this smile through our efforts to live according to the word of her Beloved Son, just as a child seeks to elicit its mother's smile by doing what pleases her. And we know what pleases Mary, thanks to the words she spoke to the servants at Cana: "Do whatever he tells you" (cf. *Jn* 2:5).

Mary's smile is a spring of living water. "He who believes in me", says Jesus, "out of his heart shall flow rivers of living water" (*Jn* 7:38). Mary is the one who believed and, from her womb, rivers of living water have flowed forth to irrigate human history. The spring that Mary pointed out to Bernadette here in Lourdes is the humble sign of this spiritual reality. From her believing heart, from her maternal heart, flows living water which purifies and heals. By immersing themselves in the baths at Lourdes, so many people have discovered and experienced the gentle maternal love of the Virgin Mary, becoming attached to her in order to bind themselves more closely to the Lord! In the liturgical sequence of this feast of Our Lady of Sorrows, Mary is honoured with the title of *Fons amoris*, "fount of love". From Mary's heart, there springs up a gratuitous love which calls forth a response of filial love, called to ever greater refinement. Like every mother, and better than every mother, Mary is the teacher of love. That is why so many sick people come here to Lourdes, to quench their thirst at the *"spring of love"* and to let themselves be led to the sole source of salvation, her son Jesus the Saviour.

Christ imparts his salvation by means of the sacraments, and especially in the case of those suffering from sickness or disability, by means of the grace of the sacrament of the sick.

For each individual, suffering is always something alien. It can never be tamed. That is why it is hard to bear, and harder still – as certain great witnesses of Christ's holiness have done – to welcome it as a significant element in our vocation, or to accept, as Bernadette expressed it, to "suffer everything in silence in order to please Jesus". To be able to say that, it is necessary to have travelled a long way already in union with Jesus. Here and now, though, it is possible to entrust oneself to God's mercy, as manifested through the grace of the sacrament of the sick. Bernadette herself, in the course of a life that was often marked by sickness, received this sacrament four times. The grace of this sacrament consists in welcoming Christ the healer into ourselves. However, Christ is not a healer in the manner of the world. In order to heal us, he does not remain outside the suffering that is experienced; he eases it by coming to dwell within the one stricken by illness, to bear it and live it with him. Christ's presence comes to break the isolation which pain induces. Man no longer bears his burden alone: as a suffering member of Christ, he is conformed to Christ in his self-offering to the Father, and he participates, in him, in the coming to birth of the new creation.

Without the Lord's help, the yoke of sickness and suffering weighs down on us cruelly. By receiving the sacrament of the sick, we seek to carry no other yoke that that of Christ, strengthened through his promise to us that his yoke will be easy to carry and his burden light (cf. *Mt* 11:30). I invite those who are to receive the sacrament of the sick during this Mass to enter into a hope of this kind.

The Second Vatican Council presented Mary as the figure in whom the entire mystery of the Church is typified (cf.

Lumen Gentium, 63-65).Her personal journey outlines the profile of the Church, which is called to be just as attentive to those who suffer as she herself was. I extend an affectionate greeting to those working in the areas of public health and nursing, as well as those who, in different ways, in hospitals and other institutions, are contributing to the care of the sick with competence and generosity. Equally, I should like to say to all the *hospitaliers*, the *brancardiers* and the carers who come from every diocese in France and from further afield, and who throughout the year attend the sick who come on pilgrimage to Lourdes, how much their service is appreciated. They are the arms of the servant Church. Finally, I wish to encourage those who, in the name of their faith, receive and visit the sick, especially in hospital infirmaries, in parishes or, as here, at s hrines. May you always sense in this important and delicate mission the effective and fraternal support of your communities! In this regard, I particularly greet and thank my brothers in the Episcopate, the French Bishops, Bishops and priests from afar, and all who serve the sick and suffering throughout the world. Thank you for your ministry close to our suffering Lord.

The service of charity that you offer is a Marian service. Mary entrusts her smile to you, so that you yourselves may become, in faithfulness to her son, springs of living water. Whatever you do, you do in the name of the Church, of which Mary is the purest image. May you carry her smile to everyone!

To conclude, I wish to join in the prayer of the pilgrims and the sick, and to pray with you a passage from the prayer to Mary that has been proposed for this Jubilee celebration:

"Because you are the smile of God, the reflection of the light of Christ, the dwelling place of the Holy Spirit,

Because you chose Bernadette in her lowliness, because you are the morning star, the gate of heaven and the first creature to experience the resurrection,

Our Lady of Lourdes, with our brothers and sisters whose hearts and bodies are in pain, we pray to you!

30

APPENDIX VII

Key excerpts from SAINT JOSÉ MARÍA ESCRIVÁ DE BALAGUER, *The Way*[177]

852. Try to know the 'way of spiritual childhood' without forcing yourself to follow this path. Let the Holy Spirit work in you.

853. Way of childhood. Abandonment. Spiritual infancy. All this is not utter nonsense, but a sturdy and solid Christian life.

854. In the spiritual life of childhood the things 'children' say or do are never puerile or childish.

855. Spiritual childhood is not spiritual foolishness or flabbiness; it is a sane and forceful way which, due to its difficult easiness, the soul must begin and continue, led by the hand of God.

856. Spiritual childhood demands submission of the mind, more difficult than submission of the will. In order to subject our mind we need not only God's grace but also the continual exercise of our will, which says 'no' again and again, just as it says 'no' to the flesh. And so we get the paradox that whoever wants to follow this 'little' way in order to become a child, needs to add strength and virility to his will.

857. Be a little child; the greatest daring is always that of children Who cries for... the moon? Who is blind to dangers in getting what he wants?

To such a child add much grace from God, the desire to do his Will, great love for Jesus, all the human knowledge he is capable of acquiring, and you will have a likeness of the apostles of today such as God undoubtedly wants them.

858. Be a child. Even more so. But don't stop at the show-off stage: have you ever seen anything sillier than the little fellow playing the man, or a grown man acting like a baby?

A child, with God: and just because of that, very much a man in everything else. Ah! and drop those lap-dog manners.

859. Sometimes we feel inclined to act as little children. What we do then has a wonderful value in God's eyes and, so long as we don't let routine creep in, our 'little' actions will indeed be fruitful with the unfailing fruitfulness of Love.

860. Before God, who is eternal, you are much more a child than, before you, the tiniest toddler.

And besides being a child, you are a child of God. — Don't forget it.

861. Child, enkindle in your heart an ardent desire to make up for the excesses of your grown-up life.

862. Silly child, the day you hide some part of your soul from your Director, you will cease to be a child, for you will have lost your simplicity.

863. Child, when you really are one, you will be all-powerful.

864. Being children you will have no cares: children quickly forget what troubles them and return to their games. With abandonment, therefore, you will not have to worry, since you will rest in the Father.

865. Child, each day offer him... even your frailties.

866. Good child: offer him the work of those labourers who do not know him; offer him the natural joy of those poor little ones who are brought up in pagan schools.

867. Children have nothing of their own, everything belongs to their father..., and your Father always knows best how to manage your affairs.

868. Be small, very small. No more than two years old, three at the most. For older children are little rascals who already want to deceive their parents with bare-faced lies.

It is because they have the inclination to sin, — fomes peccati — but they lack the experience of evil, which will teach them the science of sinning and show them how to lend an appearance of truth to the falseness of their deceits.

They have lost their simplicity, and without simplicity it is impossible to be a child before God.

869. But child, why do you insist on walking on stilts?

870. Don't try to be grown-up. A child, always a child, even when you are dying of old age. When a child stumbles and falls, nobody is surprised; his father promptly lifts him up.

When the person who stumbles and falls is older, the im-mediate reaction is one of laughter. Sometimes this first impulse passes and the laughter gives way to pity. But older people have to get up by themselves.

Your sad experience of each day is full of stumbles and falls. — What would become of you if you were not continually more of a child?

Don't want to be grown-up. Be a child; and when you stumble, may you be lifted by the hand of your Father-God.

871. Child, abandonment demands docility.

872. Don't forget that our Lord has a special love for little children and those who become as little children.

873. Paradoxes of a little soul. When Jesus sends you what people call 'good luck', feel sorrow in your heart at the thought of his goodness and your wickedness. When Jesus sends you what people call 'bad luck', be glad in your heart, for he always gives you what is best and then is the beautiful moment to love the Cross.

874. Daring child, cry out: What love was Teresa's! What zeal was Xavier's! What a wonderful man was Saint Paul! Ah, Jesus, well I... I love you more than Paul, Xavier and Teresa!

31

APPENDIX VIII

Key excerpts from JOSEPH RAZTINGER, *Mary, the Church at the Source*[178]

In Bernard of Clairvaux we find the wonderful statement that God cannot suffer [leiden], but he can suffer with [be compassionate, mit-leiden].12 With these words, Bernard brings to a certain conclusion the Fathers' struggle to articulate the newness of the Christian concept of God. Ancient thought considered the passionlessness [Leidenschafts-losigkeit] of pure intellect to be an essential attribute of God. It proved difficult for the Fathers to reject this notion and to think of "passion" [Leidenschaft] in God. Yet in the light of the Bible they saw quite plainly that "Biblical revelation. . . upsets [everything]. . . the world had thought about God." They saw that there is an intimate passion in God, indeed, that it even constitutes his true essence: love. And because he loves, suffering [Leid] in the form of compassion [Mitleid] is not foreign to him. In this connection, Origen writes: "In his love for man the Impassible One suffered [erlitten] merciful compassion,"13 We could say that the Cross of Christ is God's compassionate suffering with the world. The Hebrew text of the Old Testament does not draw on psychology to speak about God's compassionate suffering with man. Rather, in accordance with the concreteness of Semitic thought, it designates it with a word whose basic meaning refers to a bodily organ, namely, rahamim. Taken in the singular, rahamim means the mother's womb. Just as "heart" stands for feeling, and "loins" and "kidneys" stand for desire and pain, the womb becomes the term for being with another; it becomes the deepest reference to man's capacity to stand for another, to take the other into himself, to suffer him [erleiden], and in this long-suffering to give him life. The Old Testament, with a word taken from the language of the body, tells us how God shelters us in himself, how he bears us in himself with compassionate love.14 The languages into which the Gospel entered when it came to the pagan world did not have such modes of expression. But the image of the Pieta, the Mother grieving [leidend] for her Son, became the vivid translation of this word: In her, God's maternal affliction [Leiden] is open to view. In her we can behold it and touch it. She is the compassio of God, displayed in a human being who has let herself be drawn wholly into God's mystery. It is because human life is at all times suffering that the image of the suffering Mother, the image of the rahamim of God, is of such importance for Christianity. The Pieta completes the picture of the Cross, because Mary is the accepted Cross, the Cross communicating itself in love, the Cross that now allows us to experience in her compassion the compassion of God. In this way the Mother's affliction is Easter affliction, which already inaugurates the transformation of death into the redemptive being-with of love. Only apparently have we distanced ourselves from the "rejoice" with which the narrative of Mary begins. For the joy announced to her is not the banal joy clung to in forgetfulness of the abysses of our being and so condemned to plunge into the void. It is the real joy that gives us the courage to venture the exodus of love into the burning holiness of God. It is the true joy that pain does not destroy but first brings to its maturity. Only the joy that stands the test of pain and is stronger than affliction is authentic.

32

APPENDIX IX

Meditation of His Holiness BENEDICT XVI[179]

Dear Friends,

This is a moment to which I have been looking forward. I have stood before the Holy Shroud on various occasions but this time I am experiencing this Pilgrimage and this moment with special intensity: perhaps this is because the passing years make me even more sensitive to the message of this extraordinary Icon; perhaps and I would say above all this is because I am here now as the Successor of Peter, and I carry in my heart the whole Church, indeed, the whole of humanity. I thank God for the gift of this Pilgrimage and also for the opportunity to share with you a brief meditation inspired by the subtitle of this solemn Exposition: "The Mystery of Holy Saturday".

One could say that the Shroud is the Icon of this mystery, the Icon of Holy Saturday. Indeed it is a winding-sheet that was wrapped round the body of a man who was crucified, corresponding in every way to what the Gospels tell us of

Jesus who, crucified at about noon, died at about three o'clock in the afternoon. At nightfall, since it was *Parasceve*, that is, the eve of Holy Saturday, Joseph of Arimathea, a rich and authoritative member of the Sanhedrin, courageously asked Pontius Pilate for permission to bury Jesus in his new tomb which he had had hewn out in the rock not far from Golgotha. Having obtained permission, he bought a linen cloth, and after Jesus was taken down from the Cross, wrapped him in that shroud and buried him in that tomb (cf. Mk 15: 42-46). This is what the Gospel of St Mark says and the other Evangelists are in agreement with him. From that moment, Jesus remained in the tomb until dawn of the day after the Sabbath and the Turin Shroud presents to us an image of how his body lay in the tomb during that period which was chronologically brief (about a day and a half), but immense, infinite in its value and in its significance.

Holy Saturday is the day when God remains hidden, we read in an ancient Homily: "What has happened? Today the earth is shrouded in deep silence, deep silence and stillness, profound silence because the King sleeps.... God has died in the flesh, and has gone down to rouse the realm of the dead" (*Homily on Holy Saturday, PG* 43, 439). In the *Creed*, we profess that Jesus Christ was "crucified under Pontius Pilate, died and was buried. He descended to the dead. On the third day, he rose again".

Dear brothers and sisters, in our time, especially after having lived through the past century, humanity has become particularly sensitive to the mystery of Holy Saturday. The concealment of God is part of contemporary man's spirituality, in an existential almost subconscious manner, like a void in the heart that has continued to grow larger and larger. Towards the end of the 19th century, Nietzsche wrote: "God is dead! And we killed him!". This famous saying is clearly taken almost literally from the Christian tradition. We often repeat it in the *Way of the Cross*, perhaps without being fully aware of what we are saying. After the two World Wars, the *lagers* and the *gulags*, Hiroshima and Nagasaki, our epoch has become increasingly a Holy Saturday: this day's darkness challenges all who are wondering about life and it challenges us believers in particular. We too have something to do with this darkness.

Yet the death of the Son of God, Jesus of Nazareth, has an opposite aspect, totally positive, a source of comfort and hope. And this reminds me of the fact that the Holy Shroud acts as a "photographic' document, with both a "positive" and a "negative". And, in fact, this is really how it is: the darkest mystery of faith is at the same time the most luminous sign of a never-ending hope. Holy Saturday is a "no man's land" between the death and the Resurrection, but this "no man's land" was entered by One, the Only One, who passed through it with the signs of his Passion for man's sake: *Passio Christi. Passio hominis.* And the Shroud speaks to us precisely about this moment testifying exactly to that unique and unrepeatable interval in the history of humanity and the universe in which God, in Jesus Christ, not only shared our dying but also our remaining in death the most radical solidarity.

In this "time-beyond-time", Jesus Christ "descended to the dead". What do these words mean? They mean that God, having made himself man, reached the point of entering man's most extreme and absolute solitude, where not a ray of love enters, where total abandonment reigns without any word of comfort: "hell". Jesus Christ, by remaining in death, passed beyond the door of this ultimate solitude to lead us too to cross it with him. We have all, at some point, felt the frightening sensation of abandonment, and that is what we fear most about death, just as when we were children we were afraid to be alone in the dark and could only be reassured by the presence of a person who loved us. Well, this is exactly what happened on Holy Saturday: the voice of God resounded in the realm of death. The unimaginable occurred: namely, Love penetrated "hell". Even in the extreme darkness of the most absolute human loneliness we may hear a voice that calls us and find a hand that takes ours and leads us out. Human beings live because they are loved and can love; and if love even penetrated the realm of death, then life also even reached there. In the hour of supreme solitude we shall never be alone: *Passio Christi. Passio hominis.*

This is the mystery of Holy Saturday! Truly from there, from the darkness of the death of the Son of God, the light of a new hope gleamed: the light of the Resurrection. And it seems to me that, looking at this sacred Cloth through the eyes of faith, one may perceive something of this light. Effectively, the Shroud was immersed in that profound darkness that was at the same time luminous; and I think that if thousands and thousands of people come to venerate it without counting those who contemplate it through images it is because they see in it not only darkness but also the light; not so much the defeat of life and of love, but rather victory, the victory of life over death, of love over hatred. They indeed see the death of Jesus, but they also see his Resurrection; in the bosom of death, life is now vibrant, since love dwells within it. This is the power of the Shroud: from the face of this "Man of sorrows", who carries with him the passion of man of every time and every place, our passions too, our sufferings, our difficulties and our sins *Passio Christi. Passio hominis* from this face a solemn majesty shines, a paradoxical lordship. This face, these hands and these feet, this side, this whole body speaks. It is itself a word we can hear in the silence. How does the Shroud speak? It speaks with blood, and blood is life! The Shroud is an Icon written in blood; the blood of a man who was scourged, crowned with thorns, crucified and whose right side was pierced. The Image impressed upon the Shroud is that of a dead man, but the blood speaks of his life. Every trace of blood speaks of love and of life. Especially that huge stain near his rib, made by the blood and water that flowed copiously from a great wound inflicted by the tip of a Roman spear. That blood and that water speak of life. It is like a spring that murmurs in the silence, and we can hear it, we can listen to it in the silence of Holy Saturday.

Dear friends, let us always praise the Lord for his faithful and merciful love. When we leave this holy place, may we carry in our eyes the image of the Shroud, may we carry in our hearts this word of love and praise God with a life full of faith, hope and charity. Thank you.

33

APPENDIX X

Address of His Holiness BENEDICT XVI[180]

Dear young friends,

In our pilgrimage with the mysterious Magi from the East, we have arrived at the moment which St Matthew describes in his Gospel with these words: "Going into the house (over which the star had halted), they saw the child with Mary his mother, and they fell down and worshiped him" (Mt 2: 11). Outwardly, their journey was now over. They had reached their goal.

But at this point a new journey began for them, an inner pilgrimage which changed their whole lives. Their mental picture of the infant King they were expecting to find must have been very different. They had stopped at Jerusalem specifically in order to ask the King who lived there for news of the promised King who had been born. They knew that the world was in disorder, and for that reason their hearts were troubled.

They were sure that God existed and that he was a just

and gentle God. And perhaps they also knew of the great prophecies of Israel foretelling a King who would be intimately united with God, a King who would restore order to the world, acting for God and in his Name.

It was in order to seek this King that they had set off on their journey: deep within themselves they felt prompted to go in search of the true justice that can only come from God, and they wanted to serve this King, to fall prostrate at his feet and so play their part in the renewal of the world. They were among those "who hunger and thirst for justice" (Mt 5: 6).This hunger and thirst had spurred them on in their pilgrimage - they had become pilgrims in search of the justice that they expected from God, intending to devote themselves to its service.

Even if those who had stayed at home may have considered them Utopian dreamers, they were actually people with their feet on the ground, and they knew that in order to change the world it is necessary to have power. Hence, they were hardly likely to seek the promised child anywhere but in the King's palace. Yet now they were bowing down before the child of poor people, and they soon came to realize that Herod, the King they had consulted, intended to use his power to lay a trap for him, forcing the family to flee into exile.

The new King, to whom they now paid homage, was quite unlike what they were expecting. In this way they had to learn that God is not as we usually imagine him to be. This was where their inner journey began. It started at the very moment when they knelt down before this child and recognized him as the promised King. But they still had to assimilate these joyful gestures internally.

They had to change their ideas about power, about God

and about man, and in so doing, they also had to change themselves. Now they were able to see that God's power is not like that of the powerful of this world. God's ways are not as we imagine them or as we might wish them to be.

God does not enter into competition with earthly powers in this world. He does not marshal his divisions alongside other divisions. God did not send 12 legions of angels to assist Jesus in the Garden of Olives (cf. Mt 26: 53).He contrasts the noisy and ostentatious power of this world with the defenceless power of love, which succumbs to death on the Cross and dies ever anew throughout history; yet it is this same love which constitutes the new divine intervention that opposes injustice and ushers in the Kingdom of God.

God is different - this is what they now come to realize. And it means that they themselves must now become different, they must learn God's ways.

They had come to place themselves at the service of this King, to model their own kingship on his. That was the meaning of their act of homage, their adoration. Included in this were their gifts - gold, frankincense and myrrh - gifts offered to a King held to be divine. Adoration has a content and it involves giving. Through this act of adoration, these men from the East wished to recognize the child as their King and to place their own power and potential at his disposal, and in this they were certainly on the right path.

By serving and following him, they wanted, together with him, to serve the cause of good and the cause of justice in the world. In this they were right.

Now, though, they have to learn that this cannot be achieved simply through issuing commands from a throne on high. Now they have to learn to give themselves - no lesser gift would be sufficient for this King. Now they have to learn that their lives must be conformed to this divine way of exercising power, to God's own way of being.

They must become men of truth, of justice, of goodness, of forgiveness, of mercy. They will no longer ask: how can this serve me? Instead, they will have to ask: How can I serve God's presence in the world? They must learn to lose their life and in this way to find it. Having left Jerusalem behind, they must not deviate from the path marked out by the true King, as they follow Jesus.

Dear friends, what does all this mean for us?

What we have just been saying about the nature of God being different, and about the way our lives must be shaped accordingly, sounds very fine, but remains rather vague and unfocused. That is why God has given us examples. The Magi from the East are just the first in a long procession of men and women who have constantly tried to gaze upon God's star in their lives, going in search of the God who has drawn close to us and shows us the way.

It is the great multitude of the saints - both known and unknown - in whose lives the Lord has opened up the Gospel before us and turned over the pages; he has done this throughout history and he still does so today. In their lives, as if in a great picture-book, the riches of the Gospel are revealed. They are the shining path which God himself has traced throughout history and is still tracing today.

My venerable Predecessor Pope John Paul II, who is with us at this moment, beatified and canonized a great many people from both the distant and the recent past. Through these individuals he wanted to show us how to be Christian: how to live life as it should be lived - according to God's way.

The saints and the blesseds did not doggedly seek their own happiness, but simply wanted to give themselves, because the light of Christ had shone upon them.

They show us the way to attain happiness, they show us how to be truly human. Through all the ups and downs of history, they were the true reformers who constantly rescued it from plunging into the valley of darkness; it was they who constantly shed upon it the light that was needed to make sense - even in the midst of suffering - of God's words spoken at the end of the work of creation: "It is very good".

One need only think of such figures as St Benedict, St Francis of Assisi, St Teresa of Avila, St Ignatius of Loyola, St Charles Borromeo, the founders of 19-century religious orders who inspired and guided the social movement, or the saints of our own day - Maximilian Kolbe, Edith Stein, Mother Teresa, Padre Pio. In contemplating these figures we learn what it means "to adore" and what it means to live according to the measure of the Child of Bethlehem, by the measure of Jesus Christ and of God himself.

The saints, as we said, are the true reformers. Now I want to express this in an even more radical way: only from the saints, only from God does true revolution come, the definitive way to change the world.

In the last century we experienced revolutions with a common programme - expecting nothing more from God, they assumed total responsibility for the cause of the world in order to change it. And this, as we saw, meant that a human and partial point of view was always taken as an absolute guiding principle. Absolutizing what is not absolute but relative is called totalitarianism. It does not liberate man, but takes away his dignity and enslaves him.

It is not ideologies that save the world, but only a return to the living God, our Creator, the guarantor of our freedom, the guarantor of what is really good and true. True revolution consists in simply turning to God who is the measure of what is right and who at the same time is everlasting love. And what could ever save us apart from love?

Dear friends! Allow me to add just two brief thoughts.

There are many who speak of God; some even preach hatred and perpetrate violence in God's Name. So it is important to discover the true face of God. The Magi from the East found it when they knelt down before the Child of Bethlehem. "Anyone who has seen me has seen the Father", said Jesus to Philip (Jn 14: 9). In Jesus Christ, who allowed his heart to be pierced for us, the true face of God is seen. We will follow him together with the great multitude of those who went before us. Then we will be travelling along the right path.

This means that we are not constructing a private God, we are not constructing a private Jesus, but that we believe and worship the Jesus who is manifested to us by the Sacred Scriptures and who reveals himself to be alive in the great procession of the faithful called the Church, always alongside us and always before us.

There is much that could be criticized in the Church. We know this and the Lord himself told us so: it is a net with good fish and bad fish, a field with wheat and darnel.

Pope John Paul II, as well as revealing the true face of the Church in the many saints that he canonized, also asked pardon for the wrong that was done in the course of history through the words and deeds of members of the Church. In this way he showed us our own true image and urged us to take our place, with all our faults and weaknesses, in the procession of the saints that began with the Magi from the East.

It is actually consoling to realize that there is darnel in the Church. In this way, despite all our defects, we can still hope to be counted among the disciples of Jesus, who came to call sinners.

The Church is like a human family, but at the same time it is also the great family of God, through which he establishes an overarching communion and unity that embraces every continent, culture and nation. So we are glad to belong to this great family that we see here; we are glad to have brothers and friends all over the world.

Here in Cologne we discover the joy of belonging to a family as vast as the world, including Heaven and earth, the past, the present, the future and every part of the earth. In this great band of pilgrims we walk side by side with Christ, we walk with the star that enlightens our history.

"Going into the house, they saw the child with Mary his mother, and they fell down and worshipped him" (Mt 2: 11). Dear friends, this is not a distant story that took place long ago. It is with us now. Here in the Sacred Host he is present before us and in our midst. As at that time, so now he is mysteriously veiled in a sacred silence; as at that time, it is here that the true face of God is revealed. For us he became a grain of wheat that falls on the ground and dies and bears fruit until the end of the world (cf. Jn 12: 24).

He is present now as he was then in Bethlehem. He invites us to that inner pilgrimage which is called adoration. Let us set off on this pilgrimage of the spirit and let us ask him to be our guide. Amen.

Notes

AUTHOR'S PROLOGUE

1   Saint John Bosco, Letter of March 19, 1885: "A good book can find its way into homes where the priest is not welcome. It will be kept as a souvenir or accepted as a present even by a bad person. A good book enters a home without blushing. If rebuffed, it is not discouraged. If taken up and read, it teaches the truth calmly. If set aside it does not complain, but patiently awaits the time when conscience may rekindle the desire to know the truth. It may perhaps be left to collect dust on a table or on a library shelf, and given no attention for a long time. But then comes the hour of solitude, of sadness, of sorrow, of boredom, of need for relaxation, of anxiety about the future–and this faithful friend shakes off its dust, opens its pages, and, as was the case with St. Augustine and St. Ignatius, it may bring about a conversion. A good book is gentle with those that are hampered by human respect and addresses them without arousing suspicion in anyone. It is on familiar terms with good people, and is always ready to make meaningful conversation and to travel along with them at any time anywhere. How many souls have been saved, preserved from error, encouraged in the practice of virtue through good books. The person who gives a good book as a gift may only barely succeed in awakening the thought of God thereby. In most instances, however, the good that is done is much greater. Once brought into a family, if it is not read by the person to whom it was given, the book will be read by a son or a daughter, by a friend or a neighbor. In a small town that book may touch the lives of one hundred people. Only God knows how much good a book can do in a city, in a public library, in a workers' association, in a hospital, where the friendly gift of a book is much appreciated."

INTRODUCTORY LETTER

2   This letter was sent to all the women preparing to participate in the retreat.

WIDOW AT THE TEMPLE & QUEEN ESTHER

3   St. Teresa of Avila, *The Interior Castle*, Fifth Mansion, Ch. II, Stanza 1-2: "You have heard how wonderfully silk is made—in a way such as God alone could plan—how it all comes from an egg resembling a tiny peppercorn. Not having seen it myself, I only know of it by hearsay, so if the facts are inaccurate the fault will not be mine. When, in the warm weather, the mulberry trees come into leaf, the little egg, which was lifeless before its food was ready, begins to live. The caterpillar nourishes itself upon the mulberry leaves until, when it has grown large, people place near it small twigs upon which, of its own accord, it spins silk from its tiny mouth until it has made a narrow little cocoon in which it buries itself. Then this large and ugly worm leaves the cocoon as a lovely little white butterfly. If we had not seen this but had only heard of it as an old legend, who could believe it? Could we persuade ourselves that insects so utterly without the use of reason as a silkworm or a bee would work with such industry and skill in our service that the poor little silkworm loses its life over the task? This would suffice for a short meditation, sisters, without my adding more, for you may learn from it the wonders and the wisdom of God."

4   Saint Paul VI, *Pastoral Constitution on the Church in the Modern World Gaudium et Spes* (December 7, 1965) 22.

5   Saint John Paul II, *Apostolic Letter on the Dignity and Vocation of Women Mulieris dignitatem.* (August 15, 1988), 12.

6   Saint John Paul II, *Apostolic Letter on the Dignity and Vocation of Women Mulieris dignitatem.* (August 15, 1988), 13.

7   Edith Stein, *The Collected Works of Edith Stein,* vol. 2, *Essays on Woman* (Washington DC: ICS Publications 2017), 132-133. "Gestalt" refers to the form of a thing (here the soul of woman) that makes it greater than the sum of its parts.

MARTHA AND MARY

8   Saint Teresa of Jesus, *Book of her foundations* 5, 2.

9   Saint John of the Cross, *Spiritual Canticle*, stanza 1, 9-10

10   Saint John of the Cross, *Spiritual Canticle*, 1, 7-8

11   Edith Stein, *The Collected Works of Edith Stein,* vol. 2, *Essays on Woman* (Washington DC: ICS Publications 2017), 134.

12   Saint John of the Cross, *Spiritual Canticle,* stanza 28, 1

13 *Super Ionannem* XV, 1, 1985.

14 See Paul Türks, *Philip Neri, The Fire of Joy,* New York (1995), 112.

15 St. Paul VI, Homily on September 11, 1965.

16 *Expositio Evangelii secundum Lucam* VII, 85: PL 15, 1720

17 See Appendix II.

18 I use this term throughout to describe the act of visualizing in one's imagination the physical setting of different events in Scripture, as a means of entering more deeply into its meaning. See Appendix I.

WOMAN'S EUCHARISTIC LIFE

19 Edith Stein, *The Collected Works of Edith Stein,* vol. 2, *Essays on Woman* (Washington DC: ICS Publications 2017), 125.

20 Ibid, 56.

THE SAMARITAN WOMAN

21 Saint John Paul II, *Catechism of the Catholic Church* (August 15, 1997), 293.

22 St. Therese of the Child Jesus, *The Last Conversations of St. Therese of Lisieux,* Novissima verba, 87-88, August 6, 1897.

23 San Irenaeus, *Against heresies,* book IV, 13-14.

24 Luis María Mendizábal, *Los misterios de la vida de Cristo,* Biblioteca de Autores Cristianos (Madrid 2016), 137-147.

25 Benedict XVI, Meeting with the Young people during his pastoral visit in Poland, May 27, 2006.

26 Benedict XVI, Meeting with the Young people during his patoral visit in Poland, May 27, 2006.

27 Saint John Paul II, *Catechism of the Catholic Church* (August 15, 1997), 2560.

28 Saint John Paul II, *Catechism of the Catholic Church* (August 15, 1997), 2559.

29 Liturgy of the Hours, Office of Readings on the Memorial of Saint Bernard, August 20.

30 Edith Stein, *The Collected Works of Edith Stein,* vol. 2, *Essays on Woman* (Washington DC: ICS Publications 2017), 134.

31 John Paul II, *Apostolic Letter on the Dignity and Vocation of Women Mulieris dignitatem.* (August 15, 1988), 12.

32 Edith Stein, *The Collected Works of Edith Stein,* vol. 2, *Essays on Woman* (Washington DC: ICS Publications 2017), 133.

JESUS' LOOK

33 At the end of this day, the participants were invited to watch a short excerpt from the Franco Zeffirelli film, *Jesus of Nazareth.* I offer here the presentation that was delivered just before viewing the film in order to follow the path of these Exercises as closely as possible and for the benefit of the reader.

SINFUL WOMAN

34 Benedict XVI, General Audience on February 17, 2010, Ash Wednesday.

35 Saint Teresa of Jesus, *Way of Perfection* Ch.6.3

36 Pedro de Ribadeneyra, *Obras del Padre Pedro de Ribadeneyra de la Compañía de Jesús,* Madrid 1605, 330.

37 Ibid.

38 Saint John of the Cross, *Spiritual Canticle,* Annotation 1.

39 Paul VI, Encyclical Letter *Humanae Vitae,* On the regulation of birth, July 25 1968, 17.

40 Edith Stein, *The Collected Works of Edith Stein,* vol. 2, *Essays on Woman* (Washington DC: ICS Publications 2017), 95.

41 Saint John of the Cross, *Spiritual Canticle*, Stanza 29, 2.

THE CONSEQUENSES OF SIN

42 Thomas of Kempis, *Imitation of Christ*, Book I, chapter 23.

43 See Appendix III.

44 See Appendix IV.

THE WOMAN CAUGHT IN ADULTERY

45 Saint Francis de Sales, *Introduction to the Devout Life,* Part III, Chapter 9.

46 Saint Teresa de Jesús, *Way of Perfection,* chapter 1.2

47 Saint John of the Cross, *Ascent to Mount Carmel,* Book I, 9.3.

48 Edith Stein, *The Collected Works of Edith Stein,* vol. 2, *Essays on Woman* (Washington DC: ICS Publications 2017), 94.

49 Santa Therese of the Child Jesus, Letter 226 (203, May 9, 1897, P. Roulland); *Story of a Soul,* Manuscript A, 83v.

50 Saint Augustine, On the Gospel of John XXXIII, 5.

51 Saint Therese of the Child Jesus, *Story of a soul,* X, 159.

MARY AT THE ANNUNCIATION

52 Saint John of the Cross, *Ascent to Mount Carmel*, Book I, chapter 13,3.

53 Edith Stein, *The Collected Works of Edith Stein*, vol. 2, *Essays on Woman* (Washington DC: ICS Publications 2017), 119.

54 Edith Stein, *The Collected Works of Edith Stein*, vol. 2, *Essays on Woman* (Washington DC: ICS Publications 2017), 201.

55 Edith Stein, *The Collected Works of Edith Stein*, vol. 2, *Essays on Woman* (Washington DC: ICS Publications 2017), 201. 241.

56 Saint John Paul II, Encyclical Letter *Redemptor Hominis* (March 4, 1979), 9.

57 These marian meditations owe much to Father Luis María Mendizábal S. J.'s priceless book *Con María,* BAC Popular (Madrid 2014), as well as this venerable Jesuit father's teaching in presentations, retreats, and spiritual exercises.

58 Saint John Paul II, Encyclical Letter *Redemptoris Mater* (March 25, 1987), 3.

59 See Appendix V.

60 Edith Stein, *The Collected Works of Edith Stein*, vol. 2, *Essays on Woman* (Washington DC: ICS Publications 2017), 119.

61 Saint Augustine, *Confessions,* Book IV, chapter 4.4.9.

MARY AT THE VISITATION I

62 Edith Stein, *The Collected Works of Edith Stein*, vol. 2, *Essays on Woman* (Washington DC: ICS Publications 2017), 21-22.

63 Edith Stein, *The Collected Works of Edith Stein*, vol. 2, *Essays on Woman* (Washington DC: ICS Publications 2017), 47-48.

MARY AT THE VISITATION II

64 Saint John of the Cross, *Spiritual Canticle,* explanation of the stanzas, song 1, 7.

65 *Confessions* III, 6, 11.

66 Pius XII, Encyclical Letter *Mystici Corporis Christi* (On the Mystical Body of Christ), 44.

67 Saint Augustine, *Homily* 256.

68 St John of the Cross, *Ascent of Mount Carmel*, Book II, Chapter V, 7.

69 St. Thomas Aquinas, Commentary on the Gospel of John, Ch 3, Lecture 3, 456.

70 Saint John Paul II, Apostolic Letter *Novo Millennio Ineunte* (January 6, 2001), 26–27.

71 *Confessions* III, 6, 11.

72 Saint Therese of the Child Jesus, *Letter 197* to Sister Marie of the Sacred Heart.

MARY AT THE VISITATION III

73 Edith Stein, *The Collected Works of Edith Stein,* vol. 2, *Essays on Woman* (Washington DC: ICS Publications 2017), 51.

74 Saint John Paul II, Encyclical Letter *Redemptoris Mater* (March 25, 1987), 17.

75 Saint John Paul II, Encyclical Letter *Redemptoris Mater* (March 25, 1987), 27.

76 In the past and in many cultures, the woman never opened the door of the house because she was considered to be under the custody of her husband. The meaning of this caution had to do also with the awareness that she was the heart of the home and her hiding inside the house ensured the protection of the most valuable and necessary member of the family. I have been able to witness this, even today, in the Holy Land. Remember that, for example, in Muslim countries, women only remove their veils inside their homes and in front of their closest relatives.

77 "Of flowers and emeralds,
      in the cool mornings chosen,
      we will make garlands
      in your love blossomed,
      and in a hair of mine woven."

78 Saint Ambrose, *Expositio Evangelii secundum Lucam*, Libro 2,23: CCL 14, 41.

79 Saint Paul VI, Apostolical Exhortation *Gaudete in Domino* (May 9, 1975), 12.

80 Saint Augustine, *Sermo* 171, 1.

81 Saint Ambrose, *Expositio Evangelii secundum Lucam*, Libro 2,26-27: CCL 14, 41-42.

82 Saint Ignatius of Loyola, *Autobiography*, 96.

83 See Appendix VI.

MARY IN THE NATIVITY I

84 Edith Stein, *The Collected Works of Edith Stein*, vol. 2, *Essays on Woman* (Washington DC: ICS Publications 2017), 45.

85 SAINT BERNARD, 2. Homily on Missus est, PL 183, 68.

86 Jacques Philippe, *Searching for and Maintaining Peace* (New York, NY: St Pauls 2006), *Part II, chapter 16: Unrest When We Have Decisions to Make.*

87 Saint John Chrysostom, *In Matthaeum* 4, 12.

88 Saint John Paul II, Apostolical Exhortation *Redemptoris Custos* on the Person and Mission of Saint Joseph (August 15, 1989), 3.

MARY IN THE NATIVITY II

89 Venerable Pius XII, Encyclical Letter *Haurietis Aquas* on the Sacred Heart of Jesus (May 15, 1956), 35.

90 Saint John of the Cross, *Ascent to Mount Carmel, Book II, chap. V.*

91 Saint John Paul II, *Memory and Identity* (New York, NY: Rizzoli International Publications Inc 2005), 19-20.

92 Saint Thomas Aquinas, *De coelo* I, 22.

MARY IN THE NATIVITY III

93 Tertulian, *De carnis resurrectione*, 8, 3: pl 2, 806.

94 Luis María Mendizábal, *Con María,* Biblioteca de Autores Cristianos (Madrid 2014), 177-180.

95 Author's translation from Saint Alphonsus' *Opera Omnia* in its original version as can be found in http://www.intratext.com/BAI/

96 Saint Ambrose, *De Mysteriis* 53.

97 Saint Ignatius of Loyola, *Spiritual Diary* 31.

98 Taken from the Office of Readings for the Solemnity of the Immaculate Conception of Mary, December 8.

THE HEALING OF THE HEMORRHAGIC WOMAN AND THE RESURRECTION OF THE DAUGHTER OF JAIRUS

99 Saint Augustine, *Serm.* 169, XI; *PL* 38, 923.

100 See Saint Thomas Aquinas, *Lectura super Ioannem* VI, III, VII, 901/902.

101 Saint Augustine, *Sermo 130A, 5.*

102 Saint Thomas Aquinas, *Lectura super Ioannem* VI, III, 901.

103 Taken from the Ofice of Readings on the commemoration of Saint John Vianney, on August 4th.

104 See Appendix VII.

ENCOUNTER WITH THE CANNANITE WOMAN

105 Saint John Paul II, Encyclical Letter *Veritatis Splendor* (August 6, 1993), 71.

106 Thomas of Kempis, *The Imitation of Christ,* book 3, chapter 3.

107 A reflection by St. Augustine on Psalm 61 that is featured in the Roman Catholic Office of readings for the First (1st) Sunday in Lent (Commentary on the Psalms Ps. 60, 2-3: CCL 39, 766).

108 I am going to make use of the extraordinary commentary by Thomas Keating that can be found in his work *Crisis of Faith, Crisis of Love*, which I read in the edition translated by Desclèe and published in Spain in 2001. I would highly recommend reading this brief writing where the well-known Trappist monk from the Abbey of Saint Joseph reflects, based on various biblical figures, on overcoming the spiritual crises that God allows on the way to the union of the soul with Him.

109 Saint John of the Cross, *Dark Night,* Book I, chap. 1,2.

110 Benedict XVI, *General Audience,* March 7, 2012.

111 Saint Teresa of Jesus, *Interior Castle,* The Sixth Mansions, Ch. X, 6.

112 Saint John of the Cross, *Spiritual Canticle,* Stanza XXXVI, 13-14.

MARY IN BETHANY

113 This meditation was prepared and delivered on June 28, 2019, the eve of the Solemnity of the Sacred Heart of Jesus.

114 Edith Stein, *The Collected Works of Edith Stein,* vol. 2, *Essays on Woman* (Washington DC: ICS Publications 2017), 188.

115 Saint Augustine, *Confessions,* Book IV, chapter 6.

116 See Luis María Mendizábal, *Los misterios de la vida de Cristo,* Biblioteca de Autores Cristianos (Madrid 2016). 212.

117 See Appendix I.

118 Max Zerwick, *Analysis Philologica Novi Testamenti Graeci,* Pontificium Institutum Biblicum (Roma 1953).

119 See Santa Catalina de Siena, *Obras. El Diálogo. Oraciones y soliloquios,* Biblioteca de Autores Cristianos (Madrid 2002), 457.

120 Saint Bernard, *De diligendo Deo,* 1,1.

THE GRAIN OF WHEAT

121 Saint John of the Cross, *Spiritual Canticle,* stanza 12.

122 Saint Faustina Kowalska, *Diary: Divine Mercy in my soul* (Stockbridge MA: Marian Press 2004), 369.

123 Saint Bernard, *In Cantica Canticorum*, Sermo 20.

124 Saint Teresa of Jesus, *Book of her Foundations,* chapter 22, 5-6.

MARY AT THE FOOT OF THE CROSS

125 From a conference by Saint Thomas Aquinas, *Collatio 6 super Credo in Deum.*

126 Liturgy of the Hours, Office of Readings on the memorial of our Lady of Sorrows, September 15.

127 Saint John of the Cross, *Spritual Canticle,* manuscript A, song 36, 2.

128 Saint John of the Cross, *Spiritual Canticle* 36, 3.

129 Saint John Paul II, Encyclical Letter *Redemptoris Mater* (March 25, 1987), 20.

130 Edith Stein, *The Collected Works of Edith Stein,* vol. 2, *Essays on Woman* (Washington DC: ICS Publications 2017), 36.

131 See Appendix VIII.

132 Saint John Paul II, Encyclical Letter *Dominum et vivificantem* (May 18, 1996), 10.

133 Hans Urs Von Balthasar; Joseph Raztinger, *Mary, the Church at the Source* (San Francisco: CA, Ignatius Press 1997), 78-79.

134 Saint Faustina Kowalska, *Diary: Divine Mercy in my soul* (Stockbridge MA: Marian Press 2004), 163.

THE OPEN HEART OF JESUS

135 Saint Teresa of Jesus, *Book of Her Life,* chapter 11, 15.

136 See Appendix IX.

137 Pius XI, Encyclical Letter *Miserentissimus Redemptor* (May 8, 1928), 3.

138 Venerable Pius XII, Encyclical Letter *Haurietis Aquas* (May 15, 1956),15.

139 Ignace de La Potterie, *El misterio del Corazón traspasado,* Biblioteca de Autores Cristianos (Madrid 2015), 103-115.

140 Saint John Paul II, *General Audience* (April 22, 1981), 3.

141 Saint John Paul II, *General Audience* (December 19, 1979), 5.

142 Edith Stein, *The Collected Works of Edith Stein,* vol. 2, *Essays on Woman* (Washington DC: ICS Publications 2017), 46.

SAINT MARY MAGDALENE

143 The original Spiritual Exercises concluded on June 28, 2019. That day, the Church was celebrating the solemnity of the Sacred Heart of Jesus.

144 Saint Paul VI, Apostolical Exhortation *Gaudete in Domino* (May 9, 1975), I.

145 Saint Augustine, *Homilies on the first letter of Saint John, homily 4, 6.*

146 Paul Türks, *Philip Neri, The Fire of Joy* (Nueva York: NY, Alba House 1995), 5.

147 Benedict XVI, *Angelus* (7-23-2006).

148 Benedict XVI, *Homily* (4-15-2007).

149 Saint Paul VI, Pastoral Constitution *Gaudium et Spes* on the Church in the modern world (December 7, 1965), 22, 2.

150 For an in-depth explanation of this topic, see Pope Benedict XVI in his *General Audience* (June 25, 2008).

151 Benedict XVI, *Address to the Fathers of the General Congregation of the Society of Jesus* (February 21, 2008).

"IN ALL THINGS LOVE AND SERVE"

152 Saint Teresa of Jesus, *Way of Perfection,* chapter 25.

153 San Ignacio de Loyola, *Obras,* Biblioteca de Autores Cristianos (Madrid 1997), 886.

154 See Jean Lafrance, *My Vocation is Love* (St Paul's, Homebush Australia, 1994), 109: "One day when Thérèse was speaking with Céline on the subject of union with God, the latter asked her a question: 'I asked her if she sometimes forgot the presence of God. She answered me

quite simply: *Oh, no, I do not think I have ever been three minutes without thinking of God.* I manifested my surprise that such application was possible. She said: *We naturally think about someone we love'* (CSG)".

155 Dante Alighieri, *Divina Commedia,* Paradiso XXXIII, v. 145.

156 Saint John Paul II, Apostolical Letter *Mulieris Dignitatem* (August 15, 1988), 31.

157 Saint John Paul II, Apostolical Letter *Salvifici Doloris* (February 11, 1984), 30.

158 Liturgy of the Hours, Office of Readings on the memorial of Saint Alphonsus of Liguori, August 1.

159 See Appendix X.

160 Liturgy of the Hours, Office of Readings on the memorial of Saint Bernard, August 20.

161 Saint John Paul II, Encyclical Letter *Redemptor Hominis* (March 4, 1979), 10.

162 See Saint John Paul II, *Catechism of the Catholic Church* (August 15, 1997), 292.

APPENDIX I

163 Jacques Philippe, *La oración, camino de amor,* Rialp (Madrid 2015).

164 Saint John Paul II, *Catechism of the Catholic Church* (August 15, 1997), 2559-2561.

165 Saint John Paul II, *Catechism of the Catholic Church* (August 15, 1997), 2683-2684.

166 Saint John Paul II, *Catechism of the Catholic Church* (August 15, 1997), 2562.

167 Saint John of the Cross, *Dork Night,* Book I, chapter 6,6.

168 Saint Teresa of Jesus, *Book of her Life,* chapter 9, 1.3.

169 See Charles Lebrun, *The Spiritual Teaching of Saint John Eudes,* Sands and Co (London 1934), 93-94.

170 Saint John Paul II, *Catechism of the Catholic Church* (August 15, 1997), 519. 521.

171 Saint Teresa of Jesus, *Book of her Life,* chapter 8,5.

APPENDIX II

172 Edith Stein, *The Collected Works of Edith Stein*, vol. 2, *Essays on Woman* (Washington DC: ICS Publications 2017), 143-145.

APPENDIX III

173 Saint Teresa of Jesus, *Book of Her Life*, Chapter 32, 1-8.

APPENDIX IV

174 Translated from José Luis Martín Descalzo, *Razones para el amor*, Sociedad de Educación Atenas (Madrid, 1987), 211-214.

APPENDIX V

175 Liturgy of the Hours, Office of Readings, fourth week of Advent (December 20).

APPENDIX VI

176 Benedict XVI, *Homily* during his pastoral visit to Lourdes (September 15, 2008).

APPENDIX VII

177 All of Saint José María Escrivá's works can be found in: https://www.es crivaworks.org

APPENDIX VIII

178 Hans Urs Von Balthasar; Joseph Raztinger, *Mary, the Church at the Source* (San Francisco: CA, Ignatius Press 1997), 77-79.

APPENDIX IX

179 Benedict XVI, *Pastoral Visit to Turin* (May 2, 2010).

APPENDIX X

180 Benedict XVI, *Address of the Holy Father at the Youth Vigil* during XX World Youth Day in Cologne (August 20, 2005).

CPSIA information can be obtained
at www.ICGtesting.com
Printed in the USA
JSHW051140030522
25522JS00001B/1